FOREVER
REMEMBERED

Also by Irv Broughton

Hangar Talk: Interviews with Fliers 1920s–1990s.
The Fires of Tangerine: Poems
A Good Man: Father and Poetry and Prose
The Writer's Mind (Three Volumes)
Producers on Producing
Reindeer Don't Eat Trees: Anti-Drug Poems
The Art of Interviewing for Television, Radio and Film
The Blessing of the Fleet: Poems

FOREVER
REMEMBERED
THE FLIERS OF WORLD WAR II

Interviews by

IRV BROUGHTON

EASTERN WASHINGTON UNIVERSITY PRESS

SPOKANE, WASHINGTON

Book Design by Joelean Copeland
Cover Design by Scott Poole

Library of Congress Cataloging-in-Publication Data

Broughton, Irv.
    Forever remembered: the fliers of World War II: interviews / by Irv
Broughton
    p. cm.
    ISBN 0-910055-71-8
    1. Air Pilots, Military--United States--Biography. 2. Flight Crews--United
States--Biography. 3. World War, 1939-1945--Aerial operations, American.
4. World War, 1939-1945--Biography. I. Title

    D736.B74 2001
    940.54'4973--dc21

                                        20041040401

Special thanks to my wife Connie, for the support on the long journey of this book, as well as to my daughter Callie, who helped me with the photographs. Thanks also to Bob Zeller, Stormy Rodolph, Kathy Homer, Patsy Horvath and Tom Davis for their assistance and encouragement along the way, and to Christopher Howell and Scott Poole of Eastern Washington University Press. Special thanks go to Joelean Copeland, Managing Editor of the press, for her good work and solid dedication. Finally, my appreciation goes to the fliers, for without their generosity and openness this book would not be possible. Lastly, I would like to point out that each flier has had the opportunity to review the interview transcript for any additions or corrections. Still, I take responsibility for any errors herein.

IB

For all the men and women who served the country during WWII
and for George P. Garrett, Jr.

CONTENTS

CONTENTS

X

"I met you thirty years ago. I met you on a sparkling, sun-swept afternoon of horror. I have known you through a balmy tropic night of fear. I will never forget you."

Adrian Marks
Pilot, U.S. Navy Reunion Speech

FOREWORD

There is a beauty in their silence — these WWI veterans, for it represents the silence of modest, everyday men and women were sent to fight in a great war and returned home, as if they had done nothing much special. In fact, what they did was extraordinary beyond words — and certainly beyond thanks.

One day, though, you may find yourself chatting with a neighbor or someone you met by chance and, through an unanticipated turn of the conversation, you learn about that person's past. Yes, he or she was in the war. But it wasn't much. What did the person do? Did his or her duty, you are told. That's about it. What was that duty? Then suddenly you sense you are in the midst of greatness. Even as he or she tries to downplay the experience, you find yourself wanting to know more. Quite often, if you are lucky, this veteran of WWII, ground or air, busts out into the stories that have been waiting to be told all these years. The silence of the past is broken. Lucky for me, these men and women of WWII have spoken—openly, candidly, sometimes painfully, about these early chapters of their lives.

For close to 30 years, I have sought to capture many of America's recollections, but most important of these efforts, I believe, which was done over the past 18 years, has been to attempt to capture many of the personal stories of America's WWII fliers. We know what they did. The history books register it. We may know what German Field Marshall Albert Kesselring said of them, "Allied air power was the greatest single reason for the German defeat." But even comments like that do not do them justice. My goal has been to put a face on some of these neighbors, colleagues, acquaintances, or strangers, who have reached the twilight of their years or have passed away already.

I hope this book is representative of the WWII flight experience, of the thousands and thousands of men and women who donned uniforms and took to the skies, as well as of what these brave people faced — and what sustained them. It is my hope that in this book — and in other books and other ways — the words and deeds of pilots, copilots, gunners, navigators, bombardiers, flight engineers, and aerial photographers — will continue to speak for a generation not to be forgotten, a generation forever remembered.

INTRODUCTION

Joseph Blotner

The verses of some old songs are just as memorable as the choruses. So it is with one we sang nearly sixty years ago as cadets on sandy drill fields and concrete runways after Saturday morning inspection and parade. We were not much for harmony but we were strong on volume. These are some lines from one of the verses:

> *Here's a toast to the host of those who love the vastness of the sky.*

> *To a friend we will send a message from his brother men who fly. . .*

The full-throated chorus that followed began with:

> *Off we go, into the wild blue yonder*
> *Climbing high, into the sun. . .*

As I read these pages, the sounds and sights of these days came flooding back from the "Hubba-hubba" choruses of enthusiasm generated under scorching sun, to the anxiety that we might somehow foul up and wash out. So too, starkly vivid, did the memory of aerial warfare — the ear-shattering sound of roaring engines and the gut-tightening sight of black bursts exploding flak — the reality to which our youthful aspirations had led us.

When Irv Broughton asked me to write this piece I didn't realize three of the fliers interviewed were men I had known for almost fifty years now, men I had flown with in the sleek mono-

INTRODUCTION

Joseph Blotner

The verses of some old songs are just as memorable as the choruses. So it is with one we sang nearly sixty years ago as cadets on sandy drill fields and concrete runways after Saturday morning inspection and parade. We were not much for harmony but we were strong on volume. These are some lines from one of the verses:

> *Here's a toast to the host of those who love the vastness of the sky.*

> *To a friend we will send a message from his brother men who fly...*

The full-throated chorus that followed began with:

> *Off we go, into the wild blue yonder*
> *Climbing high, into the sun...*

As I read these pages, the sounds and sights of these days came flooding back from the "Hubba-hubba" choruses of enthusiasm generated under scorching sun, to the anxiety that we might somehow foul up and wash out. So too, starkly vivid, did the memory of aerial warfare — the ear-shattering sound of roaring engines and the gut-tightening sight of black bursts exploding flak — the reality to which our youthful aspirations had led us.

When Irv Broughton asked me to write this piece I didn't realize three of the fliers interviewed were men I had known for almost fifty years now, men I had flown with in the sleek monoplanes of peacetime, friends with whom I had exchanged stories, wonderful raconteurs whose imaginations had been excited like mine as an adolescent devotee of *Daredevil Aces* and *G8 and His Battle Aces*, men who went on to experience far more than I had of the battles in the sky we fought in our turn. To read these accounts is to hear their voices as if we were sitting together over coffee again and to experience once more the remembered thrills and fears.

One of the qualities that makes this book so remarkable is its extraordinary range. The United States Army, Navy, Air Force, Marine Corps, and Coast Guard fliers are all here, and the ships they knew that ranged from the flying Jenny of the First World War to the jets of today — not to mention balloons, blimps, and helicopters. And the cast is not exclusively male, including as it does, pilots who would remove their helmets to shake waves of blonde or brunette hair after long flights piloting bombers or fighters in the Women's Auxiliary Ferrying Squadron. Voices from other outfits tell what it was like to serve in theatres of war around the globe, from the Aleutians to the Hump in Burma and from Okinawa to Flak Alley along the Rhine.

Broughton skillfully begins each segment with a biological sketch, followed by a question-and-answer sessions and first person narratives. There are portraits of the Aces, such as Gabby Gabreski, dodging bomb bursts on the ground at Pearl Harbor and supporting the troops with a machine gun fire from his cockpit at Normandy, victor in twenty-eight air combats in Europe and six more in Korea. The big names are here too, with tough old Claire Chennault and his Flying Tigers in China, and brief appearances by the Big Brass who shaped the air force: Hap Arnold and Jimmy Doolittle, with cameo appearances by Dwight D. Eisenhower and George S. Patton.

Valor and suffering abound. Men like Ben Hillman plotted to escape from the biggest German POW camp for fliers, even knowing that the Germans had shot scores of Royal Air Force men who had tried to pull off the Great Escape. Charlie Mott hit the silk, only to wind up with his chute dangling from a tree, before he was captured and sent to the River Kwai to work under the Japanese masters building a bridge in the jungle. The tale of gallantry and misery advances with the war in the almost unimaginable suffering of men like Hap Halloran, who bombed Tokyo in his B-29 only to be shot down, imprisoned in a cage and tortured under the constant expectation of imminent death.

The other heroes who appear on these stages show other kinds of courage, bravery and skill. These interviews are the highlights of an era of brave men and women who lived on the thin edge between life and death, on the ground as well as in the air. The least self-aggrandizing among those who tell their stories here partook of the heroism of their generation. So it was with my three friends I mentioned earlier.

Jim Colvert is a big Texan who was checked out in the two-engine Mitchell B-25 that Jimmy Doolittle and his men made famous over Tokyo. He flew those hot airplanes, the B-26 Martin Marauder and the A-26 Douglas fighter-bomber in the skies over France, Belgium, and Germany. Alone one day, he climbed to altitude and flipped his plane over on her back into a vertical dive, to see what she would do, only to find the controls wouldn't respond when he tried to pull out. He survived only in the last desperate stratagem, when he used the trim tabs to pull up from the all-out dive. As English teachers, Jim and I talked about books more than planes, and about his specialty, Stephen Crane, long after Jim had won his own "Red Badge of Courage" in twenty-two combat missions.

Jerry Hammond was an Iowa farm boy he trained to become an aerial gunner, bombardier, and navigator. A throwback to the roisters of World War I, he survived crash landings, and the unpredictably of the Belgian Maquis who committed their own atrocities, mutilating a German soldier caught in disguise within the lines. They lynched him. Jerry reached his apotheosis when he led a group of orphaned B-17 bombers home on instruments, breaking out of the soup at a thousand feet over the Thames Estuary, headed straight for the Tower of London with the guns of the Royal Navy home fleet tracking them. By the time I got to know him, he was a fascinating, profane, and generous psychiatrist specializing in the treatment of children. He had become a writer too, and some of richest material came from the days when he flew out of England with the Eighth Air Force.

I met Jimmy Faulkner through my writing about the man he called Brother Will: his uncle, William Faulkner. Knowing Jimmy enriched me professionally and personally. He provided insights no one else could have given me about the great novelist, about his state of Mississippi, and about the region that has been the focus of my work for the last forty years: the American South. Jimmy and I are almost the same age, and one of our bonds has been our shared military experience, though his as an F4U Corsair pilot in the Marine Corps in the Pacific and in Korea was longer and more extensive than mine, more daring and glamorous, protecting American warships off Okinawa against kamikaze suicide pilots and providing ground support on strafing missions such as the one when flak bought him down into shark-infested waters for hours before he was rescued. One of the most likable men I ever met, he was a throwback to the hell-raising devil-may-care fighter pilots of the First World War, commanding a fire truck and driver for a celebratory procession through newly captured Tokyo. Neither Korea nor peacetime tamed him, when as a reservist, he buzzed the campus of his alma mater, Ole Miss, and nearly earned a cashiering to go with his DFC.

This book introduced me to men I never met, others who flew in my 306th Bomb Group out of Thurleigh, north of London, some who survived to fly all of their youth as "guests of Luftwaffe," in our circumscribed view from behind the wire of Stalag Luft III, or on guided tours of Germany under the rifles of Luftwaffe guards, before General Patton and the 14th Armored Division arrived one sunny morning to reunite us with the United States Air Force.

This book gave me back these experiences with new vividness. I hope it will do the same for you, whether you were there or never experienced any of it. You can understand why I am moved by Irv Broughton's title: *Forever Remembered: The Fliers of World War II.*

FRANCIS "GABBY" GABRESKI
Flying Ace

Early in life, Gabby Gabreski had the opportunity to witness the glories of flight at the Cleveland Air Races. He was fascinated by it and thought he'd enjoy being "like a bird up there." That wish would come true. Gabreski became one of America's premier aces. Remarkably, Gabreski was an ace in not only one war, but two.

Gabreski was born in Oil City, Pennsylvania, in 1919, the middle child of Polish immigrants. He attended Notre Dame for two years, but when he saw the war coming, he opted to join the military. He chose to fight the war in the air, as he explains, preferring it over the war on the ground.

Gabreski was sworn into the Army Air Corps, and went to Parks Air College, and then to Maxwell Field for basic and advanced training. On March 15, 1941, he became a second lieutenant. At that point he chose to become a fighter pilot. Then, asked where he wanted to go, he said, "Hawaii." As it turned out, he got both of his choices and a great military career was begun.

During World War II, in his duty with the Fifty-sixth Fighter Group of the Eighth Air Force, Gabreski shot down 28 enemy planes and killed three others on the ground. In addition, during the Korean War where he spent a year, he shot down six and one-half enemy planes, becoming an ace in two wars.

After World War II, Gabreski went to Wright-Patterson and became a test pilot, then to work for Douglas Aircraft for eight months. He returned to the military less than a year later, where he received a regular air force commission and served for twenty-seven years. Next, he worked for Grumman Aerospace for 20 years in marketing and as assistant to the president. At Grumman, he did development work on the F-14. His last career move involved three years as head of the Long Island Railroad, which he describes proudly as the "greatest commuter railroad in the world." Gabby says, "I talk about the past; I talk about the present; and I talk about the future." I sit back in an easy chair, ready to span time with one of America's truly remarkable fliers.

Did the recruiter say anything specific that helped you decide to join the military for World War II?

No, there was nothing specific, because I had already made up my mind. Years before, when I watched the Cleveland Air Races, I saw Jimmy Doolittle flying around the pylons, and I thought to myself how fascinating flight was. I was about twelve at the time, but flight was only in the back of my mind until World War II broke out. Finally, I had a choice, a wonderful opportunity. I could go and join the Army Air Corps and have the government pay me for flying— for doing what I wanted to do anyway.

What was the most memorable thing you saw at the Cleveland Air Races?

The speed and the precision that they flew those aircraft with. As a child, I had never made models or done anything like that, but it made me feel that I wanted to be like a bird.

In training what was the hardest thing for you to learn?

It was the chandelle. I could never catch on to the chandelle. I had a pretty hard time just getting the feel of the airplane. The chandelle is nothing more than getting a feel for the airplane at high speed, at moderate speed, and at stalling speed.

Any early lessons you learned that later might have saved your life?

There was no particular point, although I will make one very broad statement: there's no magic to flying. Flying's something you build up to gradually. It's not something you can buy off the shelf—if you have a million dollars—and put into practice like a business. With time you get experience, and with experience, you become a professional. Of course, there are little things you can learn right along. For one, you can learn that all airplanes are a little different, that each has its own personality and weaknesses. I was very fortunate I flew the P-2, P-26, B-10, B-12, P-36, and P-40 over in Hawaii in my training from April 1941 to December 7, 1941. We didn't have any magic wand. You just built up airtime. When I left for Europe from Hawaii, on the strength of being able to fly every day because of the weather, I had 500 hours of flying, which was unprecedented.

Through training you pick up confidence, and this is the most important thing you pick up. You then can do things with that airplane that you don't even think about—it becomes a part of you.

When did you get confidence?

When I got the P-47D, with the paddle propeller, water injection, and bubble canopy, I was able to do combat at treetop level over Germany, where I engaged 25 to 30 airplanes. That happened shortly after we got the P-47D. I was leading the Sixty-first, with 16 airplanes. We broke off from escorting the bombers. (Somebody else would escort them as we broke off.) We saw a train. We were deep in Germany, north of the Ruhr valley. I asked four of the planes to go down and attack the train, and we'd provide cover. I went down to 1400 feet. The airplanes strafed the train and blew up the engine. Just about that time, I headed down where things looked a lot larger. For example, now I could see the aerodrome, which was well camouflaged. I could just barely make it out. I could also see movement—Focke-Wulf 190s taking off. I called in to my squadron that the aerodrome was north of Dummer Lake and that planes were taking off. I announced that I'd make the first run. "Just follow me in," I said. So I nosed the airplane down, and as I came down over the airfield, I observed that the airplanes were accelerating like you know what. Their wheels were coming up into the wheel wells. Because of my rate of closure, I overran a plane right in front of me, and I shot it down. Then I picked another plane that was just getting its wheels into its wheel wells, and I shot him down. By that time, there were already Focke-Wulf 190s coming in at me. I had to break off my third attack and defend against the plane heading toward me, firing its 20 mm. I broke right into him and turned into him sharply. Just then, the other men came in and started shooting down airplanes. It was a hell of a melee over the aerodrome. I pulled up, trying to get position on another airplane. When I rolled over, down to the ground, I noticed there were two more airplanes coming in on me. I had to break in toward them. Those two airplanes tried to turn in with me, because I had lost my speed. Fortunately, I had water injection, increasing my power by 15 percent, so I started spiraling and climbing up to altitude, turning tightly, up to 10,000 feet. After I reached 10,000 feet, I looked back and there was nobody behind me. I had outrun them all.

There was a time before that when I couldn't keep up with the 109. The 109s thought they had the same speed advantage, but this time, with the P-47D, I pulled right up on his tail and shot him right out of the sky. They never tried that again. This illustrates what I'm trying to say about how the improved technology helps the individual pilot destroy the enemy.

Somebody might say that you are a little too modest.

I wouldn't say so. Everybody has his own philosophy. I knew what my job was. What made it a little easier to do some of the things I did, was that I had faith. I was ready to go, I was ready to do what the good Lord wanted me to do. I had a lot of faith—100 percent faith.

Did you pray a lot?

You bet. I went to communion right before the mission. I was ready to go if the good Lord called me. I wasn't afraid of anything. I didn't have fear. You had a reasonable fear, of course, the controlled fear, but you felt you had the good Lord on your side, and that if you died, you were going to go on to heaven.

You have a reputation as a great flight leader.

I was trained that way in Hawaii. Woody Wilmot demanded nothing but the best. When I flew up in flight formation, he made me work. In fact, when I came down from a 45 minute or hour mission, I was soaking wet. He was demanding. If he lost you, he'd be all over you, wondering if you were doing your homework. I'd tell him, "Sir, I just couldn't keep up with you." He'd say, "Well, we'll try it again. I'll take it a little easier, and we'll work into it."

Did you anticipate all those "kills"?

There was only one thing I was thinking about: I thought, "My God, here we are enjoying our life in Hawaii, and my country's in a war, and my chances of returning are fifty-fifty, maybe less. In fact, I figured I'd never get back home. I was scared to death at this point, but I also knew it was my job. That was my mission. After all, I had wanted to fly fighters, and I had gotten fighters.

What was the strangest image of Normandy?

All you could see were the wakes behind the boats. The landing craft were hard to see. You didn't see the horrors. But we knew there were horrors. We knew that was the day we had to end these horrors.

How pumped up were you?

We got up at first light and took off then. We were really looking forward to this. We knew what the mission meant, because Intelligence had talked to us. It had to be successful. By this time I had about 650 hours.

The last mission I had was after I had received orders to go home. I was going to get married. Anyway, I went to the briefing for the next mission, and because it looked like a good mission, I decided to go anyway. After all, the weather looked perfect, and I figured there'd be a lot of fighters showing up from the Luftwaffe. I asked Dave Shilling, who led the group, if I could make my last trip. He said, "If you really want to, you can. Why don't you go ahead and lead the squadron."

We headed out and stayed with the bombers all the way around Frankfurt, around the horn, and were heading home. Then another group came in and picked up our relay with the bombers, and as I was heading home, I looked down and spotted an airport loaded with planes—He 111s, the twin-engine airplanes. I called out for the squadron to make one pass at the field, so we made our pass. On that pass, I burned up a couple of airplanes, and the others did the same. Off to the left sat a lot of airplanes that had not been shot up. I decided on my own to make a 360-degree right at treetop level and destroy the other airplanes on the other side of the airfield. As I dove down to treetop level, I pulled up to keep from running into the ground, then started firing at the aircraft in front of me. I decided to bring my gun sight down. Now I wasn't paying much attention to the ground at this point. So I brought my sight down and just before firing, I felt a thump. The propeller had hit the ground. When that happened, it threw everything out of sync. There were tremendous vibrations. It felt as if the airplane was going to tear itself apart. I pulled back on the throttle and managed to gain a little altitude. Nonetheless, I figured I'd never make it home. Either I had a choice of trying to make it home at low level, where I was vulnerable to light arms' fire, and of course, fighters and flak—or I could bail out.

In a split second, I decided to belly-land the airplane. I started looking for a field, but there weren't any, except a little patch of wheat between the trees. As I touched the ground, I turned the plane up on one of its wings. I figured if I hit something solid at least there would be something between me and the object. As the plane skidded along, I dropped my arms and laid my head on my arms on the gun sight, so I wouldn't be decapitated by it, if my head fell forward from impact. There was terrible noise, and I felt the airplane go up onto its nose. I thought it was going over onto its back. It didn't; it settled down and stopped.

I was in Germany, and my airplane was starting to smoke from the oil and fluids running all over the hot cylinders. That scared the living daylights out of me. To make things worse, the canopy wouldn't go back, because the rails it slid on had gotten warped along with the whole fuselage. As the smoke increased, my adrenaline really started to kick in. I was energized, and I managed to force the canopy just enough to get my head through. Now I could get the rest of my body through. I dropped my parachute to the ground and slid out of the cockpit and started running away from the airplane.

As I was running for the woods, I heard a whistling sound past my ear—a zing. After a second, I heard another zing; I looked behind and saw three soldiers shooting at me. I realized the bullets were coming pretty close to my ear. At this point, I played cat and mouse. When I saw the soldiers kneel down to get a better aim at me, I'd fall down, and when they got up to run toward me, I'd get up and run like a jack rabbit. It turned out I was much younger than these guys, who moved slowly and seemed like old, retired soldiers.

I came to a path in the woods and followed it until I came to a little shed with a statue in it. I got under the floor, deep enough so they couldn't see me, and covered myself with leaves and twigs. When they got to where I was hiding, they went right by me. I could almost touch their boots as they passed. The statue in the shed was of a saint. I didn't know which, but it saved my life. I stayed there under that floor until evening. When I got out, I saw these little airplanes out looking for me. I decided that I'd better get out of this area as soon as I could. By now the farmers had put away their cows and had headed to dinner. I started walking as fast as I could; however, I made a mistake. Instead of staying in the woods, I hit one of the dirt roads, which wasn't really a country road but a main road. Soon I confronted a little village that I would have to go through. I saw villagers visiting in the street. I hoped they wouldn't suspect me. I dragged my foot, so they'd think I was 4-F and couldn't serve in the military. Immediately, I could tell they were in deep conversation about me, talking a little louder, more excitedly. All of a sudden, the whole group started coming my way, intending to pick me up, so I started running as fast as I could. I made it over a little rise and into a small corn field, where I hid myself from the road. I watched some of them go to the right and some to the left. By that time, it was a little bit hazy and murky, and a slight rain had begun to come down. I lay there in that corn field, as they searched. One came so close I could have touched his feet.

It got dark enough, so they decided to give up the search and return to the village. I decided I'd walk a bit further, but as I did, it suddenly got really dark. There was no moon, and I couldn't see anything. I found myself stepping into holes and stumbling over myself. I made up my mind that there was no way that I could go on at night. After that, I stayed on the road for five days. On the fifth day, I saw the farmers bringing the cows down to the field. One of them saw me before I saw him and suspected me immediately and came after me. I slid off the side of the road and hid myself, but I wasn't very well hidden.

The farmer and his little boy each came up one side of the path, and in a short period of time, the boy's sharp eyes had picked me out like a bird dog, and I was captured. The farmer took me into his home. He gave me a little bread and tea, then called the constabulary from the little jailhouse in the village. The officials came out and picked me up. I stayed in the little jail in the village for one night, and the next day two Luftwaffe officers took me down to the railroad spur, a two-hour walk away. We got on the train with all the civilians, and I was taken to Frankfurt to the interrogation center for a couple of weeks of questioning. The interrogators finally gave up and sent me to prison camp in Bonn, Germany, right on the Baltic.

Going back a bit, did you fight with the farmer?

I had left my .45 in the plane. I wouldn't carry it as a weapon in Germany, because they might use it on you. After five days on the road, there was absolutely nothing I could muster, although I did make one attempt to get free. As soon as I came into his house and saw the Blessed Virgin and the Crucifix, I pulled out my rosary, which I had with me in my pocket and showed it to the German. I said, "I'm one, too." He knew what I was driving at, but he just shook his head and said, "Nein, nein."

Remember the little boy?

He was a blond-headed kid. Cute. About nine years old.

How long were you imprisoned?

I was imprisoned for ten months. I stayed there till the Russians overran the prison site and liberated us. There was a rumor after a few days that Stalin wanted us to walk down to Odessa and that the Russians would then send us home by ship, but none of us could walk. Finally, a stream of airplanes—B-24s, B-17s, and others—came in and picked us up. We had 10,000 people evacuated in one day.

There was a time when the Russians first came in, that we didn't know how we'd be treated. The Russians were rough and tough, but they also were kind to us. When the Russians overran us, we decided to venture out to a little forced labor camp that the Germans had right next to Barth. There they built a portion of the fuselage for the Me-262. When I walked into the forced labor camp, it was really a sad sight. You had a charged barbed-wire fence. The eyes of the people showed no expression whatsoever. The prisoners consisted of Russians, French, all nationalities of political prisoner, and those that I saw were on their last legs. In the barracks we saw feces all over. Then you'd see people dying or dead, with a little piece of crumb bread that they still hadn't devoured in their hand. The Russians brought their medical staff in and tried to bring back a good number of these people.

How'd you happen to go there?

I was the squadron commander, and I was just curious as to what was around in the area. Though we were told by headquarters that we shouldn't leave, I went anyway.

Talk about your dramatic flights.

The one that really was the most gratifying, was after I had the opportunity to fly the K-14 gun sight that came in toward the later part of the war. The K-14 taught me a lot. I went up with one of my P-47s with the new sight on it. I found out something important. Pulling three or four Gs, if I'm tracking you, I found that my bullets would fall behind you. Now, if I saw the bead go to the bottom and out of sight, when I could barely see you, I would pull the airplane through till I couldn't see the airplane. That would be the best time to fire. So I used this knowledge on my next mission. I wound up with a Focke-Wulf 190 on a tight turn, turning for all he was worth. I was in behind him, and I pulled my nose through him to where I couldn't see him. Then I pressed my trigger, and I let him fly into it. When I could see him, he was smoking and starting to burn.

That gives you an idea of how little I knew about gunnery, as well as how successful we became with the K-14 gun sight after D-day. Then all our young guys didn't have to go to gunnery school. All they had to do was learn to fly the airplane and put the bead on the target.

In one episode, there were a bunch of 110s with rockets, coming in behind the B-17s. (My group was just arriving at the B-17 rendezvous area.) In a perfect setup, we saw the B-17s and the 110s coming up. The 110s didn't see us, or know we were in the vicinity. As the 110s climbed up behind the B-17, I said to my squadron, "Flight leader here; 110s below; pick up your target." We headed down and just then I saw a huge explosion. I thought it was one of our P-47s shot out of the sky by a 190 or 109. I was spooked. I broke off from going down and looked for other enemy aircraft. The other pilots kept going on down. Anyway, what happened was that one of my new pilots, in crossing over, had hit another airplane. Both went up in flames.

Once I realized that there were no other aircraft in the area, and saw a 110 flying away, I went down at full speed, with throttle wide open. I came down on him and blasted him out of the sky. Pieces flew in all directions. I looked around, and I was the only one there— the only one in the sky that I could see. The others had their targets and had gone left or right, after them. I looked around again, and this was very strange, but I saw six airplanes heading east. I thought they were P-47s, so I immediately roared toward them. When I closed in, I found out they were Focke-Wulf 190s. Immediately, before they could see me, I made a 270-degree turn and headed west.

As I was headed west, I realized I was using a lot of fuel by going full throttle. Then I noticed one more airplane—a 109—above me and heading east. I had hoped that the pilot didn't see me, but all of a sudden, he made a quick 180-degree turn, and he started heading my way. My thoughts were that I didn't have enough fuel to get into a dogfight. I said to myself, "I'll run you out of ammunition," and I did. As he came down, I left my throttle at a little better than cruising speed and went up and did a chandelle. I would watch him as he followed me up, and just the minute I saw his muzzle spitting fire, I gave him a 90 degree deflection shot—the hardest shot you can have. (For me an impossible shot.) He fired one time. As I lost my speed, I'd knife it down again, picking up my air speed. I'd come up again in the same maneuver. I was watching him all the way, until he started firing. Then I'd go into a 90 degree deflection shot again. The third time I did the same thing and was at the top, taking the deflection shot, I saw the guns firing and felt all hell break loose. There was a huge explosion in the cockpit. I didn't know specifically what it was. Then I lost my power. I figured I'd better get out of the airplane. I didn't want to look at my foot because I felt a numbness there, and I figured if I saw blood, I might pass out. I had control of the plane, so I coasted down, ready to bail out. I noticed I still had good rpm, but I decided to fold the canopy and bail out. As I did, I looked down and saw a blanket of clouds under me over Germany. I didn't know if there were mountains below, covering the terrain, but I went into the clouds where I hid before the enemy could get his last shot at me. From that point, I flew in the clouds on instruments until the English Channel. I called, "Mayday." I had just enough fuel to get in on the shore of Dover. When I landed at Manston, I found out I had one 20 mm that went through my oil tank and one 20 mm that went through my turbosupercharger. Also, I realized that the explosion in the cockpit had torn my boot. The shot had hit the rudder pedal and shot it away. I had a big fur-lined boot on and that was the only thing that saved my foot. I'd been shot up on other occasions, but not as badly as this. This time I thought I'd really bought the farm.

WAFS pilot Teresa James during World War II.

TERESA JAMES
WAFS Pilot

Teresa James earned her private pilot's license on October 12, 1934. After her solo, she flew air shows in Pennsylvania as a barnstormer. She performed stunts such as loops and spins and transported parachutists, including a man known as "Bat Man," who unfolded his bat wings and landed to everybody's amazement. About this time, she won the title of Pittsburgh's Number One Woman Stunt Pilot. When at the Puxsutawney VFW Post Air Show, she performed 26 and one-half complete flat spins, which she followed with ten loops. In 1939, she received her transport license.

In 1942, Teresa was working as a flight instructor in Pittsburgh, when she received a telegram from General "Hap" Arnold, requesting she report for a flight check at New Castle Army Base in Wilmington, Delaware, for possible work ferrying army aircraft. Teresa reported and became one of the first 25 women to pioneer as part of the WAFS (Women's Auxiliary Ferrying Squadron). There were two main objectives of the women pilot program: 1) To see if women could serve as military pilots, and if so, to develop the nucleus of an organization that could be quickly expanded. 2) To release male pilots for combat. The WAFS proved their capabilities, which led to a school for female trainees in Houston, Texas. Then in August 1943, the women pilot trainees merged with the WAFS to form the WASP, the Women Air Force Service Pilots. A total of 1,074 women in the WASP organization flew about 60 million miles in the service of their country.

During the 27 months Teresa flew for the military, she had to check herself out in such planes as the P-51 and P-47. The reason was that there were no piggyback seats for instructors in those two planes.

She was deactivated in December 1944 and returned to Pittsburgh, where she managed her parents' two flower shops. In the interview, she tells a bittersweet story about a stranger who came in to her shop to tell her of her husband who was missing in the war.

Teresa was commissioned a major in the air force reserve in 1950. Her duties included special services officer to the 375 Troop Wing at Greater Pittsburgh Airport, and an assignment to the 5040 Air Base Group, Alaska Air Command, Anchorage, Alaska. It was while in Alaska that she received two commendations for casualty assistance.

She is a member of the Ninety-nines, International Organization of Women Pilots, OX-5 Aviation Pioneers, WASP, Silver Wings, the P-47 Thunderbolt Pilots Association, Women's Military Pilot's Association, and the Grasshoppers and Florida Race Pilots.

Tell me about your solo flight.

It was a long, long time ago, in September 1933. Can I tell you how scared I was? My solo flight was one frightening experience. I didn't know that I was going to solo that day. It happened after four hours of instruction in an OX-5 Travelair. It was on a Sunday, early in the morning, at seven o'clock, when the air is real still, and there are no crosswinds or up and down drafts that you normally have during the day. It was the kind of a morning that the airplane would really fly itself.

My instructor, Harry Fogel, said to me, "We're only going to shoot a few landings early this morning." And I said that whatever he was going to do was okay with me, however, on my second landing, he pulled up. We weren't flying out of an airport. I think the field was 1,800 feet long and about 800 feet wide. There were trees and wires on one end of the field and it sloped on the north side. On my second landing, Harry got out of the airplane and said he was going to check something in the back of the plane. All of a sudden he picked the fuselage up and turned it around. We didn't have a tail wheel at that time; we had a tail skid that dug into the ground. That's how you stopped the airplane. So, after he swung the tail around he said to me, "Okay, take her up. It's all yours."

Before I even had second thoughts about it, I pushed on the throttle and was in the air. I took the plane up to 200 feet altitude, made a turn at Garham Boulevard, climbed to 400 feet to William Penn Highway, and then 600 feet over Churchill Country Club. This was in Wilkinsburg, Pennsylvania. Of course, without Harry's weight, the airplane got off faster and climbed higher. As a result, I was 200 feet higher than I should have been at each turn. So on my final approach into the field, I dove down and had to slip the airplane. I don't know where I learned that, unless from Bill, the man that introduced me to flying.

Once I landed, I taxied up to the fence and jumped out of the airplane, and that was it. I said, "Never again will I ever get up in the air. Never, never, never again." On my final approach, I kept hitting my leg above my knee to keep it from going up and down on the rudder pedal. No one could get me back in the airplane until much later. Someone said to me, "Do you realize that you got up and down?" That thought had never occurred to me. I was terrified, really. I said, "I will never again go up."

How do you explain that fear, if you can?

Later, I told some of my students that I could almost pick up the fear in them—I guess maybe due to my own fear. I could tell that when we made it turn, they pulled away from the turn, not wanting to look out. I related my experience to some I taught and told them how apprehensive I was about turning and approaching a field. I'd say, "That's a normal reaction, I think." It is hard to explain fear when you are the one in control of the airplane. You don't know whether you are doing it right or wrong, especially when you have had only eight hours of instruction.

Who was this Bill that introduced you to flight?

I had no thoughts about airplanes, but my brother bought into a club with two other guys and the three of them bought this OX-5 Travelair. They were flying out of Bettis Airport in Pittsburgh,

Pennsylvania, also known as Bettis Field. One time they decided they were going on a cross-country flight up to Detroit, Michigan, to see my uncle, who was in the florist business up there, but they didn't have enough fuel to cross the lake in Cleveland, so they had to go through Cleveland to get up to Detroit. I didn't know this at the time, but they encountered a headwind and then ran out of fuel, so they made an emergency landing in a field in Cleveland. As they landed, they hit the electric wires and totaled the airplane. The hospital called and said my brother had been in an accident. I went to see him. His leg was so bad that the doctors thought they'd have to amputate it. He was in the hospital for a month or so.

We brought my brother back to Pittsburgh. Later, he asked me to drive him over to the Wilkinsburg Airport, to talk to the pilots over there. I can remember telling him how crazy he was even thinking about going back to flying because he almost died. Strangely enough, driving him back and forth to the airport is really how I got into aviation, because I met some of his friends. This one particular friend, named Bill Angel, was the best looking fellow I had seen in a thousand years. Oh, he was the man of my dreams. At that time, any guy who owned an airplane and had a girlfriend or wife, would get up early on Sunday mornings and fly some place. They would land and play cards or baseball and then return. I remember that I was terrified, absolutely terrified on every Sunday flight that I went on. Still, I guess my infatuation over Bill helped me overcome my fear. Later, Bill took a job as an airline pilot in Chicago. A fellow at Wilkinsburg Airport had just come back from Park College and knew I was crazy about this Bill, so he said, "Why don't you learn to fly and surprise Bill when he comes back to Pittsburgh?" That's finally how I got into aviation.

I learned to fly, but in the meantime Bill got married. He wrote a letter to one of his friends at the airport and told him the news. So I learned to fly, and Bill got married, and that was the last I saw of Bill. But I still was absolutely terrified of flying. It took me a long time, almost up to my private license, to get over that fear of flying.

I remember when I was a kid about age six and my dad took me to a balloon convention in Aspinwall, Pennsylvania. Dad took me up in a balloon and all I remember was squatting in the bottom of this basket. I also think that affected my attitude toward flying.

Another time, when I was about 12 or 13 years of age, I saw an airplane come over our home. The plane was sputtering, and the engine was cutting in and out. As the plane dropped lower and lower, it scarcely cleared our neighbor's house. Our neighbor's house was almost a 90-degree angle from where I was looking. My dad had a Ford truck, so I jumped in the truck and went out to where I thought this airplane was. About five minutes or so from when I first heard this sputtering, I got to this plane and watched it burn. There were two guys in there. I didn't know it was an army plane at that time.

Were the men lost?

Yes, they were killed. That could have contributed to my fear, too.

Did you your family have any misgivings about your interest in flight?

My dad never said anything to me about flying. My mother and dad used to go flying with me. In fact, I used to go to air shows where I'd be gone all day on Saturday and Sunday. My mother and dad would fly with me, and they'd stay there wherever I was. I'd be flying passengers. They never asked me not to fly. I do think they were alarmed at what happened to Franny, my brother, but my mother was philosophical. She said, "You know, what's going to happen is going to happen."

When my mother was in her 50s, she said she'd like to learn to fly. Then she had a heart attack. It was a mild heart attack, but it was the end of her aspirations of flying. But my parents were really wonderful. They supported me all the time.

41

Did you ever come across any non-supporters over the years?

I took the heat as a female when I went up to Buffalo, New York, when I was taking my instructor's rating. There were a bunch of guys up there, but that was the only time I heard a little criticism on the side. I don't know whether it was funny or not, but I remember there were comments made. I also heard criticisms later when I got in the service.

What did you hear?

I can't remember exactly, but I believe it was sort of a resentment that we women were taking their jobs, particularly from the ones that were coming back from combat. I could understand that. I didn't understand it at the time, but they were afraid that they'd be returned to the ground; they wouldn't be flying any more—especially the instructors who were teaching the CPP [Civil Pilot Training] program.

I did try to get on with the airlines when I came out of the Service, but because I didn't have training in exactly what the airlines were flying, they wouldn't hire me. Also, the airlines maintained that public opinion wouldn't permit a woman flyer in the cockpit. Some people were highly opposed to women flying.

Barbara Poole Shoemaker and I even tried to get in the Chinese Air force. I still have the letter from the Chinese Embassy. Excuse me for laughing, it was really funny, when I think about how dumb we were trying to get in the Chinese Air Force. The letter said, "I wish to advise you that the Chinese Air Force has no unit similar to the WASPs of the U.S. Army Air Forces and that it is not in the practice of engaging women pilots. It is therefore, that no action can be taken on your offer. However, you may be assured that your desire to serve in China is deeply appreciated." It was funny. That's how desperate we were. Don't you think that's funny?

I think it's funny, yes. I can just picture you trying to communicate. You were a WAFS.

I was one of the first 28 women in the Women's Auxiliary Ferrying Squadron. That was in 1939, when Nancy Love and her husband Robert could see that there was apparently going to be a war. After the invasion at Pearl Harbor, Nancy Love went to the Civil Aeronautics Association, which is now known as the FAA, to see how many qualified women pilots would be available to fly airplanes. Now this is before Jackie Cochran. Apparently Jackie Cochran had talked to Mrs. Roosevelt about this, but Cochran had gone on to England, I think, in 1940. She took some of the girls over there to fly. Anyway, Nancy Love went through the CAA [Civil Aeronautics Association] records and got the names of the commercial women pilots here in this country. She was the one that started the WAFS, the Women's Auxiliary Ferrying Squadron. Unfortunately, the WAFS as an entity is lost today in history.

We started in 1942. And then later Cochran initiated the women's military training program, with the first group of 28 being trained at Houston. Later in 1943, the WAFS merged into one organization called the Women's Air Service Pilots (WASP). Jackie Cochran was named director of flight school. Nancy Love, who started the WAFS, was named the WAFS executive for the Ferrying Division of the Air Transport Command.

How do you explain the idea of being lost entities?

How do I explain the lack of recognition? There existed probably some conflict there in Washington D.C. Irv, I can't tell you. All I know is that Cochran came back from England and she was hell-bent on starting this school for women pilots. Remember that the WAFS were experienced pilots. Okay? And what we were supposed to do was to ferry small aircraft to air bases. This would release the men to fly bigger aircraft and go into combat. Anyway, Cochran, who had been in England, found out that Nancy Love had started this group, so she flew back and went to Washington, D.C. and asked permission to start this school in Texas to train women pilots. Now, her idea was to take the women who had maybe thirty-five hours of flying time and to bring them up to the specifications and to where the WAFS were.

And so by the time the WASPs came along how many hours did you have?

I had 1800 hours when I went in. By the time the WASPs came along, we had flown for a year. But I don't know what the WAFS time was, because Cochran came back and started this school and started taking private pilots who had to have at least 35 hours flying. And then she would bring them up training on heavier aircraft.

Did the WAFS feel kind real anger or resentment at any stage?

Oh, never. Never, because they were needed. There was never any jealousy or resentment.

Tell me about your early WAFS flying experience.

Thank you, Lord, I never had any forced landings. But I happened to be the first WAFS to ferry an airplane from one coast to the other. That was a PT-19 for a movie they were doing, called *Ladies Courageous*. The movie starred Loretta Young, who played the part of Nancy Love.

At the time I'd never flown past Chicago. For some reason or other I got the job of flying the PT open cockpit airplane west. It was in March and when I left from Hagerstown, Maryland, the temperature was 15 or 20 degrees. My log reads that it took me from February 17 to February 24 to get to Burbank. We didn't have any radios when we first started out. All we had were maps, and we drew a line and marked off every ten miles en route. That to me was the most outstanding trip I ever had in my life. It was also when I was the most scared. On the way out I never knew where I was going to land at night. That was my famous trip.

44

Where was the strangest place you landed on that flight?

There was one place I landed, Pyote, Texas, which I never had heard of. The reason I'm laughing is that when I landed at this field, I can't remember the name of the field, they had no place to put me. They took me to the sheriff's office, and the sheriff took me to his home. Now this sheriff happened to have about eight children and in this town, he was the sheriff, the druggist, the doctor, everything. It really was one of the highlights of my whole life. That's all I can tell you.

Now, what else happened on that trip that was strange or unusual?

When I got to Long Beach, I found that the government had camouflaged everything. When I say camouflaged, the buildings, the roads, everything. So I was looking for a Lockheed Aircraft in Long Beach, California. I pinpointed, based on time, where I should be. I found Long Beach. As I started to approach what I thought was the field, I realized that it was the roof of Lockheed Aircraft. And then I saw the runway. But that was how well camouflaged it was.

Did you get any strange reactions when you landed, as a female?

Oh, boy, did I ever. First of all, people couldn't believe a female was flying an air force airplane. I was the first WAFS out on the West Coast. At the time Paul Mantz, God rest his soul, was one of the big guns out there in aviation. He had done a lot of flying for the movies. Paul took me in tow because I was delivering this airplane for a movie. (I never did see the movie, as a matter of fact.) Paul took me to all the studios. At one point I had to call the base in Wilmington, Delaware, to talk to my C.O., who gave me a pass for two weeks. I met Bob Hope and many, many movie stars out there. Oh, I tell you, the uniform made a hit, not me. It was the uniform and the fact that I flew. It had nothing to do with me.

Do you have a favorite celebrity story?

I attended a lot of parties. My big thrill was going to Coconut Grove, where they had at that time, all the big bands. The girls out there were hosting the men who were going overseas. Every night was a party night at the Coconut Grove. Coming from the east, I had never heard of all this stuff. Benny Goodman was playing there that night. I don't know how many movie stars I met. Gary Cooper and Ingrid Bergman were my favorites. I wanted to meet Bing Crosby, but never did. But, boy, people wined and dined me. The manager of the Beverly Hills Hotel took me up to his suite and said, "You must rest now and we're going to give you rent-free the bungalow that the wife of the owner of the Palmer House in Chicago is vacating." I don't know how familiar you are with the hotels out there in Hollywood, but the prices were sky high. Anyway, that is where I met Spencer Tracy. Oh, I've got a lot of stories. You're really dragging them out.

Did anybody take a liking to you, sort of romance you?

Romance me? No. I was extremely careful. And being a Catholic, listen, I really kept my head on my shoulders. You could really get carried away out there if you listened to all the stuff that they poured into your head. You know, you'd hear how gorgeous you were and that you were a flyer and blah, blah, blah. It was really something else. And Gary Cooper, God bless him, he was the shyest person I ever met in my life.

Did you have a conversation with him finally?

Yeah. He was really interested in flying. He would look down and I remember the way he shuffled his foot and he'd say, "Oh, shucks," and look up. And I said to myself, "Oh, God, just like he does in the movies." Anyway, the people out there thought I was something else. After all, I was flying an airplane.

You must have been sorry to leave, huh?

Oh, was I ever. Before I left, I went to see my husband who was at that time in Santa Maria, but he couldn't get off the base but for the night. I was really disappointed, because they were getting ready to go overseas. He was a B-17 pilot.

Do you have any stories about him in the B-17?

You know I never got too much information. His letters to me said he was trying to learn as much about instrument flying as possible. He would say that things were really getting heated up and that he had to wear a flak suit every day. He would offer me different little hints about how bad things were getting. Also, he was worried about me flying, especially when I got into P-47s. He said, "Make sure you check everything." I was extremely worried about him in a B-17. He had been an instructor pilot at Roswell, New Mexico, and volunteered to be part of a crew that was going overseas. They sent them over as crews. He disappeared over there.

There was an article that appeared in a New York paper, like *The Daily News*, which had a picture that looked like a side view of my husband and two crew. The picture's caption said: "American Airmen Captured by Nazis." But the paper never identified any of the crew by name in that picture. That is the reason I thought "Dink," which is what I called him (George Martin), had been captured. Later, I got word that he was missing in action. I figured that maybe he was a prisoner of war all those years. Also, I got letters about what supposedly had happened to my husband, about how his plane had gone into a spin and then come out of a spin, then gone back into a spin and back out. I heard he was buried in Selars, France. But it was the kind of thing that was never verified. You know how in war nothing is easily verified.

It wasn't until 1984 ,when I went to France, that I learned the truth about my husband. I belong to the P-47 pilots' organization. We were having a reunion in Paris. I found out there was a WWII plane that had landed in Joinville le Pone on this narrow street named for George Martin. The mayor of Joinville le Pone got in touch with the head of the local veterans' association, and they both invited me there.

It turned out that these years since the war, the local people had kept his plaque on a fence outside this home honoring him. He was honored and remembered all these years. Apparently, during the war, there was an air raid, and a man and his two young sons heard the air raid sirens and ran into the garage. My husband, George, had crash-landed the airplane, and the man and his sons came out and salvaged some of the plane, including a part of the landing gear that they'd kept.

When I got there, I met the lady that lived in the house where the wing of the airplane hit. The woman was in her 80s. I saw the plaque on an iron fence gate that read, "In memory of Lieutenant George L. Martin and crew." I don't know how long it had been there. Then I met the two sons, who with their father, had run in the garage to escape the crash. The sons were in their 50s when I met them. The father had a coin, supposedly from my husband's pocket, and had kept it as a talisman. After the father died, the kids kept it. Now I have it. They presented it to me in blue velvet.

How did that make you feel?

Oh, God. Listen, that was one of the saddest moments of my life. On this Mother's Day in the 1980s, they gave up their day to meet this woman coming from America, whose husband had crashed an airplane, but who had saved them from a bridge being blown up. This I didn't find out until that day.

47

How did that happen? He'd saved them. Explain that.

Apparently the B-17 that my husband was flying around alerted the people of the imminent crash. The local people sounded the alarm and he diverted the bombs away from the bridge that would have cut them all off from civilization, if destroyed. They had this reception for me and that's what I walked into. In the mayor's office they had part of the landing gear and it read, "In Memory of George L. Martin." They had a presentation of the most gorgeous flowers I've ever seen in my life. During all these presentations I stood up and I couldn't say a word. I just stood there and cried. Really, that's exactly what I did. I just stood there and cried because I couldn't believe it. It was almost like a movie that was happening. Then the mayor and his wife took me out for dinner. It was the most moving thing that has ever happened to me.

I wondered how after all these years, how could anybody ever remember or how did this ever come about? The mayor's wife explained that "in France, nobody ever moves."

It sounds like you were kind of in limbo all those years, not totally knowing where your husband was.

I had no idea. I still have a letter from this friend of mine, Helen Richie, who was a WAFS. She and Jimmy Doolittle were real good friends. So Helen said to me, "I'll write to Jimmy" because he was head of the Eighth Air Force. She wrote to him, and Jimmy responded by saying that my husband had crashed, at least according to the information that was given by the pilots who were flying with him. Someone had seen him go into a spin.

So, did you ever re-marry?

No. No. You know why I didn't? People ask me that. It was because of the picture that was in the paper. I thought that he was still a prisoner of war. What really put the bug in me was this: I was working in my mother and dad's flower shop one day. My family's been in florist business, and still is, in Wilkinsburg, Pennsylvania—James Flower and Gift Shop—for 98 years. Anyway, after I got out of the service and couldn't find any other work, I went back to work at my folks' business. One day this stranger came in to the shop. "Is a Mrs. George Martin here?" he asks. My ears perked up, because nobody had called me Mrs. George Martin for a thousand years. He told me he was a waist gunner on my husband's airplane. He claimed the plane was hit and the explosion blew off the entire front end. He claimed that George, who was pilot, as well as the copilot and the navigator never knew what had hit them, and the man admitted to having memory loss, himself. He said, "Listen, I'm on my way to New York." He was with a friend and they were driving. He wanted to be sure that I'd be there, because he would stop on the way back. We would talk some more then. I never did hear from the guy again, ever. I guess he was another reason that I thought Dink might be still alive.

How do you reflect on that? In a way your loyalty and your devotion worked against you, didn't it?

It did. It really did. But then again I think about it and I've been active in a lot of things in life that I normally probably wouldn't have been active in. As I reflect now and I look back on it, who knows? What I miss is the children; they are my only regret. When you think about it, though, maybe it was for the best. Oh, brother. I'm telling you. Parents are bitching today. They should be bitching with what was going on. It's a crazy world. What can you say about it? I've lived so long and I reflect. I don't reflect too often. I'm reflecting now, talking to you. This world has changed so much in the past 30 years that it's unreal. It really is. I don't know. It really is scary. I busy myself with a lot of things. I am still flying.

What was your favorite stunt? Any stories about doing stunts or air shows, or any unusual things that happened?

Well, my favorite one was my 26$^1/_2$ turn spin that I used to do. I started out doing maybe three or four or five turns and I kept adding them on. I finally got up to 26$^1/_2$ turns in a spin. I used to ice skate. I used to dance a lot, and I used to spin. You're so young you wouldn't remember about spinning around the floor dancing, such as in a

Spanish dance where you spin, spin, spin, but we used to do that a lot when we were younger. We would see how many turns we could make on the dance floor without getting dizzy. That's where all this started, really.

So you were better at spinning in airplanes because of your dancing?

I really think so, because I could really spin around the whole dance floor. Of course, your partner had to do it with you. I didn't have any fear of airplane spins until different pilots told me that it looked like my airplane had flattened out. Instead of the nose being below the horizon on an angle, it would almost flatten out like it was flat, spinning flat.

At one of the air shows, Walter Beech, who made the Beechcraft, said to me, "Teresa, you ought to quit doing it. Some day you're going into a flat spin." And I said, "I've heard that many, many times before." But after he told me that, I quit doing it. I quit doing the 26 turns. I backed off.

How many did you do from that point on?

I maybe did 10 or 12 spins. I felt like this is crazy. I might as well get back to my 26½ turns, but I didn't get to, because the guy who owned the airplane sold it. Then after the guy sold the airplane, the new owner cracked it up. I knew that one wing was put together with piano wire. Anyway, that caused me to say, "Thank you, God." You know me. I'm so close to the Lord, though you'd never know it. I was glad then that I had quit.

How many hours do you fly nowadays?

Oh, I just go touring to pancake breakfasts and barbecues maybe once a week.

I fly with a gal named Robin Harris. She's the state chairman of the Florida Aircraft Association. She calls me the Eighth Wonder of the World. No, kidding, I'm telling you. I could kill her. I said to her, you tell one more person how old I am and I am going to strangle you. I'm doing okay though. I still have all my teeth. Thank you, God. The Lord's been good to me. Both eyes are working. I wear glasses flying or reading. I spike my holy water when I drink it. I try to keep my weight down.

What keeps you going?

The Lord and the Blessed Mother keep me going. I depend on them for everything.

So you're a pretty religious person still, aren't you?

I wouldn't say I'm pretty religious. I depend on the Lord so much. Everybody asks me, "Why do you go to daily mass?" I say, "Listen, the Lord keeps me going and I have to make an effort to get my butt out of bed to go." So you figured that out, that I'm a mackerel snapper. I do depend on the Lord.

Has your sense of humor helped get you through?

If I didn't have a sense of humor, I don't know what I'd do. Thank you, God, for that. Also, I always try to look at the best side of everything. It really has gotten me through life looking on the bright side.

51

GAIL HALVORSEN

"Candy Bomber"

Learning to fly in Utah as a young man, Gail Halvorsen learned to wiggle his wings to communicate to folks on the ground he was about to fly over. Later, during the Berlin Airlift, Halvorsen used that same device to signal a young man below which plane contained the tiny parachutes with candy and gum for the children. Thus came the name "Uncle Wiggly Wings."

Mostly, thought, Gail Halvorsen is the "Candy Bomber," a legend for his kindness in the dark, shadowy days following WWII. His gesture, which he describes in detail in the interview, of flying low and delivering small chutes of treats into the waiting arms of the suffering children, is remembered throughout the world and in relationships that continue today with those who caught or tried to catch his offerings.

Halvorsen received his wings in June 1944 at the #3 British Flying Training School in Miami. He then worked as a foreign transport pilot in the South Atlantic, returning to fly in the U.S. in 1946. Two years later, he joined the Berlin Airlift where he flew 126 missions and made history as a goodwill ambassador.

In 1952 Colonel Halvorsen was assigned to Wright Air Development Center, Wright Patterson AFB, Ohio, as an engineer and program manager. The next year he went to Hill AFB in Utah, and then to Command and Staff College at Maxwell AFB. From there, he travelled to Inglewood, California, where he worked in research and development of space boosters.

Halvorsen then worked for the Directorate of Space and Technology at the Pentagon. In 1970, he became the commander of the 7350th Air Base Group at Templehof Central Airport in Germany.

Halvorsen retired in 1974 after 31 years of service. In his outstanding career he received the Legion of Merit, the Cheney Award for 1948-49, Meritorious Service Medal, the Medal for Human Action, and the German Service Cross to the Order of Merit from the President of Germany—among others.

In 1989 Halvorsen flew over Templehof for the *Good Morning America* show to commemorate his last flight over 40 years earlier. He has chronicled his life in the book *The Berlin Candy Bomber.*

You trained with the Royal Air Force. Any anecdotes about an American by training with the British?

The instructors at the number three BFTS, British Flying Training School in Miami, Oklahoma, were American instructors. The check pilots and the commander and the staff and training people—as well as the administrative staff and teachers for ground school — were British. It was a very interesting experience. The instructor pilots were mostly "Battle of Britain" guys. They didn't like being stuck in a training situation. I remember on my final check ride, Flight Officer Handley took me over Miami, Oklahoma, for my final aerobatics check and said, "Do all the aerobatics Joe Weblemoe ever taught you over the city here."

I said, "You can't do that because it's against regulations."

He says, "Look, I'm in charge of this airplane. Do as I say." So I proceeded to do Immelmanns and cubic-eights under an overcast that was about 5,000 feet high, right over the middle of town. When we landed, of course, the flight officer was met by the commanding officer and sent home. This was just what he wanted to have happen. It was an unusual experience. That final check ride was something I will never forget. The fact is, after we finished the aerobatics over the town – the town wasn't far from the airfield – all the other student pilots, pilots at the airfield that weren't flying, the ground personnel and maintenance people—everybody—was out at the airfield watching this aerobatics show.

54

When we got through, Handley says, "You passed. Give me the controls." He took that machine and headed right straight for the airfield. I mean, he went right under the overcast and aimed it at the flight apron where all the people were gathered, watching. He was at full power, headed right for that group. At the last minute he pulled up, straight up, in a vertical roll right into the overcast. This guy was an ace of a pilot and recovered on needle, ball, and airspeed. Then he said, "We had better bugger off for awhile." We flew around, and he made a letdown on the radio range in Neosho, Missouri.

My fellow students were from Scotland, Wales, England, and Australia. It was a great mix. In fact, that's one of the reasons they asked for volunteers. They wanted us to work with the Brits and help them with culture shock in the United States. It was also to evaluate the British training program, which was quite a bit different.

If you can pick out one thing that was different between the British and American systems, it would be that the British system eliminated the basic trainer. With the American system, you started in the primary trainer, which was a Fairchild, or some similar type of aircraft. Then you would go into a basic trainer, which was more horsepower, but with fixed gear. Then you went into an advanced trainer. The British just eliminated the basic trainer. They went straight from a primary trainer to an advanced trainer.

55

What sort of things did you do there to entertain yourselves.

Rugby was the British fliers' favorite sport. I had never played it before, and I really got laid up. I missed a couple of weeks of flying with a bad leg because of a rough rugby match. You know, they don't have any padding or anything with that game, and the Brits were a pretty hardy crew.

One of my other buddies was coming back from a flight with one of these Battle of Britain guys and came into the flight pattern at one thousand feet. The RAF [Royal Air Force] instructor just rolled the plane over on its back and flew around the pattern upside down. When he came to the final approach, he just rolled it over and came in and landed. They sent him home too.

The British were a great crew. Many were fantastic for their knowledge of arts and history. That's what really surprised me. They seemed to be more well-rounded in the arts than I was. In fact, they put on a little theater in Miami, Oklahoma. It was just like they were professional actors.

Did you make any long-term friends out of that group?

Duncan Ireland is a great friend of ours. He owns a metals business in Glasgow, Scotland. We've been back there with our family and stayed in his lovely house with a fireplace in every room. He didn't have central heat, but he had fireplaces. Freddie Meeks, an Englishman out of Liverpool; Jimmy Marnie, a Scot out of Dundee, were and are still good friends.

A lot of my best RAF buddies were killed after graduation. They went to the invasion forces, where there was a need for pilots to both tow and fly gliders. Of course they needed the pilots, after they cut them loose. Besides the murderous ground fire, the Germans put up spiked poles and other ground obstacles. I lost some of my buddies in that operation.

When I graduated, the Americans needed transport pilots to move stuff around, so I was sent to South America. After a time, I got a letter from one of my buddies, telling me about the invasion and how many of our guys were killed. I was flying to Ascension Island, the main support base for getting our aircraft on the southern route into England. I also flew a number of ferry trips to England. Here, I was a noncombatant, although there was an outside chance, coming up the African coast, that we might get jumped. We didn't have any guns. It kind of made you feel like you were on the sidelines and not doing what your friends were doing to win the war. That made me feel guilty—along with feeling bad about my buddies.

Did you ever have any forced landings?

Yes, I was flying in South America and this was my first flight as first pilot. I was flying a C-47. I was checked out to Rio de Janeiro—one of our destinations. We had military operations out of Rio and were flying supplies in to them. The airport in the harbor there is named after Santos Dumont—Santos Dumont Airport. It's just a postage stamp to land on, with the harbor at both ends. The strip was about 3,000 feet long, which was plenty for a C-47, but it's still a pretty short strip.

I had a bunch of Federal Aeronautics Administration guys aboard, who were putting in navigational systems up and down the coast. There was a cloud deck just over Sugar Loaf Mountain when we took off from Santos Dumont. We had just gotten into the cloud deck and had passed the mountain when my whole left engine, all of a sudden just flared up in flames. My whole wing was covered in flames. I cut the gasoline off, pulled the firewall shut-off valve and feathered the engine. Then I hit it with an extinguisher. We had to come in a little hotter with one engine out. It was a challenge with a short runway, but we made it. It was exciting.

I was flying a Vultee Vengeance (single-engine) dive bomber on the deck for recreation—out of Natal, Brazil, one day when the engine konked out. I was only a couple of hundred feet off the ground, but I managed to get back. It was hit-and-miss for about three miles. Whatever it was that caused the problem cleared up some, and the engine ran enough to get me back. These were two of the closest calls I've had.

That saying, "flying is hours of boredom, filled with moments of stark terror" is true. When I was on the Berlin Airlift, we were coming into Berlin with a big load of flour. It was August 12, 1948, and the weather just went bananas. The GCA wasn't working. We were trying to get people out of the stack over Berlin. It took about 12 or 15 minutes to get an airplane down on a radio-range approach, and you had airplanes coming in to the stack every three minutes. In the soup, control just lost track of us, and we had three aircraft in that stack holding over the wedding beacon at ten thousand feet. We were flying along, and all of a sudden, right there, smack dab in front of us, riding in the same weather with us, at the same altitude, was another C-54, headed in the opposite direction. We nearly had it. You could see the eyeballs of the guys in the cockpit right in front of us.

Did you have any trouble with loads during the airlift?

Yes, a couple of times. Of course, things got wet because there's quite a bit of rain over there. For example, they would weight the coal in dry, and it sat out in the open cars in sacks and got saturated. We flew it in sacks. Anyway, before people got wise to it, we had some near crashes—guys struggling out through the treetops.

Finally, they got back, and what they found was that they hadn't taken into account the added weight due to water. It was a miracle that more guys weren't killed because of that.

One of the best cargoes—a noisy cargo—was crates of fresh milk in bottles. We would kid each other about a bad landing with that stuff because you could hear it way past the cockpit—all those crates and rattling bottles in the back. Of course, the crates were tied down, but they were really noisy.

One of my buddies said he heard about some guys flying out of Fassberg. We had a lot of American planes in the British sector, flying the northern corridor into Berlin. They flew mostly coal out of the Ruhr area. This crew lost several engines and had to dump out sacks of coal to keep the plane in the air.

Tell me about the "Candy Bomber" origins? How did you get started?

When the airlift started, I didn't think it would last too long because the world press was really pounding on the Russians for the blockade, talking about how they were starving over two million people. I figured they wouldn't take the heat for long. We were flying to Berlin out of Rhein-Main, the main air base near Frankfurt. We would land in Berlin and deliver our goods, then immediately, as soon as the cargo was unloaded, we would take off and get another load. In fact, General Tunner—who was in charge of the airlift—said, "You are not to go into the terminal building anymore." Those were his orders. We did go in at first, but he said, "No more of that. You stay right with your airplane at the ramp, and when that last sack of coal or flour is unloaded, get going." So from then on we didn't get into the terminal, let alone the town. (Then there was only one building in five that was partially serviceable.)

I wanted to see the Brandenburg Gate and the Reichstag and Hitler's bunker. But that was impossible. When I first got there, we would fly three round-trips. That would take from 16 to 18 hours, depending on delays. Then you would go to bed for six hours—or, if you were lucky, seven or eight. Then you'd turn around and do it again. So you weren't going anywhere, except getting that stuff to Berlin. We were too short of planes and crews. But one night I decided not to go to bed, and instead, to get on a plane with my buddy. I had a friend in Berlin that had access to a jeep, so I thought,

"I'll just go around town and get some pictures. Then, when they send me home, at least I will have seen Berlin."

One of the pictures I wanted especially was a picture of the approach to Tempelhof Airport. The principal approach was right over some five-story apartment houses that had been partially bombed out but were still standing. With the heavy load, it made for a hard approach because we couldn't get low enough, soon enough. As a consequence, we would come over that apartment house and have to stick the nose down and use power to flare, so we wouldn't bang the runway too hard. I wanted pictures of planes making that approach.

The first good day, when I finished my three trips by noon—instead of going to bed—I jumped on a plane with my buddy and headed back to Berlin. I hiked around the perimeter of the field. The approach was on the opposite side of the terminal about two miles across the field. I went with my movie camera inside the barbed-wire fence. As I started taking the movies there, a bunch of kids—about 30 of them—came up to the fence. They saw me in uniform and started talking. We must have talked for about an hour. The thrust of what they said was, "Hey, don't worry about us. If you just keep trying, we are going to get enough food some day, but if we lose our freedom, we're not going to get it back—and we know about freedom."

These little kids were saying this?

Yes, they were giving me a lecture—kids 8 to 14 were. They said, "We know about freedom because of our relatives in East Berlin over there." Of course, this was long before the Berlin Wall went up, so naturally the East Berliners could come over and visit their relatives in the West. The visitors would say, "We want to use your library; we want to find out what is going on in the world." In East Berlin they were being told what they could do. These kids were saying, "We don't want it." They gave me a lecture. I stayed longer than expected, then I started to run back to catch the jeep before the driver got tired of waiting. It was then I realized how different they were from other kids I'd seen. For example, they hadn't asked me for any gum and candy. I had flown in South America, Africa, and England during the war, and when you walked down the street in an American uniform, the kids would chase you. They would shake you down for gum and candy. Here these kids didn't have anything, and yet they didn't ask. That blew my mind. So I stopped, and I turned around and went back to the fence. All I had was two sticks of gum, and I broke them in half and passed the four pieces through the barbed wire. Boy, they looked like they had gotten a million dollars. You just couldn't believe the looks on their faces. The other kids, who got no gum, didn't fight them for it either, which I was worried about at first. Instead, they asked for a piece of wrapper. The kids that got the gum just tore off the wrapper and the tin foil and passed it to the rest. They smelled the wrapper and their eyes got big. I stood there dumbfounded. I thought, "For 30 cents I can give them a full pack of gum, and they can have the wrapper and everything." Then I got to thinking of how I'd been flying 24 hours without sleep, and that I couldn't get back there soon. I didn't know when the schedule would match again. About that time, an airplane flew in over the building, which was right over our heads. This was right at the end of the runway. I suddenly got this idea. I said, "Hey, kids, if you will come back tomorrow, I'm going to drop enough gum and chocolate out of the airplane for all of you." Boy, they had a consensus on that in a hurry.

60

I started to leave again, and they stopped me and said, "Look, we've got to know which airplane you are in. If you don't come until late, we are likely to miss it. We can't miss that little package— we've got to know which airplane to concentrate on." I told them I didn't know, that I would be flying a four-engine airplane—a C-54. The planes had different markings, and I told them I would fly whichever one was ready. They said, "That's not good enough. We've got to know which plane." Then I remembered, when I learned to fly in Utah, I would fly up over the little farm and wiggle the wings to let the folks know I was going over. I told the kids when I came over the field, I would wiggle the wings and that would be the plane with the stuff in it. Then I went all over town and got my pictures. When I got back, I couldn't get enough candy by myself because we all had ration cards which meant we could only buy so much each week. I convinced my copilot and my engineer to give me their ration. Then we took three handkerchiefs to help mark it and to slow it down. We would be just 90 feet over their heads. The first time we returned to Berlin was at night, but the next flight was at about 10 A.M., and there they were at the end of the runway. The kids hadn't told another soul. I wiggled the wings, and they almost blew up with excitement. We came around and dropped it, and when we taxied out for takeoff, I looked and there were three handkerchiefs waving through the barbed wire. All the kids' mouths were chomping like crazy, so we knew they had the gum. That's how that got started.

Wasn't your idea opposed by your commander?

Well, he was opposed at first. I wasn't supposed to do it. I mean, you are supposed to get permission to do things like that. I rationalized that if I was going to get permission, it would take forever, and we would never get the stuff to the kids. We were only 90 feet in the air, so I decided to take a chance. We made two more drops before we got caught. A newspaper guy had heard about it and, I guess, he was waiting one day and got a picture of the drop. We made all the German newspapers and the wire services, and the general heard about it. He called my commander, Colonel Hahn, and congratulated him. (In fact, Colonel Hahn had been caught flat-footed and was concerned about not being advised.) Colonel Hahn called me in and chewed me out for about 10 or 15 minutes. Then he pulled out the newspaper with the picture in it and said, "You almost hit a German newspaper guy in the head with a candy bar in Berlin. A general called me up, and I didn't know anything about it. Didn't they tell you in ROTC to keep your commander advised?"

I said, "Yes sir."

Then he said, "Well, the general thinks it's a good idea, and I think it's all right too." Next, he said, "Look, we've dropped thousands of sticks of bombs on that city. Do you really think I'd object if you dropped a few sticks of gum?"

I said, "Well, I wasn't sure. I didn't want to take a chance."

Then he said, "The general says, 'Keep it going.' I think it's a good idea, but keep me informed." We went bananas with the effort from then on, and my buddies in Germany gave me supplies.

The kids in Berlin soon heard we were out of handkerchiefs, and they sent back the old ones for refills. Finally, they started making handkerchiefs and sending them to us. The people in the U.S. sent us mailbags full too. In the States, radio stations were playing tunes for handkerchiefs. It just went crazy from then on.

Do you remember any of those little kids, especially? Is there one face you remember?

Peter Zimmerman was one. He wrote me a letter and said, "Look, I can't run very fast, so I am not catching any of this stuff. I have seen, but have not gotten a hold of a parachute. Here is a parachute." He had made one. Then he had a map and he said, "When you take off, come down the canal to the second bridge, and turn right one block. I live in that house on the corner." He told me he'd be in the backyard every day at two o'clock, and that I should drop it there." So I tried. I saw someone down there and dropped it. But he kept writing me each week, "I haven't got any yet." Finally, he said, "Look, you are a pilot. I gave you a map. How did you guys win the war anyway?" I finally took a big package of gum and candy to Berlin and mailed it to him in the Berlin mail.

Peter was eventually adopted to a family in Pennsylvania. His parents had been killed, and he was living with relatives in this bombed-out house. I had a big barracks bag with the names of German kids who wanted to correspond with Americans and vice versa. We started a lot of kids communicating.

I tell of a little girl in the start of my book, *The Berlin Candy Bomber*. Her name was Mercedes, and she wrote that we were causing her trouble because we were scaring her white chickens. They lived by Tempelhof, and when we flew in, apparently the chickens thought we were chicken hawks. They would run in the coop and molt and not lay eggs. In her letter, in the last paragraph, she said, "Look, when you see white chickens, drop it there. It won't matter."

We couldn't find her. We looked. I had my buddies look for the chickens. In fact, we saturated the approach and still didn't hit her. That was in November, 1948. In 1970, because of those two sticks of gum, I was sent back to Berlin as a full colonel and as commander of Tempelhof in Berlin. The Germans had heard I was still in the air force and wanted me back as commander. While there, I kept getting invitations out to dinner, but I found I couldn't accept them. We were so busy every night with official functions, representing the air force in the city. Meanwhile, it seemed everybody in the town who ever caught some gum or candy wanted my wife and me to dinner. Sadly, we had to turn them down. Finally, we went ahead and accepted this one invitation.

It was at an old apartment house not far from the airfield. The couple took us up to their apartment. The lady went to the front room and reached into the china cabinet. She brought out an old letter and handed it to me. It was dated November 1948. Anyway, the letter said, "Dear Mercedes, I can't find the chickens in your back yard. I hope this will be all right." The woman said, "I'm Mercedes. You silly pilot, come here and I'll show you where the chickens were." So I took five steps and looked down below in the courtyard, and there was where she had kept the chickens.

My wife and I and our kids have slept many times in the bedroom Mercedes wrote that letter from. In September 1989, we were in Germany and flew over Tempelhof and dropped parachutes to their four kids and seven of our grandkids, commemorating our last vittles flight into the city 40 years before.

After I came back from being the commander in Berlin, we had Mercedes and her husband, Peter Wild, a high school chemistry teacher, come to visit us. We introduced them to a German teacher in Provo, Brent Chambers, and started an airlift from West Berlin to Provo. Since 1980, we have had several hundred West Berlin students come to Provo, as well as students from Provo and Timpieu high schools going to West Berlin. This is an ongoing exchange program—all as the result of two sticks of gum.

Sounds like you have been a real force for internationalism.

It's been a real wonderful experience.

Tell me about making the parachutes for the candy drops. Did you have in experimentation while making them?

Yes, I did. I had a test program. There was an old barn that I lived in when we got over there. When we first got there, they put us in some tar paper shacks, which had nothing but a stove. The place looked like a concentration camp. Being a farm kid, I gravitated to an old barn near the shacks instead, and put my cot up in the loft.

There was a reasonably good attic in the barn. Anyway, before I started dropping candy and gum to the kids, I took a couple of blocks of wood to simulate the candy and tried different ways of rolling up the handkerchief. I would throw it out and see which way would open more quickly. I needed the parachute to open pretty quick because it didn't have much time to open before it hit ground. This guy saw me doing this and thought I was losing my mind. He said, "Hey, I see you're trying to go back to the States early." I couldn't tell him what I was doing; I had to keep it a secret. Finally, I figured the best way to wrap it was using a continuous roll. The top of the parachute was clear on the inside and the strings and candy were all on the outside. That way, the weight of the thing would pull it down quickly, and it would open up. So I did have a research program—though limited in nature.

Do you remember your last flight?

Yes, yes. The last flight I took into Berlin was in the middle of January 1949. I went back there with an extra load besides the flour—a big load of candy and gum—and dropped it. Then, I hitchhiked back to Berlin just to make a few contacts with people. Kids would come to Tempelhof and give crew members flowers, teddy bears, and other gifts. I just stood there and reminisced for awhile just before I got into the airplane for the ride out of West Berlin. I thought it would be the last time I would see the city. I remember this little girl who came up to me with a little teddy bear. It was not a new one—it was a used one with worn elbows. She said, "Look, I have had this with me through the war when the Americans and British bombed our city. I held this close in our cellar and then, later on, when the Russians came and finished destroying the city, I also held it in my arms in the cellar. This is my good luck symbol, and I want you to fly with it—to give you and all of your friends good luck in bringing us supplies to keep us alive in the city." She was crying. I tried to give it back to her because it was a special possession, one of the four she had left in her life. She wouldn't take it. She said, "Oh, no, it's for what you are doing for the people of Berlin." Boy, that shook me up! I'll never forget that. In fact, that same memory surfaced again, standing on that same ramp at about the same place but on September 3, 1989 when the kids and grandkids of the 1948-1949 children came back to Tempelhof to catch the candy on the 40th anniversary of the last vittles flight. Many Berlin Airlift veterans were with us on the ramp celebrating the 40th anniversary.

How many airlifters were there?

Over a hundred with their wives. That was one of the greatest, but the moment I will never forget is of that little girl, giving me the bear. It was the depth of her understanding and the appreciation of what was going on. When you give up something that is part of you, there is a communication that can be affected in no other way. It is the same kind of feeling that I and other pilots, got, working to save a people who, not long before, we were trying to obliterate. Here we were, working in every type of weather, and under terrible circumstances, for these people because they were dedicated to the cause of being free no matter what the discomfort.

Did you run into any harassment there?

Yes. We didn't know what was going to happen. We were there at the beginning, and we didn't know how the Soviets were going to react. We were going right over the top of big fighter fields that were loaded with Yak-3 fighters. They were everywhere. We didn't know if they were going to shoot or not. They would come right up under your nose and do a vertical roll right in front of your windscreen. Or they would fly right off your wing tip—or come head-on and pull up at the last minute. Buzzing was one of the most obvious forms of harassment. After they didn't shoot, we heard that President Truman had sent B-29 bombers into the airstrips in England. He had warned the Soviets that we had our atomic bombers over there, and they had better keep their hands off the transports. For that, we felt much better. After that, we didn't think they were going to shoot, it was kind of fun to see those jokers come along—as long as they didn't come too close. The other harassments were things like searchlights at night—right on the border in West Berlin where you would be letting down. This was especially true at the Royal Air Force Field at Gatow, located right on the border.

Was there one type of harassment that really bothered you?

The main harassment was the one I described—being buzzed and wondering whether or not you were going to be shot at. That was the main one for me. The second one was the placement of a false radio beacon outside of Tempelhof. It had the same frequency as the Tempelhof homer. One night we actually got lost in bad weather and picked up this radio beacon that was on the same frequency. We could have been in Poland, for all I know, before we turned around and realized where we were. It was a very bad night. We missed Tempelhof altogether. We finally got turned around. It took us quite a long while flying west to get back in Berlin.

Who held the record for flights in the airlift?

I had only 126. That wasn't any record. I think Jack Bennett probably has the record. He was a civilian, an American Overseas Airlines pilot. He was there with C-54s when the airlift started. The blockade officially ended the twelfth of May 1948. The airlift kept going until September 30, 1949 to insure adequate supplies were available.

What would you have done without flight? What has flight meant to your life?

It really has provided the basis for what I have done in, and with, my life. It has been a long, real dream that I've had since I was a kid working in the fields on the farm—to get up in the air and go. It's led me to a better understanding of people in different parts of the world, a greater respect for the beliefs of others, for how they live and how they think. It's given an enrichment to my life to be able to span this distance between people and ideas and way of life. Not only that, there is that special quality I've always felt since leaving the ground on my first flight: the disconnect feeling. It just seemed like another world. My mind would leave a lot of things behind. Anytime I flew, it sort of released me to be up there in the blue—even in bad weather concentrating on the gauges. It seemed like an elevated feeling of existence, just like when you go out on a camping trip and get caught in really bad weather, inadequately prepared, and you are freezing and miserable for a week. You come home, and boy, there is a thermostat, running water, and a dry bed. I guess flying has added a flavor to my life that I sure would have hated to miss out on.

Howard Baugh with a P-40 Warhawk in Sicily during summer 1943.

HOWARD BAUGH
Tuskegee Pilot

Howard Baugh entered the U.S. Army Air Corps in March 1942 at Tuskegee Army Air Field, Alabama. He received his pilot wings and commission as a second lieutenant in November of that year. Baugh flew combat missions in the European theater from July 1943 through September 1944. Following WWII, he remained in the air force, finally retiring in 1967 after 25 years of active duty.

Baugh was born in Petersburg, Virginia, and attended public schools there and in Brooklyn, New York. He graduated from Virginia State College (now University).

For the interview, we sat down in the kitchen of my house, around an oak table, and Baugh, a man of modesty, strength, and grace, settled into a hard, oak chair as if it were a cockpit.

Tell me, how did you decide to become a Tuskegee pilot?

The idea wasn't to become a Tuskegee pilot. The idea was to learn to fly. I had always been interested in flying. As a teenager, I read many stories about the air war over France and Germany during WWI. I heard an airplane, and I would run out and look up and see what was there. Flying was something that I'd always wanted to do. At that time, of course, the Army Air Corps wasn't taking applications for pilot training from African-Americans. As soon as I found out in 1941 that the military had changed its policy, I made application and was fortunate enough to qualify on the written exam and the physical, and to be accepted for pilot training. Then I went to Tuskegee.

What is your earliest memory of Tuskegee?

The earliest memory was the railroad station nearest the base where passengers were let off the train. The station consisted of a small wooden shack about the size of this room. There was—nothing no station master or anything. The train just let you off and went on. There was no transportation from there, and it was three or four miles from the base. Fortunately, there was a telephone, so you could call the base and get somebody to come out and pick you up.

It wasn't exactly what I expected. It was a total disappointment at first. When I did finally get to the base, I found out that the base was still under construction. The roads had not been paved. There was red clay in the streets, and everywhere you went you picked up the red clay on your feet. Things were crude.

Oh, yeah, I got adjusted all right. The biggest adjustment was to the hectic training schedule—classroom, instruction, close order drill, physical training, etc. The construction people continued to build the base. They paved the streets and completed a lot of buildings while I was in pilot training. Then, by the time I came back from overseas and went to Tuskegee Army Airfield again, it had been completely finished.

Although it wasn't mentioned in the movies, a lot of the tough part of the training was the hazing that we got from upperclassmen. And of course, the training itself was tough. We attended classes for half the day, and we flew the other half. I thought I could learn to fly, and evidently I could, because I didn't have a very difficult time with the airplanes. There were things to remember and things to master, but it went well and I got along very well with my instructors. I think they were pleased in general with my performance and my progress.

Was there any time you had doubts, though? Did you ever have any doubts?

I think everybody going through there had doubts. We didn't know if we would master the training as quickly as was necessary. We knew that some things could come up and we could make mistakes in the air that would get us eliminated. We saw our classmates being eliminated and knew we could be next. There were doubts right on up to the end.

Did you have any buddies that washed out that you felt really badly about?

Oh yeah. A fellow from Brooklyn, New York, whom I had known as a teenager, when I was going to high school up there, washed out. He had finished all the training and had gotten so close to graduation that his name was on graduation special order, but for reasons that were never made clear to me, he didn't graduate and didn't receive his commission and his wings.

Was that a racial thing, do you think?

I have no idea. I don't really have any reason to believe it was racial. We were all black. There were originally 20 cadets in the class. Only four of us graduated. Of course, the instructors at that time were White, because we didn't have any qualified Black instructors at that level of training. We had Black instructors in primary and light airplanes, but after that, we had all White instructors.

71

What is the biggest misunderstanding that people have about the Tuskegee flyers, in this day and time?

I don't know that they have a misunderstanding. It's just that a lot of people didn't know about us until the movie came out; not even Black people. The movie was successful in making the public aware of the Tuskegee Airmen. It was a commercial venture that made money. It was entertaining. It was done well. There were a few things that were put in it for dramatic effect and some artistic license was taken.

Do you wish they didn't put in the fellow crashing in the film?

You have to understand that was for dramatic effect, for the audience. It gives people false ideas, but I don't have any objection to that. The only thing that was objected to by others that I know of was that Black civilian contract pilots were not depicted in the movie. Those that are still alive resent that, since they were an important part of our training.

*Tell me about the civilian contract pilots who taught you. Did you
have any friends who you knew real well?*

We weren't friends with the instructors. I don't think we were
supposed to be. We went to the airfield. We lived on campus at that
time, at Tuskegee Institute. We were driven to the airfield and we
met our instructors, and we were briefed on what we were going to
do individually with the instructor. We got in the airplane and we
flew. Then we left the instructors there, and we had no other contact
with them.

I was one of the first four replacement pilots for the Ninety-
Ninth Fighter Squadron, which had gone overseas a couple of
months earlier, in April 1943. I had been a pilot and a second
lieutenant for about six months. Three other second lieutenants
also brand new pilots, and I went down to camp Patrick Henry,
near Newport News, Virginia. They must have been expecting us
because they had a great big empty two-story barrack to put us in.
We were the only four in the barrack. At the end of the building
there was the usual latrine, with all the stools and basins and things
right side-by-side. Of course, we had plenty of room. But the other
White junior officers were housed in a similar building all jammed
up in double-deck beds on both floors, with the same-sized latrine.
They had to line up to go to the bathroom, and when they did, they
probably had to sit on a warm seat.

Everybody was confined to the base because the brass didn't trust
us to keep our mouths shut if we went off base. The saying in those
days was "Loose Lips Sink Ships!"

The military wasn't going to give us an opportunity to say where
we were going and when we were going and what ship we were
going on. Ironically, we didn't know in the first place. But everybody
was confined to the base. One of our pilots didn't like that idea and
wanted to get off base. So he went to see the base commander and
told him he'd like to have passes for the four of us to go off base in
the evening, until we shipped out. And he got the usual lecture
about loose lips sinking ships, and that everybody was confined.
He said, "But sir, we need to socialize with somebody and there
aren't any Black women on this base to socialize with." The guy
said, "Well, I'm sorry." He said, "Well, if we can't socialize with
Black women, we'll have to socialize with the White women." That

night, and every night thereafter until we shipped out, the four of us were the only ones that had passes to go off the base! He forgot all about the sinking of the ships and the loose lips. He had to protect the White women, who were quite capable of protecting themselves, I'm sure. That's a true story.

When we got on shipboard, we still had to be segregated. They put all the junior officers down in the hold of the ship, sleeping on hammocks, stacked one on top of the other. They had to line up to use the wash basins. In order to segregate us, they put is in the two state rooms on one of the upper decks of the ship—with built-in bunks and wash facilities right in the cabin. As it turned out we had some of the best accommodations on the ship because we were Black [laughs]. When I told that story on C-SPAN, I started out by saying, "most often, segregation is cruel. But, sometimes it's ridiculous, and that was ridiculous."

Anytime you got out of the plane and took that mask off and shocked people with the fact that you were black?

That mostly happened back in the States. In the late 1940s, and early 1950s, we would fly around the country to different air force bases, and people were surprised to see a Black pilot climb out of an airplane—especially if he had a White crew. In the 1950s, I was assigned to an outfit at Sacramento, California, McClellan Air Force Base, and our job was to ferry airplanes all over the states and overseas. I had occasion to lead a group of about eight B-26s down to Lima, Peru. We picked the airplanes up in Mobile, Alabama, flew down to Miami and spent the night there. Then we flew to Panama and spent a couple of days there, waiting for the weather down in Lima to clear up enough for us to be able to land. All the airplanes had two crew members on them: an engineer and a pilot, so we had a total of 16 people, and I was the only Black in the group, but I was their leader and I was a major, everybody else was of lower rank.

We were asked to land at three o'clock in the afternoon, because that was the time that the president of Peru was going to be there to see the airplanes come in. We landed on time. The next morning, the newspaper made a great deal out of the fact that this Black guy was leading these White people, with no sign of rank visible [laughs].

Who was their commander? I had one of those little envelope hats on, so when I went to greet the president, I took it off and put in it my side pocket. The photographers were there and they didn't see any rank at all. (That was before we started putting the rank on our flying suits.) As a consequence, I didn't have any name or rank showing. I was just another guy in a flying suit. They were surprised that a Black guy could do this. And I'm sure that occurred because of the stories they had heard prior to our arrival, over the years, of how Blacks were treated in this country.

What was your proudest moment flying?

I was leading a divebombing mission down in the valley between mountains. When we got over the target area, we found that clouds obscured the target. The peaks of the mountains were sticking up through the clouds. I wasn't accustomed to going to a target with a bomb and not dropping it on the target. We could have gone out to sea and thrown it "bombs away," but we didn't want to do that. So I was looking at my map really carefully, checking the peaks. I was able to determine that if I could find a hole, I could find the target. So I went under the clouds and left the other airplanes on top of the clouds, circling. I wove my way through the valleys, under the clouds, around the mountains, found the target, put my bomb on it, and then zoomed up through the clouds. Then the other pilots in the flight were able to dive down through the hole I had made with my bomb. That was fantastic!

Our divebombing targets included artillery gun emplacements like that. Once I was scraping along the road instead of across the road, as we were taught, and we went back for a second pass, which we shouldn't have done. We were told not to do that, but we did. The fellow that was flying with me got hit. He had enough air speed to zoom up to an altitude to where he could bail out, but he was captured and went to a POW camp in Germany and spent the rest of the war there. His name was Lewis Smith. He died a couple of years ago. Lewis and I both had motorcycles over there. He had gone to a dump where they dumped old vehicles and had picked up just enough damaged parts from Harley Davidson motorcycles to put one together. So it was an unregistered vehicle that he owned. The government didn't know he owned it. They probably would have taken it away from him. But he owned it and when he was shot down, I inherited his motorcycle. The motorcycle I had was an Italian motorcycle, a Bianca, and his was better, so I took over his. I don't know what happened to the Bianca.

So, what did you do with this? Did you terrorize the hills?

No, we'd just drive around to the different villages and visit with the people and see the countryside, in Sicily and in Italy. When we moved from Sicily to Italy, we just put the Harley Davidson and the Bianca on the C-47 and brought them with us.

What's the most fun you had with the local people over there?

We didn't have much fun with the local people. In Naples, we did have what they called a rest camp of our own. It was up over a hill overlooking Naples Bay and the Isle of Capri. We could visit there in the evening and get drinks and some of the fellows would have dates with girls. I was married at the time. It was such a nice diversion for some of the guys. Some flew combat in dress uniforms so that when they came back from a mission they could go straight to town without going back to the barracks and changing clothes. It was so much better than fighting the war on the ground. We could go up and fly an hour and a half or two hours, and then come back. We were free until the next day. We had a good time, except for the times we were being shot at.

Talk about the remarkable record in terms of the escorts.

The four of us joined the Ninety-Ninth Fighter Squadron at Licata, Sicily. We were in the Twelfth Air Force, which was a tactical air force. Our job was to support the ground troops. We did divebombing and strafing in proximity, but in front of friendly forces. We had to be precise in our navigation so that we didn't dive-bomb or strafe our own forces. I felt confident that we were able to navigate well enough to find the right targets.

When the Thirty-Second Fighter Group, with three squadrons, came overseas they were stationed at Capodicino Air Base near Naples, Italy where we were also stationed. They were assigned P-39s. Their mission was shore patrol, on the lookout for enemy aircraft and submarines. I don't know whether they found any or not.

Although the Ninety-Ninth Fighter Squadron was flying out of the same airfield as the 332nd Fighter Group, the Ninety-Ninth remained with the Seventy-Ninth Fighter Group flying P-40s. We continued our tactical mission, divebombing, strafing, and flying cover over the Anzio beachhead.

After I'd been over there a year, we were moved over to the east coast of Italy and given an air base. We occupied the whole thing. The four squadrons joined the other three squadrons to make us the only four-squadron fighting group over there. All the other fighting groups had three squadrons. But they didn't know what else to do with us. We were then assigned to the Fifteenth Air Force, which was a strategic air force. They had fighter groups and bomber groups. We had P-51 Mustangs. The heavy bombers were AB-17s and B-24s, doing high altitude bombing of places in Germany, Austria, northern Italy, Vienna, Ploesti, Romania, and places like that. Then we went over to the Ploesti Oil Fields a couple of times.

We escorted the bombers over there. Sometimes the missions were so long that we had to use two waves of fighters to escort one wave of bombers, because the bombers were so much slower than the fighters. On the way we had to weave over them to stay with them. Then we'd get out so far, and then we had to leave the bombers to come back in a straight line, instead of weaving, to get back to base before we ran out of fuel. Before we could leave the bombers, another fighter group would come up and take over the escort work.

The flights to Ploesti were memorable to me. Not just because it was a long flight, but we would fly at high altitudes, sometimes up to 35,000 feet. Our airplanes weren't adequately heated. We had cabin heat off the manifold, but it was cold by the time it got to the cockpit. We actually had some frostbitten feet, but that never happened to me.

Over Ploesti, the escort fighters—that's us—did not have to stay with the bombers, because enemy fighters could not attack the bombers on the bomb run because of danger from anti-aircraft fire—

their own anti-aircraft fire—from the ground. The bombers had to start their bomb run on what they called the Initial Point [IP], when the bombardier takes over the control of the airplane to be sure that it's straight and level and he can align his bomb site to get the bombs on the target. When that's going on, the bombers are sitting ducks for the anti-aircraft fire. There was so much anti-aircraft fire over Ploesti on each bomb run that it looked like a big, big, black cloud that they had to fly through. Although it's said that we lost no bombers to enemy fighters, I saw a lot of bombers get shot down by anti-aircraft fire over Ploesti. I saw people at 25,000 feet, or above, bail out of airplanes. Some of them had their parachutes on fire, and they'd plummet to the ground. And, of course, they wouldn't die until they hit. That's a long time to think about their home and to think about their life—a horrible way to go.

Of course, there were 10 to 12 crew members on each airplane. Every time they lost a bomber that many people went down. What the bombers were doing with the four-engine airplanes was a lot more dangerous than what we were doing with the single-engine airplanes.

There were times when I did foolish things with the airplanes, not just on the fighters, but even the B-25s, which was a two-engine bomber We were stationed at a base in Italy, and at the time they were putting down tar on the runway. We had a mission to do. I made my takeoff and when I did, I flew right over the workers. They fell face-down in the tar. By the time I got to the base, there was a new regulation that we couldn't do that anymore.

What did you like about the P-40?

There was very little to like about it. First of all, when you first got in it, it was extremely frightening. It was a big leap from our advanced trainer and finishing pilot training to getting in the P-40. You see, the trainer had two seats. You had an instructor on the first time you took off. Modern-day fighters have fighters with two seats, although the combat airplane—the tactical airplane—is a one-seat airplane. There are two-seat trainers for training in an airplane you first fly. Also, there are flight simulators to train you to fly the airplane before you get in it the first time. That wasn't true with the P-40 and P-51. The first time you got in the P-40 or P-51 or P-39 or P-

47, you soloed it. After studying the operational manual you got in the airplane, sat in there for a while to familiarize with the cockpit, and started the engine. Off you went.

Do you remember your solo in the P-40?

Oh, yeah. It was hair-raising. It was the first time that I had an airplane that had a friction lock on the throttle. A friction lock is a wheel on the throttle that you can tighten, or loosen, so that the throttle would either be hard to move or easy to move. I forgot about the friction lock and as it turned out mine happened to be loose. So, when I went down the runway with my hand off the throttle to lift the gear—the throttle flew back! I had to take my hand back up again without getting the gear up and push the throttle forward again. The right hand is on the control column, and I could not turn that loose. So here I am in a dilemma. Every time I took my hand off the throttle to get the wheels up, the throttle would come back and the engine would slow down and I'd start sinking. I had to push the throttle up again. I had to wait before I got a pretty good altitude, with the wheels down, before I could turn the throttle loose and let the throttle slide back—retract the wheels and then push the throttle up again and tighten the friction lock with my other hand.

Tell me about your solo in the P-51.

The solo in the P-51 wasn't any problem because the cockpit and the handling of it were actually a little bit easier than a P-40. We were accustomed to flying the high-powered airplanes with the power that the P-51 had. That was no big transition. There were slight differences between the two airplanes. The main difference in the P-51 was that it had much more power and that it had a four-bladed prop instead of a three-bladed prop. It had a lot more power so you also had to have more torque. On the takeoff roll with high rpm the torque would try to pull the airplane to the left. The P-51 had a steerable tail wheel. The rudder pedals were used to steer the tail wheel to keep the plane on the center-line until the airspeed was built up. The idea was to get up to enough speed so that you had air going over your vertical stabilizer, and so that you could maintain direction by using the rudder rather than the tail wheel. You had to get a pretty good speed with tail wheel still on the ground. If you didn't do that, the propeller would pull the plane right off the runway.

We had been trained in the other airplanes in stalls, to become familiar with the airplane and build up confidence in it. You'd get up into a power-off stall, a power-on stall, a flaps-down stall, a wheels-down stall, and stuff like that. So I was in a P-40 and wanted to go through this series of stalls and build up my confidence in the airplane and get familiar with it. I did all my stalls okay, and recovered from them. When you stall an airplane that means you get down just below the flying speed. You don't have enough forward motion to keep the airplane flying, so the airplane falls and you recover. So I decided I wanted to do a power-on stall. With the normal cruise power, I pulled the nose up and the airplane climbed and climbed and climbed. I got up to around 15,000 feet before the airplane stalled. Then the torque took over on the right, when the airplane lost flying speed, and put me into a violent power-on spin. It threw me all around the cockpit. I finally got to the place where I could pull the throttle off and straighten out the airplane. I must have lost six or seven thousand feet. It was a good thing I was that high to start with. Of course, I never tried that again! That occurred at Tuskegee, when I was still transitional in the airplane. I never told anybody about it, either.

It seems like you had a few secrets back then.

Oh, I did. I did some things that I didn't want people to know about.

You weren't the only one, though.

No, I certainly wasn't.

Why do you think it was that you were secretive? You were afraid really...

...that I would get eliminated. That it would get out that I had done something stupid. Something stupid like that would get you eliminated. No one wanted to be eliminated. I think it would have crushed me, personally.

Do you remember any unusual situations while you were teaching?

I was never comfortable while teaching academic subjects in the classroom. I was always confident and comfortable teaching flying to cadets, teaching instruments, giving instrument check rides, and things like that. But in the classroom, I felt that my being there as an instructor was a gross injustice to the students.

That isn't entirely logical, is it?

80

No, it's not. The last couple of years I've gone back up to Howard University on invitation where I was an assistant professor of air science. Howard was my first ROTC assignment, starting back in 1946. I stayed there for three years. Many of the people who where students in the ROTC program at that time went on active duty, and three of them became generals. They think that I was the greatest thing that ever happened to them, as a role model. I didn't think that. I told them that they give me credit I wasn't due. I still think that.

You're sure you're not just a little bit modest?

No, that's not it at all. I really, honestly feel that way. When I got the second assignment down to Tennessee State, I was a good commander. I had some excellent ROTC instructors working for me. They did the bulk of the instruction. I didn't do much, because I wasn't comfortable with it. I didn't have to do too much, so I did the minimum I could get away with. We had three or four pilots assigned there. I was the only one that would take the cadets out and go fly with them. I'd take them up in a T-33. That was a two-seat, single-engine, jet trainer. I'd take them up and fly them one at a time. I'd also get a C-47, which is a civilian DC-3, and we'd load 15 or 20 of them and take them places. I was always the pilot. They admired me for that. They felt I was a role model in presenting examples for them, and a lot of them went on active duty and did well—a lot better than I did. A four-star general that was in the program is still on active duty. He stood up in front of a big audience of about one thousand people at our convention a couple of years ago and pointed me out. He had me stand up and gave my name and said that I taught him all he knows. I replied that, because he said that, he had the greatest sense of humor in the world [laughs].

You seem to be a people-person.

I don't let things upset me. A little girl did something that she thought would make me mad. I said that when you get to know me better you will find that I never get mad at anybody about anything. That's the truth. I don't have any reason to get mad with people. They may do things I don't like, but getting mad only hurts me. People ask me, after I give them my story about the segregation and the treatment we got and the prejudice that we encountered, if I'm bitter about any of that. Bitterness only hurts the person who is bitter. It doesn't hurt anybody else. It's foolish to be bitter. There's nobody around now for me to be bitter at. That was the way back then. If you understand the social conditions in the United States at that time, understanding that will ease your mind about bitterness. You understand what the situation was, so you don't let it bother you.

81

Did you fly after retirement?

I didn't fly as a pilot after retirement. First of all, I was raising a family, had a wife and three kids. Civilian flying is expensive, and I never felt I had the money for it. Then a couple of years ago, after my wife passed, I thought I might like to get back into flying again, so I went out and took a couple of lessons in a Cessna 170. I found that the whole time I was up flying the airplane that I was thinking that I'd rather be on the golf course. I didn't understand that for a long time. After giving it a lot of thought, I determined that the reason that I didn't care for it was because that kind of flying didn't have a purpose. When I was in the air force, every time I used an airplane it had a purpose: to go some place or do something or carry somebody.

I think that I've had a wonderful life. I've had wonderful experiences. I say to a lot of people that life treats me better than I deserve. That's close to the truth. Life is good to me. I've been really fortunate.

KEITH MATTAUSCH
Troop Carrier Command

Keith Mattausch's uncle was a pilot at Felts Field, in Spokane, Washington, and that, he says, influenced him to become a pilot himself. When WWII came along, the National Guard was called into active duty. Keith had joined the 116th Observation Squadron of the Air National Guard, flying fabric-covered airplanes—twin-wing Douglas 038s. Next he trained in Santa Ana, Oxnard, and Chico, California, then went to Douglas, Arizona, for advance training and on to Austin, Texas, as part of the Troop Carrier Command. In the war he flew C-47s in the Troop Carrier Command and his duties included dropping paratroopers and towing gliders.

What were some important things you transported during the war?

After the invasion, Patton started through Europe with his tanks and no one could keep up with him. The ground supply couldn't keep up with him, so we were flying gas to Patton. I never saw him. We would fly to the front lines with 100 five-gallon cans of gas. We would drop off the gas and pick up the wounded and return them to hospitals in England. During this time, we flew for 45 days. Each morning, we'd rise at about four and fly down and pick up a load of gas and then fly to Europe, unload, and fly back. We would get back to base at about two in the morning and get up at four and repeat the scenario. I learned to sleep on an airplane. We would have three planes per flight. The lead plane would have the navigator. I would just tell the copilot to follow the lead plane. It was a long flight—about a 400 mile trip depending upon where the front lines were.

Once, I was flying back with a load of wounded and my crew chief tapped me on the shoulder and said, "Look out there." There was a German Fighter M-109 sitting on my wing flying formation with me. I thought we were dead. We had no armor and no guns. We had pistols that we carried, but they were of no use here. The only thing you can do in a C-47 is head for the deck or get down right over the water. We were right over the English Channel so I got right down on the water which made it harder for him to shoot me down. He peeled off to his left and came back at us. I thought he was going to shoot us down but he went under me and pulled up in front of me and did about five slow rolls. He took off and I never saw him again. The only thing we could figure out was that he had either run out of ammunition or he was flying a photo reconnaissance plane. He never fired a shot at us.

I did about three resupply missions for the Holland Invasion. Our first group of paratroopers landed up by Eindhoven in Holland. We dropped others by Nijmegen. We would fly in at about 400 feet at about 100 miles per hour. It was slow enough that you could see the faces of the Germans shooting at us. We were pretty low and slow. We dropped paratroopers both times. It was a big fiasco. The army intelligence didn't know that there was a German tank division sitting in the woods on rehab. We dropped the paratroopers within a mile of the tanks. Nobody knew that they were there. The poor paratroopers—half of them—were dead before they hit the ground. We did not find out what had happened until we returned to base. We blamed the generals.

When we towed gliders, we would fly in an echelon of four airplanes. There were four airplanes in the first flight, and I was the second airplane in the second echelon of four. Three of the airplanes in the first flight were shot down. We were flying down a little valley, up a corridor. Britain's General Montgomery was supposed to run a tank division up there to open the corridor, but screwed up. He ran tanks up and the Germans would just close in behind him, so the corridor wasn't really open. The Germans would perch on the side of the hill and put up a curtain of fire. U.S. planes would fly through and be shot down. The Germans had success, but at a cost. When they realized that they were hitting their own on the other side, they put up a curtain of machine-gun fire. They had 88s. We could see so many tracers that it looked like the 4th of July. I watched the guy I was following get shot down. Fortunately, though, as I flew through, the curtain of fire just suddenly stopped. Apparently the German guns got too hot and needed to cool, so I was able to fly safely through, but the guns started after a pause and two guys behind me were shot down. At that time, you don't really think about the loss. You are young and figure it is the luck of the draw. I flew on all those missions and never got a hole or even a mark on my airplane. On the other hand, I could stand on one side of some airplanes and look through them. They looked like a screen door; they were so full of holes. I liked the C-47, though. It was sturdy airplane and it would bring one back a lot of times when others would not.

Tell me something crazy you did.

About once a month we used to go to London on Friday night and pick up a plane load of girls and bring them back to base for a big party. Our Saturday parties would start at noon and last until we took the ladies home on Sunday night. We would put them in the hospital ward to sleep. About once a month, we would take three airplanes and fly to Scotland. We would return with three airplane loads of 30 gallon kegs of scotch. We got *real good* scotch for the Officer's Club. We would sell one plane load to the hospital four miles away, and we would sell a plane load to the fighter pilots four miles off in the other direction. Eventually, I got so sick of scotch that to this day I cannot drink it.

A few of the guys married English girls. Ken Wakely married an English girl, but was shot down and killed in the Holland Invasion. He was only married about two months. I don't care what anyone says. When you fly unarmed and slow, as we did, it takes guts.

How did the war change you?

I'm not sure it did. Some guys came home just shot. They did no more than I did, but they couldn't deal with it. For some reason it didn't bother me. I had fun. I learned to fly. I loved to fly. Though I did fly for awhile afterward for the National Guard, I am sorry that I didn't fly more after the war.

When you got back home did you buzz anyone?

Yes, I did. My granddad and uncle had farms down by Rosalia, Washington. We used to fly down there and work them over every other Sunday. Colonel Frost was our C.O. He had been in the old Observation Squadron and had flown with my uncle. He was a character. Once, before the war, he got an observation plane called the O-47. It was a low-wing all metal monoplane.

Colonel Frost had a girlfriend near Yakima. He flew down there one time and landed the O-47 in an alfalfa field and got stuck in the mud. His girlfriend's dad was a farmer and had a big tractor. In the back of the O-47, there is a big hole through the fuselage where you would put a steel pipe through to lift the tail up and aim the guns. The farmer put a pipe in the hole, thinking he could just pull the plane out of the mud; however, when he hooked the Cat to the pipe and pulled, he ended up pulling the whole tail end off of the airplane.

How'd you stay out of trouble?

At the time the war was coming on and no one really got in much trouble doing anything.

After the war, Bill Burns a flyer, whose dad had an auto-parts store in Colfax, Washington, did slow rolls down the main street of Colfax. He was only up about 200 feet. Everyone was awake after he came to town. Usually, the people there would get mad and call the National Guard and talk to Frost. He would assure them that he would take care of it. Half the time, Frost was leading the way when they pulled stunts like that.

We had three young men in the guard, who had just graduated from Idaho State. One Saturday, during the Washington State-Idaho game, these guys took up some P-51s and worked over the field during halftime. They buzzed it and did slow rolls. They dived and generally woke everyone there up. The school, the sheriff, the state patrol, everyone, called the squadron. Of course, C.O. Frost assured everyone that these pilots would be disciplined, but ended up telling the young men something like, "You guys don't do that again."

Did you have any close calls in the air shows you flew?

None in the guard, but overseas we usually had 40 or 50 planes flying into the same grass field with steel landing mats. As you landed, the mats would move up and down because of the weight of the airplane, and the mud would come through and make the mats slicker than hell. When you landed, you couldn't stop. You would just skid. If you landed in a crosswind, you would slide and crunch into other guys. We had quite a few accidents that way, but no one ever really got hurt.

For landing we always had a guy in a jeep with a radio. One time, I was preparing to land and he said to go around because a B-17 was due in. It was all shot up. We went around and the B-17 came in and plowed up the field and blew up. Everyone in it was lost.

The Germans had taken all of the grease and lard from various countries to use in ammunition, so in Holland, there was no grease or lard to be found for years. After Holland was liberated, the military had to fly in a load of lard to Holland. There were actually nine airplanes. We flew 5,000 pounds of lard in each airplane. The Dutch people were so grateful. They insisted that we stay the night. In fact, they had a party that wouldn't quit. It was wild. Now, every year there is a celebration of the Invasion of Holland. A few years back, they had a 50th anniversary celebration. I know someone who went and he said that he still was a hero. Everyone who participated in the Holland Invasion is a hero. Though the Holland Invasion was a big fiasco to begin with, we ultimately liberated Holland and the people of Holland have never forgotten us.

Did you face a lot of flak going in to Holland?

Yes, on the Holland Invasion, we had quite a bit of flak. I remember when I first flew in, I looked out the left window and saw a flak tower two miles ahead. At the time there was a P-47 strafing the tower, but the tower was nonetheless shooting at us. We were level with the top of the tower at about two to three hundred feet. I don't know what happened. But I watched the P-47 fly right into the flak tower. That ended the flak tower too. The pilot must have been shot.

Any memorable characters?

I had a crew chief from Texas. He was redheaded and had a red handlebar moustache. He had hash marks up his sleeve from his wrist to his shoulder. One time I asked him what he did before he got in the service and he laughed and said, "I was a baby." Anyway, he was like Sergeant Bilko—a scrounger. We would haul 10-in-1 rations over. They were ten meals for one man or one meal for ten men. He would sometimes commandeer maybe five boxes for our own use. They had some pretty good stuff in them. It helped, because the food in England was lousy. He would trade some of the stuff to the French or English for fresh eggs or pork. One day I saw he had made himself a hotplate from a piece of the plane's armor plating. It was rather like a grill with two little burners. We had fresh pork chops, eggs, and potatoes he would cook for us. We ate pretty well.

Many of the crews had their own jeeps. Once I asked him why we didn't have a jeep. He said he would try and get us one the next time we were in France. After dumping off our supplies in Paris, we went and picked up wounded in Orly. One night at about 3 A.M. we were sleeping under the wings in sleeping bags on air mattresses when I awoke to hear a jeep roar up. The crew chief was in it. He said, "Get the ramps down, we need to load this jeep right now!" So we did. I asked where he had gotten it and he said, "Oh, I just borrowed it." The jeep said "MP" on the side. He had actually stolen an MP's jeep. We flew the jeep home, and he painted it over. He got us bicycles the same way. He was incorrigible. We would go over there and he would throw a couple of bicycles on the plane. He was a real scrounger.

We had a full colonel who was the C.O. of the base. He was 26 years old and had come up from campaigns in North Africa. I guess he had been in England about six or seven months. After the invasion of North Africa, some men ran an airline along the north coast of Africa. The rich Arabs, who wanted to get to England paid the guys one thousand dollars per person just to get their families out of the country. The troops said, "Sure we will put you on board but if you get caught, you are stowaways and they might shoot you." If a fellow had two wives and seven children, it would cost ten thousand dollars to escape. The crew would split the money equally. They did this for two years. The colonel, who ran the airlines, lived in the barracks with me. I don't know how much money he made, but one guy had a money belt with 26,000 dollars in it. Everywhere he went, that belt went with him. He didn't want to send the money to his wife because there would be a record of it and he would have to pay taxes. Occasionally, he would send a letter to his wife and would put three or four hundred-dollar bills in the letter. He had sent about half of the money back when she wrote him a "Dear John" letter that said, "Thanks for sending the money. I'm divorcing you and marrying the neighbor."

As officers, we had to censor the mail of the enlisted men. This one enlisted man wrote his wife, "Honey, I hope you are true to me but if you're not, at least sell it and save the money so we can buy a house after the war."

91

Did you enjoy flying in the National Guard?

I enjoyed flying in the National Guard the most. We could go anywhere within the radius of 1,000 miles without prior permission from the Guard Bureau in Washington, D.C. Los Angeles and Las Vegas were 997 miles away. We traveled there a bit. We would tell Frost that we were going to Las Vegas and we needed the A-26 to go there. We had requirements in the National Guard. For example, we had so many hours a year of navigational training that we had to take. We also had night flying, instrument flying and cross-country flying. If we went somewhere, we would log instrument flying for part of it to meet our requirements. We would fill our requirements that way, rather than just boring holes in the clouds over Spokane.

How would you like to be remembered as a WWII flier?

I would like to be remembered as one of the guys who survived.

Alex Vraciu aboard the USS Lexington immediately following the Marianas "Turkey Shoot" June 19, 1944. The six victories he made that day made him the leading Navy Ace for four months.

ALEX VRACIU

Navy Ace

Picture this: a navy flier parachutes from his damaged aircraft into the Philippine jungle where he is met by USAFFE guerrillas. They eventually appoint him brevet major, and for the final week of this episode, he finds himself in command of 180 troops, dodging Japanese and heading to meet General Douglas MacArthur's advancing Americans.

Made ace-in-a-day during the Marianas "Turkey Shoot" when he shot down six enemy planes, Alex Vraciu is modest about his remarkable achievement, attributing much of his success to being at the right place at the right time. Overall, he achieved 19 victories and destroyed another 21 planes on the ground—being the United States Navy's onetime leading ace for four months in 1944. He ended WWII as the fourth-ranking navy ace. Despite his brilliant record, his achievements may not have received full or adequate measure. He was nominated for a Medal of Honor, but that nomination never got acted upon, due in part, to the foibles of internal politics and careless government record keeping.

The son of a policeman, Alex was born and raised in East Chicago, Indiana, and attended DePauw University on an academic scholarship. He trained under the Civilian Pilot Training (CPT) program, and first carrier-qualified on the USS *Wolverine*, a converted excursion ship, on Lake Michigan. From there his journey took him to places like Wake Island, Rabaul, Tarawa, Kwajalein, Truk and the Marianas, the Philippines, and to carriers like the *Independence*, *Intrepid* and *Lexington*. In all, he survived service on six carriers, two of which were torpedoed.

While he served as commanding officer of Fighting Squadron Fifty-One, he won the high individual air-to-air competition in the 1957 Naval Air Weapons Meet at El Centro, California, where he out-shot all navy and marine pilots. He received the following message from the commander of the Pacific Fleet:

> I AM DELIGHTED TO HEAR THAT YOU ARE TOP GUN IN JETS PEACE AS YOU WERE WITH HELLCATS IN WAR X. CONGRATULATION AND WELL DONE X,
> ADM STUMP X CINCPACFLT

Had you always planned on becoming a pilot?

I knew I was going to fly after sensing a war coming on in 1940. Once the military started drafting people in 1940, I declared for the navy. I had an instructor in CPT who had been a naval reserve pilot, and he got me thinking Navy during the summer vacation between my junior and senior years.

You flew with Butch O'Hare. Any lessons learned from him?

We needed heroes badly early in the war, and the military had a pretty good one in him. O'Hare was given command of his own fighter squadron, flying F6F Hellcats. A friend and I had occasion to toss a coin to see who would be one of the first assigned to the squadron. I won the flip and for five months served as Butch's wingman and later, section leader in his division. I consider myself most fortunate to have learned my trade from this remarkable man. Having one's first combat while flying wing on this kind of leader gives one the necessary confidence to fight competitive-smart against a highly dedicated enemy. Without even thinking, I found myself, time and again, using the techniques that he advised, like developing a swivel neck; looking back over one's shoulder before commencing a run; conserving fuel and ammunition; firing close-in and aiming at the wing roof of the enemy plane. Once in a practice dogfight with him, I could see that he was getting closer to my tail, so impulsively I headed up into the sun to escape. I'll always remember him telling me afterwards, "You can go up there and possibly spin out, killing both of us, and that is not going to serve either of us too well." Also, I had been the kind of guy who wanted to fly other kinds of planes. When we were in Maui, I wanted to fly a local P-40. Butch tried to talk me out of it. He said, "Why do you want to do it? Is it just to say you did it?" And that was basically true.

Were you in awe of him?

I think all of us were. Butch was a natural-born leader who easily instilled learning and confidence in his squadron pilots, primarily stressing gunnery and teamwork. He had a quiet demeanor—never said much—but then, he never had to. We listened to him, because of his experience and service reputation.

What exactly happened to him?

In November 1943, Butch O'Hare moved up to air group commander, assuming command of Air Group Six, taking Bombing and Torpedo Six aboard the *Enterprise*. Butch's Fighting Six remained divided on three light carriers. Butch was lost on November 26, 1943 on an innovative, but tragic night encounter forty-five miles west of Tarawa. At the time he was pioneering a way to counter the repeated enemy night aircraft torpedo attacks against our carrier task force. Butch and the C.O. of Torpedo Six devised a plan—two Hellcats flying wing on a torpedo-plane equipped with radar were used to intercept the enemy night torpedo attacks. It was primitive, but it worked! What happened to Butch in the rendezvous that night, following the breakup of the enemy attack, has never been determined. The turret gunner on the TBF asserted that when a fourth plane (enemy) tried to join up on their formation, he fired on it, and that the turret gunner on the enemy Betty bomber shot down Butch in the cross-fire. It was a *bitter* loss to us all! I later had to tell his wife about the incident.

Could you describe the situation where you told her?

I just related to her what I had learned from others. Obviously she had received letters, but one of the hardest things emotionally that I have ever had to do in my life was to tell about 17 gathered O'Hare family members about Butch's death. Later in 1992, I was able to

95

meet 28 O'Hares when the city of Chicago commemorated the 50th Anniversary of Butch O'Hare's legendary Medal of Honor flight off the old *Lexington*, which eventually led to the naming of Chicago O'Hare Field.

How did you feel after you got your first Japanese plane? Did you think you would get another eighteen?

I felt pretty damn good! Remembering Pearl Harbor was foremost in my mind, but thinking in terms of total numbers in the war wasn't in the picture. It was strictly day-to-day. A lot of it was pure luck, and frequently depended on which flight you were assigned. Surprising though, as it may sound, some guys went through the whole war and didn't see an enemy plane. Then again, there were a number of bomber pilots who would have made darn good fighter pilots, but they were assigned to bombers.

When I went through training, it was no secret that I wanted "fighters," and if the navy had not given me the choice, I would have gone for a transfer to the Army Air Corps. It was possible to do so early on in the war. When I shot down of the Betty at Tarawa, it occurred when our flight director vectored our division onto a low-flying Betty or Snooper. I had the "fastest" Hellcat that day and burned the Japanese plane on my first pass. Prophetically, the plane turned out to be the very type enemy plane that I was to be gunning for, if humanly possible, after learning that Butch was lost. I vowed to down ten of those bastards for Butch, but ultimately had to settle for only five by war's end.

What about Kwajalein?

The January 29 raid on Kwajalein came about after the VF-6 squadron would be rejoined as part of Air Group Six on the *Intrepid*—our initial deployment with the *Intrepid*. I wasn't scheduled for the first two flights, but was on the third of that day—a 10 A.M. mission, a target over Roi Airfield. The first strikes ran into some air action, but I wasn't too hopeful of any action continuing, until it was our turn. Arriving at the Roi Airfield, there did not seem to be any enemy planes airborne, so we prepared to strafe targets of opportunity—in this instance, parked aircraft on

the airfield. I had hardly started my dive with my wingman, Tom
Hall, when I saw a string of Bettys flying low over the field. They
had arrived from Lord-knows-where. So I immediately aborted
our dive and positioned my section for a "high side" run on the "tail
ender," who was flying straight and level. I barely touched the trigger
to fire my six .50 caliber guns, when the Betty started flaming around
the starboard wing roof and immediately crashed into the sea. I
had fired out at a distance of three hundred yards and it seemed
right—I had a perfect shot. Looking ahead I saw another Betty
flying at about 300 feet. He dove down to 100 feet as I came in on
his stern. On my first burst, the port engine and wing exploded,
and the Betty crashed into the lagoon. In retrospect—I don't know
exactly when—I probably caught a round in my hydraulic system
from his tail gunner, because something affected my ability to fire
at the next plane. But this one made number two. Just before he
crashed, I saw bodies dropping or jumping out of the plane into the
water. The plane was burning so badly that they probably had no
choice. Again, I looked ahead—two more in line. I headed after
the nearest one, and Tom Hall pursued the farthest one. The Betty
that I was approaching started turning west, and "poured on the
coals" low on the water. I headed out after him. I pulled up abeam,
out of range and could see the tail gunner already shooting at me—
I had to be respectful of his 20 mm cannon—that "stinger" back
there. So I did what I had practiced against friendly planes while
going from island to island in Hawaii, but this time it was "for
keeps!" I pulled up abeam, intent on making high deflection runs
from one side to the other, trying always to be on the move. I made
a run with no visible effect. On the next run, I found that only one
of my guns was firing. I continued to make runs using flat-sides,
with the Betty jinking and turning into me. Even with constant
charging, only one of my guns was operative for the rest of the
attack. I would get out about one or two rounds and the firing
would stop. It was exasperating, because I could see the pilot's damn
tracers heading my way practically each time I made a pass. But I
didn't want him to get away. I would have chased him back to
Eniwetok. I made about seven or eight runs. All of a sudden—I
don't know whether I was just lucky after my last run—but I saw
the Betty nose toward the sea and crash from an altitude of about
80 feet. The Betty pilot must have been hit.

97

I returned to the carrier after notching three Bettys, and that made me feel really good! A good start on my vow! We had subsequent hops after that, but just to show how ironic things can be in war, my wingman, Tom Hall, was killed the next day on a pre-dawn launch. His Hellcat was spotted forward of mine, so he took off ahead of me. His left wheel appeared to hit a stanchion off the port bow of the *Intrepid*, and his belly tank blew up in the collision. His plane ended up in a big fireball falling off the port side into the water.

Talk about the first Truk raid on February 16, 1944.

When we first heard of the planned raid on the fortress of Truk, there was a great amount of speculation floating around about it. The place was highly touted as the Imperial Japanese Navy's main fleet anchorage outside the home islands. Admiral Marc Mitscher had indicated that all he knew about Truk was what he had read in *National Geographic*. The two-day operation began at dawn on February 16 with a fighter sweep by 72 Hellcats. It was a new experience for us—all fighters with no bombers to protect. Our main purpose was to take control of the air and destroy all enemy aircraft.

Three divisions of our squadron's Hellcats (12 planes) from the *Intrepid* were on this fighter sweep, with my two-plane section at the end of the group. When we arrived at 13,000 feet over the atoll, the flight leader, not seeing any enemy planes airborne, started to spiral our group down to strafe. Just before my wingman, Lou Little, and I pushed over into our divers, I remembered to look back over my shoulder. Good thing that I did! I saw a group of enemy fighter planes two to three thousand feet above and on the port side. I "tally-hoed" but the first ten planes of our flight by that time had proceeded far down toward the airfield. The leader of the enemy planes (Zeroes) and his group had started this attack on my section. I could see the enemy leader was already firing by the light flashes from his guns. I turned my section into the attack, causing him to break off his attack and head downward. From that time on there were Zeroes all around our Hellcats. We had built up enough speed—a good 250 knots—so we pulled up in a steep chandelle, and then aileron-rolled over and dived back down on a Zero that had tried to stay on our tail. He pulled up into a climbing turn—but spun out at the top. We jumped him but had to let him dive on down, because of the other Zeroes preparing to strike from above. Finally, by scissoring with other friendly planes, we were able to work all the enemy fighters down to our level and below. By fighting in the vertical, we were learning to deprive the more maneuverable Japanese fighters of their inherent advantage.

Until this time, we had not had much opportunity to press home the attack, but from then on the picture changed. We noticed that the Japanese were not reluctant to attack, but once cornered, they would dive steeply for the deck or cloud cover. The Hellcat at altitude can definitely outmaneuver the Zero at speeds of 250 knots or better, so we began to follow them down. I was able to follow three planes in this manner and set them on fire. All of them hit the water inside Truk atoll. While climbing back for altitude after one of these attacks, I noticed a Zero skirting a not-too-thick cloud, so I made a pass at him. He promptly headed for a thicker cloud, and after playing cat and mouse with him for awhile, I climbed into the sun and let him think I had departed. When I came down on him for the last time—from five o'clock above—he never knew what hit him, I'm sure. His wing-tank and cockpit exploded. The four kills raised my personal score to nine, in what I still consider the wildest action I ever participated in—the later "Turkey Shoot" included.

I had a couple of more hops that day. As a matter of fact, I flew 8.4 hours that day. That night the *Intrepid* was torpedoed by a "Kate" torpedo bomber, forcing the carrier to withdraw due to serious rudder trouble. With the provisional aid of a sail in the forecastle, the *Intrepid* returned to Ford Island, Oahu, on February 24. Air Group Six was ordered to return stateside. Not wanting to go home at this time, I requested continued combat duty. The navy obliged by assigning me to Fighter Squadron Sixteen aboard the *Lexington*. The squadron was temporarily ashore at Kahului, Maui, so I reported to VF-16 on February 16, 1944. But before I did, as Air Group Six was departing Hawaii for the mainland on a CVE, I naturally could not resist the temptation to borrow a Hellcat from Ford Island, and give VF-6 a farewell salute "buzz job."

On the second Truk raid on April 29, it was another squadron and another carrier; however, without the earlier mysticism surrounding the atoll. While returning as escort on a morning bombing strike, our flight was attacked by a small group of enemy fighters. We pounced on them quickly and destroyed them at their best-performance altitude—down low. It was a no-contest affair—after we had them boxed in. I was fortunate enough to down two Zeroes. We preferred not to fight the Zero at low altitudes, but obviously, we had no choice when we were escorting SBDs at 3,000 feet on the return leg to the carrier.

My afternoon session was a little more exciting, and it ended with me spending the night on one of our task force destroyers. Again, I was on an escort mission, and while I was setting up at nine thousand feet for a strafing run on one of the Truk Atoll airfields, my Hellcat was hit by medium-altitude AA [Anti-Aircraft] fire. Part of the flak passed through my cockpit just in front of my face, showering the cockpit with Plexiglas. My hydraulic system was riddled and the landing gear was dropped down part way. Aborting my run, I was escorted back to the task force by my wingman. Being unable to fully lower my landing gear, I was given the choice of parachuting over the fleet or ditching in the water alongside a destroyer, which I did. I was high-lined back to the *Lexington* the next day. Amazingly, although some Plexiglas had embedded into one of my eyes, I never felt it until the middle of the night. The ship's corpsman deadened the eyeball and scraped out the offending glass. So here I am, having returned to the carrier after ditching for the second time in a five-week period.

You had a reputation for that?

Yes. This was one of the reasons I was starting to be labeled as "Grumman's Best Customer." The first water landing was a "power-off" emergency ditching while on a CAP, while this one was "power-on," where fortunately I could use the tail-hook to feel the water and land on the backside of a wave in heavy seas. Hitting a wave head-on could have turned out disastrous.

Next came the Battle of the Marianas, didn't it?

Yes, the big one, in June 1944. The Marianas (primarily Saipan, Tinian and Guam) lay 1500 miles south of Japan. With B-29s on those islands, the enemy's homeland could be brought under constant attack, which could thus bring about an earlier end to the war. Both sides knew that a fight was coming. In fact, just prior to the battle, making use of staff intelligence, Commander Gus Widhelm bet our VF-16 squadron a thousand dollars that we would have a fleet engagement in seven days. (Personally, I was to lose $125 on that bet.) With the initiation of recapture of the Marianas Island—and its naval aspect, the First Battle of the Philippine Sea— the stage was set, not only for the largest aircraft carrier engagement of all time, but probably the greatest aerial battle as well. We had not had a fleet engagement since the crucial battle of Midway, June 1942, and we were ready.

In June 1944, the Japanese fleet containing, nine carriers, sailed to the Marianas. They were relying on land-based naval air groups in the Marianas. They were also counting on reinforcements from the Bonin Islands, halfway between Guam and Tokyo. On the other side, the U.S. Navy fielded 15 attack carriers, plus eight CVE escort carriers, which embarked spare support planes, and three more CVEs transporting U.S. Army fighters, which were to be put ashore to operate after securing the island airfields. The preliminary action noticeably began on June 11, with our TF-58 fighter sweep around Saipan and Tinian, followed by our strong interdiction of enemy air reinforcement from the home islands. On June 15, we put our first assault troops on Saipan beaches, while two of our task groups took on Iwo Jima's garrison air force, neutralizing most of the Iwo's runways in a two-day strike. Then they steamed south to rejoin TF-58.

Our particular squadron assignment at the Marianas started on June 11 doing CAPs, followed by escorting our bombers on strikes at Saipan. Of particular note, my flight logbook indicates that on the June 12, I sank a large AK in a strike at Saipan.

You sank a large enemy merchant ship in Saipan harbor?

Yes, there was still enemy shipping around, and from time-to-time, the military would strap a 500-pound bomb on our fighters and let us have at it. As a fighter pilot, skip bombing seemed a hell of a lot wiser than dive-bombing. Anyway, I took my section down. We picked the back half of the ship. I brought us in on a low approach with a lot of speed, then lobbed my 500-pounder into the side of the vessel, hitting it right at waterline. The ship went down quickly.

On June 18, we had still not located the Japanese fleet—they were out of range of our search planes. A lot of things were transpiring that we didn't know about in the ready rooms, but ultimately it was determined that the fleet attack would occur on June 19.

You shot down something like six planes in eight minutes about this time.

Incredibly, yes. That was on June 19, 1944, in what was the Marianas "Turkey Shoot." On that morning, Bogeys were picked up on radar as they approached in several large groups. Carrier fighter aircraft were scrambled to supplement the combat air patrol already aloft. I was part of the VF-16 standby alert group of twelve Hellcats launched from the *Lexington.* As we climbed for altitude at full military power, in a "running rendezvous," I heard Sapphire Base, *Lexington's* fighter direction officer (FDO) broadcast, "Vector 270 degrees, angels 25, pronto." VF-16 skipper Lt. Commander Paul Buie led our three divisions of four planes each. I led the second division of F6F-3 Hellcats.

Overhead, contrails of fighters from other carriers converged and could be seen heading in the same direction. After awhile, the C.O., who was riding behind a brand-new engine, began to steadily pull ahead until he was out of sight. We had seen his wingman drop out. The full-power climb was too much for his engine, and his propeller froze, causing him to ditch in the water. Luckily, he was picked up 12 hours later by a destroyer.

On the way up, my wingman Brockmeyer kept insistently pointing to my wing. Thinking he had spotted the enemy, I attempted to turn over the lead to him. I signed that by tapping my head and pointing at him, but he would only shake his head negatively. He did it three times, but I finally shook him off in order to concentrate on the immediate task at hand. I found out later that my wings were not fully locked—the red safety barrel locks were still extended, which explained Brocks frantic pointing.

My engine was throwing an increasing amount of oil on my windshield, forcing me to ease back on the throttle. My division stayed with me, and two other planes joined up. When I found that my tired engine would not go into high-blower, that meant our top altitude was limited to 20,000 feet. Our predicament was reported to the FDO. But apparently it was all over before our group reached this particular wave of attacking aircraft, so I was ordered to return my group to the task group and orbit overhead at 20,000 feet. We had barely arrived at our station when the FDO vectored us on a heading of 265 degrees. Something in his voice told us that he had a good one on the string. The Bogeys were 75 miles away, when reported. We headed outbound in hope of meeting them halfway. I saw two other groups of Hellcats converging from the starboard side; four planes were in one group and three were in the other. About 35 miles away, I "tallyhoed" three Bogeys and closed toward them. In the back of my mind, I figured that there had to be more than the three, as I remembered the seriousness in the fighter director's voice. Spot-gazing intently, I suddenly picked out a large, rambling mass of at least 50 enemy planes 2,000 feet below us, port side and closing. My adrenaline flow was high. The Japanese were about 35 miles from our forces and heading in fast. I remember thinking that this could develop into that once-in-a-lifetime fighter pilot's dream. Puzzled and suspicious, I looked about for the fighter cover that one would expect over their attacking planes, but none was seen. By this time we were in perfect position for a high side run on the enemy aircraft. I rocked my wings and began a run on the nearest inboard straggler, a Judy dive-bomber. Peripherally I was conscious of another Hellcat having designs on that Jap also. He was too close for comfort and seemed not to see me, so I aborted my run. There were enough cookies on this plate for everyone, I was thinking. Streaking underneath the formation, I had a good look at the enemy planes for the first time. They were Judys, Jills and Zeroes. I radioed an amplified report.

After pulling up and over, I picked up another Judy on the edge of the formation. It was mildly maneuvering, and the Japanese rear gunner was squirting away as I came down from behind. I worked in close, gave him a burst, and set the plane afire quickly. The Judy headed for the water, trailing a long plume of smoke. I pulled up again to find two more Judys flying a loose wing. I came in from the rear to send one of them down burning. Dipping my Hellcat's wing, I slid over onto the other and got it on the same pass. It

103

caught fire also, and I could see the rear gunner continuing to pepper away at me as he disappeared in an increasingly sharp arc downward. For a split second I almost felt sorry for the little bastard.

That made three down, and we were now getting close to our fleet. Though the number of enemy planes had been pretty well chopped down, many still remained. It did not look like we would score a grand slam, and I reported this to our flight director's office. The sky appeared full of smoke and pieces of aircraft, as we tried to ride herd on the remaining enemy planes in an effort to keep them from scattering.

Another meatball broke formation ahead and I slid onto his tail, again working in close, due a great deal to my inability to see clearly through my oil-smeared windshield. I gave him a short burst, but it was enough. The rounds went right into the sweet spot at the root of his wing. Other rounds must have hit the pilot or control cables, as the burning plane twisted crazily out of control.

Despite our efforts, the Jills started their descent for their torpedo runs and the remaining Judys prepared to peel off for their bombing runs. I headed for a group of three Judys flying in a long column. By the time I had reached the tail-ender, we were almost over our outer screen of ships, but still fairly high when the first Judy was about to begin his dive. As he started his nose-over, I noticed a black puff that appeared beside him in the sky—our five-inch guns were beginning to open up.

Trying to disregard the flak, I overtook the nearest bomber. It seemed that I had scarcely touched the gun trigger when his engine began to come to pieces. The Judy started smoking, then torching on-and-off, as it disappeared below me. The next plane was about one-fifth of the way down in his dive before I caught up with him. This time a short burst produced astonishing results. Number six blew up with a tremendous explosion, right in my face. I must have hit his bomb. I have seen planes blow up before, but never like this! I yanked the stick up sharply to avoid the scattered pieces and hot stuff, then radioed, "Splash number six! There's one more ahead, and he's headed for a BB (battleship). I don't think he'll make it." Hardly had the words left my mouth than the Judy caught a direct hit that removed it permanently. The pilot had apparently run into a solid curtain of steel from the battlewagon.

Looking around, it seemed that only Hellcats were in the sky with me. Glancing back along the route from where we had come, in a pattern 35 miles long, I saw flaming oil slicks in the water, and smoke still hanging in the air. It did not seem like eight minutes, but that's all it was—an eight-minute opportunity for a flight of a lifetime.

I was satisfied with the day's events and felt that I had contributed my personal payback for Pearl Harbor. However, this feeling began to dissipate in a hurry when some of our own ships' gunners tried to shoot me down as I was returning to my carrier. Although my IFF [identify friend or foe] was on, my approach was from the right direction and I was making the required two 360-degree right turns, it did not seem to matter to some of the trigger-happy gun crews in the heat of this fleet battle. I would like to think that the choice words I uttered on the radio stopped all that nonsense, but I know better.

So I came down and landed aboard the *Lexington*, and I flashed my "six" fingers at the bridge as I was taxiing up the deck. As can be expected, there was a great deal of excitement later in the ready room—including the liberal use of hands to punctuate the aerial victories. Because this was Admiral Mitscher's flagship, the war correspondents were having a field day. As I remember, VF-16 scored very high in the total number of victories that day in the "Turkey Shoot," topped only by VF-15 on the *Essex*, under the CAG (Commander Air Group) leadership of Commander David McCampbell.

The "Mission Beyond Darkness" followed, didn't it?

Yes, the next day. Early, on the morning of June 20, TBM search teams were sent out to locate the Japanese fleet, which was withdrawing westward. It was not until 3:38 P.M. that one of the teams was successful in locating the enemy fleet. Less than an hour later, TF-58 began launching 227 effective sorties. Aside from the late launch, which meant a nocturnal return, everyone was concerned about fuel. Admiral Mitscher, after recognizing that it was going to be extremely tight distance-wise, still decided to launch his strike. He said, "Launch 'em!"

We had been in and out of our ready rooms all day long anticipating a launch. We had been released from "ready alert" when we finally received word of the search plane contact. Our flight was to be so long that we had to go half scale on our plotting boards. We figured that our Hellcats would have enough fuel for this mission, but recognized the bombers would be running on fumes for the return. After a few last minute "aborts," we ended up launching nine fighters, which escorted 15 SBD bombers and six TBMs. The latter carried bombs instead of torpedoes. The first plane launched of this group from the *Lexington* was at 4:24 P.M. It utilized a running rendezvous to conserve fuel.

We knew that by the time we got there and back, it would be pitch-black. Personally, I was not worried about landing aboard at night because of my night-fighting "But Team" training with VF-6, but a lot of the other pilots had never made a night landing aboard a carrier. Frankly, that's why it was such a melee and why so many of our planes went into the water. Many were low on fuel, desperate, or had combat damage. Then, of course, we had the problem of the upwind leg of one carrier interfering with the downwind leg of another carrier—in the landing patterns. But the fact was that the fleet was not prepared to fly at night. Later, we had specific carriers designated to provide night-flying capability for each of our task groups.

En route to the target, our fighter escorts had to make *S-turns* or weave frequently (Thatch weave), because of the slower cruising speed requirements of the bombers. Eventually we got there, after an hour and forty-five minutes, and because of intervening clouds, I lowered my low-cover planes to keep our bombers in sight. Our group leader's flight course—as we arrived over the Japanese fleet—took us along side of a huge cumulus cloud buildup, which separated our top cover from those of us down below. Almost immediately, my group was attacked by a large number of Zeroes. My wingman and I had our hands full trying to keep the enemy fighters off of the bombers, who were preparing to make their diving run.

Then, all of a sudden, we two fighters appeared to be surrounded by Zeroes—good pilots who knew what they were doing. Our top cover, apparently mesmerized by the clouds and rapidly developing events, lost sight of us. Brock and I were the only planes remaining with the bombers at that time. Glancing down, I saw a Zero had just set a TBM afire and sent the three-man crew parachuting into the water in the middle of the battle down below. Far too quickly, we were no longer fighting to keep the Zeroes off the bombers. Brock and I were forced into using the Thatch Weave. One of the enemy planes managed to get on Brock's tail. Brock must have been hit because he did not turn back; he normally would have on the weave. I got the Zero behind him, but the Zero had gotten Brock first. Thus I had the sad experience of seeing my wingman going down. I was able to get in another good burst at another one of the enemy planes, but couldn't take the time to see if he went down. I damaged it, I'm sure.

At that point, I had to use my last-ditch defense and dive out. I went to the rendezvous area and joined up with a damaged TBM. I didn't know what carrier it was from. The plane's bomb bay doors were dragging. I pulled along side him. He gave me the signal, which asked whether I had enough fuel to get back, and I nodded my head "yes." He signaled that he didn't have enough fuel. I wasn't sure how badly he was hit, because it was getting dark rapidly. We flew and he stayed down low and did to climb up for altitude. His wing lights were flickering, so his electrical system must have had troubles. The TBM then headed toward a group of seven of our planes that were circling low over the water. I could hear voices, one pilot saying, "I've got only 25 gallons of fuel left. I've got to ditch!" Another one said, "I've only got about 35 myself. I might as well go down with you!" The TBM seemed to join this group. I figured they all just ditched in the water. It was dark by that time, and I gave them all a heartfelt salute. I had no idea whatever happened to all these guys. We heard later that Task Force 58's search-and-rescue effort eventually recovered three-quarters of the missing crews.

So then, I was alone. I still had about 250 miles to go, but I wasn't worried about fuel. I had learned long ago that it paid to conserve one's fuel whenever possible. I knew when I was close enough to receive a signal on the YE-2B beacon—the homing device—that I would be all right. Further, I could now climb for some altitude, which would aid my radio reception. So I climbed immediately up to 8,000 feet and planned to just gut it out. Then I heard this beautiful A signal, which told me exactly where I was.

Using the coded beacon—the YE-wheel—and hearing an A signal, we could hone-in directionally on the A signal. Pretty soon, I started to see searchlights lighting up the sky. All blackout measures were suspended. When Admiral Mitscher turned on the lights, boldly ignoring the submarine threat, I was so amazed that I thought, "My God, I'm heading for Yap [a Japanese-held island]." I began to think about all those insulting remarks the bomber pilots used to make about the navigation ability of fighter pilots. I hesitate saying this, but it has been reported before. Some of the guys were real cool coming back that night, but some were breaking down on the air. It was a dark and black ocean down there! I could empathize with them, but it got so bad that I had to turn my radio off for awhile.

Eventually though, I could hear voices on our radio frequency saying, "Land at nearest base! Land at nearest base!" But I wanted to get back to the *Lexington* and my own bed that night. At the time, I was dehydrated and thirsty as hell. I kept thinking about the "scuttlebutt" (water fountain) on the ship. When I arrived close enough, I knew that I was at the correct task group, because I recognized the broad stack on the *Enterprise* as the carrier normally stationed alongside the *Lex*. Arriving overhead, I circled a few thousand feet above the wild melee below. I figured that I had enough fuel and was not particularly concerned about the carrier landing part of it, so why not let the ones short on fuel get aboard first. After awhile, things thinned out a bit, so when my fuel gauge indicator reached as low as I dared, I let down to get aboard. I phased into the landing patterns, but I quickly saw that it was a constant "wave-off" to all who wanted to land aboard the *Lex*.

What had happened was that one of the SB2C Helldivers from another carrier had made a crash landing aboard the *Lexington*. The plane had been running on fumes and was battle-damaged. The pilot was fighting to maintain low-speed control of his aircraft and ignored the "wave-off." He plowed into and through the barrier, fouling the deck. He ended up crash-landing on the plane that had landed ahead of him, killing and wounding a number of flight-deck personnel. As expected, he caught holy-hell from the flight department and some members of the admiral's staff. A "wave-off" is mandatory, you know, but he figured he could no longer "wave-off" successfully. The carrier people said, "Yes, but you could have landed in the water." I'm sure he's going to continue to spend the rest of his life agonizing over it.

So you landed on the Enterprise?

Yes, I landed on my first pass. I taxied forward of the barrier and then heard the crash horn, which told me that somebody had probably crashed behind me. In fact, the SBD behind me had taken a wave-off earlier, and the pilot forgot to put his wheels back down for his next pass. He went into the barrier. After parking my plane, I was urged to get off the flight deck as quickly as possible. Needless to say, the speaker did not have to say it a second time! I was escorted down to one of the ready rooms. The only pilots there that I recognized were some of the SBD guys from our carrier. After taking several long drinks of water, I—along with the others—was provided with "medicinal brandy" as a relaxant.

Historically, there are different figures, but I have heard that TF-58 lost a hundred airplanes that night. Some of the planes were lost in combat, but most of them were operational losses. Over the next few days, all but 34 missing fliers were rescued, in one of the finest search-and-rescue efforts in the history of the U.S. Navy. Conversely, Japanese naval aviation had virtually ceased to exist. When Japan's remaining carriers sailed again four months later in the Second Battle of the Philippine Sea, they merely served as sacrificial decoys of Cape Engano in the Philippines.

Anyway, what occurred on the "Mission Beyond Darkness" was as wild as it could come. Out of the eight survivors from our fighter squadron, apparently each of us landed on a different carrier. That was weird! Then we spent the night aboard, unwinding and sleeping. The next morning, the military decided to put all of us that had come aboard the night before with our planes, on a combat air patrol. At the conclusion of this, we were to report to our respective carriers. We had barely gotten airborne—with fully fueled belly tanks—when we were told "Return to your respective carriers, now!" Obviously, I didn't have too far to go, with the *Lexington* adjoining us. I tailed-in on two Hellcats already circling overhead. I was relieved to see that there were other survivors from our fighter squadron, although I did not recognize who they were at first.

Very shortly thereafter, we were given a "Prep-Charlie" [signal] to land. We lowered down to the carrier, broke, and spaced out in the landing pattern (I was number three in the formation), then turned into the downwind leg. The pilot, Ensign Seyfferle, who was just ahead of me in the pattern—after going through the night before and the "Turkey Shoot"—forgot that he had the weight of a belly tank full of 150 gallons of fuel. He spun-in just off the carrier ramp and crashed into the water, and all that was visible was wisps of green dye-marker coming up to the surface. I retracted my wheels, took a look at the accident scene, and told the carrier, "He's gone!" So I returned back to the pattern and landed.

For the next few days with mixed emotions, we tried to analyze what occurred on the "Mission Beyond Darkness." It was a sobering flight—probably one of the toughest hops that any of us involved had ever had—because of the way it turned out.

Then it was back to work, hitting Guam, softening it up for the landings. Agana Airfield caught the brunt of our attacks. The navy seemingly had seized complete control of the air in the Marianas.

Air Group Sixteen was then revived. They put us on the *Enterprise* at Eniwetok, and we rode the Big E back to Pearl Harbor, followed by the ride on the jeep carrier, *Makin Island* to San Diego. All of us got a 30 day leave stateside. I received my promotion to full lieutenant upon arrival at San Diego, and being the leading navy ace, I was used at will for all kinds of PR events. With further rumors of a War Bond Tour being planned for the future, I was convinced that I should request continued combat duty. By talking with Washington, he got me a set of orders to return to the fleet. The timing was right because the military needed fighter pilots. With the kamikaze threat escalating and the Japanese fleet mortally wounded, the decision was made to double the size of our carrier fighter squadrons and lower the size of the torpedo and bomber squadrons. Bombs and rockets were being hung on the F6F to make up for the bomber aircraft deletion.

At Pearl Harbor, I received orders to join the fighter squadron aboard the *Lexington*, and hitched rides practically all over the Pacific to get to Ulithi where the *Lex* was temporarily anchored after having been hit by a kamikaze. But I was soon to feel that I was not meant to be out there with VF-20.

I flew two combat sweeps with VF-20 over the Philippines on December 14, 1944. On the morning flight, around Clark Field, Luzon, we were strafing mostly, because there didn't seem to be enemy planes airborne. The afternoon sweep, likewise at Clark, started to be more of the same—dropping our bombs, launching our rockets and strafing planes on the ground. The morning hop netted me a Tojo on the ground at Angeles Field, and the afternoon flight gave me three more burned on the ground—a Betty at Clark and two Tojos [Japanese aircraft] at Bamban Field. The two tojos at Bamban were literally my downfall, if you'll pardon the pun. I learned later that six other planes were lost off the *Lex* that day to AA fire also. Suddenly, while I was pulling out of my last low strafing run at Bamban, I received a hit in my engine's oil tank. I knew that I'd had it!

Oil was gushing out of the hole just above my oil tank and coming into the cockpit. A shipboard intelligence officer had briefed us to head westward, away from the lowlands, in the event that we had to parachute. So I pulled up to about nine hundred feet and headed westward toward the Mt. Pinatubo area. It's hard to head away from the direction of your carrier, but I had to. Besides, a possible submarine pick-up was available on the west side of Luzon.

I could see the oil pressure gauge needle steadily lowering. Trimming the plane to fly "hands-off," I opened the cockpit canopy and rapidly threw out items from the plotting board and flight suit pockets—things I didn't want to have on me when I landed in my chute. When I dared not wait any longer, I climbed out on the wing of my plane and held onto the side of the cockpit and trailing edge of the wing. I was waiting so I could get even farther out of the lowlands, up into the hills. It probably was just a matter of seconds, but it seemed like a long time. When the plane started to feel "mushy" in flight—about ready to fall off into a stall—I let go and fell free of the plane, instinctively raising my hands to ward off the horizontal stabilizer. I let go at about 400 feet, quickly pulling the ripcord and saying to myself, "Alex, what have you gotten yourself into this time?"

You cannot take time to weigh matters when you have to do something like this. If you're not ready to act promptly, you are likely to kill yourself. I didn't have a chance to fully swing the parachute risers around, so I could land into the wind. As a result, I hit the ground harder than I wanted, dazing myself slightly. I had my mind made up that I was *not* going to be captured. I had heard what the Japs had done to some of our pilots previously at Saipan—gouging their eyes out and cutting off their ears before killing them. This was not just bravado talk from me, for I had my .45 caliber pistol out. Suddenly, in the distance I saw some men running toward me who didn't seen like Japanese soldiers, though I was in enemy territory and visualized everyone as being the enemy, at first. Then I heard the words, "Filipino! Filipino! No shoot!"

In no time at all, the Filipinos got me out of my oil-soaked suit and helmet, stuck a straw hat on my head, and had me put on a shirt and a pair of trousers—I could get the bottom two buttons done up. Later on, I was able to get a pair of the mayor's trousers—he was bigger. A couple of men, both USAFFE guerrillas, gathered in my parachute and picked up my backpack. They said we had to leave quickly because the Japanese had an encampment nearby and they would be converging there in ten minutes. We started off in the direction of the hills. Eventually, were into taller grass. We would run 50 and walk 50 paces—like "Scout's Pace." The men had a young, pygmy Negrito boy leading our group. He could see the path in the tall grass. The men picked me up a few times along the way, then would put me back down. I asked why, and they showed me. There were bamboo traps set in the tall grass to discourage any Japs from heading up that way. The trap would rip the whole calf of your leg off, they said. This little Negrito boy could see where the bamboo-sprung line was set, and everyone would step gingerly over that.

I wrote that day in my diary:

"Walked 18 kilometers first afternoon, backtracking six kilometers and slept on haystack till it started raining. Could hardly move from stiffness and wrenched back . . . Hesitated drinking local water till canteen emptied, then didn't mind. . . Major Stockton joined us later in day. . . . Reached Captain Bruce's camp only to find he had moved farther up in hills anticipating raid. That's why we backtracked—thought too dangerous to stay at this deserted camp. Native guides look young but seem able enough. Carry all types of rifles: WWI, Jap, shotguns, .32s, etc, whatever they can get. Majority of them didn't even have ammunition. . . ., kept thinking of missing-in-action telegram to Kay [wife] and its effect. Also of the

112

disposition of my gear back aboard the CV, the X-mas party I was going to miss after all my planning. Wasn't planning being taken alive in case of capture. Canteen and .45 getting heavier, legs and back and neck stiffer till felt like sleeping anywhere. Later in day learned that Lieutenant j.g. D.N. Baker squadron mate in VF-20, was killed by AA that morning, chasing an enemy plane. [I was] with him on the hop and he didn't come back. Major Albert Stockton brought his dog-tag along and he said he buried remains near plane."

I relaxed a little bit when two of the younger guerrillas, obviously movie fans, sidled over to me as we were walking and said they wanted to know about movie stars. They asked if Diana Durbin had any children yet, and whether Madeleine Carroll was married for the second time. Can you imagine? I thought at this point, "If that's all they're concerned about, why am I worried?"

The next day I wrote:

". . . kept seeing purple wild flowers and thinking of Kay and orchids."

And several days later, on December 18:

"Time dragging. Read English language book. Ate bat meat for breakfast along with pork chops. Appetite enormous and getting used to rice. Twenty-one Jap planes came in from the north. Some passing overhead. Seeing [Japanese] meatballs makes me ache to be flying—fighter pilot in me."

Another excerpt from my diary for December 20:

"Bruce predicts U.S. bombing for lowlands today. Lelut and Bukayo breakfast again. Reading 25-cent novel and killing flies, morning. Japs warming up planes at Pacalcal. Low fog layer covering all lowland. Breezier today. Party from lowlands reported early noon. Confirmed U.S. landing on Mindoro. Jap heavy guns. . .moving north in Manila area. Talk of Lingayen Gulf landing high now. Eight bombers (Bettys and one Helen) and seven fighters flew in. Four of fighters *new type*. Straight edge of vertical tail piece and belly tank. Couldn't recognize them and I know my recognition, I believe. Occasional escorted single bombers (two to five fighters) fly in. Bruce's prediction wrong—no action. Perfect view from "front yard" too. Misery loves company, I guess. My flying suit brought to me—Daling promised to wash it for me tomorrow. Lot of oil from plane on it. Hadn't realized I had that much thrown on me before

113

bailing out. People carry toothbrushes in pockets. I wish I had one. Salamander made direct hit on arm from top of shack. Good for laugh."

I was taken up into the hills northwest of Clark Field—in the general area of Mt. Pinatubo—in the USAFFE camp of Captain Alfred Bruce, a Bataan Death March survivor, who headed the guerrilla camp in the South Tarlac Military District. Bruce had another navy torpedo pilot there, who had been shot down a month earlier. He was off the *Hornet*. Visitors could always tell how long we had been in the Philippines by the length of our beards.

I occupied part of my time keeping notes on the air activity over the seven Japanese airfields in the valley below. When the frustration level built high enough, I would take a potshot with my .45 caliber pistol at some low-flying Jap plane. Somehow, I would feel better afterwards. But I sure didn't feel good one day when one of the visiting guerrillas, almost matter-of-factly, mentioned that the Japanese soldiers down below had already killed 22 of the men from the village near where I had parachuted, trying to get them to tell where I had been taken.

After another downed pilot was brought into the camp, we learned that the Lingayen Landings were commencing. Captain Bruce soon thereafter decided to send a group of 150 guerrillas up north—with all the vital information on the Clark Field area—to join General Douglas MacArthur's advancing army heading down from Lingayen Gulf to Manila. That peaked my interest, so I asked Bruce if I could go with them, rather than waiting for the army to come down our way. He quickly said, "Sure! Fine! Do it!" As it developed, it was a good thing I decided to go, because on the eve of departure, the designated leader, Major Stockton, had a recurrence of malaria, and I was asked to lead the group. Just like that, I found myself in charge—a navy lieutenant. I had been made an honorary brevet major by Captain Bruce prior to departure, but I didn't take it seriously. I didn't even know what it meant. I do know the men called me "Major."

One learns to assume new roles in hurry under military conditions like that. I was in command—with an aide-de-camp I called "Wednesday," who carried my gear. On the way up north, we picked up new men—approximately 30 that wanted to get in on the action, with the Americans coming.

How long before you met the advancing Americans?

It took us about a week overall. We had the opportunity to visit and spend the night at another one of our guerrilla camps on our way into the North Tarlac Military District. Captain Elliseo Mallari headed this group. They had six American airmen in their care. It was an enjoyable meeting and we talked well into the night. Some of the men were from my own carrier. For varying reasons, I could not convince any of them to join us on our Junket. Mallari's group was also part of the USAFFE guerrillas and USAFFE guerrillas authorized by General MacArthur and manned volunteers: Filipinos from Luzon and Bataan survivors in leadership roles.

Continuing our trip to contact the Americans, we arrived at Mayuntoc, and were preparing to eat lunch when gunfire erupted nearby. At that very moment, I was in the company of the mayor of the village and an American woman who was married to a local Filipino man. We were reading a leaflet that had been dropped there by our planes. The leaflet related General MacArthur's "I have returned" proclamation. We were being attacked by another Filipino guerrilla group. All of a sudden, there was a guerrilla from the other group facing me. He had a Jap pilot's helmet on his head, half-cocked, and his rifle partly pointed at me. He could see that I had my hand on my .45 caliber. I said, "Don't get any ideas."

The guerrilla could see that I wasn't a Filipino, and he appeared a little puzzled about what to do. He asked, "You Huk?" That's short for *Hukbalahap* (communist Filipino, the People's Army.) I said, "No, I'm an American! What's going on here?" He wasn't trying to do anything at that point, so I took over and began to bluff my way. I said, "Okay, take me to your leader!"

You said those exact words?

Honestly, I don't lay claim to that phrase. It just came out that way.

So we started downhill on the trail. One of my men suddenly ran toward me for protection. This other guerrilla group appeared well supplied with carbines. Anyway, they practically cut this man in half with a short burst and he bled to death there, in 10, 15 seconds. Seeing that, I got royally angry. Then I was brought together with their leader, Captain Cleto—who was in charge of this detachment from another USAFFE North Tarlac guerrilla group under the command of a Captain Hendrickson, also a Bataan survivor. By now, two of my guys were killed. I said, "Goddamn it, Captain Cleto! Here we are trying to get your country back for you, and you spend more time killing each other than you do fighting the Japs!" I had heard—and still believe it now—that there were about 125 different guerrilla groups in the Philippines back then, and they each thought they were MacArthur's "chosen few." Anyway, they stopped the shooting, and we combined forces and headed for their camp. I rode a smallish horse all night. The horse tried to bite me all the way. About 200 yards from the camp entrance, that animal just laid down and would not go another step—made me walk the rest of the way.

We arrived at this North Tarlac guerrilla camp, and I spent about four days with them. Captain Hendrickson had suffered cerebral malaria earlier in the war, and I'll give him the benefit of the doubt in discussing him. He was living like a Capone [Chicago gangster] off the land, telling the local people that if they didn't contribute three types of meat daily and all the liquor that he wanted, that the guerrillas would have them adjudged as "pro-Jap" when the Americans arrived. He literally passed out drunk the four nights that I was with them. One day he said, "You don't like me, do you?" I said, "No, it's not that. You're just enjoying this too much. You're going to have a helluva time when you get back stateside."

He had been a Bataan survivor as a private first class, and over time he apparently had worked himself to a captain via the battlefield promotion route—I was told. Anyway, after four days of inaction about heading to meet the Americans coming south, I reminded him that I had some material I had to deliver and asked him why we were not going up north. Not hesitating at all, he answered, "Well, they're coming into my territory! They should report to me!" He had developed that kind of an ego.

I said, "Well, okay Hendrickson, if you're not going, I'm going to take my guys. We'll head up north by ourselves."

He said, "No! No! No! We'll go. We'll go tomorrow."

That night we had an alert. Some retreating Japanese reputedly were going to be coming across the river just to the west of us. So, I was handed a carbine, and shortly thereafter, I was laying on my stomach on the side of the river, waiting for the Japanese. I thought to myself, "What's a good fighter pilot doing on his stomach in the middle of this God-for-saken country, at war?" Anyway, the Japanese didn't come across. Thus, we did not have to use our password, "Seven" and if they did not answer, "Eleven," start shooting. Back to camp we went, but no one slept much that night.

Late the next morning, we started up the National Highway, would you believe, with a bugler leading the way, in front of a row of three flags—American, Philippine and guerrilla. Following the flags came twelve of us "chosen few" on horseback. I was back on a horse, a larger one that did not try to bite me. Then came a goodly number of his guerrilla group on foot—followed by a scattered array of women and children, and a few dogs, all of which we had attracted passing through the little villages and up the highway. Every once in awhile, a navy TBM would come down to take a look at us, trying to figure what we were all about. We would just wave the plane, so they wouldn't shoot at us.

We continued on up the National Highway, and eventually came to an advance outpost manned by a huge army private. It was obvious that he didn't know what to do with us. He said, "Da sergeant's down the road." So we passed on and soon reached the advance elements of the U.S. Army, 129th Division, at Paniqui. The 129th Division was an Illinois outfit, and when they learned that I was from the Chicago area, there were warm feelings all around. They quickly broke out coffee, wafers and beans. I then told them that I had some material that I'd like to turn over to the commanding general. I prepared to say good-bye to my gang and to my aide, "Wednesday." In no time at all, a one-star general showed up in a jeep with an aide, and we headed off to Camiling. The general was driving, and I was sitting in the right side of the jeep. We talked while going up the line and I explained a little of the situation. His aide, sitting in the back seat—during a little lull—suddenly said to me, "You're Vraciu, aren't you?" We both had attended DePauw University. I didn't recognize him, for he was several class years in back of me. Talk about small world!

At Camiling, I turned over my central Luzon-area material and made my report about the guerrillas and the recent affair at Mayuntoc. I was then taken to the colonel's tent for some much-needed sleep. I had very little rest during the last four days. In the next few days, I had to tell my story to intelligence three times.

Captain Hendrickson never made it like the rest of his peers—everything caught up with him and I learned that they bounced him.

I remember having lunch with General Beightler, and I know it sounds funny, but I ate practically a whole loaf of bread. Having eaten a lot of rice while with the guerrillas, I wouldn't eat rice at home for three years. My wife had orders on that! After a day or so, I was taken over to the navy receiving ship *Wausatch* in the harbor, to report back into the navy. Going up the gangway, a war correspondent named Waite, who had been on the *Lexington* at the Marianas, recognized me—beard and all. He said, "Can I get a story from you real quick?" He held up his departing boat, while I gave him the story fast—with the condition that he would get word back home to my wife that I was okay. The next day, I hitched a ride on a PBY-5A Black Cat, over to Leyte Gulf.

From Tacloban at Leyte, I took a six-hour plus, open-boat ferry ride to Samar, where I had to spend several days in a personnel pool awaiting word from the *Lexington* on their plans for me. Captain Shoemaker, a previous carrier man, stopped in and expedited a transport flight to Peleliu. I reached the Ulithi forward anchorage eventually and reported back to the *Lexington* After a few days back aboard, the ship's executive officer tactfully presented me with a razor. He didn't want me to have a beard on-board the ship. That was not accepted back then.

Then, Air Group Twenty was relieved, and I attempted to stay out there and get in on the first Tokyo raid. The plan was to pick up my "missing in action" gear at Pearl Harbor and get assigned to another squadron, but when I got to Pearl, the military said, "Oh, no! You cannot operate over enemy territory until the area you were underground with is secured." So, that ended my war. For the last few months of the war, I served as a test pilot at the Naval Air Test Center, Patuxent River, Maryland, helping evaluate tactical performance of U.S. and enemy aircraft.

Logan Urice with his C–47 as part of the European Air Transport Command.

LOGAN URICE
Glider Pilot

Logan Urice enlisted in the Air Corps in October 1942. At the time he was attending Coe College in Cedar Rapids, Iowa. The government sent him to Des Moines, Iowa, for exams and screening to see if he was acceptable. He passed with flying colors. Logan was sent back to school in October, and was called in January 1943 to go into the service. The military shipped him to Jefferson Barracks, Missouri. Conditions were anything but desirable, as Logan explains, "We spent a miserable winter there in tents. Heat was from a potbelly stove with minimal fuel. We had a five-gallon bucket filled with water in case of a tent fire, but the bucket was always frozen in the morning." Next Logan was sent to a college training detachment at East Lansing, Michigan, followed by a period of extensive physical conditioning at San Antonio, Texas. Then he went back to Sikeston, Missouri, for primary flight training. After that he would go to Winfield, Kansas, for basic training and then Eagle Pass, Texas, for advanced flight training.

What was it like training in Texas?

We were out in the middle of nowhere. Flying there was interesting because the uniform for the day was shorts and sneakers. That was what we wore all day, everyday. We were given tremendous amounts of physical conditioning to the point where we could run all day, if necessary. It was amazing! Following graduation at Eagle Pass, my first assignment was with a cavalry. My time was taken up in a jeep, running around the flat land, hunting hay for retired cavalry horses. How is that for a single-engine pilot's first assignment? Later, I was asked if I would be interested in a flying assignment. I said "you bet." It turned out I was shipped to a glider school at Lubbock, Texas, for ten hours of in-flight training, which qualified me as a glider pilot. Then they hurried and shipped the contingent off to New York because they wanted us in Europe.

Do you remember your first landing in a glider? Were any of your landings rough?

No, the glider's model number was CG4A. It's a big beast with about a 95 foot wingspan. There were always two pilots per glider, so if one should be disabled the other one could save the day. There was no problem putting them down, because the glider lands more slowly than power craft. You just wouldn't do it without training.

122

Did you have any trouble braking?

No! On a combat glider mission, your objective was to get your load on the ground as quickly as possible and to leave the glider, as it would be a target for ground fire. To accomplish this, the glider had an airfoil brake, hand-activated by a lever between the two pilots. It was a means of breaking the wing lift, which resulted in a steeper descent without increasing landing speed. Once on the ground, steering and braking control were accomplished by individual wheel brakes and the option of putting nose skid pad to the ground.

How far did you have to figure for stopping?

That was your option. If you took the glider in just above a stall speed, you could stop it in 50 yards or less very easily. We were trained bring the glider to a halt on a specific spot.

Then gliders were not a hard transition for you?

No, not with the power-flight training. Student pilots were weeded out during power-flight training. If you could handle a military plane, you could handle a glider. I don't know if you know it, but glider troops were all volunteer troops.

So you're on your way to Europe then?

We went across the ocean on the ship, the *Aquatania*. There we were served two meals a day, and that was it. Because of the number of troops on the ship, we slept in hammocks, decked four high. Mighty crowded, but this was war. Landing in Scotland, they took us by train through England to a base. That wasn't the most pleasant because the hoarfrost, which was quite common, could be two and a half to three inches thick. We would consider it a snowstorm here in the United States. That cold, wet penetration was quite miserable. The thing that was the most memorable for that brief period in that setting was that the latrines were just a series of what we called "honey buckets" or five-gallon buckets.

We were then supposed to be flown to a base in France, which would be our operating base as glider pilots. When we got to France in C-47s, we landed on a metal landing strip. All the buildings were tents. We carried our dinner plates with us daily. Outside of the mess hall stood three buckets. The first bucket was food scraps, the second was sanitizing solution, and the third was boiling rinse water. After awhile they made arrangements to move us from tents into civilian French homes. The government reimbursed the French for putting us up.

Did anything funny or unusual happen there?

The gentleman who owned the place was basically bedridden. There were about a half dozen of us living in his home with him and his wife. He didn't speak English, and we didn't speak French. He loved his wine! I don't think I ever saw him drink water. Seeing their waste disposal, I can understand why! We walked to our mess from the French home where we slept. We had to pass a grave identification station before we got there—dead GIs stacked like cordwood, waiting to be identified and taken care of. It was a very grim reminder of man's mortality.

The Battle of the Bulge was my first real exposure to warfare. We flew injured troops from the Battle of the Bulge to England,

123

approximately 20 per load. That was not exactly a pleasant duty. There were temporary metal landing strips in Belgium. We'd come in to those strips to land and pick up injured troops. I will never forget seeing the line of military ambulances stretched as much as a mile. It was sickening. There was one ambulance after another bringing wounded personnel, both ambulatory and stretcher cases. By the time we got to them, the men had received some sort of medical assistance, so we were spared that part. We flew for about a week during the Battle of the Bulge.

To get one flight in a day was about as much as we could manage, because December daylight was short and there were no landing lights on our single landing strip.

That must have been tough emotionally.

I didn't feel it beating me down. It felt like I was fortunate when I saw what some fellows went through.

At Christmas 1944, the Germans dropped paratroopers in the immediate area of our glider base, so we were cautioned to be on the alert. We carried arms at all times. On Christmas Eve, we went to a little church in the village, and I think every soldier on the base attended church that night. It was standing room only. The irony there was that we were singing about "peace on earth" and there we stood shoulder to shoulder, everyone armed, singing Christmas carols! Luckily, nothing ever came of the German paratroops supposedly in that area at the time.

From then on, until early spring, we did flight training with our gliders in central France. Usually we were on a "single tow," which is one glider per towing-plane. One day on a practice formation tow, suddenly the tow ship cut us loose. I never learned why. We ended up with a forced landing in wheat stubble. Shortly thereafter, coming over a hill we saw all these Frenchmen. We wondered what was going to happen. As the Frenchmen drew closer, we noticed they all had wine bottles with them. They were so happy to see us. They wanted us to have a drink with them. To this day I never did know how I got back to my base!

They got you intoxicated?

Thoroughly! Wiped out! I wasn't used to drinking.

My first and only glider combat mission was the crossing of the Rhine. All the bridges had been destroyed as the Germans retreated. The mission was to put 1000 troops on the ground across the Rhine near Wesel, Germany. The anticipated loss numbered 300, so 13,000 went over by glider. To soften enemy opposition, paratroopers dropped by C-We went across the Rhine on "double tow" as I remember, and we went in at an altitude of about 500 feet. We met a lot of ground fire from machine guns and small arms.

How many troops per glider?

It varied depending on the load weight. Some could carry nine, ten, or 11 fully-armed troops with all their gear. You could actually roll a jeep in there if you wanted to! There was a weight load limitation of personnel/gear.

If you're bringing in that many people, and you've got a lot of gliders going, how does one keep from getting in each other's way?

We were taught to get your load safely on the ground, be it troops or materials. The gliders were considered expendable. If you were coming down between the trees, put the main portion of the glider through the trees and sheer off the wings. I mean they didn't care how you got it on the ground. Just get your load on the ground safely. There were a few errors though, let's face it.

What do you remember? Give me an example of an error.

I lost my best buddy there. The glider he was taking in flew right into a hidden German 88 gun field and it just disintegrated.

The paratroopers had a job to do once we were on the ground. Believe me, we saw many dead troopers on the ground.

Did you see your friend?

Luckily, no. I didn't know what had happened to him until quite some time later.

We had landed our glider near a plowed field, and I spent the better part of the day down in a furrow because there was small arms fire all over. When the fire ceased, we pilots grouped up a bit to find some idea where we were, which way to go. We were instructed not to engage in any firefights. The troops that we took in were to do the fighting, even though we carried firearms. If you're getting shot at, it's needful to shoot back. I know I had the option of a .45 pistol or a .30-caliber carbine. I opted for the carbine. I was qualified with a pistol, but let's face it, I was born and raised doing a lot of shooting. In fact, I hunted all my life. If I wanted to hit something, I wanted something other than a pistol.

The first night across the Rhine we came to a farmhouse, abandoned except for an aged woman in an iron bed, apparently left to die by her fleeing family. We "liberated" several mattresses from the house and slept outside, fearing the house could become a target for mortar fire.

There were gliders after our flight still coming in. It was spectacular to view, to see tracer bullets tracking the gliders as they came across the Rhine. The Germans had a lot of firepower and shot many craft down. You would feel for the boys that didn't survive. We watched from about three-quarters of a mile for less than an hour as several waves of gliders arrived, spilling out their loads as quickly as possible. We couldn't see the actual landings beyond our immediate drop zone. Squadron after squadron, but I can't tell you numbers. Wave after wave of gliders.

Tell me a little more about that battle. Did it wage for a long time?

It was pretty well whipped in a day. We were put on the ground early in the morning. From then on things were more organized. Troops seemed to come together. Squadrons, that is, troops you took in, took over in essence and worked hard, as they needed to get things better organized. While this was going on, there was continuous cover by American fighters in the sky above us, to insure that no German aircraft would sneak in. Our planes came in from all directions, at different altitudes, to provide the most complete cover. A second Allied airborne assault was anticipated, so we glider pilots were "pulled out"—that is, ordered from the drop zone, back across the Rhine on foot using a Seabee-built pontoon bridge—so as to be available for a possible second glider assault.

Who was your friend that was killed? Was he a good friend?

His name was Johnny Keiser and he was quite a guy. We'd gone through all of our flight training together, from primary to basic, advanced, and gliders. After I came back home following the service, Johnny's parents looked me up. They knew my name at least, and they wanted to know what I could add to their information about their son. We spent an afternoon discussing how we went over from the States, where he had been based and such. They wanted to give me all of Johnny's flight equipment. I told them no thanks, because the war was behind me.

One friend of mine, Randy, who flew a tow plane on the Rhine hop, got shot out of the sky. At 500 feet one doesn't have much time to get into a parachute or get out of a plane and pop a chute, but luckily he did. After that, he was indoctrinated into what they called the "Caterpillar Club". Anybody that had to make a parachute landing from a plane was an honorary member of the "Caterpillar Club".

Later on, I was assigned to a Ferrying Squadron. We used to draw some of the darnedest assignments. I can remember, once we were dispatched from France, and my assignment that particular day was to fly to England to pick up a load for a lieutenant colonel based down near Munich. The load turned out to be just a bar stool—an excellent example of abuse of rank. Another time, I had a flight to England to "pick up a load"—that's what the manifest said—and fly it to Germany. My load turned out to be approximately two and a half tons of navy beans. They weren't even bagged! They were just shoveled into the plane. Oh, what a mess! Later, I flew a French general from Paris to Reims for the signing of the Armistice, 1945.

When Patton made his tank drive across Germany, we flew fuel to him for his tanks in C-47s. We would take 53 five-gallon jerry cans. For landing we'd get assigned two areas. The plan would say for us to fly to the first one, and if we didn't draw enemy fire, we would put our plane down and unload and get back in the air as quickly as we could. If we drew fire, we would go back and set the load down at the second area. When you get 53 supposedly sealed cans in the turbulent air, the heavy fumes from them in that plane are just as nauseating as can be. Any spark introduced by a live round would take care of you and your plane immediately.

Did you ever see Patton?

Yes. After the shooting was over, I had an assignment as a private pilot for Major General T.B. Larkin, theater chief of supply. He and about 43 other general officers were billeted in the George V. Hotel in Paris. I got to eat in their mess. That was choice duty. As a general officer's personal pilot, I got the same food the troops in the field got, but it was served on a clean plate, with a tablecloth. We had tuxedo waiters who delivered coffee and drinks and even we enjoyed live orchestra music.

128

Patton was there, of course. I shared an elevator ride with him alone one day. He was immaculate in dress—a very dynamic, commanding person. He always had a pearl-handled .45 strapped on. Even under those conditions, he wore leather everything, boots and all. He was a friendly, warm person. He wouldn't mind you saying hello to him, like "Hi, George," but if it was a kind of military situation it was "Yes sir" or "No sir." He was a true military man.

So the ferrying wasn't quite as much fun, or was it?

Oh, there was fun! For awhile, I flew mail between the continent and England. Based in Paris, I'd fly mail to England and pick up a load of incoming mail and fly it back to France. Then after lunch I'd take another load to England and bring another back. That was interesting. After the shooting was over, I was stationed at a base in Paris. We would fly leave troops from Paris to the Riviera. Then we'd pick up returning troops from the Riviera and fly them back to Paris. That was nice duty. I had a little bit of seniority in our squadron, and I'd always ask for the last flight down. That way, I could spend the night on the Riviera. Later, I remember I was flying troops from Paris to Rome, and we were asked to brief those on board, because they weren't familiar with a parachute. I had several nuns in their garb. They had their long dresses on and all. I thought, "How am I supposed to show these nuns how to strap on a parachute around their torso?" Finally, I put the suit on myself in hopes that the nuns, if they had to use a chute, would figure out how to do it. I felt uncomfortable with that. Another time, I almost ran out gas flying troops from Paris to Munich. I was overloaded and had flown beyond the turnaround point. When we got to Munich, the landing field was socked in with fog. I could remember the field because I had landed there before. I remembered there was a big smokestack on one side of the field. If I hit that, there would be no second chance. We had to land. The tower talked us in. "We can hear your engines," they said. "We know roughly where you are." We had a ceiling of about 100 and as we came in on approach, we broke out of the soup, but my glide angle was too sharp, so when we touched down, I bounced back into the soup. We went around again and landed. When we got on ground, I couldn't move. I couldn't get out of the plane. My body was too tense. It puts a tremor in me even now, just to recall it. I primarily flew C-47s, but also flew C-45s and C-64s. The only mechanical problem I had was when I landed in the Riviera once and blew a tire. Luckily, it didn't "ground loop" as they call it, where the wheel would dig and spin you.

What did you think of the C-47?

It was a good old kite. My mother was killed in one in 1953. She was flying to see us on a commercial flight. Still, if I had to pick the safest plane in that period, it would have been the C-47.

That must have made you feel extra strange when you lost your mother like that?

Yes. To the best of my knowledge, the plane was not at fault. It was a severe thunderstorm and *possibly* pilot error.

Where did your mother crash?

Near Mason City, Iowa. She'd taken off from Waterloo and was headed to Minneapolis.

Any more stories about serving in Europe?

On the continent, commercial laundries weren't available so you were on your own. Some of the guys would get French women to do laundry for a fee, like cigarettes or chocolate, since money didn't mean anything really. A pack of cigarettes would go a long way to get things done. I had misfortune after misfortune in that department. Since I was a small person, the French girls could wear my GI shorts and I'd never get them back! I'm telling you, the quartermaster and I got to be old friends. He knew what I was coming for whenever I came to see him. It was always for shorts!

When I got out of the service, I went back to the farm. At the time I was almost afraid to get in a car. I had no desire to go anywhere. I remember when I returned to college, my first impression of the coeds of the time, was "what a bunch of lamebrain, silly willies—sheltered and naïve."

It sounds like the war had sobered you?

How could one not be affected by the experience I had? Yes. Among my treasured mementos are a carved duck from St. Moritz, alabaster bookends from Rome, and cameos from Naples. Also, I still have a compass, issued prior to the Rhine hop.

Upon graduation from advanced flight training, it was customary that you would hand a dollar to the first person saluting you as an officer. That was part of the game. My friend, Johnny Goyen, got his wings a month before I did, and I saluted him. He handed me a dollar. He'd written on it, "keep your head out," meaning if you are flying and get too absorbed in your cockpit, you could be a "dead duck." In training our instructor was always telling us "get your head out." Anyway, I still carry that dollar in my wallet. See. Here it is. [Logan digs deep into a compartment of his wallet and pulls out the signed dollar. The dollar appears weathered, but not so much considering the time it has been there.]

In France I was dating a girl by the name of Josette Phillipe. She spoke English so we had it covered, because everywhere we went she could translate! She was just a good friend. Before I left, she made me a white silk scarf and embroidered a little bird on it. It read in French: *Le Petit Oiseau.* ("The Little Bird.") I still carry a picture of her in my wallet. And I still have the scarf, after 50-plus years of marriage to one of the "sheltered and naïve" coeds I met in college in 1946.

Charles Huppert during WWII.

CHARLES HUPPERT
The Great Escape

Remember the classic movie, *The Great Escape*? Charles Huppert's experiences in helping to engineer equipment used in the tunnel inside Stalag Luft III, were shown in the movie.

Huppert was born in Dale, Indiana, December 18, 1918. He went to grade school and two years of high school there, but then left home. His father had died and he didn't want to be a burden on his mother. In Indianapolis, he got a job and returned to high school, graduating from Arsenal Tech. During that time, he went to school only four hours per day and worked at several jobs. Later he ended up at UCLA which led to his working in the movies.

Charles learned to fly when he was 18, and when WWII broke out, he was called up from the reserve. Charles left the military in March 1946 as a Lieutenant Colonel.

Tell me about your first flight.

I had a friend who was an instructor at the old Metropolitan Airport in Van Nuys. That was back in the 1930s when the airport was nothing more than a cow pasture. Anyway, my friend was always after me to go with him to fly. One Sunday afternoon, I went with him. He took me up and let me fly and immediately started in with some instruction. Before we had taken off he said, "I want you to look at the nose and see where it cuts the horizon. That will be your altitude of the plane you land." When we were up in the air, he said he would show me how to land. I did what he showed me until he was satisfied. Then he let me go around and he talked me through the first landing. We taxied back down to the end of the runway and then he talked me through the take off. We then circled around on the pattern and he let me land by myself. Then he said, "This just comes natural to you. Why don't you go ahead and start flying?" So I did and it was easy. I just loved to fly.

Whenever I went overseas, we flew from the states via the southern route to Africa and ended up at El Kabrit Air Base [British] on the Suez Canal. The main runway ended at the edge of Big Bitter Lake and the canal ran through the lake.

On takeoff once we lost power halfway down the runway. There was a big drop off to the lake. We went off and recovered just above the water. We flew about ten feet above the water across the lake before we could gain a few more feet and go south across Sinai and back to the base.

You really don't have time to be frightened until the situation is over. We had many times when you would really sweat. Anyone who says they flew combat and didn't sweat is lying. One time we were hit by a large piece of flak. It came in one side of the plane and went out the other. It passed between our stomachs and the wheel, taking out the radio.

We flew ground support for the British Eighth Army. In the lull between battles we would go back of the lines and hit airfields. On April 26, 1943, we went in on one called Solimon South, which was across the bay from Tunis. Here's something I wrote about it: "The first and second missions were called back at the last minute while we were setting in formation for takeoff. On the third try in the middle of the afternoon, we were finally on our way. After forming up, we headed east over the Mediterranean Sea, turning south of Malta toward the Bay of Tunis. We flew right above the water. Just before we reached the Bay we went up to 10,000 feet, with full power and at 200 miles per hour. The flak was so bad that we went up another 2,000, leveled off and started the bomb run. After spreading out a little we were immediately hit and blown out of formation. A 120 mm shell had gone off right under the plane. It took out both engines. We feathered and quickly found that the controls were not harmed and we could still control the plane. Since we still had a full bomb load and all our .50 caliber ammunition, we

134

could still turn toward the target and accomplish our mission. We were going down no matter what. So Dorrance [navigator] got the bomb doors open and we bombed the airfield. We still had air speed and altitude so we again dived on the field. As we swept across, we unloaded all our .50s at all the 109s we could see. Then we crashed a very short distance from the field on the beach. The problem was that the beach was covered with large boulders, and I believe we hit them all. We dropped the tail section first, both engines, then the nose right up to the control panel. The upper turret gunner was in the tail section. He had been told to stay in the turret but he didn't. The bomb bay moved up to the pilot's section, and the navigator was pinned upside down with his legs over the pilot's seats. The lower turret gunner was still in his seat, but his legs were pinned in the wreckage and he couldn't get out. Davis [crewmate] had crawled out of the plane and was lying by the side of the plane, dazed. I flipped the upper hatch off and crawled out, lifting Dorrance up by the legs and pulling him out through the hatch. He was cut very badly from his head to his stomach. I looked for a bag of sulfa and found one. I poured the powder in all his wounds. The big problem was how to get Galate [gunner] out. About that time a jeep arrived with a German lieutenant and driver. He first asked if I had gotten everyone out and then said, 'For you, the war is over.' He spoke very good English. I told him that Galate was pinned in and couldn't get out. I also said that gasoline was everywhere, and I was afraid that someone would light a match. By that time there must have been 50 people running toward us from the field. He sent his driver back for an axe and he ran toward the people to halt them. He set up guards around the area to keep everyone away. When the driver came back he chopped Galate out and we saw that his legs were hurt."

By the time ambulances had arrived and the rest of the crew was sent to a hospital. The lieutenant took me with him in his jeep. I asked him what his job was. He said he was the commander of the battery that had shot us down. He said that it was a 120 mm shell that shot us down. I had heard of 88s and 105s but never 120s.

135

So you miss those old boys?

It took me years to find any of them. A few years ago I found out from the Veteran's Administration that the top gunner had died about a year after the war. Last year the navigator, Sam Dorrance, was killed in a boating accident in Long Island Sound. Radio/lower turret gunner, Bill Galate, and I are the only two still living.

The doctor examined me and said that all he could find was an injury to the left jaw. He thought it could be taken care of later. On all missions I wore my field boots. I had to take them off so he could look at my feet and legs. After that he looked inside the boots and immediately found my assassin's knife. He said it would be a good one to take home.

The lieutenant reappeared just before dark and asked me if I would like to go with him to a movie. He said that he would take me if I would wear a blanket around me so the soldiers wouldn't know I was an American. Also, he wanted me to promise I wouldn't laugh when they showed the newsreels. It seems that they always showed the Germans whipping the hell out of the British and Americans. I promised and off we went to the movies. It was a very good comedy.

The next morning he and a driver drove me to Tunis. They had converted a building into a jail. Others were also bringing prisoners who had been captured the day before. He turned me over to an officer in the street in front of the jail. A sergeant wrote your name on a clipboard, and then stood you in a line on the street. After awhile they started down the line asking each prisoner his name and marking them off on the board. When the major came to me, he did not ask me my name. Instead, he stuck out his hand to shake mine. I wouldn't, but the sergeant marked a name. He said, "Lieutenant Huppert, how are you." I didn't speak. He saluted me so I returned the salute, and he went on. I was then lodged in a cell in the jail. The cell had one window and faced the street.

About every three hours my door would be unlocked and opened. A soldier would stick his head in and ask if I wanted anything or if I wanted to go to the bathroom. It didn't matter what I told him. A little later he would bring a sandwich and coffee. I saw several other prisoners in the latrine and they said they were fed three times a day and that was all. I figured there must be a reason for all the attention and that I had better be on guard at all times.

On the third day they came and got me. They said the major wanted to interrogate me. My thoughts—here it is! I went in and the same major stood up and saluted. I returned the salute. He told the three soldiers in the room to leave—to go get some coffee—and he would call them back as soon as he was through. He looked at some papers on his desk and finally said, "I'm supposed to interrogate you, but I'm not going to." He then told me he had enough information on me already. "We have good intelligence on all you people. I want to talk about something else," he told me. "I know that your home is in California. I'm a college professor and a geologist. I have been in the States many times. I have visited Yosemite and Sequoia in California, and Yellowstone. But I want to know if you have been to Lake Louise in Canada. I would like to visit there and also the Jasper Ice Fields." I told him I hadn't been to any parks in Canada.

The major went on to talk of the war. He said that Hitler was crazy and anybody with brains would know that the war has been lost. He wanted to get it over so he could go back to teaching.

He then said, "I threw you a curve the other day, didn't I? I bet you wondered how I knew your name without ever seeing you before." I said he had. "I saw your name on the clipboard and knew it was a German name. I looked up and down the line and you were the only German out there." Because of this you have been well taken care of so far, but I must warn you that when you get to Frankfurt it will not be so easy. They can be rough up there." Then I went back to my cell.

About midnight they came and told me that they were moving me to the airport. An officer met us and told me that I would be flying to Naples with a Ju 52 pilot. He said he had a special cargo that had to get through. They had lost over a 100 planes the night before. He wanted me to tell the pilot how to avoid being shot down. And that I had no choice, for I was going with him. When we took off I was surprised at the amount of vibration and noise. But the minute we lifted off, it was very quiet. Since I had no choice, I told him to fly very low. When we came to the water, I told him to fly right on the water. We landed right after daybreak at Palermo without incident, and refueled. We then flew to Naples. During the trip I tried to figure out a way to take over, but the opportunity never came. It is hard when there is one against four. We landed in

Naples and I was taken to jail close to the railway station. I then joined a small group of POWs.

After two days our small group boarded a train to Frankfurt on the Main. On this trip none of our group found a way to escape. When we arrived we were taken to Stalag Luft. We were immediately searched again and my leather jacket was taken from me. That left me with only warm-weather clothing. They took me to be interrogated.

The interrogator said he had a few questions to ask me. I told him my name, rank and serial number, and that was about all I could give him. He laughed and said that was all right because he knew everything anyway, but just to verify some things. He held up a paper and started reading my history—where I was born; where I attended schools. Also, he knew when I joined the army and even recited my route to my overseas bases. He told me when and where I was married. "Now, are you convinced?" he said. "Now, where did you come from on your last mission?" I didn't answer, and he said, "I think Malta—right?" So I said, "I have read all about the German army and how well trained every soldier is. They have one of the best-trained armies in the world. You are one of them. Now if we traded places would you answer any of my questions?" Without hesitation, he said "No." I waited a moment and said, "good."

He grinned and asked if I would like to send a message to my wife and to tell her I had been forced down in enemy territory, and was a POW, but was not hurt. He explained that it would take several weeks for the U.S. government to let her know. He said, "This is no trick. You will be broadcasting yourself, and you can write your own message. We will send it right away." I told him to give me a few minutes. He said okay and that he'd be right back. I went to the restroom. When I got inside there was another pilot, a major from England. He said that he was a squadron commander and had been shot down. I asked if he had been offered a chance to broadcast to his folks. He said no, but he knew of it. He said that they were told in England that if they were ever shot down that it was okay to do it. He said the Germans used it as a propaganda tool, but it didn't harm, because people knew what it was and it had no effect. I wrote a message.

Don Lee TV Studios on top of Mt. Hollywood set up a shortwave recording station and brought my wife up to listen to the broadcast. My relatives in Indiana also heard it. As a result, my wife received over 850 letters, many telegrams and recordings, even from ships at sea.

I was put back in solitary for several days. I timed the march of the guard up and down the hall so I would know where he was at anytime. I always knew when he went to the restroom. When they put you in solitary, you were naked and they supplied you with wooden shoes. They'd placed my clothes in a locker and I remembered the number. So early one morning when the guard went to the restroom, I took one of my wooden shoes and broke the wooden door to my cell and got out. I went to the end of the hall where there was a vault door and worked the mechanism to open the door from inside. I opened the door and got out, closed the door and reset the lock, then tried to find a way out, but all the doors were steel and locked, and all the windows were barred. I ran upstairs to the second floor—all barred windows. Then to the third floor—all barred windows there too. There was, however, a ladder to a roof hatch. I went up, but to no avail. It was steel and padlocked. I just couldn't find a way out. By this time I could hear dogs barking and men yelling. They had discovered I was gone. I could hear them coming up the stairs. I ran to a large bathroom on the third floor, opened a stall door and sat on one of the stools. In short time, they found me. I pulled up my pants and came out when ordered to do so.

A big argument started between the officers, about who was going to pay for the damage to the door. One of them asked me if I had any money. I said yes and reached into my pocket for a coin that the Germans had missed when they first searched me. It was an Egyptian piastor (about five cents). I gave him the coin. He looked at it, then threw it across the room. Then they took me down to the first floor, but not to solitary. They told me that I was a bad apple and said that they were going to send me to a high-security camp where there would be no escapes.

139

That was Stalag Luft III in Uder Silesia, Poland.

Yes, that was the north compound, Stalag Luft III. To me the conditions were better than any place that I had been before. They were getting Red Cross parcels of food and it helped greatly. You have to remember that it was the beginning of the war and the Germans were still in pretty good condition. Escape activities were in progress and very well organized. I was assigned to work with the group who designed and built all the equipment that was used in the tunnels. Late in the afternoon in August, the Germans found one of the tunnels. They had just built another compound south of the north camp. So the Germans took all of the Americans out of the north camp and moved us to the south camp. They believed that the Americans were responsible for the tunnel.

Now we had to resettle, reorganize, and start all over. We found our new camp to be very similar to the old one. I set up our factory and recruited about 15 to 20 fellows who could build things.

Any disagreements with anybody?

Not really. The head of the German security was a fellow by the name of Glimnitz. He was always trying to catch us doing something forbidden. After the war, on our 25 reunion, the committee brought Glimnitz over. At the time I knew nothing of it. I attended the reunion and the first night I woke up very early and went down to the hotel lobby to get a cup of coffee. As I walked across, I heard someone call out "Hooppert." My hair stood up on the back of my neck. After all those years, I knew that voice: it was Glimnitz. Sure enough, there was Glimnitz sitting on the couch waving, with a big smile on his face. I went over to him, shook his hand and sat down. We talked things over and he said, "We can be friends now—it's over and long past now. I was always trying to catch you but never could." I agreed and told him we both were just trying to do our jobs. I shook hands again and went on.

In the south camp my mess mate was the senior American officer and camp commander, Colonel Goodrich. I worked closely with the camp interpreter, Dick Schrupp. On January 27, 1945, we were ordered to vacate the compound. We started marching to the west at 2200 hours. A couple of weeks later we arrived at Stalag VIIA, Mooseburg. The two of us were ordered to stay as close as possible to the colonel, in case he needed us. We learned that the Germans were going to separate the field officers from the rest of the men. Schrupp ran back to me and said Colonel Goodrich had just promoted both of us to major, so we could be close by.

Stalag VIIA was a terrible camp. There was little food, not enough latrines for all the men. There were about 500 men in each barracks. About half of them had to sleep on the floor.

A few days before April 29, we were preparing for the Germans to leave the camp. The American senior officers were negotiating with the Germans on how to take over. We were up all night on April 25 operating radios and taking messages. We were also in contact with the Fourteenth Armored Division. They were Patton's unit that was coming in to liberate us. The next morning the battle for Mooseburg started and lasted for about two hours. At 12:40 P.M. the American flag was raised. We were free again.

After a couple of weeks, we were flown to Le Halle and Camp Lucky Strike. I hadn't eaten for about ten days. In fact, at that point, looking at food made me nauseated. I was immediately taken to a field hospital where I was fed on glucose. After a few days I was sent to a hospital in Dieppe where I stayed until I could eat solid food. I had weighed about 210 pounds when shot down. Now I was less than 100.

I arrived in New York on June 3, 1945. I then was sent to Indiana and given a 60 day leave. After the leave I was sent to Santa Monica, California for two weeks. From there I was sent to a hospital at Santa Ana Air Base. Just before Thanksgiving, I was released and spent the rest of my time on terminal leave. I was released from service March 2, 1946.

How many years were you in prison?

Two years. I was shot down April 26, 1943, and liberated April 29, 1945.

What don't people understand about life in prison?

Mostly they don't understand prisoner of war treatment. It is one of neglect. The Germans put you in a camp and give you a table knife, fork, spoon, bowl, and mug. They give you a sack and shredded wood to put in it for a mattress—and one blanket. Now it's up to you to survive. You must improvise, have ingenuity, and have the desire to live. You must have perseverance. Never give up. Always think positive. There is nothing impossible. My motto has always been, "If it is said and done that it can't be done, just watch some fool come along and do it."

Give me an example.

I studied the German mind and figured out how it works. The Germans are very methodical. When you learn how they think and operate, you can stay one jump ahead of them. You know what they are going to do and how they operate. Improvise—I've done that all my life. On the farm my father always said, "Thank God for baling wire." In lieu of nuts and bolts, use wire. In the camp we had no tools—they were forbidden. So, you made hammers out of wood, tin shears out of the two bed-boards, a nail and a table knife.

When I first came into the camp, the men were having a hard time getting their solder to stick. So I made a small cup out of a tin can and put a spout on it. We had several pine trees in camp so I drilled a small hole in one of them. Before dark I would go out and stick the spout into the hole and catch the draining sap. In the morning I would go out and get it and then boil it down into resin flux. We saved all the tin foil off the cigarette packs and melted them down into solder. This cured the solder problem. After I made a percolator, I couldn't find any glass for the lid. Some of the fellows got coffee in their parcels and perked was better than boiled. I finally found a glass bottle in the trash. It would have to be cut—but how? I knew a fellow who had a small bottle of gasoline. I got a string and the fellow let me dip it into the gas. Then I tied the string exactly where I wanted it cut. I lit the string and let it burn and then put the bottle in cold water. It cracked just where the string was. I had a perfect cut.

Did these tricks make you popular around there?

I really don't remember but in a large group of people there is always some fool around—don't you think?

JIMMY FAULKNER
A True Pilot

James M. Faulkner is a Mississippian whose hobbies include hunting and horses. He has Tennessee Walking horses and his daughter shows them. "Is riding horses like flying planes?" I ask. "I guess a little," he replies. He tells me he thinks the nearest thing to flying is sailing, and he's done that too.

Faulkner was born on July 18, 1923. He started college at Ole Miss in the fall 1941. When the war started in December of that year, he went into the Navy Cadet Program and graduated from Pensacola in late 1943. He went to Okinawa in April 1945. When the peace treaty was signed with the Japanese, Faulkner was with VMF-224 (a marine fighter squadron), in Marine Air Group Thirty-one, and flew up to Yorosuka where he stayed until December 1945. After WWII, he remained in the reserve program and was called back to active duty in October 1951 during Korea. He went overseas to Korea in March 1952 and returned home in December. He again returned to the reserves in the summer 1954 and retired in 1978, though he quit flying in 1965, as he said, "to make way for somebody else."

Faulkner's uncle William is *the* William Faulkner, the great American writer and Nobel Prize winner for literature. James M. has some of the same story-telling abilities it would seem. He starts by telling how "Brother Will" helped introduce him to flying:

"Well, 'Brother Will'—as I call my Uncle William—had an airplane in Memphis about 75 miles from here. He took four of us boys—his stepson Malcolm, my younger brother Chooky, Arthur Guyton and me—to Memphis for a day's flying. He had an open cockpit, bi-wing Waco that he flew. Malcolm and I flew first that morning. That was 1932, I believe. We took turns all day long flying with him, maybe 20 to 30 minutes at a time."

Did Uncle William ever tell you any flying stories?

He told us the one he told a lot of people. That was when he was in Canada and training for the Royal Air Force. He said he flew through a hangar and got stuck upside down in it.

When we were boys at his house, he would sit on the floor and turn a straight-back chair level with his chest and say, "This is what it feels like being in the cockpit of an airplane." He had a knobby walking cane that he held up in the middle of the floor as the stick, and he would say, "This is what we fly with."

Any other memories or things that stand out in your mind?

Well, William Faulkner was the pilot in my first flight in an airplane, and I was the passenger. On his last flight, I was the pilot, and he was the passenger.

He flew into Memphis on an airline from one of his trips for the State Department. I met him in a Cessna 150, a two-seat single-engine airplane. I let him fly back to Oxford. Just before we got back to the airport, a light snow started. He turned to me and tapped the yoke with his hand and said, "You land it."

What about your service flying?

I joined in June 1942, about six months after the war had started. I had always wanted to be a marine pilot. I went through navy training because the marines didn't have a flying school. I went to primary in Memphis and then went from there to Pensacola, and got accepted into the Marine Corps. When I graduated from Pensacola, I went to Daytona Beach, Florida, and started flying Wildcats— those little mid-wing F4F fighters they had at the beginning of the war. I flew about 100 hours in the Wildcats, then went into F4U

Corsairs. I flew Corsairs about 150 hours in the States, then went to the Pacific and flew Corsairs in combat until I came home after the war was over.

Any problems with the Corsair?

It had awful bad spin characteristics. You go on board a carrier, and it would stall quick and do a torque-roll. They found out after it had been with the marines for about a year, that you could take something that looked like an engineer's triangular ruler and tape it to the leading edge of the right wing, and it would stop the quick-spin characteristics it had.

The first ones that came out—the tail wheel was low. It had a 13 or 14 foot nose on it—in front of the cockpit. Once you got in the groove to land, you couldn't see. You had to look to one side. They raised the tail wheel a little, making the pilot sit a little higher, so when you landed, you could see a little better. When you were in the groove, you looked out the left side.

Isn't that a little frustrating?

Well, you get used to it. I didn't know any different for a long time.

You liked the airplane, though.

It was a fantastic airplane. It would fly itself. All you had to do was sit there and think, and it would do it. It had counterbalanced controls on it—there were boosters on the ailerons and elevators. Little boosters are what they were, making the controls work easier. And, at one time, it was the fastest airplane in the world.

How fast?

The book said 437 knots, but we cruised them when we were on patrol at about 160 knots. You could turn as tight as you wanted to on a dime. And that plane would hold together—it was a strong, tough airplane. I've seen them come back with holes all over in them, and they still flew.

147

The Marine Corps would load it down with rocketrails. We had two bomb racks we'd carry along with external tanks. We would carry eight rockets, two 500-pound bombs, an external 185 pound tank and 2,400 rounds of .50 caliber ammunition. That was quite a load. I believe we had a little edge on the P-51 in terms of speed, except for the load, all of which slowed us down a lot.

Did you do a lot of coordinated strikes?

SBDs and TBMs—we escorted those. And, when we got to Okinawa, a couple of months before the war was over, the army brought in some B-24s, so we escorted them to Japan. The Marine Corps had B-25s, we called them PBJs, and we'd escort those.

What happened when you escorted them?

We had a lot of flak. Most of the time it was ground fire that we were involved with. In Okinawa, the kamikazes would come out against the fleet and we would try to keep them away.

I saw a kamikaze hit a destroyer once. The destroyer went down in about one and a half minutes, I believe. There were so many kamikazes coming in that you couldn't get them all. You couldn't find them. They would come in low on the water. We'd have a four-plane division stacked up every 3,000 feet, from about 500 feet on up to about 10,000 or 12,000 thousand feet.

The destroyer escorts had picket patrol out around Okinawa—eight or ten of them. One picket patrol would have two or three destroyers in it and three or four destroyer escorts around it. So it would be about a five, six, or seven-ship patrol. We would fly air patrol for them as much as four hours at a time. Then we would be relieved by four more planes. That went on during daylight hours, then they had the night fighter boys who flew F6Fs. They would go from dark to daylight the next morning.

Tell me about a dogfight.

One morning we were up north of Okinawa, and about six Jap planes all of a sudden appeared. We jumped them and got all six of them before they got to our ships.

What was the name of the ship that went down?

I don't know. I know it was a destroyer. I just saw it. I was at the 5,000 foot level then, and this plane came in low. I didn't actually see it until it pulled up and dove. They would pull up to about 400 feet and then go straight towards the destroyer. I saw it just before it hit—I saw the explosion, and I saw it go down.

What's the most frightened you were over there?

I had aftershock once, I suppose, when I went down and was picked up by a destroyer. We were strafing up north, and I took a hit and almost made it home. I landed in the water. The destroyer came along beside me and picked me up that afternoon. I was good and wet when I crawled over the side. The skipper was a full lieutenant. He said, "Come on down to my room"—the stateroom. He gave me his room and I got a shower and some clothes. The doctor came down with a big water glass full of brandy. Just about that time I was feeling sort of funny. I drank that and got normal again [laughs]. Then they took me down to the ward room.

They rolled out the carpet because fighters had been flying cover for them for about three months. They said, "What do you want?"

This big old colored fellow came in the room—he was the cook. And, with a more southern accent than I have, he said, "How you want yo' steak?"

And I said, "Where you from?"

He said, "Coffeeville, Mississippi." That's about 30 miles from Oxford.

I said, "I want the thickest, best you got." He brought that steak out, and it was fantastic. Late that afternoon, they put me aboard a hospital ship for a check-up, and I was back on the field the next day, flying.

Talk about your ejection—what you did.

I landed in the water. I was too low to jump. I wanted all the speed I could get, so I could get as far as I could back toward home—I didn't want to lose any distance by climbing and losing air speed.

When the airplane finally quit, I was maybe at 500 feet. I got it all set up and hit the water. It was a real easy landing. My right wing hit first, and I was thrown into the instrument panel. There was a plane (Bob LeeSun) circling over me, and when the water hit me, I undid my seat belt. I had heard about the suction pulling people down, so I ran as hard as I could off the wing and jumped, parachute and all. I put my head out of the water and turned around and watched my airplane go down. The next day I asked Bob LeeSun, who was flying over me, how long it took the airplane to go under water. He said, "The cockpit was underwater in about ten seconds; the whole plane went down in 56 seconds."

That was a comforting thought, wasn't it?

Yes, I was way out in the water, watching it.

How long were you in the water?

I was in the water for a few hours. I got picked up the same day.

Who was your most memorable character from the war?

John Sharbrough. It just so happened that he and I were together during World War II and Korea both, and he was born in Mississippi, too. He was a hell of a good pilot.

What sort of mischief did you get into?

John and I would go out on four-hour flights and come back and we would be tired. He'd just be sitting there doing nothing, and he'd be happy. We'd carry a canteen of water with us—this is off Okinawa. Anyway, I'd see him in the cockpit—he'd take a sip of water every now and then. He'd come back, just seem good and happy as when we left four hours before. I couldn't understand it, even though he was 20 years old then.

One time when we landed, his left leg was wet all the way down. He said, "Damn people are cheating the government, selling them bad canteens."

I said, "What's the matter?"

He said, "They leak." Well, what he was doing—and I didn't know it at the time—he had gin and grapefruit juice he was carrying in it—and the grapefruit juice just ate through the metal in the canteen!

Give me another of your old flying buddies.

There were a lot of them. I guess a Major Don Stapp, who was our C.O. for the squadron here in the States would be one. In fact, I went overseas with him. He'd been out before, and he already had 12 Jap planes to his credit.

We were on a transport, going out of San Francisco, to Honolulu, when he called me down to his cabin. I'd flown with him before in the States, and we got along real well. So he says, "I'll keep them off your tail, if you keep 'em off mine." He wanted me as his wingman. I said, "Yes, I will." I felt about ten feet tall then. So we got to Peleliu and flew together a few times. Then some of us got a chance to go to Okinawa. That's when we were getting ready to invade Okinawa. Four of us out of the squadron got to go, so I grabbed at the opportunity and went. He stayed back.

What happened at Okinawa—any stories?

Well, for one thing I was there the night they had the big suicide landing on the field. I was sitting on the ground watching it.

What time did that happen?

It was, I guess, ten o'clock at night. It was a real bright night. Outside of our tent area was a big courtyard that was about four feet deep—about 20 by 20 feet. Then there was an entrance to the tomb where they buried the people. We used that as a foxhole. We had been having raids every night, but this particular night the raids came in real high. There were two or three planes that looked like they were 20,000 feet high. The searchlights on the field pinpointed them way up there. Then everybody started shooting at the high planes—which was a diversionary thing. We shot back and while that was happening, the Japanese sent 18 or 20 transports down loaded with suicide troops. These turned out to be about 15 or 20 suicide troopers

151

per airplane. Two of them that survived the night, fighter boys who landed wheels up, had come in over to where we were sitting on the ground. These guys got loose right around the flight lines and were putting satchel bombs in our planes. You know, we left our oil coolers open at night, and they stuffed them up in the engines to blow the engines up. When they ran out of bombs, they had knives and attacked the planes with them. Our control surfaces were fabric— the elevators and outer wing panels and the ailerons. They took the knives and cut slits out of them. We were grounded the next day until we got some new airplanes in and got those fixed. There was a field down south—Yontan Kadena—that had another marine air group on it, and they doubled up until we got new planes in.

How did you wipe the Japanese out?

The ground defense finally shot them all. It took all night. They finally killed the last one the next morning at about daylight.

Kind of amazing, wasn't it?

Oh, yes, it was unreal.

Did you know when you went to Japan after the war that the Japanese had executed our B-29 fliers—after the war was over?

I didn't know it until I got back to the States. When the war was over, we were in Marine Air Group (MAG) thirty-one and we flew to Japan and landed at Yokosuka, a Jap navy field right on Tokyo Bay. We got there in early September when they signed the peace treaty. We didn't know a whole lot. In fact, when we were flying strikes over Japan—or anywhere—we were never told much— anymore than we absolutely had to know, because if we got shot down and we didn't know anything, we couldn't tell anybody. But when I heard that had happened, I was pretty mad about it.

People talk today about flying in the old days—the regulations then?

Overseas there weren't any regulations except you fly, you stick together, you fight together.

Any anecdotes of doing what you wanted to do?

There was one boy I was flying with. We were coming back from a flight, and things had been sort of dull. He and I were just flying low over the water. It turned out there was an island—Japanese-owned—about 50 miles north of us. We hadn't done a lot on this day. I was flying on his wing and he said, "Let's shoot in this hole." There was a cliff down to the water with a hole like a cave. So we were up there fat, dumb, and happy and he started shooting up in the hole. I was off to one side, just watching, when the biggest part of the island blew up. He had hit an ammunition dump. He came back, and his eyes were big—his expression—you know when Pluto's surprised, his ears stick up. Another time a boy, Bob LeeSun, and I were flying together on a strike down south. We carried eight rockets with us, and the idea was to hit this kamikaze airfield. I guess there were 24 of us, and we were going to make one pass and fire all the rockets at one time at this kamikaze base. Bob was off to one side. We all fired off our rockets and were coming back, and Bob told me that as he shot, he looked up and saw all eight of his rockets go in an outhouse (privy).

What was your fondest memory of flying?

There are two times that I remember. One is the first strike on Japan. We took off before daylight one morning. We were going on a fighter sweep. There were 24 of us, and we were going up to 20,000 feet. Just at sunrise, we could see the southern Japanese island off in the distance and the white sand on the beach at Kyushu. We could see the real green trees and fields, white clouds like you see in the Pacific. I thought how could a people living in a place as pretty as that is cause so damn much trouble. Then the Japanese started shooting at us, and the whole complexion changed. The Japanese had different-colored anti-aircraft shells. Some were orange, some red, some yellow, some blue, and some black. It was so the ground crew could, I suppose, identify the shell and know how to lead when shooting, So these things started exploding on us—the complexion changed.

I stayed in the Marine Corps, retired, and I went back and spent three years in Korea. Then I stayed in the reserve program until I retired. The last jet I flew was an FJ4—a navy version of the F86. Then I flew the Cougar—it was a Grumman swept-back jet—a real nice little airplane. Anyway, the navy has a storage yard, a pickling yard in Arizona, where they can store airplanes outside in the low humidity, which helps preserve them. We'd fly planes out and deliver them there. In ferrying, you can't fly at night, so I left Memphis one afternoon and got as far as El Paso in the Cougar. I wanted to get back to Memphis as soon as I could, so the next morning I took off at sunrise. I was going from El Paso to Tucson and up to Phoenix at about 30,000 feet. As you climbed up to 30,000, the visibility in that part of the country is fantastic. I was halfway between El Paso and Tucson, when I looked down.

Over the years I've liked to read a lot of history, especially the history of the west. As I looked down, I could see White Sands, New Mexico—the sun was really hitting it for the first time that morning—and El Paso, both of the Chiricahua Indian strongholds, Tucson, and down into old Mexico. I said, "Here I am. I can see the history of the west at one sweeping glance!"

Is flying ever boring to you?

Oh Lord, yes. That's when I started smoking, flying in Okinawa. When I stopped flying, I quit smoking.

What does flying mean to you?

I use it as a getaway. I can get detached from the world, almost.

What about unusual things that happened flying around Mississippi?

Every pilot wants to fly over his hometown—flat-hat over it. The University of Mississippi is here in Oxford, of course, and I was born in Oxford. In 1946, I was flying out of Millington—about 100 miles north of here. I was in the school at Ole Miss then. Anyway, one Sunday afternoon I went to Millington and got a Corsair and came down. It was my first real flying over Oxford. I said I was really going to put on a show, so I made one pass over the university, then I went down south about five miles and got at about

6,000 - 7,000 feet and started down. I got all the speed I could get, and I got right on the ground, going from south to north. I jumped over fraternity row, over my fraternity house, and right to the side of the drill field. One the other side of the drill field is a little rise and the university hospital. Then there was a gap, and then the boys' dormitories. As I got over the Sigma Alpha Epsilon fraternity house, I rolled upside down—I was going pretty fast—and I went between the hospital and the dormitories upside down. Then I pushed up and rolled back over and went back to Millington. I knew I'd done wrong, so I came home right quick. Well, it didn't take long before the authorities came investigating me. They found out who it was because the number was on the side of the plane. They might not have done anything, but a nurse fainted on the second floor when I went past the window upside down. I was grounded for a year.

The nurse didn't get hurt badly, did she?

No, she just fainted and fell on the floor.

How'd you feel during that forced retirement?

I was just hoping I could get back and start flying again the next year. I got a letter from the commandant of the Marine Corps, and he was really mad at me. The C.O. of marine aviation wrote too. He said, "If you ever do anything like that again, you'll be grounded and have your commission taken away from you." So I was real good for a year. Then, a couple of years later—before Korea started—I got a letter from both of those men I mentioned—telling me all was forgiven.

When the war was over we went up there to Japan. We kept our guns hot when we landed because we didn't know whether the Japanese had diehards there or not. So we sat in the cockpits a few minutes and then shut the planes down. But they wouldn't let us off the base the first day. I wanted to see what was going on in Japan. At 21 years old, you're curious. They said, "You can't go off today, but tomorrow you can, but you'll have to wear a sidearm." So we wore .45s off the base until I came home. The next day we had this skipper—a heck of a nice fellow—who called us in. He made a mistake when he gave us passes. They were mimeographed, and he filled in our names on them. What it said was, "The below named officer is under verbal orders of the commandant of the Marine Corps," and he signed it. I saw what he had done and I said to the boy next to me, "Bobby, look what I got." I said, "I'm gonna use mine 'til they figure out what they've done." So we went off base that day. I went by myself. I'd heard about Japanese beer and how good it was—18 percent alcohol, I think, and I wanted some. I walked down the road to this little town of Yokosuka, and I found a fire truck. The Japanese had a manned fire truck in the station. So with my pass, I confiscated the fire truck in the name of the commandant. There was a lot of screaming. The Japanese guy couldn't speak English, and I couldn't speak Japanese. He drove the fire truck and I sat beside him, directing him. I finally got across to him I wanted some beer and ice. We found an ice house and kegs in a warehouse. We loaded the beer on the fire truck, and I went back to the base and pulled up in front of the building we had taken over as BBQ. We hauled the beer upstairs and iced it down. I kept the driver—he was going to be on call for me. I wanted transportation. The driver didn't say anything—he just sat there. We couldn't fly because gasoline hadn't come yet. So I said, "Come on, let's go riding in my fire truck." I had a quart of beer by then, and we hadn't had anything to drink in about four months, so it had really hit me.

My driver and about six or seven guys jumped on the truck. We rode around the base—drinking—and looking at all the bomb marks and holes that had been shot through the hangars. Colonel Munn, our group commanding officer, caught wind of this and sent an MP down in a jeep.

The MP said the colonel wanted to see me. I went up to see him and, when I walked in, Admiral Halsey was there and he was sitting, talking to Colonel Munn. (We were in the Third Fleet.) Colonel Munn said, "You've got to give the fire truck back."

And I said, "No sir, it's mine. We won and it's mine." I knew the colonel pretty well—I had been flying his Corsairs for him for several months.

Anyway, he said, "You've got to give it back."

I said, "The spoils of war. It's mine." And he got so mad, but Admiral Halsey got tickled. I knew I had it made then.

The colonel finally said, "Give that damn fire truck back."

I said, "Yes, suh." But I'd always wanted to own a fire truck, and I did own one for about four hours [laughs].

Charles L. Brown in May 1943.

CHARLES L. (CHARLIE) BROWN

One Lucky Guy

Imagine this: the B-17 bomber you are piloting on a combat mission is severely damaged. You are wounded and many of your men have been also hit by machine gun or cannon fire; one mortally wounded. Based on the damaged condition of your airplane, you wonder if you can make it home to England. Then the nightmare that would haunt even the boldest of aviators materializes just off your right wing, in the form of an enemy fighter. What can you do? You can surrender, or refuse to surrender and expect to be shot down. In this interview, Charlie Brown tells how he made it back to England despite the conditions detailed.

Charles Brown volunteered for military service just before his seventeenth birthday by joining the West Virginia National Guard while still in high school. During his senior year the State Insane Asylum caught fire and his national guard company was activated to guard the patients who had been moved to the State 4-H Camp. Charlie found himself trying to do homework between tours of standing guard duty. He enlisted in the regular army in June 1940 and by early 1942 he was a staff sergeant in the Signal Corps. He decided that he wanted to be a pilot, applied for and was accepted both as a flying sergeant and an aviation cadet. He chose the aviation cadet route and was commissioned a second lieutenant upon graduation. When he completed cadet pilot training, he was offered a job as an instructor pilot, but refused and volunteered for combat duty. At that point he was absorbed into the U. S. Army Air Forces Bomber Combat Crew Training Program, and the rest is the stuff of legend.

Today, Charlie is the Founder/CEO of an environmental research company, the Mobile Energy Research Center, CBE, Inc. His discoveries have led to the creation of an essentially "smokeless diesel" and methods to improve the chemistry of combustion of all internal combustion engines, for which his work has won several awards.

When did you get into the war?

I arrived overseas in early November 1943, just as the Eighth Air Force was starting continuous heavy air raids on targets in Germany proper. Previously, two out of three Eighth Air Force missions had been on targets around the periphery of Germany, including France, the Netherlands, Belgium and the coast and near coastal areas of Germany. Then, we started hitting deeper into Germany proper.

In my view there were three air war phases, but I've never seen these defined in writing. This first phase started in August 1942 when we started the testing of the daylight strategic bombing concept by flying into France. Eventually, by summer 1943, the military leaders said "Let's conduct a major raid to a real priority target deep into Germany." In my view this started phase two of the European Air Offensive. They chose the aircraft factories at Regensburg and the ball-bearing plants in Schweinfurt—and they went after them in full force on August 17. The Germans gave us a real good licking. I don't know how many airplanes the U.S. put into the air, perhaps 300 or 350. [Research confirmed 310.] It wasn't a massive number, but we lost 60 of them, with four more damaged beyond repair. Furthermore, 168 of those planes that came back were badly beaten up—not to mention the near 600 fliers who became casualties on those airplanes, including seven killed in action (KIA), 21 wounded in action (WIA), and 552 missing in action (MIA).

The unexpected Regensburg/Schweinfurt heavy losses required some re-evaluation and some regrouping. Meanwhile they had the aircrew replacement pipeline going full force. After a brief lull, they tried Schweinfurt again in mid-October. And damned if the same thing didn't happen. Again we lost 60, had 8 damaged beyond repair and 138 damaged. Aircrew losses were a staggering five KIA, 40 WIA, and 594 MIA. At this point they had a real conundrum in trying to determine if this strategic bombing approach was going to work. At that point the Eighth Air Force did not have long-range fighter escorts to the targets. They had nothing to defend the bombers on deep penetrations of Germany. The Spits could only get to about the coast of Holland. And P-47 Folks, without drop tanks, couldn't get too far into the continent. Despite the now demonstrated weaknesses, the "powers that be" conferred and decided, "We've got enough people and airplanes in the pipeline. We'll do it regardless of the cost."

When I got there in early November they had just selected Bremen, Germany as one of their prime targets. Starting on October 8 and including my two missions to Bremen on December 13 and December 20, the Eighth Air Force hit the Bremen complex a total of seven times. Our aircraft losses, on just those seven missions, were approximately 150 bombers and slightly over 52 fighters, with about 1,200 aircrew casualties. We moved the first P-51 group into England in December 1943 and things began to improve a little. We could get escorts fairly far along the routes and sometimes all the way to the targets. Any time we had good escorts, they accomplished a lot in terms of shooting down German fighters and saving bombers from Luftwaffe fighters. Later, in early 1944, the fighters pulled off direct escort a little bit, but when they changed their escort tactics, the Germans again came after the bombers in force.

In February, we did five major missions into Germany in seven days. It was called "Big Week" and it was so big that it almost finished off all of us. Finally, we tried for Berlin on March 3 and 4 and finally hit it on March 6, 1944, with massive losses. From that point up through May, it was really the strategic war, with losses of over 60 bombers on a single mission as late as April 11, despite improved fighter escort.

Phase three began after the Invasion of Normandy in early June 1944. It was then a different war, because when bomber crews and fighter pilots went down, they had a friendly place they could either land or bail out. Prior to that there was no safe place to land on the German occupied continent. On each mission you invaded Europe, and you fought your way in and then fought your way out. Any time you went down in either Germany or German Occupied Europe the odds of successfully evading capture were small to nil.

After my last bomber mission on April 11, 1944, I was assigned as a ferry pilot to fly bombers, fighters, and transports between North Ireland, Scotland and England until mid-August 1944, in support of both the strategic bombing and the invasion forces.

Describe a couple of your toughest missions. Was that the Schweinfurt Mission?

No. My first mission as an aircraft commander to Germany on December 20, 1943, was my toughest. Prior to my first mission, an experienced pilot had told me that when you saw the red center of a flak burst you were in deep trouble. As we approached Bremen the flak was black and really heavy. On this particular mission my group was leading the entire Eighth Air Force. My aircraft was down in the second element of the low squadron (lower left corner of the formation), and as we turned on target the flak grew even worse. Suddenly, I saw this incredible red burst immediately in front of me. It was brilliant, almost like a beautiful orchid. I thought "Damn, we're in trouble." At this point both my navigator and bombardier came on the intercom simultaneously and said, "We're hit, we're hit—there is a large hole in the nose." As they were describing the nose, they saw the number two engine propeller slow down and go into a feathered position.

As we completed the shut down of number two, number four had also been hit and was running away (overspeeding), so we started to shut it down. Despite the problems, somehow, I was able to keep the plane in formation until the bombs were dropped in conjunction with the other aircraft. (We were near the target.)

We were in the process of feathering the number four engine, but never got it totally feathered. For some reason I said, "Let's try to hold the feathering and see what we can do with it." We were fortunate that the engine still turned, producing partial power at about 1,600 rpm. For the next two hours we kept feathering/unfeathering and working on that engine and fortunately it got us back to land. Otherwise, we would never have made it.

162

Just after the target, the formation left us due to our reduced speed. That is when the German fighters hit us. I looked up and saw eight of them in a line above us, approaching from the right front. I knew we were in pretty deep trouble at that point because the Germans had been shooting down 15 or 20 of our bombers each mission. As we were alone, I figured we didn't have much of a chance of survival. When the first two came in, I just said, "Oh, the hell with it," and I pulled up directly into the second fighter attacking from the 12 o'clock position. The first fighter was over a little to the left, at about the 11 o'clock position. As our top turret gun started firing, I pulled up into a collision course with the second fighter. The navigator fired a blister nose gun and hit the plane attacking us from the left or number one position. I saw that plane catch fire as it went under us. Then I just turned into the others who were in a line. I thought that maneuver would give them shorter aiming and firing time, which turned out to be true.

By then, seven more planes had come up from the back. As it turned out, we only had three functioning guns—the one nose blister gun and the two top turret guns—with the other guns frozen. The intercom and radio were knocked out early, and I was basically flying blind to anything behind me. At some point the Germans hit the oxygen, knocking it out. I had started dogfighting, with three forward-firing guns, which made my survival chances much less. At that point I was dogfighting with 13 German fighters, and all I had was an old beat-up B-17, which by now is without communication. It was the most incredibly stupid thing anyone could possibly do. I remember being in a Lufberry Circle and saying, "Well, I'd better reverse the circle because the fighters have the advantage." We can only go so tight, maybe 70-80 degrees of bank.

The last thing I remember was trying to reverse the circle, being unable to stop the roll, and then looking up at the ground. The next thing I was conscious of doing was pulling up over trees, five miles lower. Apparently, I passed out and then came to and somehow got the airplane out of the spin or the spiral without a rudder or a left horizontal stabilizer/elevator. With the left horizontal stabilizer and elevator shot off, it was highly unlikely that it was in a full spin, but apparently it was enough of a spin or spiral that the German fighters thought my plane was going down. I was trying to get my mind together—trying to gain some altitude. With no communication, I

163

sent the copilot, engineer and bombardier back to check on the crew in the rear. As I looked out the right window, there sitting on my right wing was another damn German fighter.

At this juncture, I thought that I'd lost my mind. So I closed my eyes, opened them and looked to see if he was still there; he was. Then the German pilot started motioning with his hands. That meant absolutely nothing to me. Then he started nudging me, by flying across my front, trying to get me to turn around and land. My mind just wouldn't accept that. I could not accept surrender. Why doesn't he shoot me? I thought. Then I figured he must be out of ammunition. Then I thought, "I know he carries a .38, if he pulls out his .38, he can still shoot me down." So, he stayed with me for some time and gradually just fell back on the wing. He stayed there and continued gesturing with his hands. None of this made any sense to me. By this point we had flown out over the North Sea. When the copilot came back he reported that the tail gunner was dead, two of the crew couldn't walk and one could not use his hands. In other words three of the crew could not safely bail out.

I thought we were high enough to bail out. In fact, I told my crew that I would fly back over land and that any of the able-bodied crew who wanted to bail out could do so, but I would try to make England. My crew all chose to stay on board. At this point the German pilot was still motioning and I figured that since he was not going to kill us, I turned toward England. He gave a salute/ wave rolled over and left.

Describe your aircraft. Was it badly shot up?

I hear of people who counted holes on damaged planes. In this instance, there was no part of the airplane that wasn't damaged. The Plexiglas portion of the nose was shot out, which made it extremely cold. The temperature at that altitude was probably 75 degrees below zero Fahrenheit. The right wing showed evidence that an 88 mm, or possibly a 105 mm shell, had gone through the wing without detonating, so there was a big hole. It was two or three feet in diameter, on the topside where it came out. A 20 mm or 30 mm cannon shell had blown the top out of one of the gas tanks, but luckily the tank did not explode. Several cannon shells had destroyed the radio room, as well as the waist gun positions, and the tail gunner's compartment. The rudder was 90 percent missing and the rudder cables were severed. The whole left stabilizer and left elevator had been shot away. There were machine-gun bullet holes throughout the entire aircraft, including the remaining right horizontal stabilizer and elevator.

How chaotic was it? There were a lot of wounded people. Were you wounded?

Yes. I had a bullet in my right shoulder, but I didn't know it. I was the only one hit in the front of the aircraft. I was in good shape, relatively speaking, but not in good enough shape to make intelligent decisions.

The tail gunner, Hugh Eckenrode, was just about decapitated. He must have taken a direct hit with a 20 mm or 30 mm. The radio operator, Dick Pechout, had a concussion and a cannon shell fragment in his eye. Ultimately, what saved our lives was that most of the wing areas were in good shape. The ailerons had escaped hits by flak or cannon fire and were in pretty good shape, although they had several machine-gun bullet holes.

Furthermore, the skin along the left side of the airplane had been torn away by cannon fire. Cannon shell explosions had destroyed all of the radio-room equipment. The plane really was a "flying wreck." That's one way the German pilot, Franz Stigler [later] described it. In addition, he described it as being "the most badly damaged aircraft that he ever saw, which was still flying."

He actually looked in and saw all this chaos, didn't he?

Yes.

What else did he tell you?

Franz explained that he had shot down two B-17 bombers in the air battle. My Lord, that's a major feat in itself. Then he had landed to refuel and rearm. Apparently, when I was trying to regain altitude after the spin/spiral recovery, I flew right over the edge of the German airfield where he had rearmed and was finishing refueling. Franz then took off and came after me, but by the time he caught up with me, I was close to the coast. As he approached, he held a position high at the rear. With his hand on the firing button, he waited for the tail gunner to raise his guns. Of course, he didn't. Then Franz dropped down and kept getting closer and closer, until finally he was within about 20 feet of the rear of my plane. Then he saw the tail gunner was gone and he could see a lot of blood. As he started pulling up along the right side, he could see that the waist-gun positions were unoccupied and that patches of fuselage skin had been shot off. He actually could see the people moving in the airplane. By the time he got up close on my right wing, I was alone in the cockpit. That's when he started trying to signal to me. He said he wanted me to surrender or go to Sweden. When he nudged me to surrender and I didn't respond he figured that I was at least bright enough to go to Sweden, and he would have escorted me part of the way. But he wasn't able to get that message to me. Surrender just didn't appear feasible to my muddled mind, and going to Sweden didn't enter my mind or decision making process.

166

It was your second mission?

Yes. My first combat and orientation mission was also to Bremen on December 13. This was my first combat mission as an aircraft commander. They sent me over there to fight. They didn't send me over there to become a prisoner. Now the decisions I made were not that heroic. They were incredibly stupid. But you know, looking at it in hindsight, my mind really stopped when I lost consciousness at 25,000 thousand feet and probably began to function somewhat when we got down below 12,000 feet. Somehow I became conscious enough to bring the aircraft out of the spin or spiral just above the ground.

One of the weird aspects is that I had nightmares about coming out of a spin in a four-engine aircraft probably a thousand or more times for years and years, up to the point when I located Franz. After we had talked the experience over a few times, I was convinced that he was the man who could tell me what happened on his end. After meeting Franz, I never had that nightmare again.

That's strange?

That is strange, having had the dream over and over for years

How do you know a thousand?

Oh, it's at least a thousand. I had the dream for 47 years, sometimes nightly, weekly, monthly or bimonthly. I never discussed my dream with anyone, including my wife. In fact, she had no knowledge of either the incident, or the nightmares.

As we approached the English coast, I was looking for any place to land because I didn't want to drop below our 250 foot altitude. We were in the latter stage of the flight, when I saw the coast. I started to breathe again. Anyway, it turned out to be a rough part of the coast.

About that time two P-47s flew by at my altitude and scared the daylights out of me. The reason for the sudden appearance of the P-47s became evident when they pulled up to about one thousand feet and began to circle. Below them was an airfield, just inland. I'd already decided I couldn't or didn't want to land on the beach, and at about 10 - 15 degrees to my port, under the fighters, I saw a beautiful runway and was able to get the gear down and land there.

I had a lot of help from my "third pilot" in landing. I had no control over engines three and four. The copilot cut the ignition switches and fuel supply on engines three and four just before we touched down and I cut the power on number one. That worked out pretty well. Despite not having a rudder or brakes the aircraft stopped, still on the runway. Apparently the P-47s had alerted the tower and the people on the field, because they had fire rescue there by the time we stopped rolling. They took the casualties away from the rear of the airplane. I dropped down under the nose and couldn't stand up. As I sat there people were speaking to me, but all I could say was, "What a hell of a way to start a war! What a hell of a way to start a war!" I had blood on me, but thought that it was caused by a nosebleed. I had been in an auto accident as a kid and had fractured my nose which left me with thin membranes. Luckily, the military didn't find that out before I got over there. Because of this condition, I bled on almost every mission. The truth was that I should never have been flying high altitude, but it is the kind of thing that once

Oblt. Franz Stigler Luftwaffe Fighter Forces May 1944.

168

you're in you can't quit. The British had an expression called "lack of moral fiber." I didn't want to report the problem and possibly be branded a coward. So I stuck with the high altitude, combat flying.

A little bit after landing, they hauled the remainder of us off for an intelligence debriefing. I never really looked at the airplane before they took me away. After the debriefing, the commander of the newly arrived B-24 outfit, took me back to my aircraft. When I looked at the tail I couldn't believe its condition. The colonel then asked me "Lieutenant, why would you try to fly an aircraft damaged like this?" I replied that I had one already dead aboard and three who couldn't survive a bailout, and besides I didn't know that the tail had been shot off the aircraft. The colonel then said "Young man, I'm going to recommend you for our nation's highest award." Although I was still in shock, I knew what honor he meant. I then went deeper into shock.

That evening at about 11 o'clock my bomb group sent an airplane to take us back to Kimbolton. Earlier, at just about dark, a couple of German fighters had come down out of the clouds and made a run up the airfield, which was really weird. They just came in and flew up the runway. They just machine-gunned the runway area, but they didn't drop bombs. When the siren went off and everybody started running, I didn't know what was happening, so I ran into a hangar-like building. I hadn't seen in there but a few seconds or minutes when I heard a loud bang on the metal wall beside me. I thought it was a bomb. I also thought that if the bomb went off I was going to die. In my befuddled state it was as if the Germans had changed their minds and had come back for me. Actually, what happened was that someone had gotten excited and driven a jeep into the side of the metal building—I found out later! Oh, and the Luftwaffe was probably just welcoming the new B-24 outfit into the theater.

Why didn't I talk about it? I guess I expected that back at my home base there would be somewhat of a ceremony and that they would decorate my crew, or whatever. Nothing ever happened. We not only did not receive special recognition, we didn't get even a handshake. That was it. So by the time I left that base, all I wanted to do was finish and get my crew and me the hell out of there. Anyhow, I truly put the episode out of my own mind until 1985 when "A Gathering of Eagles" took place in Las Vegas. This group comprised some of the world's most experienced aviators. About ten of us (including three recipients of the Medal of Honor) were sitting at a table telling stories. When someone asked if anything unusual had happened to me I told them the story of the German fighter pilot who flew along side of us and didn't shoot us down. Then that night, I told my wife the story. I said, "I'm not sure, but I think this really happened, I need to find out."

What was the toughest thing about finding Franz?

There were no records. I formally asked the German air force and of course they had no record. Franz could have been shot for what he did, or more specifically, what he did not do. And all he had to do was hit a button and he would have blown us out of the sky. I couldn't say I was any type of a hero, because I was so damn stupid. Anyway, had I not found Franz, this story would never have been.

Apparently, the 448th Bomb Group Commander, or a senior officer at Seething Air Base, nominated me for the Medal of Honor, but nobody knew anything about it, over 40 years later. Then I found that this colonel probably started action at his first or second level for me to receive the Medal of Honor, but somebody said: My God, bury that story. We don't know how the war is going to go, and we can't have a hero in a German cockpit. Also, if this causes a flier to hesitate just a couple of seconds it could bring about disaster, because the air war is fought in seconds. My aircraft and the mission details were classified "secret" within two hours of our landing. The limited details of our crew mission remained classified "secret" for 40 years. The 448th Bomb Group Commander was killed in action on a mission to Germany within about three months of December 20.

Describe finding and your first meeting with Franz Stigler.

Eventually, after checking with the [RAF] Royal Air Force and the German air force, I learned from someone else that the editor of a German fighter pilot's organization could publish a letter in the organization's newsletter, which I did. I didn't give all the details of the episode. I did give the date and roughly what had happened. I knew it was a shot in the dark. I was looking for any of the engagement's surviving Luftwaffe pilots. Then one day I got a letter from Canada. The last thing I really expected was to get a letter from the specific German fighter pilot who let us live. It boggled my mind. I couldn't believe it was him. I called and talked to him and asked him a few questions. He had the markings on my airplane correct. Then he reminded me of something I hadn't recollected, relating to altitude. I had never combined my spin nightmares with what actually happened. The thing about anoxia is that you don't remember what you're doing. The world stops and it starts again in a situation like that.

We arranged to meet at a hotel in Seattle. When I arrived, I went to the front desk and showed a picture to the clerk and said, "When this man checks in, would you ask him if he is Franz Stigler, the famous German fighter pilot? If he says he is, would you please ask him to autograph this print." Unfortunately, after awhile, the desk shift changed, so I kept watch on the front desk from a balcony on the third floor. After a while I saw him enter and walk up to the desk. I could identify him from photographs he'd sent me. He started looking around, and then the desk clerk brought out the print. I saw the look of amazement on his face and told my wife we'd better go on down. As I came out of the elevator, he looked at me and then ran over and gave me a bear hug that almost broke my ribs. Then we all went up to his room. After we'd had a couple of drinks, Franz and I went for a walk. We were walking ahead of the ladies and Franz's wife said to mine, "Oh, thank God they like each other! Do you realize how badly he worried whether your husband survived the mission and was still alive? He has worried about it for 40 years, whether that crew survived or not." Haya Stigler then said, "In view of everything that had transpired over the years, it would be a real downer if Franz found that the guy he saved was a real SOB." I still think that's one of the funniest things.

A real SOB?

A very realistic thing, when you think about it. Who the hell is this man that you saved? That, to me, puts a real human touch on it. Anyway, we hit it off extremely well. It turns out we're an awfully lot alike. Incidentally, my mother was of half German ancestry.

What did Franz do after that incident happened?

Franz was an active wing commander twice, as an oberleutenant. Both times he ran into problems with the Gestapo. Most people don't know that the vast majority of German pilots had nothing to do with the Nazi party. They were aviators, and that was it. They were part of the old school. When a political element would come in, in the main, the German pilots would have nothing to do with it. As a consequence of his mission-orientated, nonpolitical views, he lost each wing command position.

171

What's the lesson of all this? Is it a moral or ethical lesson?

There is a moral lesson here. One is that as a military man you take an oath to first serve your country, and then you take an oath to do a job for whatever service you're in. There is a limit to how far you'll go if you have moral values—and Franz felt in this particular case that it was his moral right to do what he did. In other words, his moral right not to kill us superseded his overall orders to kill us as enemies. It's interesting to note that Franz felt that he was not brought up to be a murderer, which he considered he would be if he fired on us while we were helpless.

Franz's first combat squadron commander was a great instructor pilot, one of Germany's top pilots, and a great leader, who became a general in the West German air force after the war. He was probably a captain or major at the time when he said, "First of all, you are pilots. You are gentlemen and you are pilots. If you ever shoot at a man in a parachute, or if I ever see one of you shoot at a man in a parachute, I personally will shoot you. You are not politicians, you are pilots."

That Luftwaffe commander and the residual influence he had on his men undoubtedly saved my life and that of my crew. If an identifiable German in a parachute went down by our airplane, my gunners were never going to shoot at him. All aviators in parachutes are helpless and out of the war, at least for that point in time. In the air, it's different. On the ground in the infantry you're taught to kill people. You shoot and kill people. But in the air, at least on my crew, we basically were shooting at airplanes and not at people. And Franz, as possibly a special breed of enemy fighter pilot, definitely was shooting at airplanes.

What about the bloody nose problem?

172

Oh Lord, in combat it was real trouble. You were wearing an oxygen mask and anything that flows down your face, even perspiration, will freeze in the breathing apparatus as it comes down under your chin. And so the perspiration or blood could clog the oxygen-demand flap of the mask, and bring on anoxia, which would incapacitate or kill you. So, periodically I would have to take the mask off and bang it on the control column, to get the ice out of it, while trying to maintain position in the formation.

The first time I cleared the red ice from the mask, it scared the living hell out of my copilot. I hadn't told him about my nosebleeds, and he surmised that I had been wounded in the head, which actually happened later.

You were assigned a top-secret project?

Yes, I was assigned to a top-secret project for about a month prior to starting combat missions on December 13.

Is that still top secret, or can you talk about it?

No. The project is known as GB-1. It was for Glide Bomb One. There's still less written about it than any other highly classified project. Basically, it was a 2,000-pound bomb. The engineers wanted to put a couple of wings, a tail, and a stabilizer on it and they'd hang one under each wing of a B-17. Theoretically, you'd get up to about 30,000 feet, dive to achieve about 185 to 190 miles an hour, then release it, and it would go about 30 miles to the target. The concept was that you didn't have to fly over the target. My crew never dropped one. To carry them in formation we had to develop a new 12 ship formation, which much later became standard for all missions.

The bombs went every place except where they were supposed to go. The Germans went absolutely mad. They thought they were shooting down a large numbers of new type of American airplane. Of course, they were flying and landing all over the countryside. They never really did advance the concept to where it was accurate. The idea was good, but it just didn't work out.

What don't people understand about the Eighth Air Force ?

(1) It was an all-volunteer force. (2) It was never turned back by enemy action. (3) It fought the longest continuous campaign, with the most casualties of any comparable U.S. military unit or combat action. From summer 1942 to May 1945 we had over 58,000 casualties. Many of the losses were in phase two between fall 1943 and the Invasion of Normandy in June 1944.

Two of the real, but normally unrecognized enemies, were the extreme cold and the lack of oxygen at our normal operating altitudes. Many of our airmen died due to those factors. As an example of losses in the case of my crew, we were one of 50 crews assigned to a provisional training group during the three months of our stateside crew training. We were shipped to England as a provisional group of 50 crews. When we arrived in England 11 of my provisional group crews or 110 men, were assigned to the 379th Bomb Group (Heavy), of the Eighth Air Force. By the time that I completed my tour on April 11, 1944, all 11 crews had been shot down. Nine of them, or 90 men, were missing in action; both the other crew and my crew had made forced landings in England on one operating engine. Of the 20 members on those two crews, only eight were not either wounded in action nor killed in action. In addition, of my five crewmen who were not direct combat casualties, two of them had severe post-war mental problems, with one being medically retired and the other spending several years in V.A. medical facilities. For our little group of 11 crews, combat induced casualties were over 100 of 110 or well over 90 percent. My mentor in cadets was an older married cadet, who was always in my flight, throughout the cadet program, where I was a cadet captain from pre-flight through advanced training. His mother-in-law even pinned on my wings upon my being commissioned a second lieutenant at our cadet graduation ceremony. Jim and I ended up in B-17 transition training together and became even closer before we left each other summer 1943.

Somehow, on an early combat mission I inadvertently became the flight leader. I believe that we started the mission in the last element of the low squadron. Just as we entered Germany, we encountered massive condensation [con] trails resulting in heavy clouds and severe visibility restrictions at our altitude. The formation became extremely loose, as it was impossible to fly close formation. When we lost sight of our lead aircraft we turned to the left for a few seconds and then turned back to our original heading. Shortly after resuming our original heading we broke out of the con trails/ clouds into a small valley-like opening, surrounded on both sides by clouds. Somehow we had acquired three other aircraft who were tagging along apparently using us as a flight leader.

Unfortunately, directly above was a wing of about 30 German fighters and they immediately attacked. Although we managed to shoot down one of the fighters, the two B-17s flying on my wings and the slot aircraft disappeared during the first fighter attacks. Still aware that the clouds to my right were filled with the remaining aircraft from our group, I immediately commenced a diving turn into the clouds on the left side of the valley. I safely reached the clouds and once in them began to climb to try to fool the German fighters. Shortly after reaching an altitude at least 2,000 feet above

174

our group's assigned altitude we broke out of our cloud cover. What a beautiful sight!

Flying unmolested, well down below the con trail/cloud level was a full combat group of B-17s, in fairly clear air, and in perfect formation. Just as I started down to join them, the entire wing of German fighters reappeared and again commenced to attack us. I went into a full power dive and in desperation pulled up under the high squadron of the new group. All of the normal slots in the combat group formation were filled and I decided to fly just below the high squadron and use them as a shield against the German fighters, attacking from above and from the front.

The Germans were determined to shoot us down. During their first passes the B-17 squadron leader and the aircraft on his right wing were shot down. As the formation closed up, another B-17 of the high squadron was shot down and we ended up flying on the right wing of the slot aircraft. The attacks eventually ended, after the loss of the three aircraft, and we stayed in formation and bombed the target with our newly adopted group. We also stayed in formation with them until we returned to the English coast where we bid them adieu and returned to our home base of Kimbolton without further incident.

During the initial fighter attacks, a machine-gun bullet hit the pilot's side windshield and I felt a stinging sensation near the center of my forehead. Upon checking with my glove I found a small wound, which had started to bleed, with the blood interfering somewhat with my vision. Shortly after we had escaped the fighter attacks, and while we were flying with the other bomb group, the bleeding stopped, possibly due to the extreme freezing temperatures (approximately 55 degrees below zero Celsius).

On that mission the Eighth Air Force lost 20 heavy-bomber aircraft, including four from my group, believed to include my two accidentally acquired wingmen, with three Category "E", believed to include our slot aircraft. There were about 115 bombers damaged, and casualties included about 225 bomber aircrew, plus five fighter pilots. Rather than my losing the full thirty men in 30 seconds as initially feared, at our home base we learned that the two wing aircraft (twenty men) were, in fact, missing in action. The third aircraft flying behind us landed at an American base near the English coast, had several casualties and was damaged beyond repair due to fighter inflicted damage and the extreme stress experienced during their high-speed dive to avoid the fighters. We were the only aircraft out of our acquired flight of four to return to our home base. Our own aircraft had several .303 holes made by the German machine guns, a few flak holes, a few .50 caliber holes from the defensive guns of the bombers, a damaged nose, damaged pilot's windshield, and damage to the leading wing edge area's and engine nacelles. By far the greatest amount of damage was due to the .50 caliber shell casings from the guns of the B-17 squadron above us.

Our copilot and engineer asked me not to report my wound, as it would cause my grounding for a period and my crew could have to fly with another pilot. Since the wound was not of a major nature and in view of the extensive loyalty of my crew, as demonstrated on the December 20, 1943, mission to Bremen, I chose to treat myself with non prescription medication, later provided by a medic, and not report the injury. Even though our unusual starting position below the high squadron of the new group saved our lives it proved to be rather unsatisfactory as a normal position, and we considered ourselves very fortunate to have survived without greater damage of a fatal nature. The two combat lessons learned or reconfirmed during this mission were: 1) Friendly fire (there is no such thing) .50 caliber shell casings are dangerous to one's health, and 2) our earlier judgment to never fly lead when it could be avoided was again proven valid.

After completing college in fall 1949 I decided I wanted to become a professional officer of the newly formed United States Air Force. I applied for active duty, and despite the existing surplus of officers already on active duty, by taking a reduction in grade, I was recalled to active duty in a specialized field. I applied for, and a few months later the air force awarded me a commission as a regular air force officer.

Reporting at my new station, one of the required check-in points on the base was the finance office. I joined a small line of individuals waiting for service. Upon looking closely at the officer immediately in front of me there was my old friend Jim, whom I had not seen since mid 1943. After the normal "How are you? What are you doing here?" questions, I found that Jim was just departing the station that I was just checking into. The short line moved rather quickly, but I was able to ask Jim what had happened to him after we had finished the B-17 transition school. Our further training and combat assignments had paralleled and Jim had also been assigned as a B-17 pilot and aircraft commander with the Eighth Air Force in England. In response to my question of, "How did you make out?" Jim replied, "Well, I was doing great. I was being checked out as leader of the high squadron. Our group was flying in relatively clear air, no flak, no fighters, and in perfect formation, when some crazy SOB with triangle *K* markings came out of a cloud and brought the whole damn Luftwaffe fighter forces with him. The idiot pulled up under our high squadron and we were shot down on the first fighter pass. Fortunately, we were able to successfully bail out and I spent the next sixteen months as a prisoner of war."

Long buried memories were suddenly resurrected by a series of vivid flashback pictures. Unfortunately, recall was total. "Gosh Jim, sorry about that," was my concluding comment, as Jim moved up to the counter.

Needless to say I did not inform Jim that my aircraft tail markings included a large triangle *K* and that I was the *idiot* who had brought the *whole damn Luftwaffe fighter forces* to his unfortunate squadron. Out of the hundreds of bombers and fighters in the air that day, fate had brought two old friends together, a lifesaving incident for one, but a most unfortunate meeting for the other.

Jim, if you are still out there, I truly am still sorry about that.

Any other thoughts?

I guess being one of the early bomber pilots to complete over 20 bombing missions into Germany proper, is a matter of pride to me. I started 26 bomber missions into Germany and completed 24 of them.

What can you add about Franz Stigler?

Franz ended WWII as technical officer of General Galland's famous JV-44, Squadron of Experts, flying the M-262, in effect the first combat jet aircraft. He was either a fighter squadron or wing commander for most of the air war in Europe. At war's end he had completed 487 combat missions, was credited with shooting down 28 Allied aircraft, with more than 30 probable. He was himself shot down 17 times, well over half by bomber gunners and the rest by fighters and ground fire. He was also wounded four times. He emigrated from Germany to Canada in 1953 and is a retired businessman.

Do you still have contact with Franz Stigler?

Yes, we talk by telephone once a week and visit each other at least once or twice a year. We are now like brothers, in fact, as well as brothers in the fraternity of aviators.

Leonard Wright (middle back with mustache) with his combat crew December 17, 1944.

LEONARD WRIGHT
B-24 Pilot

Leonard Wright had a difficult time getting into the Air Corps. After finally being accepted, he did primary training in Oklahoma City on PT-19s, then went to basic in Coffeeville, Kansas, flying PT-13s, and then to Altus, Oklahoma, flying AT-17s and AT-9s. He requested B-24 transition school and was sent to Fort Worth. Then he was stationed at March Field, California, where he flew routine coastal missions. Later, he instructed at Muroc Air Force Base. A friend of his had just returned from the Aleutians, and persuaded him to join the advanced cadre of the 494th Bomb Group. After a short time in Orlando for tactical training, he went to Wendover, Utah, where he picked up crews. At the time, Wright was in the 864th Squadron with probably more hours of B-24 flying time than anyone in the group—some 800 hours. Then came time for Wright to receive his brand new B-24. His face lightened at the memory, though he was in pain at the time, rubbing his arthritic hand. From across the table, I leaned back, knowing this frail, 81 year old man was excited with the past.

How did you feel when you got that new B-24?

It was like getting a brand new Cadillac, especially after flying the beat-up wrecks we had in training command. Right then I told my crew chief that I never wanted to get into that airplane in a class-A uniform, a dress uniform, and come out with a grease spot on any of the trousers. He took my word, and we did have a beautifully maintained aircraft. Next, we staged through Lincoln, Nebraska, then went to Fairfield-Suisun, California, then to Hickum Field in Hawaii, where we went through the Seventh Air Force gunnery school, waiting for our eventual destination, Palau islands, a group of islands about 650 miles east of the Philippines. We were the second airplane to land on an island called Angaur, which is in the Palau group. We followed our group commander Lawrence B. Kelly. The 494th was known as "Kelly's Cobras."

What are your earliest memories of flight?

My earliest memories of flight were about in 1930 when I was taken flying by my dad's instructor pilot. This instructor took me on the first flight I'd ever made and scared me to death. He did a couple of wingovers, and as small as I was in the front cockpit, I found the safety belt was not fastened. It occurred to me later that I could have easily departed the airplane. Even after that, I wanted to fly. I had another barrier though. I has already been rejected by the aviation cadets program twice when WWII started.

182

How was that?

In 1938, I had finished two years at the University of Tennessee that was required for the aviation cadet program, but I was turned down for being too tall—6'4". Later, in 1940, the government increased the height to 6'4", which I was, but I was two pounds underweight, and adherence to the regulation was very rigid. At that point I said the heck with it. But on December 8, 1941, after Pearl Harbor, I was in line at Fort Des Moines for the Army Air Corps. I ended up 68 in line that day; only 64 applicants were accepted. So they sent me home for a couple of weeks and said they might call me again. My wife and I were living in Des Moines at the time. After several delays they finally enlisted the rest of us in early April.

The day after we landed in Angaur, we bombed an island in the Palau group [Babelthaup] and lost one airplane from another squadron. The Japanese controlled the entire northern end of the Palaus at the time. The army had taken over Angaur; the marines had taken over Pelileu. We basically covered the Philippine invasions for General MacArthur. We covered the Philippines from top to bottom, from Manila in the north to Zamboango on the big island of Mindano.

One of the toughest flights we had was the flight over Clark Field north of Manila. Clark had been a big base for the Air Corps. At the time the Japanese had over 400 operational fighters in the Clark strip. We were told one day we would have top cover by a P-38 group, headed by Dick Bong, a top ace in the Pacific; however, when we reached our initial point, we didn't see any P-38s. It was a blue-bird day—you could see all the way across Luzon. Suddenly, we see airplanes boiling off of Clark Field like bees coming out of a hive and figured we'd have a tough time. We were among 24 B-24s, six from each group. My group was the last squadron to cross the target. We were at 5,000 feet and just before we got to the field, three squadrons before us disappeared. It looked as if they'd run into a thunderstorm. There, we encountered about as severe resistance as I saw anywhere else in the Pacific.

Did you get hit?

We were lucky that we just lost a wing tip and had one engine banged up.

The engine had to be changed when we got back. We finished our fortieth mission on Friday, April 13, 1945. Since we were on the other side of the dateline, we knew it was April 12 in the States.

So it wasn't the unlucky Friday, the thirteenth?

It was Friday, April 13 where we were, but it was April 12 in the States. That was the day that Franklin D. Roosevelt died. In fact, when we went out to get into the airplane for our last mission, I remember realizing that several of my crewmen were just 19 years old and had never known anybody but FDR as president. The crew was quite disturbed at FDR's death. I told them that the best thing to do was to get 40 missions out of the way first, which we did.

What about when the Japanese shot the wing?

The main spar of the B-24 was just like a construction I-beam. When we landed at Tacloban in Leyte to refuel, the ground control officer came by to check with the crew to see if everyone was all right. Fortunately, they were, but he noticed some minor damage in the cabin behind the bomb bay. We had an idea that damage had been done. Then ground control asked if we had any problems, and we said no. At this juncture, I stepped out of the airplane to stretch my legs and my engineer who went on top to read fuel, said, "Skipper, I think you'd better come up here." I went up there. From the ground I could see there was a hole in the bottom of the outward wing about 18 feet from the wing tip, which was about the size of a silver dollar—obviously nothing of any consequence. Then, when I got on top of the wing, I noticed there was a hole about two feet in diameter through the top skin. Apparently, a piece of flak had hit the bottom span and made a small hole, but cut a *V*-shape piece out of the main spar, widening from about one inch to 20 inches in the top of the wing. By some miracle, that shell hadn't cut the aileron controls or hit the Tokyo tanks, or even the electric light on the wing. Also, though, we had a big hole in the propeller of the number four engine and had lost one of two elevator cables—a piece of flak had gone by the waist gunner's windows and cut the top cable. Fortunately, the B-24 had dual elevator cables, so it didn't affect the plane, and we had no knowledge of the severity of the problem until we got back down.

I had the option of staying at Tacloban to get the wing repaired or going back to Angaur. Since we'd already flown 400 miles from Manila without any major problem, I asked the engineer what he thought about returning to Angaur for repair and several days off. He concurred and we went back to home base. Unfortunately, another crew had landed wheels up several days before, so before we could really get relaxed, the ground crews had taken the wing tip from the aircraft that had just landed wheels up, and grafted it onto ours. They called me the next day and said we were ready to go.

We had received word that there was a Japanese regiment camped in a coconut grove somewhere in the middle of the Philippines. The Philippine guerrillas kept us well informed of movements of enemy troops. That time we were sent out to drop fragmentation bombs for the first time. The frag bomb is a very wicked device. Weighing about 30 or 40 pounds a piece, they were like hand grenades .

We were leading the second element just behind the first, heading toward the target area. When the lead flight dropped their frag bombs, the bombs came showering down and we flew through those pieces of metal that held those bombs together. I could see the bombs themselves skipping across the top of the wing. The propellers on the bombs were starting to unwind. It seemed to take an eternity for the bombs to skip across.

How many bombs came across your wing?

I counted four or five. I kept thinking that the prop had better not come off of that thing or we'd really be in trouble. Fortunately, they hadn't fallen far enough to re-arm themselves. So, outside of having a very serious conversation with our group C.O. about the problem of dropping frag bombs, when we returned, it turned out okay.

Basically, the weather was always a problem. There was always a front between Palau and the Philippines. Some of the thunderstorms we ran into were tremendous. We would usually take off at about three o'clock in the morning. We had no electric lights on the runways; we were lighted by flare pots. But sometimes it would be raining so hard. You'd take off in one-minute intervals and when your minute was up, you gave the aircraft the gas and tried to stay between the flare pots. When you ran out of flare pots, you'd better be flying. We'd climb out and make a turn over Pelileu where the marines were still fighting at Bloody Nose Ridge, and then on course to the Philippines.

Could you see what was going on below?

We could see flashes. I was nervous most of the time, but one time over Clark Field, our copilot, who was supposed to be our flight armament officer, didn't do one of his chores. He was supposed to see that all our flak suits were prepped. We got to the initial point of our bomb run, and I issued the order to don our flak suits and flak hats. My copilot reached behind his seat and his was there. I reached behind my seat, and it was empty. I said, "Chuck, we have a problem."

He said, "What's that?"

I said, "Where's my flak suit?"

He said, "It's right behind you," only it wasn't.

I said, "I'm the brains of this operation, so give me your hat—I'll take the helmet. You can take the body armor, because you're in a position to hide behind that." Previously, I had salvaged a piece of armor plate from a wrecked P-38, and I'd placed it under my seat. The piece was about 18 inches square. I figured that if I got shot from behind or underneath, that the armor plate would be of some benefit [laughs]. We got back from that mission without too much of a problem, though the squadron lost an airplane.

I mentioned weather conditions. I remember one time we took off at three in the morning. Our group C.O., Colonel Kelly, was supposed to go with us as copilot. We were at 8,000 feet and had broken out of the solid clouds a little, when I saw this weather front ahead of us, outlined by lightning. Our normal cruise speed was 160 miles per hour. Anyway, we hit this front and I reached up to turn the autopilot off and we hit this updraft. Colonel Kelly was sleeping. I should say that a B-24 could hardly climb 500 feet a minute, fully loaded. But when we hit this updraft our airspeed went from 160 to close to 250 miles per hour, and we started to climb at 2,500 feet a minute. I had to pull the power off to keep from exceeding the air speed of the airplane. Finally, at 13,000 feet we leveled off, but one would have thought we were on a submarine. I've never seen water as thick in my life. Meanwhile, Colonel Kelly had awoken. He looked up and said, "What's up, Len?" I said, "We've got some kind of weather." About that time we hit the down draft on the other side of the front, and started dropping at about 2,000 feet a minute. Our air speed fell off to about 130 miles per hour, which is in complete violation of the rules of flying. I had to put the nose down and add power to pick up speed, so as to keep the plane from stalling, even though we were dropping that fast. Soon the storm kicked us out on the other side at about 8,500 feet, which was about 500 feet from where we went into the front. I don't know what kept the wings on that thing. Colonel Kelly, who'd been flying for 15 years, looked at me and said, "I've never seen one like that."

How much do you love the B-24?

My candid opinion was that it was probably the sorriest airplane that was ever built. I had one member of my squadron who was from a well-to-do family, who when the war was over, was going to buy one and put it in his backyard, so he could urinate on it every morning [laughs].

It was inherently unstable. On the other hand, the B-17 was a very stable aircraft, much better suited to high altitude. The B-24 had a different wing configuration. It was supposed to be more efficient and probably was. I guess you'd say the B-24 was a good airplane, because it got us back safely.

One time transferring a B-24 from Muroc up to Hamilton Field in San Francisco, I came close to running out of gas. Since we were trading aircraft, the practice was to put as little fuel into the plane as possible, because it became somebody else's aircraft. I had only an engineer as copilot that day. We set out on the trip, which was only about 400 miles to San Francisco. After the aircraft was refueled at Muroc, we left and were out about 30 minutes. Then the engineer came over and said, "Lieutenant, we're out of gas." I said, "That can't be. We just put 1,000 gallons in it, which is adequate to get us to Hamilton." He said, "I'll check it out again." He came back and repeated what he'd said. "The gauges are about empty." I did a 180-degree turn and headed back to Muroc as fast as I could go. I leaned the engines back to get maximum mileage, then called the tower for a straight approach. Right after the wheels touched down, two engines cut out, and we were able to roll off the runway. That was close.

How do you explain it?

Engineering said it was impossible, but it seems the pumps we used to transfer fuel, which were called "positive displacement pumps" failed, so that instead of 1,000 gallons of gasoline, we got 1,000 gallons of air.

You seem to like to talk about the war.

It's only been the last few years that things have eased up. I felt like I was blowing my own horn and that people weren't interested in listening to old stuff that I had done. Now I've got nephews who are asking for pictures and stories. Also, I was elected to the Quiet Birdmen and that sort of helped.

Of what are you most proud?

I had a routine tour. We had 18 flight leads, six squadron leads and three group leads—and we never lost an airplane on any mission that we led—so I'm very proud of that. I also had the satisfaction of recognition from some of my enlisted men, who thought I was quite possibly too strict. They had come to realize that they were fortunate to be in our crew. That is most gratifying. You feel you have accomplished something when you could take absolute raw crewmen and make them into a first-class crew that had a reputation of probably being as good a crew as there was in the group. I say that because we were selected many times to carry VIPs on the tour.

My wife's father was a military man, and he told me, "Son, if you're ever in command, you take care of your troops, because your troops are going to take care of you." We always had a distinct understanding, and I always told each crew member, "I don't care what your mistakes are in the past. I don't want you if you don't want to work to be a member of the best crew." For example, I had a tail gunner who was a big rough cowhand. He'd popped a second lieutenant that he'd disagreed with, and then we had our little understanding talk. There was a feeling of camaraderie, but it wasn't like "Let's go out and get drunk every weekend."

It's just difficult to realize that life is totally different during the war—the possibility that every morning, every day that you climbed into that aircraft you might not return. You tried to avoid getting too close to people, because you never knew if they'd be there in the next bunk the next day. Early on, I lost my best friend, Steve Wood from Knoxville, in a B-24 accident in Lakeland. He had an engine cut off on a routine takeoff. We'd gone through high school and two years of college together. He was drafted early and applied for aviation training. He graduated in late 1941 and was killed in March or April 1942. Then when I was assigned to March Field, a cousin named Henry Cox—who had a good job for Alcoa, but decided to go in, after the Bataan Death March—he was coming back from his 13 mission and his navigator was sick. They ran into a mountain. Those two incidents cemented my resolve to do as well as I could.

Since the war, I've kept in touch with all my crew members. For example, I've had a practice of calling them for the past 50 years on April 13, which was the date of our 40 mission.

Several years ago, I was sitting here at home one night and got a call, not from a crew member, but from my wingman named Myron Phillips. He said, "You sound like you're next door."

I said, "What do I owe this pleasure?"

He said, "You're not going to believe this. I was walking along the balcony at the Air Force Armament Museum at Eglin Air Force Base, and I saw something that looked very familiar. It was a *V* on the tail of a B-24."

I said, "My gosh, that's our squadron."

He said, "When I got a little closer, I looked and couldn't believe it. I could barely make it out, but I had seen it for about 20 missions when I flew as your right wing. It said, *Hell's Belle*."

That was the name of our airplane. The photo had been taken in flight because all of our fans were turning. We had no idea of how this picture got there. I couldn't believe that out of more than 18,000 B-24 airplanes (and of the very few that flew in the Pacific) that we'd end up on a museum wall. I couldn't believe it.

I said, "I'm approaching the end of my path, and I'm going to try to go up and see it."

A powerful moment when you did see the photo?

Yes, it was. My sister and I went up to Pensacola and spent the night with my cousin and then headed over to the museum the next day. The visit to the museum evoked such memories— sentimental thoughts. The funny thing was that while I was standing there, a boy about eight years old came up and was looking at the photograph. He looked at me and said, "Did you fly that airplane?" and I said, "Yes, I did, son. That was my airplane." And he turned around and yelled, "Daddy, daddy, this man flew this airplane!"

Ken Barmore in Brazil on his way to Italy in March 1944.

KEN BARMORE
B-24 POW

Ken Barmore was born in Verona, New Jersey in 1921 and lived there until he went into the air corps. Enlisting as an aviation cadet in mid 1942, he graduated as a twin-engine pilot in class 435 at Turner Field, Albany, Georgia. He went to combat crew training as a B-24 copilot and then to Italy and the Fifth Air Force and 451st Bomb Group. It was there that he bombed Ploesti and was shot down, captured and held as a POW in Bucharest. Ken is modest in describing his experience as a POW, declaring strongly that it was not the same of those who were imprisoned in Germany and Japan during WWII.

After returning to the U.S., Ken was assigned to the Radar Navigation School at Victorville, California, as a B-24 pilot and assistant operations officer. Then following release from active duty, he went to work for United Airlines where he retired after thirty-five years. He lives in Soquel, California, with his wife, Barbara. The two have a daughter and son and four grandsons. Ken is still active, in music as a trumpet player, and with church and friends. He says unashamed, "Retirement is the best."

When did you have your first flight?

I had my first ride in a plane when I was 12. My dad took me to a local airport and another kid and I went up, circled around, and landed. I enjoyed it, but never was too excited about it. Then, when WWII came around, I heard a couple of my coworkers talking about joining the Army Air Corps. I thought about the alternatives: the navy (no, I couldn't swim.); the army (no, I didn't want to be on the ground.); the air corps (it sounded like a pretty good place to go, so I went.).

You're a trumpet player. You could have played in a military orchestra.

I came very close to joining a military band. One of my high school instructors was trying to get a marine band started, but I declined. His group was in the first wave at Guadalcanal, so I was very glad I didn't do that.

I was raised in a small town and having never been away from home, I found it scary to join the military. I hadn't gone to college, so I had to take a written exam to get in. The exam was a strenuous one, and I failed it the first time. I think a lot of the reason was that I was scared. Later, I came back and retook the exam. The examiner told me I had one of the highest scores he'd ever seen.

194

Any unusual tests you had to take once you were in the military?

Yes, they had some unusual ones. There was a device you held out at arms-length. It was broken halfway to the end, so if you lifted up on the handle, the other end would go up. If you pushed down on the handle, the back part would go down. The device bent in the middle and you couldn't hold it straight. But for the test you had to hold this thing and put it into a metal board that had little holes in it. You were supposed to hold it at arm's length and keep from touching the sides of the hole. If you touched the sides, a light came on, and you had to count each time. As you attempted this, a sergeant walked behind you and called you a bunch of jerks and said that you were stupid. "You'll never be able to do this," he said. Meanwhile, we were getting mad and distracted, as he intended.

Another test involved something like a 78-rpm record. The goal was to hold a needle on a mark on that record. Unfortunately, the record didn't go around in a perfect circle. It was really weird. I guess how one did on certain phases of these tests determined whether you became a pilot, bombardier or navigator.

Remember your solo?

Very clearly. I came close to ground looping. My instructor had been a copilot with the Penn Central Airlines. He thought the most fun thing to do was to get the Stearman up as high as you could, then flip it over on its back and glide down. I hated that. I was always hanging there with my feet down in my face. My instructor really wasn't much of a teacher. On my first try at a solo, I turned 90 degrees from where I intended to go, and scooted across the field. He had me do it again.

I remember my first night solo in basic even more vividly. For this, we went to a grass field that had flare pots lining the runway. An Army Air Corps instructor sat on the ground in an airplane and acted as a kind of air traffic controller. Think of the field as a rectangle. There would be four zones, one in each corner of the rectangle, and the fliers would climb to the different zones assigned to them. For example, there were three airplanes in each zone. Perhaps a lower airplane was at 1,000 feet, the next at 1,500 feet, and another at 2,000 feet. Then the control person would say, "Lower zone two, you're cleared to land." When he did that, someone would take off and climb to the top of zone two, and everyone would drop down five hundred feet. I had never flown at night and it was very dark. Even after my instructor took me up and showed me, I didn't know what was going on up there. I got through it, though. A friend of mine who was landing for the first time, mistakenly lined up on the lights of the main street of one of the little South Carolina towns. He was preparing to set down when the controlling airplane yelled over the radio for him to pull up. "That's a town," the voice said. He was pretty embarrassed.

You flew the Ploesti Raids.

I had requested to fly A-20s. But I was sent to B-24s as a copilot on a replacement crew. After combat training we went to Hamilton Field and picked up a brand new B-24, then flew it to South America, and across to Africa and up through Morocco. Once there, we had a couple of practice flights. Our first mission was to a little place called Alessandria, Italy. It was uneventful. On the second mission we went to Orbetello, also in northern Italy. On this, we ran into weather, so the flight leaders had us drop down lower and we hit our secondary target. We got the heck shot out of us. It was so bad that we had the number-one engine feathered and number-two engine pulled back so much that it was practically windmilling. Also, our aileron control cables were shot away on the left side, so we had a hard time keeping the plane flying. We had other problems. The waist was shot up badly, and the waist gunners' parachutes shredded, so we had to fly the plane back. At that point, a couple of planes dropped back and escorted us. When we arrived back at Castellucia, the C.O. said we should have bailed out and let the airplane crash. He didn't know about the damaged chutes.

Our third mission was to Ploesti and that was where we got really shot up. The anti-aircraft flak was so thick that it looked like we were heading into a rain cloud. We dropped our bombs okay, and as we were rallying off the target, we got hit. We figured we must have been hit pretty hard because immediately there was no control of the airplane. What a sinking feeling! In the distance I could see the 451st Bomb Group going home, and we were on our way down.

At the time, I was flying the airplane, and there was no control whatsoever. The pilot, Paul Kreuger, had lost oxygen. He rang the emergency alarm bell, which was the signal to get out. Then he and Stephens, Stauffer and Hawkins went out the nose. About that time, the top turret gunner, Charlie Joines, came out of the turret and had blood all over his face. He looked horrible. It turned out the Plexiglas from the top turret had shattered and he had a bunch of pin-prick size pieces of glass in his face. He was bleeding badly. I helped him clean up a little. Then Lyle Clark, the ball-turret gunner, came up. He told me that the two waist gunners had been hit badly.

Going back through the bomb bay to the waist, I noticed the plane was full of gas and hydraulic fluid squirting all over the place. I could hear the wind whistling. I tried to get through, but couldn't. The bomb racks, which go up in a *v*-configuration, get wider at a point, and I got stuck. (I was wearing a seat-pack parachute.) Boy, I thought, "This is it!" Hard as I tried, I couldn't get loose. Finally, I was able to wiggle free.

When I got there, I could see that the waist gunners had practically nothing left from the waist down. Their legs were just shattered. I saw George McDonald, the tail gunner, working on Archie Eakins. He then manage to get him out of the hatch. I told McDonald to go too. As soon as I had helped Maurice Kelly with his chute, I asked him if he could pull the ripcord once I pushed him out. He said yes.

It's funny what flashes through your mind at times like this. As I looked out and prepared to jump, I thought the ground looked exactly as it did when I had done spins in a BT-13. I jumped and as soon as I felt the wind outside, I popped the ripcord. As the chute popped open, I noticed the plane had already crashed below me, and was burning. I thought I was going to land in the fire. Fortunately, I was able to swing forward, back and forward and miss the burning plane. I was very lucky.

My diary reads:

"As I got out of my chute, I saw Kelly land about 150 feet from me. Then I saw McDonald coming down behind some trees. I was the last one out and probably the first on the ground. I went right to Kelly. He was lying just as he landed. He had nothing much left from his upper legs on down, but seemed to suffer no pain."

We had landed near a tiny village called Tirgoviste. Peasants surrounded us out in the field as we came down. They were friendly. The Germans came along soon thereafter. To our surprise, they didn't want anything to do with us. Two Romanian officers were there. Later, two of the gendarmes from the village escorted us away.

What happened then?

We were put inside this little building. Kelly was outside on a little cart. I had given him a shot of morphine, and he seemed to be comfortable, but who knows? He talked a little bit. Inside, the Romanians tried to interrogate us, but they spoke Romanian, so we didn't understand them nor did they understand us. Suddenly, someone came in and motioned for us to come out. We went out and Kelly died just a few minutes after that. An old peasant lady came up to him and placed candles in his hands and made the sign of the cross. She wept as if this was her own child. It was an emotional moment.

The next morning Kelly was still out there, but covered. They moved us to Tirgovisti in a horse-drawn wagon. On the outskirts we had seen Clark and Joines in the back of a passing truck. They interrogated us there and put us in a room where we were joined by Paul Krueger. He had landed with Eakins, who had his leg amputated and died from loss of blood.

I wrote in my diary:

"We spent the whole day here and in the afternoon we could see the bombers overhead as they bombed somewhere nearby. We saw one plane get hit and could see some chutes. We wondered if we were to spend the night here, but after dark they came in and took us outside and loaded us in a truck. There were other POWs in the truck with us, but we didn't know any of them. We had no idea where we were to be taken. I made myself as comfortable as I could on a pile of parachutes and tried to catch some sleep. Something was put in my hand and moving very slowly I saw that it was a .45 pistol. What a thing to have. It was a very bright moon lit night and a guard was sitting on the chutes just above me, and I was scared that he might see it. I slowly moved my hand until it was over the side of the truck and when we went over a small bridge over a stream, I let it go."

Later, they took us to an army garrison in Bucharest. We were put in a filthy, smelly, small room. I wrote this:

"The garrison was in the shape of a rectangle with an open courtyard in the middle. The latrines were in the center of the courtyard and we had to be taken from our room in twos with a guard. It was a long wait for each turn as there must have been 20 or so of us there. When it came my turn, another fellow and I went . . . We took the rifle from him [the guard] and marched him to the latrine, went inside, came out and marched him back to our room, went inside, and pushed his rifle back out through the barbed wire on the door. He kicked up a real fuss, and we realized it had been a pretty stupid thing to do."

Fortunately, the guards were peasants, not real soldiers. That afternoon the Army Air Force flew over. One person claimed he counted 404 B-17s and B-24s. That afternoon Charley Hawkins and Leon Stephens were brought in. Hawkins had banged up his knee some. It was great to be able to account for the entire crew.

Then we were taken to a school building near the middle of Bucharest. Here's where 16 of us POWs stayed in one room and the Russian POWs prepared our food. "Our room had a liberation lottery where we picked two dates, which would be the date we were released. There was a small supply of books to be read, including the Bible, which was very popular. Lieutenant Bill Rittenhouse (who became a minister after the War) was our chaplain. We had church services every Sunday. It was amazing how many verses we put together of hymns, from memory, so if you knew the tune, we could sing the hymns. Another form of entertainment was crushing lice that we found in our underwear each morning. We also had our share of bed bugs. I wore my flying suit most of the time, so I could tighten up the sleeves and keep the bed bugs out at night. Some fellows suffered bad bites, and some sat up most of the night reading in the hall to keep from being bitten. Every so often the Romanian colonel would round us all up in the auditorium, make two lines facing each other, and have his soldiers count us. I really believe that he never knew exactly how many POWs he had. They would count up one side of the line, and that would give one count. Another count would have four or five move into a different line, unseen. The count never came out the same twice. The colonel would slap faces, and have his men count again. This gave us a lot of fun and drove the colonel crazy."

199

Did you ever talk to Kelly's family?

I wrote to them. The pilot lived close to where Kelly lived in Illinois. Kelly had a brother there who was a priest. I felt sorry that I didn't follow up after my letter. I really liked that kid. He was a kid from a small town who'd never been anywhere. We were together for such a short time.

I had a great experience with the other waist gunner who died, Archie Eakins. Archie had gone to pilot training wanting to be a pilot, but he had washed out in Basic. Then he was sent to gunnery school and wound up on our crew. Later, when we were ferrying our plane overseas, we stopped at Memphis, Tennessee, at an Air Transport Control base there. I got out of the plane and noticed a BT-13, so I asked the operations officer, "What's the chance of flying that?"

He said, "Fine."

I said, "I've got one of our waist gunners out there. I'd like to take him up with me." So Arch went with me and he flew that plane for about an hour. He'd washed out in that plane, but he flew it there and was in seventh heaven. We buzzed cattle on the ground near the Mississippi and had a ball. I was really happy I did that.

When you were a prisoner, what did you do?

I learned how to play bridge. In the courtyard they had two baskets, so we organized basketball teams. During the night the RAF [Royal Air Force] would bomb, and during the day the Army Air Forces. After awhile, I found out that we were imprisoned right on the edge of the marshaling yards, which explained why the Allied Forces were bombing there constantly. On June 28, I was watching the skies and wrote:

"Before the B-24s came into sight, I saw a fighter get hit and start to smoke. He started to spin straight down and just as the plane went out of sight, I saw a chute open up. The heavies hit the yards and came right over us. Every plane was streaming vapor trails and it sure looked beautiful. There were a few stragglers and a few smoking a bit, but saw none go down. If the smoke we could see was any indication, they did a good job."

We would run into the basement during the raids. Half of the basement was underground, and the window was at ground level. We could stand by the window and see the formations of planes go by. One night the RAF flew over. It was a real foggy night and a couple of flares dropped in the courtyard and across the building. We didn't know what they were. We had a couple of RAF pilots imprisoned with us, and one of them said, "Oh, my God, this is the alternate target!" That night there were fires all around us, but fortunately nothing hit our building. But across the street the damage was enormous.

I wrote about that experience in my diary on July 27, 1944:

"We had no shelter except to go down to the kitchen and get under anything we could. We heard at least a dozen bombs whistle going over us. I thought I had been scared at the garrison when bombs dropped near us, but that was nothing compared to this. More flares came down on us and in the morning we heard that one flare had landed on the roof of the guard shack. We knew that the bombs hit close to us as we could see red reflection in the sky and smell smoke. For a time we thought our building was on fire.

The building in Bucharest during the 1960s where Ken Barmore was a POW.

201

When we came up to our room we could see just how close they were to us. A block to the south of us was a hit and flames were shooting up a couple hundred feet. We could feel the heat in our room. North of us about two blocks away was another big fire, and there was a smaller one a block to the east. They hit all around us. Windows were broken in some rooms and glass was all over. We all agreed that we want no more of that. It's a helpless and scary feeling hearing a bomb whistling towards you and getting louder all the time, and thinking that it has your name on it. The one that hit south of us must have cleared our building by only a few feet."

Did you ever get depressed?

I was incarcerated for four months. It was nothing compared to most POWs. You feel guilty saying you're a POW. It was no big deal. You think of the guys imprisoned during WWII in Japan and Germany. They were the ones that had it hard.

It doesn't sound that easy?

We didn't have much food. We got bombed a lot, but other than that, it was just boredom.

To get us out, Colonel Gunn made arrangements through the Romanian Air Force. See, the Russians came into Romania and took the country away from the Germans, but the Germans didn't pull out peacefully; they came back and bombed and strafed, making bomb runs in Heinkels over Bucharest at low levels from every direction. After the raid, we all got together in the courtyard and our C.O. gave us the word to seek shelter where we could. Stauffer, Weil, Pardue and I stayed near the school building for the day and slept there at night. The Germans bombed the entire night. Then the Romanians moved us out of town and took us to what you might call a ranch, which belonged to some beer baron. We would sit at the edge of the slit trenches and watch the Germans come by and bomb Bucharest. Distantly, we could hear the fighters strafing. Anyway, after this, Colonel Gunn made arrangements to fly to Bari, Italy. This Romanian fighter pilot took the radio gear out of a M-109, and the colonel stuffed himself in the vacant radio compartment. Then the Romanian pilot flew back to Bari. Once there, the colonel made arrangements for B-17s to come and pick us up. If we controlled the field, we were to fire off a flare and then the B-17 would come in and land. It was called Operation Reunion.

McCoy and I were given a pass to see if we could round up POWs in Bucharest. There we got picked up in a jeep by a Romanian, who claimed to be a part of the ruling family. I made a trade of cigarettes for a German pistol, but it turned out the firing pen was bent. Fortunately, I did not try to use it. We met a combat photographer named Woody Mark, who took pictures of the Russian tanks coming in.

I remember being out on this field. Then the P-51s came in twos and buzzed the field. Oh, the sight of those planes was just so powerful! Then we knew the B-17s would follow, which they did. Since my name started with a *B*, I think I was one of the first to get on a B-17. I went up into the nose and rode there. Years later, when I was flying with United Airlines, one of the UA captains I spoke with explained how he was involved with that operation. He went on to say that he flew with a general as a copilot. I remembered there was a general as copilot in the plane I was in. We pretty well established that this captain was flying that B-17 in Romania that had taken me home.

RAYMON IRVIN
Battle of the Bismark Sea

As early as April 1940, Raymon Irvin had anticipated war occurring with Japan. At that time he told his mother, "We'll be at war around the first day of January 1942." Later, when he told his mother of his desire to join the military, he found his prediction had backfired on him. She balked roundly at the notion of her son joining if war was imminent. Further complicating things was the fact that Raymon was not old enough to enter the service on his own. He needed his mother's signature to be able to enlist. Finally, Raymon convinced his mother that if he did not get training, he would "get killed in the war." The persuasion worked and his mother signed her permission. Raymon went to Fort Moultrie in Charleston where he took infantry training. Then he prepared to sail to San Francisco. On board were "Yankee" recruits from Fort Slocum, New York. He explains, "Never forget that the Civil War was still a real issue then to some of us Southerners. So we "Rebels" had made up our mind that if those damn Yankees on the ship said one word to us, we'd kill them." Raymon went up the gangplank, flanked by Northerners, but was surprised by what he saw. "I don't know what I was expecting to see. But those people looked as normal as we did. That surprised the hell out of me."

Irvin and the boat full of Yankees and Rebels sailed to San Francisco, then to Hawaii, landing there on July 15, 1941. There he served in the military police, but later became a flier—a change he explains in the interview. As a flier, he served in the Ninetieth Bomb Group, 321 Squadron, in Australia and New Guinea. After his tour of duty, he returned home and attended the University of Chattanooga. In what he describes as an ill-fated decision, he quit the Aviation Cadets, where he was paid as a staff sergeant. "I could have gone on and become a pilot," he says, "because I was too damn dumb to be a navigator or a bombardier." He flashes a broad, toothy grin. "I probably would have retired a bird-colonel or a two-star general—no telling where I might have gone."

Raymon is especially proud of being part of the crew that spotted the Japanese convoy that led to the Battle of the Bismarck Sea. During his career Irvin got the Silver Star and the Distinguished Flying Cross, but never the ten other medals he says he was owed. "The recording of these things was horrendous," he says. In addition to his other accomplishments, Irvin shot down nine enemy planes.

Irvin retired as a missile security superintendent for the Minuteman missile at Great Falls, Montana in 1964.

You were at Pearl Harbor when the war started.

I was at Fort Shafter, an artillery fort, when the attack started. Fort Shafter was only about five miles from Pearl Harbor. I was on the last day of the week's KP duty. All of a sudden, things got to rockin' there. Every weekend, particularly on Sunday, we had grown accustomed to the navy digging near Pearl, to put in large fuel-storage tanks. When I heard the big explosions, I made the remark in the dining room, "Oh, God, they really must be tearing up Red Hill."

In this one building we had a dining room, a day room, and a gun room, where we stored our weapons. I was in the military police at the time. Anyway, a guy named Clare Trevor from Pennsylvania happened to be in the day room, where he had the radio on. All of a sudden he ran into the dining room, yelling, "We're under attack from an unknown enemy." That did it. I ran out of the mess hall, down a sidewalk inside of the quadrangle, up a set of steps and jumped over on the roof of this community latrine where I could see the attack going on. I was standing on the roof when this Zero came right smack over the top. I was a good shot and believe that if I had my pistol, I could have shot the son-of-a-bitch. He was less than 100 feet off the ground. In fact, I could see his face. (Later, I saw the *Arizona* when it blew up.) During that time, one enemy plane came over us, strafing. I got down under the barracks. Meanwhile, some of the people who had stayed overnight in town, started arriving. We couldn't get our guns out of the gun room. We each had a .45; we had some .03 Springfield rifles; and five water-cooled machine guns. Finally, a guy named McNabb showed up and got our weapons. We set machine guns around the quadrangle. Later, we thought we were under a gas attack. I remember one of my buddies just about passed out—he thought he was gassed.

I didn't go into flying until about a year later. I was selected from 30 or 40 military police to do training. While I was doing this, the Ninetieth Bomb Group came through going to Australia. They were pretty hard-pressed in that theater. The problem for me was that the army had come out with a regulation, in which they graded all the corps, and the military police were rated low. Part of the regulation said that any time a person put in from a lower corps to join a higher one, the battalion commander had to approve it, which he did. So my friend and I went down to Wheeler Field and made application to transfer to the Air Corps.

We went down to a little dirt airstrip pushed out in the jungle, up on the Cape York Peninsula in Australia. We had a lot of internal trouble with our aircraft on those muddy runways. I can remember our living headquarters in tents on the side of the runway. One night it was raining and the flights had to take off. One of the flights clipped a tree and fell off into the jungle there and burned up, crew and all. Another time on the narrow runway, one plane came in for a landing and something happened to the brakes. It plowed into two more aircraft, destroying three aircraft in one pop. One crew member got killed. It was wild there. Once some guys killed a big python snake and it stretched halfway across the runway. He was a monster. I can remember going out and dynamiting fish and taking them up on the side of the hill and cooking them. That was a relief, because about all we were getting to eat was mutton. We might have gotten a little mule in there, too. Needless to say, our food was not too good.

We no sooner got there, when we planned on moving up to Port Moresby, New Guinea. The Japanese were about to take Port Moresby. The Australian army had turned the Japanese back from a trail coming in. All the farmers had released their animals, so the Japanese wouldn't get them. As we moved back in, the Australians were rounding up horses. They'd bring them over and sell them to us GIs. I bought one and it was the only horse I ever owned. We rode them around and hunted wallabies and other game on them. I sold it just before I left, which was relatively early. The flight requirement was 300 combat hours, wheels up, wheels down. I got my hours in pretty fast. I did 55 flights, in about a year. I would go over to operations and anytime they had someone sick from a gunnery position, I would volunteer.

I was flying nose gun on this one mission, on a plane named "Crosby's Curse." The guy who named it had known Bing Crosby. A guy named Smith was the pilot of the plane. We'd just taken off and were flying along the coast. As we approached Hollandia—we were the first crew up there since the Japanese had taken it away from us—I was sitting there fat, dumb, and happy, looking around. I hear who I think is the navigator on the radio. I was up on the flight deck, having a cup of coffee, out of my position, which I shouldn't have been. The voice said, "There are two ships sitting side by side in the harbor, unloading supplies." When he said that, I ran back under the nose wheel to get in my position. I'm hanging there ready to lift my feet on the catwalk when the bombardier opened the bomb bay doors and I find my feet are suddenly out in space. I managed to get my feet up. I heard the pilot, Lieutenant Smith, tell the bombardier that we were traveling at such-and-such a speed, that we were at 12,500 feet, and that we would start diving down to 7,500 feet long enough for him to drop his bombs. (We were limited to five or six bombs because we had Tokyo tanks in the front bomb bay.) Anyway, I was standing right over the bombardier, looking around. There was a little valley and a series of small hills up by Hollandia there. I could see at least one of the several airfields. Before long I saw Japanese fighters taxiing out like crazy, getting ready to come after us. When the bombing doors came open, I was watching the bombardier and saw two ships come right under us. I'm looking through my natural eyes—this enlisted bombardier's looking through his Norden bombsight. As this unfolds, I say to myself, "Drop 'em, drop 'em, drop 'em." Finally, he pushed the damn toggle switch. Just as soon as he did, I said, "You missed him." Sure enough, the first bomb fell right over the second ship and the bombs strung right out through the water. All of the work we had done, all of our lives on the line had gone for nothing. I was so mad at that guy.

On my fourth or fifth mission, in early 1943, I was on a reconnaissance, flying with a captain named Higgins. There was an airstrip at Buna, where we went in for an emergency landing. When we were there, I remember, the engineers were out with bulldozers covering up the dead Japanese. Troops had run a lot of them over the pass, rounded them up and killed them.

We tried to get over to Bougainville, but there was a heavy, thick storm over the whole island there. We were searching, wondering if the Japanese would reinforce their troops at Guadalcanal, Bougainville, Lae, or Wewak. We didn't know which way they intended to go. We flew that day 10 or 11 hours and we bounced all over the sky. We weren't making much headway, because we couldn't see anything. Then we turned and came back across New Britain, the island that Rabaul is on. As we came across, the clouds suddenly got thinner and the weather cleared. We could now see. Finally, I heard the navigator on the intercom. I'm flying waist-gunner and photographer. He said, "My God, there's the Japanese navy." I looked out the window and I saw a lot of ships. We were now over the west side of New Britain. I grabbed my camera and tried to take some pictures through the broken clouds. When I heard the navigator say, "Zeros," I threw down my damn camera and grabbed my gun. I looked out the window and could see at least three Zeros not far away. At the time we were trying to count the ships spread out below us, but turned when the Zeros started toward us. We made it back into the clouds. Now and again, we'd break out of the clouds and try to count them. Unfortunately, the Japanese jammed our radio for a while, so we couldn't immediately call back what we had witnessed. Finally, we got further away and Mike Lamoreau, our radio operator on the mission, got word back. The military sent another plane to shadow the convoy overnight.

The Japanese convoy was heading toward Lae. We knew if it got through, we'd be in trouble in New Guinea. We mounted everything we had and the next day started attacking them. Because my group was low on airplanes, I didn't get to go. Anyway, the Allies attacked with B-17s, B-24s, B-25s, A-20s, P-38s, and Lightening Fighter planes. The Australians had Beaufighters. Anyway, they tore the

Japanese up and sank 22 ships, which included 12 transports and ten warships. They also shot down 95 fighters, and killed 15,000 Japanese army and navy personnel. We only lost four planes—one bomber, three fighters, and a total of 12 men. That was the famous Battle of the Bismarck Sea.

You lost some close friends.

I was going to tell you about the two buddies I had that got killed. I named one of my sons for one; another of my sons for the other. I named my oldest son Raymon Rolfes Irvin; my youngest I named Kirby Ray Irvin.

How'd your buddies get killed?

Coming in from a mission, another plane came up behind them. The plane's engine hit their vertical stabilizer so the pilot had no control. The plane nosed over and crashed and killed the whole crew. I had just left on November 9, and this occurred on November 11, 1943. Tragically, the crew almost had its 300 hours in. They didn't have but a couple of hours to go to be able to go home.

How do you remember your friends?

Leroy Bernard Rolfes was easy going. He usually wouldn't drink much, except a gin fizz. The rest of us would get drunk and disorderly and raise a bunch of hell. He was always thoughtful and considerate. He was from Covington, Kentucky. Kirby Griffith was the other. He was a tail gunner and was always joking. Back then we called them "dirty jokes." Nowadays, you could almost tell them in Sunday school. He was from Peoria, Illinois. I was waiting for my pilot to come down to Brisbane and join me. When he arrived, he told me of the tragedy.

The military leadership we had didn't want us to get attached to each other. For example, our crews weren't encouraged to go over to another crew's squad tent. That way we wouldn't get overly familiar and feel the loss so much, if and when someone got killed. Whether we knew the deceased person or not, some of the guys might go over and raid their tent, and see if they had anything they wanted. People would get what they wanted before an officer came down to get the stuff to send it back to the family in the States. Hell, I came back twice from missions and had to go round up my own gear.

People thought you were dead?

They thought we had crashed. The guys would usually give it back. I should say that stuff like this didn't go on all that much.

What did you feel when you lost those friends?

Oh, Jesus. It just tore the hell out of me. What's more, I sat under the wing of the airplane in Brisbane, and lost all my money in poker. I got back to the States, flat busted.

CHARLIE MOTT
On the River Kwai

Nearly everyone who has seen the David Lean film classic, *The Bridge on the River Kwai*, remembers not only the great scenes (Colonel Nicholson struggling out into the sun after he is released from solitary) but also the unending struggles for survival. Charlie Mott has seen the movie, but he also knows the circumstances of that camp from the inside, for Mott himself was imprisoned there, at the site where the novel and film take place.

Charlie Mott was born in 1914. One of five children, he grew up in Philadelphia, where his dad worked for Bell Telephone as a manager. He attended public schools there, and at the time of the Great Depression, he entered the University of Pennsylvania Engineering School. He graduated in 1936 in civil engineering, worked in the steel fabrication and erection business for a year, then got into flying. Mott earned his wings, fell in love with a girl from Alabama named Ellen, then joined the Flying Tigers. To his surprise, he was put in charge of the first group of Flying Tigers, not an easy task, as he explains.

Imprisonment took its toll on Mott physically. At the end of the war, he went to a hospital in Calcutta, India, for awhile before returning home. When Mott got back to the States after the war, General Chennault offered him a job flying for him, which he declined. He wanted to stay closer to the home front, to pursue other career opportunities.

After he left the navy in 1967, he practiced in the field of aerospace engineering. He holds an M.A. in Engineering Management from George Washington University. Mott was also a member of a small group that designed the F-15 in 1967.

You were one of the earliest Flying Tigers over there. Could you talk about how that transpired?

Well, it starts of course with recruiting. I was at North Island, the naval air base there, though we were actually attached to the carrier, *Saratoga*. During this period when we were land-based, a retired commander came through with authority from the highest levels to talk to us, and so he did. I listened to him and decided, after conferring with my wife and talking with the skipper on my squadron, that it was a proper enterprise, and so I signed up.

The process of signing up involved two things: number one, you had to resign your commission; number two, you had to sign a contract with the central Aircraft Manufacturing Company, known as CAMCO, for one year. It involved combat flying in China. Having signed up, I received a communication to report to San Francisco, which I did. The wife and I (we had no children) left in May and took a sort of a second/farewell honeymoon. We arrived in San Francisco on July 7, 1941. There we met the assembled group at this particular hotel on July 9. We were briefed as to what was going to happen. What was in store was a passage to Rangoon aboard the Dutch motorship, the *Jaegersfontein* ("Hunter's Fountain").

What really persuaded you? Was it the adventure?

There were a number of factors to it. Certainly, the pay scale was attractive, which was 600 dollars a month, roughly over twice what we were making in the navy. But that was not the only determining factor. In my case, it was not even a major determining one for me. Those who went for the money were the first to complain that the money was not enough, really. In my own case, I had a number of Chinese friends back in the University of Pennsylvania where I had matriculated. I liked them, and so there was an element of friendship there. Also, as a professional aviator, I anticipated that we were, in

214

fact, going to be in the war—in those days, most people did—and that it was just a question of, when? I figured it would be a good professional opportunity to get some combat experience, then come back into the navy. This was part of the agreement with the service when we left. The agreement also provided that we would be reinstated without loss of rank or precedence and regardless of physical condition, as when we got there we would be shot at frequently. The spirit of adventure was present, as well as the lure of travel to a fascinating foreign country. Finally, a number of my friends, who were members of the divebombing outfit—Bombing Three—aboard the *Saratoga*, signed up too. As a matter of fact, we had a representation, as I recall, of seven pilots, as well as a number of the support personnel. So, all these things merged. I talked it over with the wife, and she agreed that it was probably a good idea and if, in fact, circumstances changed, we would go with our lives elsewhere in aviation, such as airline piloting.

What happened when you were heading over on the ship?

We had 123 individuals in the party. I do say individuals because they came from all parts of the country and with different goals and interests. The common thread was experience in military aviation. Anyway, there in the hotel after the big session of indoctrination/explanation by Lieutenant Colonel Aldworth, retired from the army (the chief recruiter), dinner was served. Then Aldworth took me to one side and said, "By the way, Charlie, you're going to be in charge of this group."

That didn't make me too enthusiastic because I knew some of the guys, and some of them were troublemakers. I said, "Well, Colonel, what do you do in the absence of 'Articles from the Government of the United States Navy' or 'Articles of War,' in terms of maintaining order and creating good things for the group?"

He replied, "Well, write them up."

So I got some hotel stationery and sat down and simply wrote out my orders in longhand. I wrote, "You will proceed with the Central Aircraft Manufacturing Company group, from San Francisco. You will take such steps as you deem necessary to maintain order and promote the welfare of the group." The colonel signed it, and that was my authority!

Any discipline problems on the way over?

Well, there wasn't too much trouble because there wasn't too much strain. The stewards were well trained Indonesians. The food was good, and it was like a pleasure cruise. So there wasn't any real difficulty. There was some objection to the assumption that the officer in charge has the authority to close the bar [laughs].

We probably hit our low point about two weeks after we arrived in Burma in August. Colonel Chennault (later Major General Chennault), God bless him, was certainly a leader and military analyst. He had a governing principle of not committing the unit to combat until it was ready, i.e. fully trained. So rather than put the men in China where we would be subjected to engagement right off the bat, he obtained permission from the British authorities to use the airport at Toungoo, a British Royal Air Force base about halfway up the Burma road up towards Mandalay. Actually, the road extended up to Kunming, China. So this is where we were to be stationed. The airplanes had not been assembled yet; the food was terrible by U.S. standards; and there was not enough to do. As a result, the muttering element sort of took over. However, by no means was this dominant. The core of our group was dedicated.

As a group we were pretty straight when you get right down to it. I mean, we did have an element of native woman chasing, hard drinking, gambling—all of that stuff, but it was a minor element. Chennault had not met us. His agent who met us, retired Captain Carney, was kind of a miserable sort of a guy. Later on, he was court-martialed and retired because he shot somebody in the course of a poker game.

I was made acting adjutant. This duty is a combination of personnel officer, a sort of a flag secretary, and general jack-of-all-trades for problem solving. So anyhow, the big day came when Chennault was to come down from China, and I was to meet him. I assembled the Flying Tiger group in what was actually the mess hall. Meanwhile, I went out to meet the general. He came in and as adjutant, I preceded him. As I entered the mess hall, I commanded, "Attention!" in a loud voice. About half of the men stood up, and some of the rest of them were muttering, along the lines of "I ain't standing up for nobody." Then, Chennault, who was right on my heels, noticed the situation. I've never heard him speak so loudly or as authoritatively. He commanded "attention" and all stood up attentively. Their reaction was like RCA Victor's dog listening to the gramophone, "His Master's Voice." Next, Chennault made a little talk. He was not a man of many words and was very much to the point. The meeting then broke up.

When Chennault arrived, things started to happen. He set up training programs. By then, the airplanes had started to arrive at Rangoon and were assembled by CAMCO. We sent pilots down to pick them up, and we gradually built up our strength because people were busy on constructive work. Very largely, these were crew chiefs, mechanics, and ordinance men who, once they had an airplane to maintain, were totally committed. However, some of the electronics people regarded themselves as something apart, and this resulted in a lot of complaining. But we got over it. We trained intensively. Not without good days and bad days.

Give me a bad day, and did you lose anybody that early?

We lost a number of airplanes in training accidents and also people. One day, we had four landing accidents, very largely the result of big airplane (army bomber and navy patrol plane) pilots learning how to handle a fighter. We had no two-seat trainers, so they were on their own in a single-seat P-40. Chennault grounded all planes that day to stop the carnage.

In another case, in our own squadron [Second] we had a pilot by the name of Armstrong. As operations officer of the squadron, I made the point to dogfight with everybody in the squadron, which would give me some idea of who was a good dogfighter and who could handle attacks. I had just exercised with Armstrong a week before that and noticed an absence of certain safety precautions that you have to take in dogfight training. Otherwise, bad things like collisions happen. For example, I noticed that Armstrong had a fixation and had a tendency to play "chicken." Anyway, the next week Armstrong and another one of our guys, Gil Bright, were up there dogfighting. Evidently, Gil wasn't too sensitive to Armstrong's proclivities, so they hit in midair. The collision took off Gil's wing, but Armstrong didn't get out, and he crashed. Gil parachuted safely.

What was the hardest funeral, emotionally speaking, that you had to attend?

All funerals are hard. I often thought that the real tragedy was back at home, not at the site of the death. Grief is for the living loved ones.

So how long before you were ready for action?

In November we were just about ready. We were up to strength, had as much as three months to train and get indoctrinated. Chennault deemed us ready for combat, even though some late arrivals didn't get a proper syllabus. He sent me and another pilot up to check up on facilities for supporting the group, at the end of November. I was in Kunming on December 7, and all the action was in Pearl Harbor! Unfortunately, I had managed to get into a quiet spot. When the balloon went up on December 7, Chennault immediately went on the alert. The only plane we had in Kunming—the Japs had not attacked there—was mine. Chennault sent one squadron down to Rangoon to work with the British Sixty-Seventh Squadron, Royal Air Force. The remainder of the group went to Kunming, except for a few airplanes that stayed at Toungoo. Though we were ready for action at Kunming, no action took place until December 20. The Japs sent a group of ten unescorted bombers from Hanoi to Kunming. We were able to put over a squadron on them, and we shot down enough of them that they never came back. Only one of them got back to Hanoi. The principal battles took place over in Rangoon. Chennault had followed the army practice of not committing the whole force at once, and committed only one squadron to Rangoon. I didn't go. Still later, we flew into Rangoon to relieve the First Squadron and secure the place. The British had radar there but wouldn't let us anywhere near it, but we did get warnings. Alex Mihalko, one of our radio men, hung around there, and when an attack developed that had been tracked by the radar, he let us know about it.

The Flying Tigers never fought the Zero. We did tangle with the army equivalent, the Hayabusa [Falcon], which actually was more maneuverable than the Zero but had a shorter range. Chennault had access to the complete Japanese tactical manuals, and he was able to work out tactics based on the manuals and the performance of Japanese aircraft. In fact, as a result of one meeting when he announced these specs, some of the faint hearts actually quit shortly thereafter. We knew that the P-40 had a rate of climb of 2300 feet per minute; the Zero could do 3200. Chennault told us to never dogfight. Just make your attack, go through them, separate, come back, and do the same thing. Also, operate in pairs and use teamwork. Sadly, they didn't release this information at the Pentagon, and a lot of fellows got killed unnecessarily. The Japanese never did solve that little problem of our refusal to dogfight.

How did you get shot down?

When we got to Rangoon, the heavy daylight raids were over, so I missed that. They had started to attack at night, and we experimented with night tactics. As I expected, it didn't turn out too well. The idea was to get in an attack group and stay over the field at 4,000, 6,000, and 8,000 feet altitude and wait for them to silhouette against the moon. The Japanese had a habit of having the lead bomber signal a formation drop by the lead-aircraft tail gunner firing. Our plan never worked. We couldn't spot them because of lack of radar control and vectoring information.

219

Because the Japanese got their noses bloodied coming over in daylight, we decided to do raids on their fields in Thailand. That was where I got my comeuppance. They had a base on the Thai/ Burma border, in Thailand, called Mesoht. One day we got the word from our reconnaissance that the Japanese had eight or ten airplanes on that field. The field was well within our range. We decided to go at noon hour when presumably their noses were in their mess buckets. I led a flight of four. We caught them all right and shot up the flight line, and then decided to look around for other dispersed airplanes. I spotted a couple there and had turned and was making my third pass when I got hit. I had just opened fire and had about 250 knots just above treetop level. My target was a plane at the edge of the field when I got hit. I'd been hit before, and a few rounds came close enough so I could hear them. At that point though, something hit the engine with a bang, and everything stopped. Immediately, there was an organized panic as I started switching tanks, working the fuel pump, flicking the magneto switch, and rocking the aircraft to clear tanks. Shortly, I was out of air speed and altitude too, so I rolled over and parachuted out. I was too low actually—about 250 feet—but my chute opened and I hit a big tree almost simultaneously.

The airplane landed maybe 150 yards away and was burning. There still was some ammunition left in the plane, which was going Pop! Pop! So we had a little local war going on. The bullets were flying everywhere. The Japanese were very sensitive to parachute troops, as everyone was in those days, so they thought this might be a paratroop landing. They deployed, and there was quite a firefight going on between them and the exploding plane ammo. I was intact, but I was about 30 to 35 feet in the air hanging from this big jungle giant in my parachute. I tried swinging and getting to the branch but couldn't. I tried to climb up the risers with no luck. I worked to get out of the straps but had trouble because there was a Chinese quick release on my chest. It was designed to release all four straps simultaneously, but it wouldn't release any. I picked up my .38 pistol and put it right up against this steel pin on the parachute release and pulled the trigger. That released one strap, and then I struggled to get out. As I got into position, trying to get free, I literally fell out. I hit the ground and broke a foot, an arm, my pelvis, and a couple of ribs. That was the end of my mobility. All I could do was lie there.

So you were in terrible pain?

No, no, that didn't come until later. So I lay there for about five minutes. I never saw the Japanese soldier that stalked me. He jumped out from behind a bush in this little clearing where I was. He prodded me in the butt with a bayonet, drawing blood. I pointed to my arm, which I was holding limp, and which was only suspended by the fleshy part. He stuck me again. I tried to get up, but I fell back. Then the rest of the squad came up and milled around, looking as if they had springs in their heels, running around in circles. Moments later, someone in authority appeared on the scene. At their command two soldiers went out and came back with a couple of big pieces of bamboo. Two of the soldiers took their trousers off, and made a stretcher with them by inserting the bamboos in the pants. They then put me on the stretcher and started carrying me for the airfield. We arrived at the edge of the field. About that time the trousers ripped, and I came in on the parallel bars. I raised up to see what had happened and could see planes burning on the flight line.

How many planes did your attack get?

The group got eight, though the Japanese claimed seven. I got two.

Anyway, at the time I looked up, a Jap I didn't see, hit me in the head with a bayonet, opening a cut. This had a curious effect of dulling the pain without affecting my consciousness. Somebody pulled him off. We went across the field, and they put me down in a tent. Then the bigwigs of the field—some eight or ten of them— came in. They stood around in a circle and just looked at me and talked among themselves. The bigwigs evidently called up army headquarters in Bangkok. Because I was the first one they had caught, the order was given to bring me in for interrogation. In the meantime, they patched me up, put a splint on my arm, and gave me a couple of shots of morphine. Later, a truck pulled up and took me to the railhead and down the railhead on the day and a half ride to Bangkok.

They took me to their headquarters. The idea was to show how beneficent the Japanese army was. I was being used for public relations purposes.

Afterward I was put on the floor in a room and after a time heard a great scurrying outside. In came this senior Japanese officer who sat down on a chair. He spoke good English, and he started a conversation. Evidently, he had some duty in America, because I noticed a New England accent. He asked, "How old are you?" "Twenty-seven," I answered. "Are you married?" I said, "Yes." I detected polite Oriental conversation, and I resolved then and there to be polite with these people at all times. It paid off handsomely because the Oriental attitude about Europeans was—and this was not confined to Japan—that we were all barbarians. Some were less so than others. We were hairy, and our manners left a lot to be desired. I also had mustered a salute, when he arrived. After more polite conversation, he said, "You are an American."

I said, "Yes."

He said, "You were flying a Chinese airplane." In view of the fact that the plane had Chinese suns painted all over it, it was pretty hard to deny. Then he said, "We can treat you as a pirate." I didn't say anything. Then he said, "But we will treat you as a prisoner of war." He had the orders written out and after that, I was taken to the Japanese hospital in Bangkok. There I was treated like any Japanese soldier, though they never put any traction on my arm, or attempted to set the bones in my foot. They did leave me alone, and my bones healed in about three months. Then I could actually walk—my foot was knit and my arm, too. Next, I was taken from the hospital and put into a guardhouse. I was there for three months where I was "bunged" in with the British prisoners from Singapore, whom they had brought up to build the Burma-Siam Railway along the river Kwai. So from then on I spent the whole three years there. Under severe duress, we built the bridge and the railway. The movie, *The Bridge on the River Kwai* and a lot of books describe the conditions there.

So you were imprisoned at the location of the movie, The Bridge On the river Kwai? What was fiction there?

The plot was complete fabrication. There were no special forces that penetrated and blew up the bridge. The bridge was blown up by B-24s. But the atmosphere and the battle of wills between the Guiness character and the Jap commander were very much realistic. The depicted condition of the troops was authentic. The filmmakers caught the atmosphere of the camp. You might question if the part Guiness plays was real, but it was. Also, there was a guy—he was a second-class sailor from the U.S.S. *Houston*, who tried to pass himself off as an officer, but that didn't work and he was not accepted. The portion of the film which relates to the British taking over building the trestle bridge, that's wrong. It didn't happen. Actually, the Japanese had a railroad company there. Today, you know how the Japanese have got the highest speed railroad in the world. Even then they were competent railway engineers, and they designed the bridges. The bridges made you nervous, but they worked.

They made you nervous?

Well, they were just big wood timbers with a couple of iron U-shaped spikes holding them together. The wood supported the weight, but the bridge would sway and creak. Still, they didn't fall down.

What were your responsibilities in the prison camp?

I couldn't walk very well, and the British took me in and made me a member of their officers' hut. I suffered the same conditions that all the rest of them did. The British were in the process of forming a prisoner of war transport company, with 62 trucks coming up from Singapore, which were the only ones we had to bring the rations up the river during the monsoon, via a dirt track. Anyway, perhaps because I was an engineer, the British put me in charge of this motor company. I then recruited 150 guys—most of them from the Eighteenth British Army Division, from the London area, but also a few Scotch Argyles (Highlanders), and several Australians. Our job was to get material and food to the upper camps—the camps way up in the jungle. Actually, I think the British didn't expect things to turn out as they did. Originally, in the Nong Pladuk camp, I was like any other junior officer there, but when I pulled out and set up operations in a separate remote place, I was pretty much on my own with the Japanese. In the camp were a lot of Koreans, which the Japanese called volunteers. They were recruited for army auxiliary service, and they were a bad lot.

As a matter of fact, the normal Jap I could deal with. They were civilized, educated, and the working level, you could establish a rapport. The Koreans there were entirely a shoddy bunch. I've seen them cross the road just to kick a sleeping dog in the ribs, to hear him yelp. They would get drunk on a holiday and try to take it our on my crew and would beat them. I ended up interceding. This resulted in a beating for me on two occasions. Fortunately, I would establish a good working relationship with a Japanese captain who had authority over me and my unit, and I was able to keep most of the situations under control, although not all of them. I had trucks and detachments up and down the railroad prospective right-of-way. I couldn't be everywhere, so it was necessary to teach my men how to get along with the Japanese (and Koreans) when they were on their own.

We did have in camp at one time a bunch of British Indian Army officers, who acted like Alec Guiness who played the British commander in the movie. They were really straight-line soldiers and dedicated. They couldn't send them out with the troops on work parties because sooner or later they'd make it worse, because they couldn't adapt to dealing with the Japanese. We called them the Imperial War Museum because they represented a type of officer who could not adapt to the new circumstance.

Because we in the transport business were on the supply line, we never really starved. Also, we could steal a little gasoline and get 16 ticals (bahts—Thai money) per gallon on the black market. When we were stealing the gasoline, we called it "bleeding the emperor," because Hirohito was the emperor, and gasoline is the lifeblood of an army. Anyway, we'd sell the gas, take the money and buy things, turn some of it over to the local British for funds for hospital supplies. We'd use some of it on the black market to buy things we needed when the opportunity presented itself. Black market items were eggs, bananas, and medicines.

How'd your men manage?

In my unit we lost only two men that first year, out of 150. One of them was a lance corporal by the name of Parrott. He got cerebral malaria, and when that hits it works fast. In about three days you either recovered or you were dead. The other case was a British Londoner. He had a little can of gasoline and was trying to prime-start a truck. A Korean came along, and he took it over. He was doing that when it backfired. He threw the gasoline over his shoulder and accidentally set my driver on fire. He was so badly burned, he expired.

How would you manage to steal the gasoline?

Well, the gasoline came in drums at first, steel drums. Later, they ran out of steel drums and shipped it in wooden barrels, and these leaked. We would unseal a drum and then take a five-gallon can-full, and pour it into the truck. In that process we could make sure that a little bit of it went into another can. Somebody would come and cache the payment at the same place you left the gas can. In the case of the wooden drums, these were invariably not full; they were always leaking, so there was no real problem accounting for the gasoline with them.

At some point spirits must have sunk to a pretty low ebb?

The lowest period was what some people called the "speedo" period. The orders from Tokyo came to complete the bridge by the end of the year. This meant long hours and little food. You got up at the crack of dawn. You had breakfast of rice gruel, then roll call where the enemy would count you. Then you formed work parties and marched off—one officer to every 20 to 30 men. You might dig dirt or crack rocks or, in some cases, work on the bridge. The piles for the bridge were driven like the ancient Egyptians did it. That is, the pile driver was simply operated by 30 to 40 guys pulling on ropes. This heavy log section would come down and hit. Then they'd pull it up again, and it would drop. The quota for dirt diggers was one cubic yard per man per day. It all had to be dug by hand. No construction machinery was available. The diggers used little wicker baskets to put the dirt in. They'd dig it, carry it up to the embankment, and dump it—do the same thing all day. When it came to making clearings, you cut down these gentle jungle giants with a handsaw. Some of the guys might later on cut the firewood for the locomotive. Troops got injured doing everything from falling off a trestle to getting in the way of a falling tree. Many men gave up the ghost during this period. In the final analysis, there were 55,000 white men who worked on the Thailand side of the railroad. One third of them died; one third of them developed long-standing health problems, and another third you couldn't kill if you wanted to.

When the railroad was finished, the living conditions in the camps definitely improved. One big thing going for the prisoners is that discipline, including sanitation discipline, never broke down. The Japanese also "shanghaied" coolies, who died by the thousands. We had British medical people who were very skilled and dedicated. Although skilled surgeons were very short on tools (they sometimes used ordinary carpenter tools), and medicines, they did a wonderful job.

One of the more prevalent things that would happen was that you would get a scratch, particularly on the shin, which is not well supplied with blood, and this would get infected. Infection would turn it into an ulcer. This ulcer would grow quickly. Also, there was beriberi because of lack of vitamins. But anyhow, we used maggots to clean them out. The maggots would crawl around in the wound and would eat the dead skin and clean it out. The only thing the camp had in quantity as an antiseptic was potassium permanganate, which was not particularly effective. Sooner or later, the leg was likely to need amputation. Medical equipment was very scarce. There were some funds available. The officers took the hospital funds to buy things like sulfur and malaria drugs. It took me awhile to get back to normal. I still have some problems, to this day. In the camp everybody got malaria once a month. We were in places the natives wouldn't go because of malaria.

Who was the most memorable guy that you met that was under your charge there of the 150, the one that you were closest to?

Well, it's hard to say. I had very fine young men. The one New Zealander, in particular, was a Malayan volunteer. These are Malayan/British who were residents of Malaya and who were volunteers for the armed forces. His name was Dunne, and he was an outstanding guy. I never had troubles with morale because the guys knew that the option was to be sent back to the line battalions. Maybe they weren't smart, but they weren't stupid.

There were a number of camps: Kanchanburi, Chung Ka Hindato, and Tarsao, for example. The camps went up the line to Three Pagoda Pass. We only went so far as the border. This was an ancient, communication trail, between Burma and Siam. The camps were at intervals along the route. They all worked at the same time to prepare the right-of-way. The whole thing actually grew from the bottom up as the rails were laid on the prepared right-of-way.

So did you bring any supplies that went to building the bridge?

No, generally speaking, but we did take work parties when they came up on the railroad from Singapore. We took them as far as we could so they would not have to march, and we would take some of their personal gear and small tools like shovels. However, our primary transport was food. We had one truck for 600 men on the line working.

They didn't pick your brain as to how to build a bridge or anything? You were an engineer.

Not with respect to the bridge, but they were very interested in how we maintained our trucks.

Is that right? And what would they do?

Well, they just wanted to know everything about it. If the truck was down, they wanted to know why, and in many cases, I would show them why. They had the attitude that we knew more about it than they did and would accept our explanation.

Did you ever try to deceive them on what was wrong with the truck or in some other venue?

No. Deceit was dangerous.

Do you remember the British officer that was in charge of the big camp at the bridge?

He was a lieutenant colonel, named Colonel Toosey, and he was a pretty competent guy. He was very resourceful. It was a big camp. He had about 4,000 to 5,000 people, and he dealt with all the Japanese. He maintained order. He was always smartly dressed, clean, in the sense that his shorts may have been ragged and a shirt torn, but they were always well washed. He was an excellent officer with fine command presence. Later, he was awarded the Order of the British Empire (OBE).

So, were there ever any false hopes if a plane came over?

Oh, we saw plenty of planes. Every time they attacked the bridge, we saw the planes. They made a number of attempts, but it wasn't until late that they really hit the bridge.

Describe liberation day—the day you got out of there.

What happened was that the Japanese actually stopped military operations on August 14, 1945. The peace treaty wasn't signed until September 2. The day that we got the word in the camp was on the August 14 or 15. We learned because we had a secret receiver, and we were current. However, we were a little shaky about the Japanese delivering on the agreement.

Some general comments: For a long while, though the conditions were miserable, they were 180 degrees away from the Vietnam experience of close confinement. During the early days, you could walk anywhere. Anytime you wanted to go into the jungle, you could. Then what? There were some organized escape parties, but none of them got through. They were recaptured, brought back, and used for bayonet practice at the place where they left, so that discouraged people from trying. You had to go one thousand miles to get to friendly lines.

I was in Kanchanburi at the time when the Japanese stopped this business of letting us—you might say—walk around. After that, we were in camps with moats and barbed wire and guard positions.

This happened about the last year. It got increasingly tight. Militarily, the reason was obvious. The only real line of communication that the Japanese had with their Burma army was the railroad. The Japanese army in Burma was taking a beating. There was only a road up further north, a dirt track. There were 2,000 POW Allied troops and officers sitting on the line of communication, so they were nervous that we probably would design a takeover. The Japanese made it impossible to do that. However, we were nervous that they would murder prisoners, which in fact happened in places like Wake Island, with about 100 of them they had kept on the island. They were just lined up and murdered before the war ended. The same was true with about 200 Americans at Palawan in the Philippines. They were working an airfield. A couple of guys got away by hiding in the rocks, a bunch of caves and so forth, until they could get out and join the guerrillas.

As a matter of fact, when the British took over Southeast Asia, the records show that the Japanese commander of the southern regions, Count Terauchi, had planned to murder the prisoners. They were very clear as to the disposition of POWs. They preferred that the commanders take orders from headquarters, but if not, they were to dispose of them locally by any feasible means.

So, then, you had secret radio receivers. Did the Japanese ever catch anyone operating one?

Yeah, as a matter of fact, the Japs were very suspicious and in one case, we were careless. This was earlier. You can understand that it's good news that keeps the guys going, but widespread dissemination was dangerous. So it was the routine to try to control what people knew, though we had rather loose control. As a consequence, the Japanese got wind of something by listening to some of the troops talk. They simply tortured their way back to the guys working the radio, and those guys disappeared. They were probably executed. The Japanese were always searching for a radio. In fact, they thought I had one.

I had no radio. Though I didn't, I knew where it was, and I was in on the news. Sometimes I furnished a car battery to operate it. I'd take the battery and carry it to the main camp, when they were low on batteries, and then bring the old one back. I would put it back in the truck and charge it up. So I was on the circuit.

What about the big day your incarceration ended?

On the big day, this strange officer came through the guardhouse. The Japanese staff administration building was right in the POW camp, which was a big one. He was spotted, and word was passed. This was at nightfall. They told senior officers to report to the headquarters, which they did. There was a group of English, Dutch, and American officers. The word of our impending release came in the presence of the Japanese camp commander, who incidentally was later hanged. His name was Noguchi.

But anyhow, we posted a chain such that if anything drastic was going to happen that the main camp could be alerted to take provision to react. But this Japanese staff officer came in and did it like a man. The Allied officers were there at the table, and he came in and put his sword on the table and said in very good English, "Gentlemen, the war is over. Japan has lost the war." With that, he turned on his heels and walked out. And this word was picked up, and after he announced it, there was a big roar of "hurrah" from the POW area, and the Japs looked a little startled. Then all of us got together for a celebration. We sang our national anthems, American, British, and Dutch. It was over.

That must have been one hell of a celebration there?

Of course. There wasn't much to celebrate with, but we did it with enthusiasm. Following that, I received a message from the American OSS group which was up in the hills about 40 miles away. We knew they were there. The Japs also knew they were there. There were three Americans there at the time and about 315 Thais. They were training and had not started active operations yet. They were supplied by airplanes operating from India and Burma and were well armed with everything from automatic weapons to "grease" guns. The Japs had run a few patrols up there to try to engage them, but had gotten a bloody nose, and so they adopted a "live and let live" philosophy. I got an invitation to join them. So I left. I sneaked out of the camp and went up the road on a dark night. I was challenged by a Thai, and I identified myself. He had a horse for me, and we went cantering up the road toward the OSS camp. I was full of malaria, and this Mongolian pony jarred it all loose. All of a sudden I had a malaria attack and fell off the horse. The Thais got an ancient, small truck from somewhere and put me in that. They drove on. We arrived at the main OSS camp. Of course, they welcomed me, and we had an old home week. The next day they made me aerodrome officer. They had cleared a strip about one thousand feet long. Nothing that a large plane could use, but you could get a light plane in there. Meanwhile, all the information about the surrender was coming over the radio. These were nice guys, and I was enjoying their hospitality, but I decided to go back to the camp and get evacuated. So they fixed me up, and I went back to camp with the first group.

The Americans went out promptly. They were flown out by combat cargo planes from Ratburi, Thailand, which had a regular aerodrome. We were flying in a C-47, a combat cargo-type, and I struck up a friendship with the pilot. He let me shoot the approach to Rangoon (Mingaladoon Airport), which is the field I left on my last mission. I got a strange sense of déjà vu. From there, we flew to Calcutta, and that's where the army put me in the hospital for six weeks. I couldn't get a plane authorization, but I finally got a bunk on a troopship going back to New York. It took 24 days.

230

We passed the Statue of Liberty and tied up at a Hudson River pier. When the telephones were hooked up, I called my parents in Philadelphia. My sweet wife had come out from Mobile, Alabama, where she had stayed for four long years with her family. I caught the earliest train to Philadelphia.

The war was over. I was home.

BARBARA ERICKSON LONDON
For the Love of Flight

Barbara Erickson London was born and raised in Seattle, Washington. After high school she attended the University of Washington and learned to fly as part of the Civilian Pilot Training Program (CPT). Half of the people in the CPT program trained at Boeing Field and the other half at Lake Union, which is where Barbara ended up. Her solo flight took place in December 1939, while Barbara was working at Sears Roebuck in the cosmetics department over the Christmas vacation. After CPT, Barbara instructed in 1939 and 1940, until the war came, which necessitated a move inland, as she explains in the interview. Later, a letter from Nancy Love invited her to try out as part of a new group of women pilots. This led to her becoming a part of history as a pilot for the Women's Auxiliary Ferrying Squadron (WAFS). Barbara got out of the military in December 1944. Commissioned a Major in the air force in 1948, she stayed in twenty years and retired in 1968. After almost three years in WWII and 20 years in the air force, the government still could not put all her time together to give her any kind of retirement. "I donated that to the government," she says. Her husband, Jack, died at 59, so he got no pension, because he did not live to be 60. She says, "Last year they passed a law called the Forgotten Widows Bill. I found out by accident. I was complaining that after 23 years in the military, I was not on active duty enough to get a commissary card." Barbara now receives $130 per month. Still, despite the setbacks, Barbara is strong and resilient and philosophical about her contributions.

Was it hard to go back to work after you soloed?

I do remember that it was pretty exciting. You shoot so many landings that you figure that you know how to do it. You do get rather excited when they finally let you go the first time. We were just all teenagers doing Christmas work. I didn't know anyone very well. I called my mother because I didn't tell her that I was going to solo until after I soloed. When I finally received my license, she was the first one that I took for a ride.

She knew it was going to happen, but I figured it would be easier on her if I did it and then told her. She never had any concerns. My folks were very, very supportive when I signed up for the program, as long as I did what I was supposed to do, like go to school and do my school work. This was extracurricular, and I could do it. I really wanted to do this. They had no fear, and neither did I.

This was CPT. Otherwise I probably never would have flown. I was never exposed to an airplane before. I didn't know anything about what it was like. When the advertisement appeared in the paper that the program was going to be given at the University of Washington, another gal friend and I thought it sounded like it would be real fun to fly. We went down and applied and took the physical. I got in and she didn't because she was too short. She was a tiny little thing, just barely five feet. At that point, there was no written rule, but I think they turned her down because she was too short. I was very, very sad because she was so enthusiastic about it. There had been two or three girls through that period that didn't make it, and I felt very sorry for them. They should have made it. They would have made very good pilots.

One girl that went with me to apply had flown, but when she went to take the physical, they found some problem with one of her ribs. The rib was either crossways, backwards or missing—or something stupid. It was the equivalent of not being able to go in the army because of flat feet.

She didn't make it, but all of my life, and to this very day, she's kept right up with me. She kept up with the program; she knew what we were doing. I've always corresponded with her. I'm still her good friend after 55 years. I remember when she was turned down. It was hard to understand because it was rather nebulous.

234

The instructors were not able to pinpoint what the problem was. Anyway, the class ended up with four girls out of forty boys. We were allowed one girl for every ten boys.

What were the seaplanes like that you flew?

We were flying Taylorcraft; little 65 horsepower side by side planes on floats, out of Lake Union. We just brought them up on to a ramp off the water and then they towed them into a hangar.

When I finally got my license, I came back to the same flight school and started instructing there in the same program. I eventually branched out from just teaching CPT students to some civilian students. In fact, the press came out and took a picture of me and the very first student that I had off the street. We were pictured in the cockpit of this airplane. A few days later, the police came out to the flight school. They told me that they had just arrested my student.

As it turns out, his picture was on a "Wanted" poster in every post office in Washington state for some sort of larceny. The police had put the two together when they saw the picture. In my scrapbook, I've still got this "Wanted" picture that I got from the post office. I never flew with him again, because they put him in jail. I still can't believe that he would have his picture taken. He was smiling and happy, and the next morning the police had him in the "cooler."

You should have gotten a reward.

His picture was my reward. He was a nice guy.

Any people ever panic or have it against females?

I didn't have very many problems. When the war got going, civilian flying stopped on the coast. Our flight school had to move from Seattle, inland, so Mr. Kurtzer moved to Yakima, Washington. We all had to go 300 miles inland. This was January, and it was the last of my senior year so I didn't go with Kurtzer. I stayed and finished school. In June I was ready to go back to flight school, but Kurtzer didn't need an instructor. As a consequence, I ended up in Walla Walla at a flight school. There was a little bit of feeling there about this 20 year old girl coming to instruct. There were several men instructors—airport hanger on'ers—older guys who weren't too sure I would fit in. There was a bit of a feeling against a young girl coming in, especially since I was teaching a class of older boys and eventually boys that were in the navy getting ready to become navy pilots. After awhile, the instructors settled back and decided I was doing the same job they were. Also, they were particularly happy because I took the 5:00 A.M. morning shift, which they didn't want. I worked from 5:00 A.M. until noon.

Was there one navy pilot that stood out?

I've kept track of a couple of them. Several of the Navy boys did become fighter pilots in the South Pacific. When I went back to Seattle in 1994, I got an award at the Air and Space Museum. This one boy, Terry Dalton, who was in my first class and whom I had not seen since he was a student, came out and had dinner with me. He became a marine pilot during the war and served in the South Pacific. He was a couple of years younger than I; he was 18 and I was 20.

When I graduated that first class of five boys, they took me out to dinner at the Olympic Hotel in Seattle. We had a neat time. I got along well with all of them. They went on from there into the navy and then they started regular navy basic training. The navy was trying to give them their original 35 hours, which at that time was a private license. It was called NTS (Navy Training Service), which kind of followed behind CPT.

Ever had a forced landing?

Never. Thank the good Lord. I have gone almost 60 years of flying without a real emergency. And I flew almost every day. I was being watched over; there was no question about that. A lot of people who were a lot more confident than I am had problems.

Tell me about becoming a flier.

I was one of the original WAFS. Both Nancy Love and Jackie Cochran knew that there was a very great possibility that if the war got critical enough that there were women pilots out there that could do the same job, at least domestically, and release the men for combat. Both of them were working on a program. General Hap Arnold had told Jackie that nothing was going to happen right away so she took a bunch of girls and went to England with the ATA. I applied for that program and was accepted. I was ready to go to Toronto to take my flight check. All my paperwork was ready. I was the right age and had enough time flying. Also, I'd gone to high school. I was ready to go to Toronto to take a flight check when Nancy Love convinced the ATC division that they should try a test group of women for the Army Air Corps. I got a letter from Nancy stating that if I had the listed requirements and was interested and willing to come to Wilmington, I could try out to be in this experimental group of women pilots to fly for the army.

I went to my boss, Herman Martin with Martin Flying Service, and told him I had a chance to try out to fly for the army. He said, "You know, what a wonderful opportunity. Pack up and go. I'll write you any letter you need."

Actually, Herman could have made me stay. I was working for a government contract school and he could have held me to that contract. Many of the girls, who didn't make the original WAFS group as I did, were unable to because their employers would not let them go. Any number of girls ended up in the third, fourth, and fifth classes that were just as qualified as I was but they were working for a contract school and the contractor wouldn't let them off.

I drove back to Seattle and packed up everything and got on a train and went to Wilmington. The girl who worked in the flight school as a secretary, Eleanor Dressen, decided it would be fun if she could go too. The train went through Spokane, and she climbed on and joined me in the upper berth. She was hoping to find a job in Wilmington. It worked out that Nancy had lost her secretary about the time we arrived. She got a job as Nancy Love's secretary.

We got to Wilmington and then we took a taxi to the base. It was midnight and pouring down rain. The guard at the gate said that there was a BOQ 14, where the girls were housed. He took us there. A housemother showed us two rooms and said, "Go to bed and we'll check in with Nancy in the morning." So there we were on these iron cots with nothing but a three-drawer chest and a window with a big black curtain over it, because we had blackouts during that time. We were 3, 000 miles away from home with not 20 bucks between us, without jobs, wondering what we were doing there.

As it turned out, the next morning I had them check my logbooks. I took a physical. I took a flight check and was accepted, and within a week Eleanor was hired as Nancy's secretary. Eventually, when Nancy got someone else to replace Eleanor, Eleanor became my secretary for the rest of the war out in Long beach. In fact, she stayed with me until the end of the war.

Did the fact that you were a pilot ever surprise any of the men?

We all have experiences when we have gotten out of an airplane and no one would believe it was a girl. I remember taking an A-26 someplace and calling in and telling the tower I was downwind and the man in the tower said, "Well, we don't have you in sight but we have an A-26 on downwind, just follow it in." They would not believe that a girl's voice was coming from an A-26. A lot of times you would climb out of a fighter and the guys would kind of gawk at you. The only time you ran across anybody that was jealous was when some guy was in an AT-6 and you were in a P-51.

Did you ever verbally spar with any men?

They didn't give us any trouble. We were all doing the same thing and we were all so busy. The average girl didn't spend five days a month on the base. She was on a trip all the time. It was hard to build up permanent, lasting relationships because you couldn't make a date. You never knew if you would be there or not. Everybody was in and out. Just as fast as you were into one place, you were out again.

In the three months I was in Wilmington, before I was transferred to Long Beach, I probably was on base a total of 12 days. We were in a new location every night. Everybody was good to us. We stayed at military bases. We ate well. Though we didn't get paid an awful lot, it was enough then. We got paid two hundred fifty dollars a month and we got five dollars a day per diem. How in the world did anybody live on five dollars a day? That's what the men got. That's what we got. Besides, we stayed in military facilities most of the time. Ninety percent of the time, you landed and refueled at a military base where your billeting was free. Your mess hall was free and Officer's Club was inexpensive.

A favorite Jacqueline Cochran story?

I'm not really a Jackie fan. I was in long before Jackie was in the picture. She was still in England while I was ferrying airplanes. I didn't go to Sweetwater. I didn't go through her training school. I'm not one of the Jackie girls. Jackie started a program and she allowed a lot of girls to learn how to fly who had not flown before. It allowed them to serve their country. This was very admirable. Those girls all thank her for the opportunity that they had. But she didn't start the program. She came in after we were already a functioning organization and started a training program. All of her trainees came back to Nancy and the Ferry Command and were under her command for the first year.

Everybody that graduated from Jackie's school was a WAFS up until August 1943. She soon ran out of girls who had the requirements to get in. Our requirements were that we had to have a minimum of 500 hours. They had to have a 240 horsepower rating, as well as a commercial license. There were only about 100 women in the United States that had those qualifications and Nancy knew that when she started.

Jackie came in with the idea that every girl in the world could be trained to be a military pilot. She ran out of those 100 very fast so the requirements were dropped to 18 years old and 35 hours. When the women graduated from the school in Sweetwater, Texas, they didn't have the required time that the Ferry Command demanded to be a ferry pilot.

Jackie had to find other places to put them. That's when they started putting them in the Training Command and Tow Target Squadrons. They put them in to do test flights on airplanes and to do all these other various jobs around the country. In August 1943, our name was changed to WASP [Women's Airforce Service Pilots],

239

which covered all of the various women's activities. Jackie was put in charge of all of that, and Nancy Love remained head of those 300 that were left in the ferry command.

Nancy and Betty wanted to fly across the Pacific in a B-17 but were stopped. It was the most heartbreaking story, because they had checked out in the B-17 and were ready to go. The two had gotten the airplane up through Maine and up to Presque Isle and were ready to jump across the ocean when General Arnold found out and stopped it. Nancy and Betty had to leave the airplane there. A guy took it across the Atlantic. They came home.

The women were very brokenhearted because it was a trip they really wanted to make. They trained very hard for it. Being civilians, we really were rather restricted to the United States.

This didn't occur because you were women?

I think Jackie found out and stopped it. Nobody really knows. It was all politics.

What about the end of the war?

Once the war was winding down, there were a lot of jobs that the girls could have given up, but we didn't want to give up the Ferry Command jobs. Every one of the girls in the Ferry Command was a fighter pilot. We had to be to stay in. The war was badly in need of those airplanes, so badly in need that we never got a break.

The ferry command pressured General Arnold very hard that if they disbanded the WAFS to at least leave the Ferry Command alone, because they were trained and badly needed. But Jackie was not about to let Nancy's girls stay in and have all of her girls go home, so the mandate came down that we were all to go home. That was really sad.

The morning I left Long Beach on December 20, 1944, there were some 60 fighters sitting at Long Beach Airport that didn't get delivered that day because we all went home. The boys that were doing the complaining about the women were Stearman pilots from the training school. In fact, the military had to go out to other commands, to fighter schools to get boys that were checked out in our airplanes. Certainly the government didn't fill our shoes that day. The boys could be trained to do what we did and checked out eventually, but we were already doing it. It was sad that we had to go home, particularly those fliers that were crucial, and anybody who could fly a fighter at that point was crucial.

At the time, some of the factories were building one and two planes a day. We had Lockheed, North American, Northrup, Convair, Boeing, Douglas, all of them sitting right here in the Los Angeles basin pumping out airplanes.

We all volunteered to stay for nothing. What the military was paying us wasn't a dent in the debt anyway. Instead, we were sent home six to eight months before the war was over. We had to go home and sit on the sidelines.

It drove me nuts. I went home. I didn't want to go back to school because I was training to become a home economics schoolteacher. That was about as wrong as anything could possibly be, but I didn't want to go back to the department store and work. I stayed home a couple of months and my folks sent me back to California because I got a job at Ryan on a test program for one of their airplanes. When I returned to California, I came back through Long Beach and met my boyfriend there. I decided to get married instead. I just stayed in Long Beach.

241

What was your favorite plane?

I loved them all. When the government gives you a million-dollar plane every morning, that is something! To me, the planes all fly alike whether it's a P-51 or a P-38. They were wonderful. I liked the A-26, a Douglas. They were very maneuverable. They were easy to fly. The A-26 was a real speeder. Very few girls got to fly it because it was towards the end when it came out. The P-51 had a nice, small, compact cockpit.

Did you ever buzz anyone?

My halo was on too tight. I was very conscious of doing what I was supposed to do right.

Never broke a regulation?

Never.

Were you tempted?

I danced around through the clouds, one billowy cloud to another, but never came close to another airplane and never came close to the ground.

There are big billowy, puffy clouds up there, and the only way you can tell how fast you are going is to race pretty close to a cloud. When it is standing still and you go by it so fast, you realize how fast you are going. We were going 400 - 500 miles per hour. That was pretty fast back then.

What does flight mean to you?

I'm pretty down to earth. It's a mode of transportation. It is freedom and ability to get up above and out of everything. That's why it was fun to fly alone. That's why fighters were fun because you were in that airplane all by yourself—up with the clouds, the sun and the rain. You had to make the decisions. You went places you had never been before and it was a freedom that you don't get any other way.

After the war, a few of us formed a small company in Long Beach called United States Aviation. It was a multifaceted business with a flight school and an insurance department and a parts department. In fact, we were so multifaceted, we multifaceted ourselves right out of business. It lasted about five years. Then we all went our separate ways.

Later, I worked for the Powder Puff Derby as executive secretary and flew in that for 20 some years. I instructed. I worked for a flight school. I went into sales working for Piper in 1966 and have been in the sales business ever since.

Talk about your daughter Terry, who flies professionally.

Terry is the older one. She always had a leaning towards flying. Very early on, she made up her mind that she would like to be an airline pilot. I applied for the airlines when I got out of the service

242

in 1944. I think of all the airlines I applied for, two of them sent me back applications for a stewardess.

They were not ready for women. My daughter, Terry, had soloed on her 16th birthday and got her license on her seventeenth birthday. Then she spent the next ten years getting background enough to be eligible to be an airline pilot. She worked in flight schools. She instructed, got her college degree, her 727 rating, and her helicopter rating. She got several scholarships. She worked at it night and day. By the time she was 27, she was as qualified as the men who were being hired. She started applying to the airlines. Her approach was that one of these days you are going to have to hire a girl, best you look at my application and be ready, because I am. When you have to make the choice, I'm here. She applied for every airline and upgraded her resume every 30 days to every airline. In 1974, the break came. She got a call from both American and Western. At that point, there were probably only about ten women pilots with the airlines. Western [now Delta] hired her. She has been there 24 years.

I was proud of her. It wasn't easy. She worked in a flight school every night through four years of high school and four years of college to get her flight time. Nowadays, the average girl that goes to the airlines is from the military. They learn to fly in the military and they are ready for the airlines.

243

Did you see yourself in her?

She had the same determination to do it and do it right. She got a degree in aeronautics at San Jose in 1972. The reaction of some of the captains when she got hired was, "There's not going to be any GD woman in my cockpit." They eventually got over it, but she had lots of rough times. The captains would leave cartoons in the cockpit and make all sorts of remarks. Some of the captains wouldn't speak to her. It was tough for the first few girls. It was hard to be accepted. She always said, "The only difference between a guy and me is out plumbing and the airplane can't tell." It seems to me the only thing that they never solved during the war and have not since is a relief tube for women. They can put us on the moon, but they have never solved that problem [laughs].

How does it feel to be a pioneer?

Pioneers were the people who flew in the 1930s. Betty Gillies, head of the WAFS in Wilmington, got her first airplane in the 1920s. She had an airplane all her life. The girls who flew back in the early 1920s were the pioneers.

You are a pioneer in the sense that you have made a substantial contribution.

I think what my girls did was outstanding. They did contribute a terrific amount to helping the war effort. That's what we were there for. Everybody was very patriotic. It is hard to explain what WWII really was. People know Vietnam and Korea, but they don't understand about WWII. Everybody was involved. My mother saved grease. They picked it up once a week. We all were on ration stamps but nobody complained. Everybody did something. I don't think we will ever see our country and our people as united again in any effort. I waited in line at the commissary to buy things to send home to my folks because I ate better than they did. They didn't complain.

I guess I am proudest of being in the right place at the right time and being able to serve my country. I met some fabulous people that are my friends today. I still correspond with a man who is 91 years old who gave me my first pilot's license in 1940. He is still alive and lives in Washington State. We still write. His name is Jack Feeney. He lives alone in Lake Bay, Washington.

When they had the *Missouri* in Bremerton, Washington, I went and gave a speech from the bridge of that ship, to 10,000 people. On that trip we stopped by and saw Jack. Up until two years ago, he still passed his physical. Now he doesn't fly. The FAA takes a dim view of us 80 years-old flying. They'd rather we fly with someone.

What is the greatest compliment that you ever received?

There is not anybody I ever met that I would be afraid to meet today. I don't think I made any permanent enemies and I didn't hurt anyone. I just finished a TV appearance for *American Experience*. We jokingly say that as years go on and all the girls keep dying, our stories get better and better because there are fewer and fewer to tell if they are wrong. There are not too many of us left. Right now, of the original 25, only nine are still alive. That is sad.

These girls came in and did their job. After the war, they returned to the same places they came from before the war. For example, I had a girl that was a buyer for Bullocks. She was an excellent pilot. The day the war was over, she was back to Bullocks and never flew again. My brother-in-law, Charlie London, was the first American ace in England in P-47s. He came back home and never flew again.

What would you be in your next life?

I have mixed emotions if I were to come back in my next life. Would I want to come back in the 1920s when they were doing barnstorming or come back now as an 18 year old, when the girls are flying the wonderful things they are flying, including the Shuttle? Then there are the girls flying all these new military planes. I am torn.

Just a few years ago, I knew a kid who had a tail dragger airplane. He was going to sell it so he advertised it. A guy came to look at it, and he brought a girl. The guy liked the looks of the airplane and said he was going to buy it. "I'm going to teach my girlfriend how to fly," he said.

The kid said, "You're not going to let a girl fly a tail-wheeled airplane like that? She'll wreck it."

I said, "Where do you think I learned? They hadn't invented the nose wheel when I learned to fly."

DUKE CAMPBELL
The Life of a Pilot

Duke Campbell is an individualist—easy going, astute. And, he's been almost everywhere. Once he offered the United States Army moving pictures of the approach and landing to a dozen major airports in China. The army told Duke they didn't want it. Duke replied, "You don't want it. You're asking all the sources you can find for this information. Why don't you want it?" The army officer answered, "We know damn well no American has gone in and out of these airports."

After four years of aeronautical engineering in college, Duke had intentions of becoming an engineer for Boeing, but when the chief pilot for Boeing lectured on the difference in salary between a pilot and an engineer, Duke was sold on being a pilot.

He explains in the interview that he planned to resign from the Army Air Corps and go to work as a pilot-engineer, but when war broke out in Europe, one was not permitted to resign. He was stuck. The Boeing job had ceased to exist. Then, in a strange quirk of fate, the United States government decided that Pan American World Airways should continue to operate to parts of Europe not at war. Pan American needed pilots in order to fly to Europe. In a sort of trade, the government allowed Pan Am to take 24 of their newly qualified pilots—and Duke was one of them.

In the early 1940s Duke flew "flying boats" out of Miami into South America for Pan Am. He later flew to Europe, the Far East— virtually anywhere that Pan Am went. During the war, Duke made important trips related to the war effort. He went on to fly 747s and was for years, a check pilot for the airline. He has seen a lot, this balding veteran of many miles and many stories.

A clipper ship flew President Roosevelt to a meeting with Churchill and Stalin in Yalta—as I recall.

A second Boeing 314 carried other government people and was also there, if needed, to assist in case of emergency. The trip was kept secret until the president returned to the United States.

That seems pretty mysterious—flying the president without fanfare.

It was just a part of wartime procedure. I was merely a part of the operation that was flying between New York, down through the Caribbean—eastward along the north coast of South America to Natal, the easternmost point in South America, and from Natal over to Fishermans Lake in Liberia; from there to ports in Europe and northern Africa. That was a standard operating procedure at that time. Somewhere along the way, when President Roosevelt came through, I was at one of the bases, enroute in the same direction—or coming back—I don't recall which.

248

Was Franklin Roosevelt disguised?

No, but the operation was kept as secret as possible, considering the circumstances. The seaplanes came and went—they were always loaded with materials for the British, before we got into the war. Once we were in the war, they made it a little more obvious what they were doing. The planes were all four-engine seaplanes built by Boeing—the Boeing 314—one was known as the China Clipper. It was not the original, however. The original China Clipper was a Martin M-130, also a four-engine seaplane. Pan American had three of those. Once they got the Boeing 314, they changed the name to the 314 and that's what they called it many years after. That was the plane—or one like it—that Roosevelt was on.

The creator of Pan Am, Juan Trippe, considered his airline to be the "merchant marine of the air," therefore, the named the aircraft Clipper after the old clipper sailing ships that were the fastest in their era. He began operations between Miami and South America. He used commodores and Sikorsky S-38s. They were used with other models until he got the 314s. The Commodores and S-38s were two-engine seaplanes.

Weren't clippers the first to fly long distances?

Not exactly, depending on what you term long range. We had been flying the four-engine planes and were the only airline, in the United States at least, that had four-engine aircraft.

And you were flying them in South America?

Pan Am flew them down the east coast of South America, out of Miami. The first four-engine was the Sikorsky S-40 model. Then came the S-42, also four-engined, a later model of Sikorsky's. Finally, three Martin M-130s were used. I enjoyed that airplane very much.

I liked it mostly from the comfort standpoint. In the earlier planes we had nothing in the way of berths for places to rest when multiple crews went long-range flying across the oceans. In the S-42 a great distance was several hundred miles, not in the thousands. So we'd have extra crew on board, but extra facilities were not available. Later, we had the B-314, with wide—about three feet wide, seven feet long—berths on board. That made a big impression on me after lots of long flights without rest facilities. One of the things that stood our more than anything else was the fact that you could walk semi-erect from the fuselage (on the upper deck, which was available to crew only), open a hatch out into the wing to the inboard engines on either side of the aircraft for minor maintenance purposes. You could go out to the outboard engines, but you had to crawl out there. The crawl space was about three feet high, but the novelty of it was that we were able to go out to the rear end of an engine inside the wing without any trouble. I don't think the other aircraft had such an arrangement.

Describe the distances the airline flew, comparing 1935 to 1937 and to 1941.

Anything prior to 1935 was not across the ocean. It was across the Caribbean, down South America on either side. Pan Am wasn't flying anything that was a long distance, compared to what they've done since. Once the Martin M-130 was built, it was guaranteed to fly to Honolulu and have sufficient fuel remaining on board to go to an alternate island, if necessary.

Meanwhile, out of Germany, they were flying a twelve-engine seaplane, the DO-X, that they flew across the Atlantic from Africa to South America, when or before we did. But is wasn't practical; it made only a trip—or two—and was withdrawn. It couldn't carry very much. The real distance aspect came in once we started flying the oceans. That started in 1935.

That was with Gib Blackmore's flight.

Gib was checking out as pilot on that trip only. In fact, immediately following that trip, he was flying as captain. The government rules at that time were that one had to make a trip with someone that had already been to your destination before flying as captain on that route. So that leaves the question: "How'd the first guy get there?" It would have been on a proving flight—the government required us to prove that the flight was feasible. Those who went on that flight showed the way to those that followed after.

Any strange experiences with pontoons?

We had two pontoons on the S-40, which we flew in the Caribbean for the most part. The S-40 pontoons were fixed. They hung down off the wing after you left the water. With the later-model aircraft the pontoon would fold up and become the wing tip. That was a more efficient operation. It didn't have the drag of the earlier pontoons. On the Martin M-130, followed by the Boeing B-314, they had sponsons—that's what Boeing called them. These sponsons stuck out on either side and were like short, stubby wings. They performed somewhat like a pontoon but were attached to the hull rather than the wing. They carried quite a bit of fuel. It was a great advantage to have a place to put a good portion of fuel. On the Boeing B-314, they stuck out around eight feet.

When you landed in the Amazon, near the city of Belem, near the mouth of the river, there were piranha fish in the river. They are very vicious—as you know. Well, one time when we landed there—I was a copilot on the airplane and was told by the captain to go out onto the sponson to take a line to be handed to me by a man in a small boat. Meanwhile, number three engine had been losing a little oil. As I stepped out on it, I quickly slid off into the river. I was well aware of the fact that there were piranha all over the place. My peers said they had never seen a person fall into the water and spring out of it faster. I came straight out of that water, thinking that my legs and anything else was going to be gone. They thought it was such a neat trick to come flying out of the water, like you see a movie where someone dives into a pool and they reverse the projector so he comes back out. That was the most thrilling experience I ever had on that aircraft.

I went into China in 1946. The war was over, and we were going in as passenger planes; previously we had gone in for military reasons. Pan American had an operation going out of the United States, down the east coast to Natal, over to Liberia, across Africa and all the Middle East and into Calcutta, then over the big mountains in that area and into China, supplying Chiang Kai-shek. One time the load I was taking there, destined for China and Chiang Kai-shek, was a three-foot cube of wire netting. In that wire netting was several million dollars in small bills, less than thousand-dollar bills—hundreds, fifties. Hundreds of thousands of twenties. You could see it—it was one big bag of money, handed over to Chiang Kai-shek.

Any other unusual flights you remember?

Juan Peron, President of Argentina, knew that his days were numbered unless he did something. He made a deal with Pan American to ship gold bars from Argentina to New York. They took all of the seats out of the DC-4s to make room—this was probably 1946 or 1947. Anyway, they put two-inch by twelve-inch planks down on the floor, then they loaded bars of solid gold so that each flight carried about ten million dollars worth of gold. These bars of gold were encased in wooden boxes and laid across planks on the floor. Then the boxes were bolted to the planks, and the planks, of course, to the floor. It looked like an empty cabin from the bow to the stern.

The interesting thing to us was that we would fly out of Buenos Aires, up to Natal, and spend the night. They would just park the airplane off to one side with ten million dollars worth of gold in it. Then, we'd take off from there and fly to Trinidad and spend the night. From Trinidad we'd go to New York. When we landed in

New York, there was a great change. The airplane would be immediately surrounded by about 50 or more men with machine guns. The gold would be unloaded into trucks with police cars in front and back of them. Then, they would take the gold to some bank. I thought, that sure lets you know how things are in one country, compared to others.

In the old days you were able to pick your routes, weren't you?

With all airlines, in fact, in all transportation, seniority is the golden word. Those that are senior are the ones that can do what they please.

When I started with Pan Am—I arrived on the scene in December 1940, right out of the army—they had about 250 pilots. There were 20 of us released from the army, for no other reason than to work for Pan Am. The draft was on—they were drafting people into the army, but we were allowed out because the State Department told Pan Am they had to continue flying to Europe and anywhere else. So the State Department told the army to release some pilots so Pan Am could have replacements for those called to active duty in the military. I happened to be one of that group. They hired about 600 in the next seven or eight months. In that period, I had almost twice as many junior to me as I had senior, because they had picked up civilians along the way, and they also hired hundreds of military pilots.

Therefore, being relatively high on the seniority list, I could generally go where I wanted to—but as copilot. I was a copilot for about 17 or 18 months. By then, there were 2,000 or 3,000 pilots junior too, therefore, I could go almost anywhere I wanted for my entire career because I was very near the top of the list. Attrition had a lot to do with it. Inability to pass flight checks, or illnesses that precluded flying, also affected things. Most of the men ahead of me were 15 to 20 years older.

How did you happen to join the military?

I was going to be an engineer for Boeing. That was my intention, while I was in college, but the chief test pilot for Boeing told me at one of his lectures at the university in 1938 about pay. He said,

"Boeing will pay you $200 a month as an engineer and $400 a month for a pilot so, if you go down to Randolph Field, Texas, the Army Flying School, and graduate, I'll hire you as a test pilot at $450 a month." That was more money than I ever dreamed of, up to that time—and that would be every month. I could hardly wait. So I went in and joined the army. Then they told me I had to spend two to four years on active duty before I could go to work for Boeing. I told the chief test pilot for Boeing about it—Eddie Allen was his name—I said, "How do I beat that?"

He said, "Oh, it's easy. Do like I did—just as soon as you graduate, you resign."

So when I graduated, I told the army, "I've had enough—I'm resigning."

They just laughed and said, "Since you joined this party, Hitler, a fellow in Europe, has started doing things, and we aren't letting anybody out of the army."

I said, "What do you mean you won't let me out?"

"You can't get out."

So I called Eddie Allen and said, "What will I do?"

His response was "Gee, I don't know what to say."

Then, all of a sudden, Pan American said they needed 24 pilots and asked if anyone wanted to get out and go to work for Pan Am.

I became one of the 24. We hadn't been with Pan Am for more than a month when four of them quit because they wanted to wear Army Air Corps uniforms and have silver wings—have all the girls chasing them. Here we were in the shops wearing coveralls while learning about engine-changing and all other associated details for about two months.

Ever run into any of your military friends flying?

During 1943 and 1944 we started flying for the navy because they were having trouble getting airplanes from San Francisco to Honolulu. Finally, someone in the navy said, "Pan Am flies this route daily without any trouble—why not have them teach us their system?"

The problem was long-range cruising. They didn't know how to manipulate the engines. The navy contracted Pan Am to fly—to teach the navy—as much as they would hate to admit. But Pan Am taught the navy long-range flying.

We flew those airplanes—one Pan American pilot, and all the other members of the crew were navy. We did that for about a year, from about 1943 and part of 1944. Once the navy said it had had enough, then General Arnold, who was in charge of the air force, made a contract with Pan American to do the same thing across the Atlantic. We went to New York, temporarily, and flew the Atlantic, using army aircraft, the C-54s, which later were called the DC-4s and used for commercial flight after the war. We flew them for the army, and were landing them at army air bases in Europe, delivering materials. But, to answer your question, sometimes when we landed, we'd see bombers or fighters there, and we'd see some of our former classmates. Boy! Those guys were mad at us. We had been selected by chance, but because we were basically flying commercially, we were paid 600 - 900 per month and were not subject to military rules and regulations. As captains or majors in the military, they said, "We're getting our rear ends shot off, and you guys are living the life of Riley. You're home every once in awhile and we haven't been home for months; you're making three times as much money. . ."

Most of them were just disgusted with us. But we didn't do it ourselves—we just happened to be the lucky ones.

Do you remember the number that you retired at?

I think I was number 12 when I retired.

You could really go anywhere, then?

Yes. There were 11 who could do what they wanted to do before I could. They made me a check pilot in about 1950 or 1952—and I was one until 1970, when I went to 747s. There was a change in chief pilots at the base in San Francisco. When a new chief pilot came along, he usually wanted men he knew to be his check pilots. Anyway, the new chief pilot had his own list of men he wanted, and we were all invited to resign. That ended my check pilot days. That was no problem, because by the time I was on the 747, I was in the first twenty on the seniority list, and there was no problem going where I wanted to go.

You took your pick though, didn't you, as check pilot?

Yes, as check pilot I could line up—or be given a list of pilots and where they were going—and I would make a point of going wherever a pilot was going, where I wanted to go. That was the person I would check. I'd check a man to Honolulu; somebody else to Tokyo; and somebody else to Hong Kong, where I was having a sailboat built. I would check to Hong Kong to see the progress of my boat.

Check your sailboat?

Usually I knew before I left that the man I was coming to check wouldn't be coming back for a day or two. I'd have this time in Hong Kong to go and watch them build my boat. I did that about six or eight times, until finally it got to the chief pilot. He called me in and said, "Just what in hell are you doing there? This is not an airline to drive in your own manner—you've got a job you are supposed to do."

I said, "I'm checking men over and I'm checking others back."

He said, "I understand you have been staying one or two days in Hong Kong and that you've got a boat being built there. I want you to know that's all over with—that you won't be going there anymore. Anytime you are in Hong Kong, it's going to be at your expense, not Pan Am's."

I said, "I hope the boat's finished." [laughs]

What was the most exotic place you've ever flown?

In 1946 I flew a bunch of engineers down to Saigon, where we landed in a grass field. Those engineers started construction of an airport—in conjunction with the French. The airport became very important during the Vietnam War.

When I took them down there to build the airport, we were more or less on our own coming back. I went over Angkor Wat. It was still in its ruined state. I wanted to see what it looked like. We went down in an empty airplane—no passengers or anything—just the crew. We circled at about 30 feet and took pictures of it. That was very impressive to me. The trees were growing out of it. It had not yet been cleaned. I believe someone was starting to work on cleaning it. The war stopped that.

I'd heard about the temple, but I'd never seen any pictures. We were very low, and we were very close to it—within a few yards. Then we'd go about a hundred yards away. By staying out a half a mile or so, we could circle it. I had previously done this same thing at Christophe's Palace in Haiti. Haiti was once ruled by Emperor Christophe. He built his palace on top of a hill—an impregnable fortress, he figured. According to legend, at least, once the thing was built, he didn't want anyone to know where the secret passages were. So he marched his army of workers right off the palisade, and they all fell to their deaths—they didn't dare disobey. That was the story I had heard. True or not, I wanted to see what it looked like. Sometime in 1942 we were flying from Port-au-Prince to the Dominican Republic, but this time we went off to the left somewhat and circled the palace—you couldn't get there on the ground because it was jungle all around, and it was on the top of a cliff.

We took pictures of it, very crude, but nevertheless moving pictures. I think I took forty feet of 16-mm footage, and they paid me over four hundred dollars for it. I thought that was fabulous. Anyway, I was over Angkor Wat for the same reason, but I couldn't sell that footage. I went to the same source and they said, "We don't do that stuff anymore."

Air routes had to be surveyed, didn't they?

There was a Captain Musick, who was doing what we called a proving flight to Manila. He was considered to be the pilot at the time. He was in a Sikorsky S-42, and he was making survey flights. He had made the survey trip out through Honolulu to Midway, and Midway to Wake—whichever comes first—and then over to Guam, from Guam to Manila, from Manila to Hong Kong.

He was lost. The S-42 had gas tanks in the cabin, because they were making long-range flights—no passengers on board. Something caused the plane to blow up. It blew as he was approaching Samoa—United States Samoa. I think they had an engine failure, and they were going to dump some of their excess fuel. In those days, to dump fuel, you pulled a lever and a chute would come down out of the wing, and the fuel in the tank would come out the chute, making a long cloud of gas as it expanded in the air. It looked just like a cloud. No smoking or anything else. What they surmised is that when he started to dump that fuel, somehow it caught fire and ran back into the gas tank and exploded.

You did a lot of picture taking, it sounds like?

I carried a 16-mm Cine Kodak Special. It had a 1,000 foot reel on it. It could run indefinitely. I kept that thing right in front of me on the glare shield, which is directly in front of the pilot on most aircraft. Anyway, I'd leave the thing there, and I'd just press the button. It would take a movie of the airport I was landing on—or of whatever I was seeing ahead of me.

I went across Marajo Island, which is in the middle of the Amazon River. It is about 100 miles across—a big island. The Amazon splits and comes out into the ocean at different places, so it had created the big island. There are all kinds of animals there. So we were running along 15 or 20 feet above the ground in a small aircraft, and I got a lot of pictures of various birds that would be scared up—or good-sized animals—some the size of small dogs.

I photographed most of my travels around the world—China, Europe, Africa, Alaska, and South America. I had done it before in Alaska, and the passengers always enjoyed it. Climbing up, I told the passengers, "We'll soon come to a lake, and I'll bank to one side and then the other and you can take pictures of the lake." As we came up, a huge bear stood up on its hind legs and pawed the air—almost in front of us.

Any other animals you saw close-up?

There was a moose swimming across the lake, and I went off over to one side, so the passengers could see it. I banked so they took pictures. But that turned the moose around. I turned the airplane so that the other side could take pictures of the same moose, which was now going back to where it started from. As I started to go back, the moose started to turn around again. So I pulled up and climbed out. Of course, the passengers on the left side didn't get to take pictures and were upset about it and said so. The stewardess came up and said, "Why didn't we give them a chance?" I said, "I

257

was afraid the moose would drown. He was halfway across the lake and our presence made him turn back. Then he was starting to turn around again because he thought he was in trouble."

What was the strangest thing about flying the Alaska route?

We would take off from Seattle and go into the clouds and we would not see anything until we landed at the next base. There we'd take off again and not see anything until the next base. All instrument flying, and you very seldom saw anything. So, when it was a nice day, it was just beautiful. That's when I would go down to lower altitudes and near mountains.

On one trip I was somewhere between Juneau, Alaska, and White Horse, Canada, going through White Pass. The vice president of the airline came up to the cockpit—this was illegal at that time. He introduced himself and said, "My wife would like to have a picture of a mountain that we will be going by. Could you get a little bit closer to it?" I said, "How close do you want to get?" He said, "Close enough so she can see it." So I took her by—about 500 feet from it. When he got back to New York, he reported to Juan Trippe, the president of the airline, what happened. But he didn't say that he asked me to do it. Juan Trippe notified my chief pilot, and he notified me that I was in trouble because I had gone so close to the mountain with passengers. I wrote a letter to Juan Trippe—I doubt if he ever read it—and explained to him that if you are working for Pan American Airways and a vice president tells you he would like to go near a mountain—that you are hard-put not to do it.

There was a homey quality to the old flying boat days.

Yes, in those days it really was nice in that respect. All the food was initially box lunches. Then it went to china and silverware. Juan Trippe, who was the chairman of the board of Pan American—and the driving force in its first 20 years or more—was always anxious to treat the passengers just like they were royalty. If he were around today, we'd still be number one. Once, an airplane took off a little more than five minutes ahead of schedule, but that was his limit—on other words, don't depart more than five minutes ahead no matter what. If we left early, someone might come along who wanted to get on, and we'd be gone without him.

On one occasion the airplane departed five minutes ahead of time. I was called along with other members of the crew to get right out to the seaplane base because we had a Sikorsky S-42 there ready to go and we had another passenger. I asked, "Why are we doing this for a single passenger?" They said, "It's orders from Juan Trippe." We went out there and everything was done as it usually was—homey as you said—and this man couldn't believe it. He'd arrived about four minutes before departure, and so he was within reason—in those days. Nowadays, some airlines close the gates at five minutes before departure, and if you aren't there, it's too bad. There is a law saying they can do it.

I'd only been with the airline a few months at that time, and I was copilot on the flight. I asked the captain, "My God, do you always take one passenger—you can't make much money at that rate." He said, "We take one if Juan Trippe says we take one." So we flew this man all the way down to Puerto Rico, just by himself.

259

What about the last time you flew a Clipper flight?

I didn't want to quit. You have to quit at age 60. That's it and there's no way in God's world to extend it. Any commercial pilot flying in the United States for an airline has to get off before midnight on the day before his birthday. The company usually would allow pilots—any pilot regardless of seniority—to take their pick for their last flight. This was early in the business when they could do that. Now, of course, that's out the window. Now it goes by seniority—it's just tough if you are retiring and not at the top of the seniority list.

On my last flight I had seniority, being number 12. I was going from Tokyo to Honolulu, where I was going to meet my wife and three of my four daughters to fly back with me on my last flight. When I got there, the man in charge of traffic told me he was very sorry, but the airplane would be full and so he couldn't take any of my family, because they would be riding as passengers for free. Free ride for the family, that's what they gave to a pilot on his last flight—but they couldn't go. I said, if they couldn't go, then I didn't know if I could go either. He said, "Of course, you are jesting." I said, "No,

I might have a problem here—if you can't provide my family this last flight. I might not be able to make it. I might get sick."

When the flight was ready to go, I came out of the airport, and looked at the passenger list. I noticed there were eight or ten company employees on that flight. That left my family to come back by themselves and not with me on my last flight. I notified the airline that I couldn't make the flight, that they would have to get someone else. They always have lots of extra crews in Honolulu, but I knew on this occasion they would have to delay the flight seven or eight hours, because when you land anywhere you have to have a minimum rest period before you are allowed to go out on another flight—that's a federal law. In this instance, I knew there was no one available for at least four or five hours or more. They said, "You've got to take it."

I said, "I'm not going to—not unless my family is there. You take off some of those company employees who are on there."

They said, "We couldn't do that because they are ahead of you."

I said, "No, they're not—they're going to be off that airplane, or I'm not going."

They said, "Well, you'll be fired."

I said, "Well, this is my last flight—there is nothing you can do about it."

So I told my daughters and my wife that there were two seats up in the cockpit. It's illegal to have four people in there because two of them couldn't have a seat for landing and takeoff. But I said, "What the heck? It's my last flight. So what if they give me trouble? I'll have you all in the cockpit." I got up there myself before departure and sitting in one of the two seats was a stranger.

Every few months the FAA has inspectors on the airplanes. They are there to see how things are going—check all crew members just like the check pilot does. I said, not realizing who it was, "I'm awfully sorry but you're going to have to sit down below."

He said, "No, no, I'm inspector so and so and I'm going to be up here for this flight."

The copilot said, "Do you know this is the captain's last flight, and he has his wife and daughters on board?"

The guy looks at me and says, "Well, why didn't you say so? I'll see you in San Francisco." He went down below, which I thought was very nice of him. Now that he was out of the way, I'd have all four of them in the cockpit for takeoff. We were soon en route and eventually, when we landed in San Francisco, they were all in the cockpit again.

I told my wife, "I will make the best landing I ever had or I will never hear the last of it from you." So I did—I made an absolutely perfect landing—one of the few—and the passengers all clapped because the stewardess told them it was the captain's last flight. We had a total of about 400 or more passengers clapping. It was quite an event.

261

DONALD RODEWALD
Freedom Flier

After graduating from high school in Baraboo, Wisconsin, Donald Rodewald attended the University of Wisconsin for one year and then joined the United States Army GHQ [General Headquarters] Air Corps, Selfridge Field, Michigan. He went to armament school and later to China as armorer for the American Volunteer Group, the famous Flying Tigers, commanded by Claire L. Chennault. When his contract expired on July 4, 1942, he received a field commission as first lieutenant Army Air Corps. After five months as an armament officer with the Seventy-fifth Fighter Squadron, China Task Force, he returned to the United States and Air Corps pilot training, graduating in 1943. He did test work and returned to China in February 1945 as a fighter pilot. After the war he remained in Shanghai, serving as operations officer of Kaigwan Field, and received his regular commission, United States Air Force.

Following several stints, Rodewald was transferred to headquarters in Washington D.C., in 1951 as research and development officer. Then he served in Korea and flew combat missions with the Fifty-first Fighter Wing, as well as the Fourth Fighter Wing.

On January 11, 1954, an already distinguished flight came to what seemed a certain end, when he crashed on instrument approach to Andrews Air Force Base: an accident the left him paralyzed from the waist down. He spent months on physical rehab—a period he describes in the interview. He took a job at Lockheed Aircraft, one he would hold for 20 years. Still, because of the accident and his diminished physical capacities, flight seemed almost impossible.

Over the years, the idea of flying burned in his mind. In 1969, he obtained the first production Blackwood hand control and received his pilot's license waiver. Then came Don's record-setting flight. In 1984, he flew solo around the world in his Comanche 260. With that, he became the first paraplegic to fly solo around the world—a trip of 31,350 nautical miles. On the way he made 34 stops in 24 countries.

When we interviewed, Don was beset with health problems, but his spirit still was strong. For his courage and accomplishment, he stands as an inspiration to fliers and non-fliers alike.

You flew around the world in a Comanche in 1984. How'd you get the idea for that?

Well, another wheelchair pilot and myself were talking about going to Europe, flying the Atlantic in formation. But that sort of fell through because of medical problems he had. So I decided to go it on my own. I had friends in Italy I hadn't seen in years. Then, it so happened I met a lady from Australia and stumbled onto the fact that we both had a birthday on the same day. And I said, "Jean, some day I'm gonna take you to dinner on our birthday." So I thought it would be damn nice to go down to Australia—I'd never been there—and take Jean to dinner on her birthday. I learned that there would be a Flying Tiger reunion in Tai Pai. Why not be there when my friends arrive?

How did you become a paraplegic?

In 1954 I was coming home from Wright Field, and the weather was pretty bad. I called ground control approach—I was flying a jet and a B-25 was in the pattern. They asked the B-25 to pull out of the pattern and allow me to let the jet down. In those days they were pretty sensitive to fuel, so they gave the jet a priority. When I broke out of the overcast at 800 feet, they said, "Well, we got another one on the ground. Okay?" Between there and the end of the runway, the engine quit, and I fell short of the runway. I don't remember that part of it. I woke up in Walter Reed hospital some days later. I wasn't very coherent for about three or four weeks.

That was a blow.

I was a really active individual, and it was a hell of a shock. Although sometimes I was on cloud nine. I had people call me up and I'd say, "Oh, I'll be back flyin' in about a month or so." I really didn't realize the seriousness of my injury.

I got to keep my legs, but was paralyzed from the waist down. It was a broken back—a spinal cord injury. They had to weld about three of the vertebrae together.

What was the hardest thing about it?

I think most of it was the negative stage. That was the toughest thing to come through. When they took me from Walter Reed, I told my wife, "Why in the hell didn't the airplane finish me off?" I had a pretty negative attitude at that time. But then you get to the VA Hospital and look around you. You find out there are a hell of a lot of people worse off than you are. You straighten yourself out pretty fast.

What kept you going?

Well, Irving, I'll be honest with you. I don't have a hell of a lot of money, but I am one wealthy son of a bitch when it comes to friends. I have a lot of friends. Those kinds of people don't expect you to quit—so you can't quit.

Let's talk about flying around the world—which was an amazing accomplishment, and a lot of logistics.

A hell of a lot. You could never do enough. The first thing I did was go to Don Taylor. He had flown around the world a couple of years before. One of the first things he told me was to write the government printing office and get a *World Flight Planning Manual,* which cost $30 at that point. It has every country in the world, including Russia, and what their ports of entry are, where they've got fuel and where they don't, who you should write, etc. Thanks to help from my daughter and son-in-law, I did all that. In 19 days, I got an answer from Tai Pai; in 22 days I got one from New Zealand. From then on it went longer and longer. Some didn't answer. The Philippines, for example, never answered. Indonesia answered with something so asinine it was comical. They asked me questions I had already answered. It was like doing it all over again. Incidentally, you can't go into Indonesia without a previous contract for fuel.

What did you do?

I ended up going back to a professional organization—Lockheed Jet Plan—which makes arrangements for executives—for a price. They deal with these people all the time, so they've got ways of breaking down bureaucratic barriers. I used them for making arrangements for entry, places to stay and fuel—things I hadn't been able to crack. I did my own flight planning, however.

Time must have been running out on you?

Yes, because hell, I had to take Jean out for dinner on our birthday—and the reunion in Tai Pai. Plus the fact that June is the best time to fly across the North Atlantic. As it was, I didn't get started till August. If I had waited much longer, it would have been too late.

Close calls on the flight?

Between Majuro in the Marshall Islands and Honolulu, I came closer than I wanted to come. I reached over and patted the dinghy, and I said, "I hope I don't have to use you." My Loran navigation system went out 200 - 300 miles north of Johnson Island. I wasn't about to go back and try to find it, because Johnson Island is about as big as a carrier. I ran into headwinds. I only had about 50 minutes of fuel left when I landed in Hawaii.

How many days were you gone?

I was out of the country three and one-half months. But I wasn't trying to set any records—I was just visiting friends and going places I hadn't been before. I'd never been to Europe or Australia—even though I'd been around the world three times in the armed services.

What about finding fuel?

I got a call from Lockheed Jet Plan. They said, "We've determined there's no fuel in Karachi. What are your intentions?"

I said, "Well, I'll have to get my charts out. I'll call you back."

Well, they said, "We'd like to suggest you stop in Dubai and from there go to Ahamadabad in India. It has fuel."

So I got the charts out and called them back. I said, "That looks good to me." I went from Riyadh to Dubai. I'd had a call from a fellow in Dubai.

He said, "I understand you're coming through our country."

I said, "That's right."

He said, "If there's anything I can do for you. . ."

I said, "Just some fuel and a place to lay my head."

He said, "That's already been taken care of."

So I landed in Dubai, and they took care of me—first class. In fact, it didn't cost a damn cent—even filling up my tanks with fuel. I stayed in one of the most exotic Hyatt Regency Hotels. I took off from there and, when I crossed Karachi, they forced me to land.

Somebody scramble up beside you?

No, they just said to land. If it had been interceptors, I wouldn't have worried because I was on top of an undercast at 11,000 feet. I would have dropped down in the clouds and gone on. But guided missiles couldn't care less about the weather, so I chickened out and landed.

What happened?

They cleaned me out of more than $800 and didn't give me any service.

Did you have the money hidden?

Well, they took me to their bank twice to cash traveler's checks [laughs].

What problems did you face because of your physical situation?

Sometimes you had a lot of help; sometimes you didn't. I landed at Dhaka in Bangladesh about ten at night. It was dark and, within a few seconds, I had about a dozen people standing around outside the airplane. I tried to communicate with them, but they just stood there and looked at me. I got the wheelchair out, a couple of tote bags, and navigation charts to review the next leg of the trip before I went to bed. They never did lift a hand. I said, "Where's the terminal?" They just pointed, and so I started wheeling toward the terminal. They followed me.

There were times when it was a problem, but in those days, I got around pretty well. I wore leg braces and could handle crutches. At my advanced age, I'm beyond that capability now.

268

It affects you after awhile.

Yes, they told me that using crutches, braces, and wheelchair for 30 years wore out my shoulders.

So you're in a lot of pain much of the time?

Once in awhile, yeah. It's better to forget about it.

You were also a Flying Tiger?

Yes, I was a ground man in the Flying Tigers' organization.

How primitive was the equipment you used?

First of all, the tool situation was atrocious. As enlisted men in the service prior to the war, a guy was pretty proud of his tool kit. The government didn't issue very good tools. Even when you're making 21 dollars a month starting out, you usually found enough left over on pay to go in and buy a wrench at Sears. Eventually, you had a toolbox you were proud of. So, when "Skip" Adair recruited us and signed us up at Selfridge Field, I asked him where we should deliver our toolboxes. He said, "Oh, you don't need any tools—we'll have all the tools over there for you." I was an armament man. We worked on guns and bombs. In fact, we worked on bombs from seven different nations.

Was there one kind that really stumped you?

Well, we sort of jokingly said we knew why the Italians lost the war. It took them so long to fuse their bombs [laughs]. You had to disassemble the fuse to put in the detonator and then you had to reassemble the fuse again, whereas with American bombs, that was probably a ten-second job.

Any things that especially bothered you?

We had one squadron that had 7.62 guns in the wings, and the other two squadrons had .30-caliber. You can imagine the problem we had with logistics. Shifting aircraft from place to place, we would end up with both calibers—so two types of ammo. You've got to realize that these 100 airplanes we had were originally destined for Great Britain, so when we got them, they didn't have our type of equipment. We would put in the guns, the gun sights and synchronize the guns. The radio people put in the radios, and they were just about as bad off as we were for equipment and tools, let alone test equipment.

I never did get used to defusing a bomb that was a dud—that the enemy dropped. That was always a very uncomfortable situation. As far as incidents, I've jumped into a hell of a lot of foxholes to save my butt from Japanese strafing and bombing.

How good were the Flying Tigers?

Most of them were damn good. Those that weren't didn't last. They went home or quit us—like Pappy Boyington, for instance. I'm not saying for a minute he wasn't good. He was just trouble, that's all. So eventually he left us.

269

Any Pappy Boyington stories?

[Laughs] Well, I've put him to bed more times than I'd like to admit. I would be one of three or four guys that would pick him up and carry him out of the bar. You wouldn't touch the son of a bitch unless he was absolutely stoned, because if he could move a muscle, he'd kill you.

Remember guys coming back after the Battle of Rangoon?

The battle of Rangoon was a highlight. Sometimes we only had seven to fourteen planes operational at any one time. Forty or 50 Japanese would come over and the guys would take off and shoot down as many as they could until the ammo ran out.

All we had time to do was for the crew chiefs to refuel the tanks, and we'd fill the .50 caliber guns and send them out again on a scramble.

I remember one time a bomb fell off a Lysander, a high-wing plane. The bomb tumbled toward us guys. We, of course, jumped into a ditch in a hurry. Then we had to defuse it.

What about rivalry between services?

Hell, yes. For example, I was in First Squad. Our chief was Bob Neal out of the navy. Eugene McKinny and I were from the Air Corps and both of us had P-40 experience. So here we were with a crew chief over us from the navy, who actually had no experience in the P-40.

What sort of differences were there?

The trigger motor, which was a critical item in the synchronization—to make sure you didn't shoot the prop—was totally different on the navy-type aircraft. So we had to teach "navy types" how to synchronize the P-40. There were other things. I personally went to the "Old Man" to get McKinny as chief armorer instead of Bob Neal.

You went to General Chennault?

Yes, I went to Chennault myself. One of the pilots got me in to the Old Man. The Old Man sort of put me at rest and said if it didn't work, he'd think about changing it. But he thought Neal was a pretty good man and said we ought to leave him there and give him a chance. As it turned out, Bob Neal was one hell of a good armorer. He turned out to be one of my best friends. There was that inner-service rivalry all over the place, though. Bob and I would laugh about it. We got along fine.

So you changed locations? How long were you in China?

I was one of 21 ground men who went back in the service in China, and the promise was that in six months the Old Man would get us home. So, after about five months, Chennault came by Kweilin, and I said, "Good morning, General, how are you doing today?"
He said, "Fine, how are you Rody?"
I said, "By the way, you told us in six months we would get to go home. Is that still going to be okay?"
He said, "Are you ready?"
And I said, "Yeah."
He said, "I'll send down orders on the next airplane."
I said, "How'll I be going back?"
He said, "You'll fly across the Hump, probably take a train to Bombay, then take a ship."
I said, "Ship? General, if it's a ship, don't bother—I'll stay here." [Laughs] I'd heard a lot about German subs and torpedoes, and I had no desire to get on a ship. So when the orders came through—it was Class Three, by air. He was a fine gentleman.

271

What else did you do over there?

One of my jobs was to go and find arms. I rode trains, looking for bombs and ammunition. Most of the time I found them in Chinese temples, one of the favorite storage spots. Many times I'd ride back to Kunming with my bedroll and whatever I had with me on the top of a box of fuses as my bed.

Meet any characters doing that?

Well, mainly the Chinese were quite cooperative because the word was out the Old Man needed it. I remember this one particular time. I left Rangoon; I think with the first convoy to go up the Burma Road. At that time we were going to set up a group armament shop at Kunming. I was looking for ammunition when I came across this stockpile. I met the Chinese colonel who was commander of the compound.

I told him I'd be back tomorrow with trucks to pick up the ammunition. That was his ammunition. The next morning when I went out to get it with several trucks, there wasn't a damn bit of ammo in the building. I took that information to the Old Man, and eventually the colonel was shot. This was because he had lost face.

That must have been hard to take.

I sure didn't have any intention of having the colonel shot. One of those things in a society that I hadn't learned. If I had known more about it, I wouldn't have approached it in the same way, and it would have saved his life.

Did you run into many missionaries over there?

There was a missionary doctor who took care of me soon after I ended up in the service. I got amoebic dysentery, and one day I found I wasn't strong enough to get up on the wing and load ammunition. So they flew me to Kunming to the hospital. I weighed 96 pounds at that point. My going weight at that time was 160 pounds.

We didn't have any sulfa drugs at that point, so Dr. Monjae, who was head of the hospital, started prescribing enemas. Regardless of how beautiful that Chinese nurse was, I hated to see her come toward me. I had about three enemas a day. Of course, each time they put it under a microscope and looked for bugs. "That's not diarrhea, it's dysentery. The amoeba's got to be killed." So after about two and one-half weeks, this Dr. Monjae walks in, looks at me, and says, "No more bugs." I was cured, and he started stuffing me with rice.

I went home and became a fighter pilot and came back on a second tour. I got as far as Karachi. The first night in Karachi I went to an American officer's club with three or four other guys and had some food. Lo and behold, the next day I had amoebic dysentery. I thought, "Rodewald, you stupid son of a bitch, you volunteered for this." But we had sulfa drugs there, and I was flying three days later.

It doesn't end there. On my round-the-world flight, when I got to Australia, I ended up with—you guessed it—amoebic dysentery, which the doctor figured I got in Singapore. My daughter, who was my main contact in the United States, sent me a telex in Adelaide, Australia, which said, "Should we tell Grandma about this?" I said, "We'll send it on telex, but be sure and send it exactly as I write it. "Judy, tell Gramm my nemesis of the Far East was patiently waiting for me." [Laughs]

Tell me about going back into the service. What was it like?

Unfortunately, when I went back over there, there were no Jap airplanes left. We bombed and strafed—the daily routine.

I didn't come away from World War II really convinced that I was a fighter pilot, because I hadn't met anyone in the air—head to head—so I had to go over to Korea and find out whether I was a fighter pilot or not.

So you met some people in the air in Korea?

Yeah, I got a taste of it both ways. I managed to damage a MiG-15 the second time I was over there. I saw both sides of it very well.

So you got knocked down?

No, but I got kind of hosed pretty well—the controls of the airplane and the engine were shot up. But I managed to get it down without cracking it up. However, the plane was a dead loss. We pushed it off in the bushes.

What happened?

Four of us took a late mission up in MIG Alley. Soon after takeoff, number four had engine trouble, so number-two man and number-four went back home. You never let a flier go back by himself. So then, there were two of us in MIG Alley. You really should always have a full four-ship flight. "Bandits," I called out, "9 o'clock high." My leader made a 180-degree, they jumped us, and I got shot up pretty bad.

What was the most inspiring scene you observed during your around-the-world trip?

[Laughs] Probably seeing Hawaii come over the horizon. Maybe the Alps. There was cloudiness. I'd like to go back and see more of them.

What does flight mean to you?

274

Freedom. Ability to go places and do things I want to do.

And that's what you did.

Plus the fact that I had to be the first paraplegic to go around the world. After I did, I got a note from a friend that read, "Jesus, Rody, if you're going around the world, why didn't you let me go with you?" I said, "Dear Art, if I hadn't chosen to go around the world by myself, I would have picked a pretty girl." Then I softened the blow and said, "If I'd wanted a man with me, I'd have picked a good pilot, like you."

First Lieutenant Jerry Hammond in February 1945.

JERRY HAMMOND
A Close Call at The Tower of London

Jerry Hammond joined the U. S. Army Air Corps in October 1942, and served as a bombardier, navigator, and aerial gunner. He left the military, June 9, 1945. During a stint as a navigator, his infamous calculations led his plane on return, up the Thames River, towards London, in an episode that would frighten even this wildly original and irascible soul—an episode he describes in the interview.

After his years in the military, Jerry E. Hammond earned his MD degree from the University of Iowa. A practicing psychiatrist for 37 years, he is now retired. He proudly proclaims, "I no longer drink and haven't smoked a cigarette for 30 years." What does he do to pass time? "I love to watch again the movies of my child and young adulthood, where everyone smoked like a chimney pot." At present, Hammond is a dilettante essayist and maker of paper-collage pictures. He also watches C-SPAN a lot. "It's the same as watching crook movies but without the violence." So much for the acerbic side of the old navigator/aspiring writer.

Hammond is the father of two children, Paul and Terrell. His wife, Lyn Smith Hammond, works as a Genetic Counselor, at the Medical University of South Carolina. "She's totally okay," Jerry explains.

Any strange things happen in training?

Lots. The Army Air Corps took us country kids and off-the-street city kids and sent us to Jefferson Barracks, Missouri in the middle of winter. It was cold, freezing and wet—either mud up to our ankles or frozen ground. Jefferson Barracks was an old, comfortable, permanent base but the raw recruits were sent to a new area with jerry-built hutment's of green jack pine with half-inch cracks in the walls. We kids froze our asses off at night and ran our asses off in the daytime—most of us sick with the flu and the vaccination shots. I got shin splints from eight hours a day marching on the frozen parade ground. I used to bite my tongue 'til it bled to cover up the pain in my legs. Some kids got so discouraged they committed suicide: hung themselves from trees in the woods. The rest of us fell off in weight and lost all our baby fat. Post-basic training we were sent to a college in Springfield, Missouri, where we learned physics and trigonometry and the history of the Third Reich, Il Duce, and General Tojo and how girls behaved around soldiers, the likes of which they'd never seen before.

278

Next stop was Ellington Field near Houston, Texas. We'd become aviation cadets and were sent out in a hurricane to hold down all the aircraft. You believe that? Seems these airplanes were diverted from San Antonio where it was believed the hurricane would go. Instead, it made landfall at Galveston and straight up the bay to Ellington Field, a more severe storm even than Hugo in 1989. As one stood out in that weather, it was easy to become contemplative, "Just what the hell am I doing out here?" The wind was a constant 150-160 miles per hour with rain warm as urine and coming down horizontally. The wind and rain slowly picked up the seams of our rubber rain gear and eventually took it off us and blew it away. Since the wind blew a steady velocity, it didn't affect the aircraft at all. They just sat still through the entire blow. Gusty and it would have turned them over and about, cadets or no cadets holding them down.

Four hours later our duty was done. We were left to make our way back to the built-up area. There it was very gusty and people were injured or killed by flying corrugated iron roofing and airborne lumber.

Where did you go from there?

Laredo, Texas, to aerial gunnery school, via troop train, one side of Texas to another on the "Katy" which was the Missouri, Kansas and Texas railroad, at a speed at times 110 miles per hour. The weather was dry and hot as Iraq and nothing to do but play cards and dice. I was on a lucky streak, hot as a pepper and drunk as a fool on warm whiskey out of a paper cup. We shot dice on our knees; I did nine straight passes! When I went to get up, my right knee wouldn't straighten, so they took me to the hospital in Laredo and took out the cartilage.

If it hadn't been for that major surgery, I would have arrived in the European Theater of Operations (ETO) months sooner. The German Air Force would still have been operational. As it was, our aircraft arrived early July 1944, and we flew our first mission in September. The same day, I believe, the Battle of Arnhem (Holland) began—a huge expeditionary fiasco as you may or may not have read about.

It failed, it was said, because of the passive resistant behavior of General Viscount Montgomery. It also was said the war continued in Europe for six unnecessary months because of the failure at Arnhem. Whatever the case, we flew often, especially during the Battle of the Bulge, and we finished our tour of duty in February 1945.

The next week, we started home on an Army Transportation Service (ATS) troopship, the *Edmund B. Alexander*, 18,500 tons. We were attached to a convoy in the North Atlantic. At that time, the ATS claimed it manned and sailed more ships than the U.S. Navy. We had a fabulous trip home, with very heavy seas. I used to stand on the fantail and watch. At the crest of the waves, the screws of the ship came out of the water at the bottom of the waves, the sea washed over the deck. Fabulous food also. We had filet mignon for lunch served with banquet napery.

Late in the war, the convoy was harried by U-boats. I still remember the crunch and the mumbles of depth charges. In spite of wartime politics, I feared for the German submarines. We sailed into New York harbor, past the Statue of Liberty, and I, one of many, shed a heartfelt tear. Then we went up the Hudson to Camp Kilmer, New Jersey, where the company streets were swept by Kraut prisoners of war, blond and arrogant.

You were trained in navigation, weren't you?

I went to Bombardier school first, then to navigation. This was another delay in my arrival in the ETO. This was very important. After the German Air Force was killed forever in April 1944, the Eighth Air Force losses of strategic bombers fell to about five percent per mission. Those kind of odds you could work around, and most men finished their tour of duty. Before that few air crews completed their missions; either killed, wounded or captured and held in Kriege (POW) camps. The German M-109s and FW-190s were devastating aircraft enemies. Especially so until the United States P-51 Mustangs were fitted with auxiliary wing tanks to accompany our bombers much deeper in Germany.

Was the navigation equipment primitive in those days?

Not at all. We were taught celestial and dead reckoning navigation in school but we used them in a minimal way or not at all. At our arrival, the British installed their system of radar navigation, called "G". It was the precursor of the Loran system which is still in place at the present [1990] as chief navigational aid for ships at sea and overseas aircraft. I'm sure they were ahead of the Krauts as well.

How long did it take you to learn that?

The whole "G" system? Just a few hours. The genius that invented it also made it easy to operate.

Do you recall any briefings that scared the daylights out of you?

Always any target in the Ruhr Valley, the Cologne-Dusseldorf area. Much heavy industry there was vital to the German war effort as well as thousands of flak installations and whatever fighter planes they could muster. Other dangerous targets were the synthetic oil and grease factories. Moorseberg in Bavaria was one that comes to mind. I saw some of their synthetic products, bright blue in color. The Krauts couldn't rely on natural petro-products. Stop and think about this a minute. With all the oil industries in place on the planet, no one ever talks nowadays about synthetic alternatives. And they won't until the oil runs dry and the petro-industry can't make any more money.

So you bombed some of these places.

Like I said, Merseberg was one. Our group got shot to pieces; lost far more than the usual five percent.

Tell me about it.

But not much to say about our own B-17. We got off scot-free. The terror came from others exploding and falling about us. Terror is why people say "war is hell, for soldiers anyway." My worst mission was to Holland late in the tour. Can't recall the primary target, but we couldn't strike it, clouded over or some such thing. We searched for the secondary, finally dumped our bombs on the tertiary. All the while we had to fly lower and lower and the flak was more accurate and tore us up in pieces.

Did you get shot down then?

That's right, but the mission was a bummer from the get-go. We'd barely made landfall when the top turret gunner was discovered dead at his post. We never knew why. Heart attack? Maybe the bends? Susceptible people sometimes got bends at our operational altitude.

Right on the plane?

Yes. And we tried to revive him. All through the mission we took turns with artificial respiration, with him on the catwalk between the flight deck and the plastic nose. Later on, we began taking hits and losing engines. An 88 flak-shell burst very close to the plastic nose bubble and blew out half of it. Lucky for me I was back on the catwalk trying to revive the turret gunner. The shell frags missed me, and the oxygen mask and earphones protected my lungs and ears. Unprotected and a shell blast can blow out the air sacs of your lungs. They collapse and you smother. This happened to Confederate soldiers holed up in the rocks in the Devil's Den at Gettysburg. No obvious wounds. Just dead. No one knew why until World Wars I and II.

By now things were pretty hairy. Only two engines left, one of the dead engines windmilled its prop, which dragged us down all the faster. Totally lost, we didn't know if we were over occupied or liberated territory. Visibility was minus zero and only 2,000 feet altitude. The wind from the hole in the Plexiglas nose was hurricane strength and very distracting. I called up the pilot, "We better call Ninth Air Force Controller Tac." Ninth Tac was a radar ground-to-air guidance system, another fantastic British invention. Fact is, it was run by Arthur C. Clarke, Royal Air Force officer and science fiction writer who was in charge of the system for a while. Our pilot broke air silence, "Ninth Controller, this is Cocksure. We need a heading."

Ninth Tac says, "Give us a long count, Cocksure." A long count was one to ten and then backward. "We read you, Cocksure. Take this heading: one, one, zero. Begin to lose altitude slowly. Instructions will follow every ten seconds."

I was still working on the dead turret gunner. Can't remember his name. Poor guy. He was on loan from another crew; our guy was sick. The reason we stayed with this man so long was that, we were afraid of the Oxygen Death Review Board. If they decided a death was due to oxygen neglect they gave the whole crew another mission.

The next few minutes I'll never forget if I live to 110. A glance ahead through the big hole in the plastic nose and there was this beautiful runway ahead of us and our wheels are down ready to land. Then I saw the unbelievable. A very large D-9 Caterpillar tractor-bulldozer was chugging across the runway directly in front of us! Its driver was oblivious.

"Bulldozer at twelve o'clock!" I yelled and made for the rear. Somehow, some incredible somehow, the pilots lifted us up over the Belgian and his unbelievable tractor and set the airplane down on the tarmac before we skidded off the runway into the mud up to the axles. All of us fled that aircraft like ants when you step on their nest.

We hung around this former Luftwaffe base long enough to debrief and we all took off for a nearby town. That actually was the most interesting part of the story. One of us, Sam, the waist gunner, was an Apache reared in Arizona. When he drank booze he did deer dances and war dances and ki-yi-yied and we all had a very good time with him. The Belgians also thought he was nifty.

Another thing he could do was crack black walnuts and pull Coca-Cola caps with his teeth. He grew up near a high fluoride water source on the reservation. Sam died last year. He'd been a cattleman and a banker and a high level federal bureaucrat, all in the white man's world.

Then you took off from there?

Not then. Some other interesting things happened. Next night, I met some infantry GIs in town on 12 or 20 hour passes.

"Sell us your clothes," they said. "We ain't got shit. Ain't seen a supply sergeant since Saint Lou." Turned it was out over two months before. One of them said, "Thirty dollars for your sheepskin boots."

"What would I get home with?" I asked and he held up his old beat up GI shoes.

A sergeant said, "Fifty bucks, lieutenant, for your pretty air force parka with the fur fringe hood." I said, "It's a deal." That was big money then.

On the way home to the base I had no coat, was quite drunk, half frozen and totally unsure where I was. Out of the dark came voices. You have no idea how unsettling this was. I spoke no Flemish, and very little French. Like a nut, I yelled back in German, can you believe that? "Wo ist das Fliegenfeld?"

In no time, I heard boots behind me on the cobblestone road. Actually, I was in serious danger. The Belgian Marquis was on the lookout for German hideouts who'd been cut off from their outfits.

Very fortunately, I stumbled onto the base. The MP at the gate turned out to speak French and calmed down the Belgians who thought I was a Kraut. This was a very damn good thing because the next day I was back in town and the folks were having a parade. Quite a turnout. The burgomaster in a shadbelly coat, a couple of nuns, the priest, the rest in whatever clothes they owned this late in the war. A little brass band with trombone and trumpet and bass drum led the way. At the rear were two Belgians holding up some guy between them. It turned out he was an out-of-uniform Kraut whom the Marquis had caught. Listen to this—they'd cut off his penis and sewn it up in his mouth!

Who did that?

The people. There was much rage that morning in that little town in back of their calm faces and the noise of their tiny brass band.

Then there was more music, probably the Belgian National Anthem and they hung the Kraut from a jury-rigged scaffold in the town square. I remember his feet were only six inches off the ground. The Krauts were very good teachers when it came to hatred. After that, I couldn't wait to get back to home base.

Then you returned to England?

That's right. There was another ragtag bunch of orphans just like our crew, who needed a way home like us, so we all piled on another B-17 and took off for the Midlands of England. "You're the navigator?" says the pilot, whom I'd never seen before. "Guess so," I said. "There's nobody else." That would have been all right except the weather immediately went to hell and the clouds socked in right down to the tops of the bushes and trees. The "G" went out—the second time for me in 72 hours—and then we had no idea where anything was. We just kept going and going and hoping and hoping but we just couldn't seem to find our way off the goddamned European continent. By then I was convinced I was born only to get lost.

Finally, we broke out of the clouds over water, altitude at 1,000 feet. But it wasn't the channel; it was the Thames Estuary and we were headed straight for the Tower of London! What the hell to do? The Royal Navy might shoot us down. In fact, I thought we should probably count on it. After being shot all to pieces three days ago, we were again terribly at risk. So we took the bull by the horns and became as obvious as possible. Identification flares poured out of the side of our airplane; we sent the password of the day over and over on all military radio bands. The pilot called me, "Who in hell are all those goddamn ships?"

"Looks to me," I said, "like the entire Royal fucking Navy."

But no one fired a round at us. You could see their ack-ack guns following us like we were a goose. So we cruised by the Royal Navy like the *Queen Elizabeth II* right over 10 Downing Street and on up

284

to the Midlands. This had to be the most incompetent piece of navigation since Wrong Way Corrigan. Couldn't even find the English Channel out of Belgium!

You can laugh about it?

I'd better be able to laugh. And forgive myself. Otherwise you can carry stuff like that around forever. I was just not cut out to do math of any sort, much less be a combat navigator. But that's the way the plan was set up. No such thing as turning in a resignation.

285

Jim Colvert in the cockpit of a Martin B-26.

JIM COLVERT
A First Look at Hitler's New Jet

Along with several other World War II combat pilots, Jim Colvert was ushered into the jet age over Nazi Germany one day in the early spring of 1945. As their bomb group approached a target on the Rhine, Jim and his crew sighted, several miles ahead, a nearly vertical condensation trail tracing the path of something climbing at an unbelievable speed. Their first thought was that it was a German V-2 rocket but when the nearly invisible object levelled off at about 20,000 feet and began rapidly tracing a wide circle, they realized it was no V-2. It was a Luftwaffe fighter, one of Hitler's awesome Messerschmitt 262 jets that the crew had been hearing about for several weeks in their combat briefings. Jim describes this unnerving experience in the interview.

Jim entered USAAF [United States Army Air Force] flight training in early 1943 at Kelly Field, Texas, continued his training at Corsicana, Texas, and Enid, Oklahoma, and graduated from the advanced twin-engine school at Altus, Oklahoma, in April 1944. He trained as a pilot on the Martin B-26 Marauder at the combat aircraft transition school at Del Rio, Texas. Later that summer 1944, he was at Brooks Field, San Antonio, where he qualified in the Mitchell B-25, the airplane General Doolittle and his raiders made famous by their attack on Tokyo in 1942. Jim trained for tactical combat in the B-26 at Barksdale Field, Louisiana, and was assigned to the Ninth Tactical Air Force in Europe in the fall 1944. In early January 1945, he was posted to France as a pilot in the 554th

Squadron, 386th Bomb Group, then based at Beaumont-sur-Oise, a village about 25 miles north of Paris. The group later switched from the B-26 to the new Douglas A-26 fighter-bomber and moved to St. Trond, Belgium, a few miles west of Liege. From these bases, the 386th attacked enemy communications and materiels centers—bridges, highways, railroad junctions and marshaling yards, ordnance warehouses, and oil storage depots. Colvert flew 22 missions with the 386th—eight in B-26s and 14 in A-26s.

When he left the air force after the war, he continued flying, and at various times, has been a part-time flight instructor and charter pilot. His principal interest since the war, however, has been English and American literature. He received his Ph.D. from Louisiana State University in 1953 and taught English and American literature for more than 30 years at various state universities, among them the University of Texas, the University of Connecticut, and the University of Virginia. He retired in 1988 from the University of Georgia, where he edited the *Georgia Review* in the late 1960s and early 1970s, taught American literature, and served several years as head of the English department.

Tell me something about the airplanes you flew in combat. What were the B-26 Marauder and A-26 Invader like?

The Martin B-26, a medium bomber, carried a crew of six—pilot and copilot, bombardier-navigator, radio operator, armorer, and flight engineer. The last three doubled in combat as gunners. It was a fast, rugged airplane.

I've heard that it was tricky and dangerous.

It was notorious—known as "the widow maker" and "the flying coffin" because of the appalling number of fatalities it scored on inexperienced pilots in combat training schools. There was even a congressional investigation, as I recall. Since it was designed to carry heavy loads at high speeds, it had a very high wingloading; that is, its short, thin, low-drag wing had to bear tremendous loads for its small size. At maximum takeoff weight every square foot of the wing had to lift nearly 52 pounds, the highest wingloading of any airplane in the world at that time. Consequently, it had an unusually high landing speed. We flew it down to the runway at 150 miles per hour and touched on at about 115 or 120. I flew eight combat missions in it.

How about the A-26?

My group switched to the Douglas A-26 fighterbomber in March 1945. It was just a coincidence that the airplanes shared the designation "26." They were actually very different, except for the engines. Both were equipped with two huge 18 cylinder, 2,000 horse powered radials, the famous Pratt-Whitney R-2800. The A-26 normally carried a crew of two—the pilot and armorer-gunner, though one version had a Plexiglass nose to accommodate a bombardier-navigator. The pilot did his own copiloting and bombardiering, and his own navigating, too, if he ever became separated from his formation. I flew 14 combat missions in A-26s. It handled like a dream.

Was the A-26 used as a fighter?

No. We tried it once or twice on low-level strafing missions, but it didn't do very well, even though it was originally designed for low-level attacks. It was as fast as some of our fighters (its top level speed in one configuration was about 360 miles per hour), and it could climb like a homesick angel. It was highly maneuverable and heavily armed—14 forward-firing .50 caliber machine guns plus four top-and-bottom swivel guns in the fuselage turret, but relatively poor visibility from the cockpit made working close to the ground at high speeds with other airplanes whizzing around too dangerous. So we used it as a medium bomber, dropping our loads in large formations from 10,000-14,000 feet.

How did the A-26 fare against enemy fighters?

Very well. It was fast enough to frustrate even the best German fighters. They couldn't attack from the front. The 14 forward-firing .50 caliber machine guns the pilot commanded with a single button on his control yoke, made head-on attacks unthinkable. Enemy fighters also had trouble attacking laterally in the classic pursuit curve. In this maneuver, the attacker, approaching from the side is obliged to fly in a constant turn during his run in order to keep his target in his gun sights. Having the greater distance to go in the engagement, the attacker must fly at least 100 miles per hour faster that his intended victim to keep up. The A-26 could cruise in formation at nearly 300 miles per hour plus if necessary, which means that fighters attacking from the side would have to maintain speeds well over 400 miles per hour, a straining performance for even such legendary Luftwaffe fighters as the Focke-Wulf 190 and Messerschmitt 109.

Luckily, I never had to endure a fighter attack. By the time I started flying combat, the Luftwaffe wasn't as formidable in western Europe as it had once been. Many of its fighter units had been withdrawn from the west to try to stop the advancing Russians along the eastern front, and it was also handicapped by a severe fuel shortage. In the west, it usually saved what gas it could scrounge for its use against the Allies' heavy strategic bombers, which by 1945, were ravaging German cities day and night. Still, just to keep us sweating, I suppose, they occasionally launched fighter attacks on tactical bomb groups like the 386th and 391st. In late 1944, the 391st, our "sister" group, based near Cambrai, was virtually destroyed in a ferocious, all-out assault by fifty-odd yellow-nose Focke-Wulf 190s of the Hermann Goering Honor Squadron. Luckily, I wasn't on either of those missions

Fighter attacks were always possible, of course, and we naturally worried about them. But what scared us most was the fierce German anti-aircraft guns, especially the famously accurate and efficient 88s.

Were you ever shot down?

No. I lost an engine once on an B-26 mission and I took shrapnel hits several times in both the B-26 and the A-26, but I was never downed. I probably came close, though, the time my bomb bay doors stuck open over the target deep in enemy territory. Open bomb bay doors hanging out in the slipstream act much like speed brakes. In no time at all, I had fallen behind my group, which had flown west, as per custom, after we got rid of our bombs. Hobbling along 100 miles deep in hostile skies, with a balky airplane, I was perfect prey for free-lance fighters on the prowl for cripples. By the time I got the doors unstuck, (by beating on the stuck hydraulic value with a fire-ax), my head was swarming with images of sharks sliding into the pursuit curves, their wings alight with the red flicker of their hammering 20 mm cannons. My gunner, Staff Sergeant James "Bugs" Callery, scanned the rear. I scanned the front, aware that fighters might come from nowhere, announced by 20 mm shell crashing through our fuselage. Luckily, no fighters spotted us. We got back to our base at St. Trond all right.

What about German jet fighters?

I saw my first jet airplane on a combat mission over Germany in 1945. That was the Messerschmitt 262, a revolutionary twin-engine jet fighter that could have altered the war, or at least extend it, if Hitler had allowed it to be used as an interceptor against our bombs. The M-262 had been operational since 1943, and the Germans had plenty of them (1,400 in existence when the war ended in May 1945). Luckily for us, the Fuehrer, acting on his crazy notion that it should be used only as a revenge bomber against England, forbade its development against Allied raiders.

In January, Captain Robert Preston Meservey, our squadron intelligence officer, the movie actor Robert Preston (from the *Music Man* and *Victor Victoria*), reported that the airplane was shortly expected to be deployed in the defense of Germany and briefed us on its incredible speed (550-600 mph in straight flight) and spectacular performance.

In mid February 1945, on a B-26 strike against a railroad bridge near Mayen, I got my first glimpse of it. It first appeared about 15 miles dead ahead as a long white con trail [condensation trail]. In my mind, it was very nearly vertical, though it probably wasn't quite that steep. I'd never seen an airplane climb like that, I simply couldn't take it in. A V-2 rocket, maybe? I got on the intercom and asked my copilot, Lieutenant Art Griffith, and my bombardier-navigator, Flight Officer Joe Cerniglia, what they thought. "Yeah, it's a V-2," Joe said. "They've launched a V-2 down there." That sounded likely. Still pushing their Ardennes offensive, the Germans were raining V-2s on Antwerp and other cities in the lowlands and this was probably one of them. But shortly the con trail levelled off at about 18,000 feet, 6,000 feet or so above us, and began turning a wide circle. "Oh, yeah!" Gif said, his voice rising. "V-2s don't level off and circle around! That's one of Meservey's jet fighters. That's a goddamn M-262!"

I'm sure that made you a bit anxious.

Well, more than a bit, creating apprehension was the jet's main game. We were approaching the point from which we would begin our run on the target, the most critical phase of the mission, and his objective was to take our minds off what we were trying to do. We understood from our briefings that a lone M-262 pointedly advertising his presence wouldn't attack. His strategy was psychological. He'd hover during our attack to unnerve us. Then as we turned off the target, he'd drop like a thunderbolt on one of our four "tail-end Charlies," plummeting at 650 to 700 miles per hour, he would train his four 30 mm nose cannon on Charlie, unleashing a tornado as the M-262 flicked by invisible, recovering from the dive far below, to then turn homeward. Meservey also assured us that there was no defense against this maneuver. The fatefully chosen Charlie wouldn't likely survive. Guess who one of the tailend Charlies was that day?

The jet lurked in a mile above us, all the way to the target. It was impossible to ignore him—even on the critical bomb run. We worried more about him than the Mayen bridge, as he expected us to do. After we dropped our bombs and dove sharply away from the target toward home, he lingered along, and tension grew. This was the position from which he would likely start his attack on Charlie. I couldn't see him from the cockpit, but my gunners kept me informed. "He's still up there, sir. He's still following us," they said about a dozen times, and about a dozen times, I said, "If he starts down, fire as soon as you can get your sights on him. Never mind range, just fire and keep firing." I knew it was a meaningless order. They could never really bring their guns to bear on an airplane dropping nearly straight down on us just under the speed of sound.

And so he came down?

No. I don't know why. But after a eon or so, Bugs said, "I think he's dropping back." Then, "He is. He's leaving! He's heading east, going home, sir!"

Grif grinned at me from his copilot's seat. Cerniglia, who hadn't uttered a word after we left the target, said on the intercom, "Boy, that jet really scared you guys, didn't it."

So that's how we were all brought into the jet age.

What else did you worry about in combat?

Our main worries, of course, were fighters and enemy antiaircraft guns—those terrible 88s, and 105s, the bigger ones that flashed a hellish red center when they burst. Then toward the end, when missions got longer as the enemy pulled back into the "fatherland," we had to worry about running out of fuel. We planned carefully, of course, and operated on reasonable margins, but sometimes long distances, bad weather, and the enemy worked together to upset our planning. Our monstrous engines normally consumed about 80 gallons of fuel per hour each, but as they aged, they tended to use even more. They aged rapidly the way we flew them in combat. We abused them, exceeding their design limits on takeoffs, running them at high power settings in cruise, and "rawhiding" them mercilessly doing violent evasive action. Before they got loose enough to scap, they could be drinking up to 90 or even 95 gallons per hour. Flying these gas hogs 800 mile round trip missions with lots of evasive action in the target area—maybe even a couple of long detours around bad weather coming and going—created some hairy situations.

What happened to us in April 1945, illustrates the point. On our way back to Belgium after an A-26 strike on an oil refinery at Stod, Czechoslovakia, we started running out of fuel even before we crossed the Rhine. We were desperately stretching for our emergency refueling alternate, the Ninth Tactical Air Force base near Worms. My situation was critical because I had been stuck with a notorious gas hog, A Able. I recall A Able's fuel gauges were bobbing on empty. I wasn't sure how far Worms was, but I was certain enough of one thing, I would have a very heavy load of dead machinery on my hands. I had a feeling I'd never make it to Worms, so I decided to abandon the airplane.

I summoned Sergeant Callery from his turret. He came up through the bomb bay, crowded into the little jump seat and listened as I gave him the bad news and described our bailout procedure. I

293

thought we had maybe five to ten minutes, though I wouldn't have been surprised if the engines had died that very instant.

But then Worms appeared on the horizon, and a moment later, off to my left, the flat, gray expanse of the air base. We had been closer than I thought. I began to rethink my plan and dropped out of the formation and heading for the airfield now, I thought I could make it. I broke radio silence to inform my box leader I was leaving the formation. He didn't acknowledge. I began waggling my wings to alert my flight, and I slid down toward the base. I became aware that some other pilot advised the leader that he was also dropping out, but I was too preoccupied to pay much attention.

I was descending now under reduced power, keeping my mental fingers tightly crossed. I told the tower (code named "Lovesick," to the briefing sheet) that I was out of fuel and approaching for a straight-in landing on the east-west runway, and he cleared me. (It wouldn't have made any difference if he hadn't, of course.) I delayed extending the landing gear until I was within a mile of the runway. Just as it thudded into its lowered and locked position, the right engine fuel-pressure gauge smoothly dropped from its normal 14 psi to zero, and the engine serenely expired. I checked the swerve it caused—increased power slightly on the left engine—and a few seconds later we were on the ground. Just as I lowered the nose wheel, left engine quit, and I was rolling down the runway at 100 miles per hour. But no matter. We held a quiet little carnival in the cockpit.

An urgent voice in my headset informed me that our celebration was premature. The pilot of the airplane that had followed us was just crossing the threshold behind and was ordering the tower to get us out of his way. The controller told him to pull up and go around. "Negative on the go-around," the pilot replied in a desperate voice. "I can't make it around. Get that guy of the runway. Clear the runway now! Get that guy off!" I was coming up fast on an exit 50 feet off to my right. I was going too fast to turn, despite heavy breaking. I turned anyway. More than anything else in the world, I wanted to get out of the way of the 12 ton airplane about to plow into me at 80 or 90 miles per hour.

I pushed the right rudder pedal to the floor and snubbed the right brake. The airplane swerved violently toward the exit, landing gear juddering under the tremendous side-load, and just as it twisted

The ruined hangar where Jim Colvert spent the night listening for werewolves in April 1945.

295

into the turnoff, lurched into a right spin—a classic ground loop. It spun into the taxiway and then, around and around, off into the open field, coming to rest finally in an ear-smashing silence and boiling cloud of dust. Exhausted and shaken, Callery and I simply sat and watched glumly as emergency vehicles raced towards us. The group formation was turning slowly above, dispatching airplane after airplane down to the runway. The airplane that landed behind us was parked, propellers still, in the open field near the far end of the runway, We were still strapped in our seats when the fire truck and ambulance pulled up. One of the medics, pointing to our bulletproof windshield, splintered by a chunk of spent flak, said, "Hey look at that. These guys are really shot up."

We exhausted the base fuel supply even though we loaded only enough gas for an hour's flight. We had to wait around for tanker trucks to haul in a new supply. Later, a line of heavy thunderstorms popped up northwest, between us and St. Trond, and the group commander spread the word that we'd spend the night. There wasn't enough room for all of us at the barracks, so several of us were issued blankets and cots and trucked several miles down the road to an abandoned German airfield. The field had been almost leveled by repeated bombing, and we were hard put to find any kind of shelter. We finally installed our cots in what once had been a large hangar, placing them behind piles of rubble under a roof that sagged on one side all the way to the ground. We walked around the field and down to a nearby abandoned village, which was completely destroyed.

The officer who drove us there warned us about local "werewolves," murderous Nazi guerillas, who stalked the night to waylay enemy soldiers. He advised us to post a lookout and sleep with our pistols in our hands. We only half believed his stories, but we nevertheless held our pistols while we dozed. I heard noises in the rubble and ruin all night long, and they were just the kind of noises werewolves make, too.

Any other particular worries besides fuel consumption and werewolves?

Well, the runway at Beaumont-sur-Oise. Built by the Germans for fighter planes, it was too short for combat-loaded B-26s, especially when we flew overloaded, as we often did. The airplane was designed to carry a 4,000 pound bomb load, but someone somewhere at sometime decided that under pressing circumstances we could manage another 1,200 pounds. Pressing circumstances are the norm in war, of course, and as it turned out, almost every time we lined up for takeoff on that sadly inadequate runway, we were overloaded. Our takeoffs were always colorful and no doubt would have been instructive to the young if there had been anyone around younger. Holding our breaths as we wrenched our airplanes into the air, we hugged the ground until we got the landing gear up and reached minimum single-engine control speed of 135 mph. I often pictured the smoking hole a B-26 might make if it stalled on lift off and slammed into the ground at, say, 110 mph loaded with 700 gallons of gasoline, 5,000 pounds of highly volatile demolition bombs, and 2,000 rounds of .50 caliber machine-gun ammunition.

What else was interesting about life at Beaumont-sur-Oise?

Our physical layout. When the Germans retreated after the fall of Paris in the summer 1944, they blew up the runways and shelled the buildings with artillery. We rebuilt one of the runways and patched over some of the gaping holes on roofs and walls of the few buildings left with standing walls. Headquarters was a narrow, three-story stone and brick building facing a small courtyard. Across was a smaller building that housed our operations office.

Both were nearly uninhabitable. A 12 foot hole in the outside wall of headquarters exposed part of the sagging staircase leading up to the squadron commander's office on the second floor. A single room was all that was left on the third floor, which we fixed up as our Officers' Club. Here we had an inexhaustible supply of captured champagne served over a bar fashioned out of a downed Messerschmitt 109 wing, and drunk straight out of the bottle, like beer. The stairs going down to the second floor led straight to the open hole in the wall, over which hung a crude sign "Pull Up Your Flaps and Go Around"—a warning that probably saved many a pilot from soaring out into empty air, champagne bottle in hand, and crashing to the ground 12 feet below.

We had no barracks. We lived in large, six-man tents, pitched in rows behind the ruined buildings. We didn't freeze to death, but we thought we might. The European winter of 1944-45 was the worst in more than 30 years, and when we were not flying—bad weather grounded us for days on end—we crowded around the orange glow of our little coal stoves and shivered. Temperatures were often near zero, and inside it was usually not much above freezing. We wore our fleece-lined flying jackets, pants, and boots day and night, in bed and out, and padded our cots with thick layers of newspapers.

Outside was a tall pole bearing two loudspeakers connected to a radio and a public announcement system in the operations office. We used the British word for the system, the "tannoy." The tannoy was almost always on, bringing us via the BBC from London, the popular music of the day, puzzling English humor, and running reports on the course of the war. We followed Field Marshall Montgomery's progress against the Germans in the Lowlands, took heart at the overrunning of the German forces at Remagen and the saving of that famous bridge, and celebrated, over the M-109 wing, General Patton's wild dash to the Rhine at Koblenz.

We were usually out of the action. Sleet and snow and thick, lowering clouds and fogs kept us on the ground, huddled and dejected in our freezing tents. We flew a day or two now and then, but it was not until the weather broke in early March that we got back into operations, just in time for the historic crossing of the Rhine and the final bitter battle for Germany.

What was the routine of a typical combat mission?

A mission actually began in the early evening of the day before it was flown. About supper time, squadron operations posted a list of the eight or nine crews and aircraft assigned for the next day's mission. Since we had some 20 flight crews in the 554th, we expected find our names listed on about half the sorties our squadron flew.

On mission days, a noncom awakened (if, in fact, anyone was asleep) the assigned flight crews around 4:30 A.M. I was almost always awake under my pile of blankets in my fleece-lined flying clothes. I watched the flashlight as he crunched through the frozen snow, knocking lightly and calling names in a discreet murmur. In ten minutes we were in the mess tent, where we ate glue-like oatmeal, under naked light bulbs. I lost more than 20 pounds that winter at Beaumont-sur-Oise. A large board sign painted in bold red letters hung over the door that said, "Smile. You Never Had It So Good."

Personnel carriers to take us across the field to the briefing room. We passed armed guards and sat on wooden benches before a curtained operational map which held the secret—where we were going and how much trouble we were going to have. When the briefing staff arrived, the chief briefed, went to the map, drew the curtain, and tapping with his pointer, said something like this:

"The Bendorf railroad bridge on the Rhine, between Neuwied and Koblenz—it's crucial to the German Ardennes offensive. They move hundreds of tons of supplies across it every day. There'll be strong resistance, approximately two hundred enemy fighters. Gentlemen, this bridge is playing a significant role in the enemy's defense of the Rhine. It must be destroyed. Good luck."

For 30 or 40 minutes we scribbled notes on our planning sheets as specialists fed us information: the flight routes, weather (which our own P-51 reconnaissance planes had scouted for us an hour or so earlier), enemy defenses, technical information about the bombs, tower call codes for bases available to aircraft in distress, the combat line, beyond which there were no friendly ground forces to worry about if we had to drop our bombs for some reason before reaching the target. We also got our engine-start time, taxi time, and first-man-off time. Finally, we hacked our watches on a countdown so that we all carried the same time to the second.

It must have still been dark after briefing. Did you take off then?

No. Briefing was usually over by 6:00 A.M., and we normally didn't launch morning missions until 7:00 or 8:00, even when we had no weather delays. There was still plenty to do before we were actually ready to go. This was the usual routine for a mission in the combat-rigged B-26:

Grif, my copilot, Joe, my bombardier, and Staff Sergeant Fred Ellis, my radio operator-gunner, return to squadron operations to pick up certain standard-issue combat items: "flak suits"—long, blacksmith like aprons ribbed with steel bars to protect us (theoretically) against machine-gun bullets and shrapnel; individual "escape kits" containing maps, money, first-aid supplies, special rations to help us evade capture if we are shot down; morphine and syringes for the airplane medical kit (these items were kept under lock in the operations office between missions); and a box of candy bars—Baby Ruths, Butterfingers, Three Musketeers—to consume on the way home to bolster our sagging blood-sugar level.

Staff Sergeants Day and Callery, my flight engineer and armorer, go with me directly to the airplane to start the inspection routines. Ground-crew specialists have already checked the engines and instruments and loaded and checked the bombs; our interest in these matters is more personal. We check again. Malfunctions can have deadly consequences.

By the time Grif, Joe, and Ellis arrive with their loot from operations, the tower has signalled with flares that engine-start time is still valid. The enemy knows we are coming, or soon will. Meservey has assured us that enemy agents in the village keep us under constant surveillance, but there is no need to make their jobs any easier. We maintain strict radio silence.

As engine-start time approaches, we begin the business of loading up. We adjust the straps of our heavy leather flying pants and jackets, check the zippers on our fleece-lined boots, each of which weighs at least six pounds, pull on the massive flak aprons, buckle into our seat-type parachutes, and squeeze through the hatches to our stations in the airplane. A ground crewman starts the putt-putt, the auxiliary outside generator that furnishes the electrical power for cranking the heavy engines. Grif, begins setting up the cockpit as I watch the tower across the field for the engine-start flare. When it goes up, I signal the putt-putt operator outside, and Grif and I begin the starting ritual. The whir of the starter flywheel rises to a high whine, and when it reaches the right pitch, I hit the engage switch. The starter slowly swings the massive 12 foot, four-bladed prop. Mixture control to full rich for two seconds, then to idle cut-off. The exhaust stack coughs a puff or two of blue smoke; the engine catches momentarily, then suddenly comes alive, sending a tremor through the whole airplane. Mixture to full rich, mags switch on both, pressures check. Set throttle to idle at 1,000 rpm. We start the right engine, and when the temperatures are right, begin our final runup tests, Grif calling the items from the checklist, I verbally confirm the conditions and settings required: magneto checks at 2,000 rpm, temperatures, carburetor heat,: fuel, engine oil, and hydraulic pressures; generators on and voltage and amp checks; propeller governors check; gyros set; supercharger in low blower; and on and on. The blue taxi flare goes up from the tower, and aircraft along the taxiway begin rolling out of hardstand position.

How many airplanes usually flew? It must have been complicated getting information after takeoff.

Yes, some genius worked it out. Getting a group of 30 to 36 airplanes off the ground and assembled in group combat formation is no mean operation. A group formation consists of two "boxes" of 15 to 18 airplanes each—high-box and low-box. Each box consists of three flights with six airplanes in a flight. The objective is to get the group airborne with every airplane in its assigned place without wasting time and fuel. The join up operation is choreographed, like a ballet routine.

The routine begins when we pull into our assigned places in the taxi line. Looking ahead as the flight I'm assigned to approaches the runway, I see that the group leader is parked in first-man-off position on the right side of the runway. Parked immediately to his left is the pilot who will fly his left wing (number two position). The pilot who will fly his right wing (number three) is at the head of the taxi line waiting to take the leader's place on the runway as soon as the leader starts his takeoff.

A green flare from the tower marks five seconds to first-man-off time. The mission leader clamps hard on his toe-brakes, slowly opens his throttles and his airplane begins to tremble. The tower fires an orange "get ready" flare, the mission leader advances his throttles to near takeoff power. At zero countdown, the tower fires the green "go" flare. The leader releases his brakes quickly and cleanly and moves his throttles swiftly to full takeoff power. His airplane leaps forward, catapulted down the runway by 1,850 screeching horsepower. The mission is under way.

The instant the leader bolts, the left wingman, holding his brakes, advances his throttles and starts a 20 second countdown. The high-box leader's right wingman pulls into the empty position on the right. When the left wingman moves, the right wingman begins his 20 second countdown. This rolling-and-filling drill continues until all airplanes are airborne. Six minutes after the leader starts his takeoff roll, the 18 aircraft of high-box are in the air, maneuvers to join their flight leader in their assigned slots.

Captain Walter Schuler, the low-box leader, is on the runway now with his left wingman; First Lieutenant Roger Amiot is in the number two position. I wait on the taxiway to pull into position as soon as Captain Schuler leaves it. Major James Reed, who will be flying the difficult number four position, slightly behind and below Schuler, is just behind me on the taxiway, and the men flying the major's left and right wings are behind him.

Grif makes final adjustments in the engine-cowl and oil-cooler flap, sets the wing flaps, toggles on the auxiliary fuel pumps, and advances the mixture controls to rich. Schuler bolts, and I move quickly into place. I keep the non-steerable nosewheel straight as I brake to a stop. Amiot is on the runway to my left, counting down. The airplane begins to quiver as it strains against the locked brakes. Grif counts—"5-4-3-2-1 Go, GODDAMIT, GO."

I snap the brakes off and glide the throttles forward until the manifold pressure gauges reach 52 inches, the absolute allowable maximum, plus four. The airplane leaps forward. Grif holds the emergency propeller feathering switches, one in each hand, in case he needs to stop a runaway propeller. He calls the speeds as the runway slides under us faster and faster—80, 85, 95, 105. I test with back pressure on the yoke for elevator resistance, feeling for takeoff lift. At 120 mph, I find it and haul her off, just as the end of the runway flashes beneath us. I give Grif the thumbs-up signal to raise the landing gear, and he moves the control lever to the up position. I touch the brakes to stop the spinning wheels as they rise and fold into the engine nacelles.

When we finally reach 135 mph, I relax a bit. Even if one of the engines fails now, I can maintain reasonable control of the airplane, and perhaps with a lot of luck, even nurse and get it back to the field for an emergency landing. At 145 mph, I reduce the manifold pressure to 40 inches. Grif sets the props to 2,400 rpm. I start a slightly steeper climb. We're at 190 now. We've got it made, and begin to get into formation, an operation requiring precision timing and turning. We know Schuler reversed his course precisely, with a standard-rate right turn, and is now on his way back to gather up his flight, which is strung out along the climb-out path at 20 second intervals. We see Amiot, 20 seconds ahead, start his timed turn to the right, and at the end of our count, we start our turn. Schuler shortly comes into view about two miles to the right, dawdling along at join-up speed of 190 mph. Amiot, turning to meet him, slides under him and slips neatly into place on his left wing. As we continue our swing toward them, near the airfield, high-box is loitering in a wide circle at two thousand feet, its three six-plane flights—beautiful. They're waiting for our low-box to fall into place.

We assume our position half a mile behind and 500 feet below height-box, headed northeast toward Germany at 215 mph.

What was it like going into enemy territory and hitting the target.

I remember the strike on the Bendorf railroad bridge. I still have the information sheet for that mission. I look at these old briefing notes, flight logs, and airplane manuals, and I can see it almost as if it's actually happening again.

We're climbing steadily at 215 mph toward Marle, a tiny village about 75 miles east northeast, the end of the first leg of our constantly shifting and dodging approach to our target. As the crow flies, the Bendorf bridge is only about an hour and a quarter from our base—about 280 miles—but we don't fly as the crow flies. We know the enemy is likely tracking us on radar, and we want keep to him guessing right up to the last two to four minutes—literally—about what target we are going to hit and how we are going to get to it. That way, he can't make any special arrangements, like deploying extra anti-aircraft guns mounted on railroad flatcars or maybe even scrambling a half-dozen Focke-Wulf 190s to greet us we turn in on the bomb run.

At Marle, cruising now at 265 mph at 12,000 feet, we turn due south, almost reversing course, and then eight minutes later, over Reims, we turn toward Thionville, 97 miles due east. A few miles west of Thionville (20 minutes out of Reims) Schuler, who's carrying the lead navigator for low-box, rocks his wings slightly to confirm that we're crossing the combat line. (We are maintaining strict radio silence, of course.) I inform the gunners, who have been readying for action at their posts in the turret and waistgun stations since we left Reims.

We're over Thionville. We turn left toward Koblenz and the target area, 90 miles northeast. The Germans might easily guess that our target is somewhere in or around the crucial communications center, but they can't be sure. There are important targets all up and down the Rhine; we could reverse our direction of flight at any moment and go to a significant target somewhere else. Fourteen minutes and 70 miles later, over the village of Bremen, we make another feinting turn, swing widely to the southeast toward Simmern, and four minutes after that, still another turn, this time far to the left toward the point from which we'll start our run on the bridge.

In bomber-pilot lingo this point is the dreadful I.P. (Initial Point), dreadful because from the I.P. to the target, we are utterly vulnerable to enemy action. We can do nothing to defend ourselves. We bore straight ahead, no matter what. We can't turn away from anti-aircraft fire ahead, we can't dive out of burgeoning flak clouds, we can't change course. Not until the bombs are out of our bays over the target. The distance from the I.P. to the target is short, usually two to three minutes, but it's by far the longest leg of the mission.

Three minutes to the I.P., we begin tightening the formation for maximum concentration of the bombing pattern. My eyes are locked on Schuler's wing, which is so close I can see two or three loose rivets in the wing skin vibrating in the air stream.

Day is on the intercom from the tailgun position: "Flak at five o'clock low, six bursts, 88s, 300 yards." This barrage, is just a feeler shot for tracking and ranging, a promise of what's to come. Then several oily black blossoms spring up silently (we can seldom hear the shells exploding over the noise of our engines) to the right and slightly below high-box. Then two or three level and fairly close on our right. A faint, dry spattering sound tells us that the airplane has been hit by shrapnel fragments. Grif looks right and left along the wings and around the engine nacelles for signs of damage. He sees nothing, nor do the gunners. So far, so good.

Neither Schuler nor the mission leader takes evasive action because we're too close to the I.P. to maneuver. In fact, we're at the I.P., and Schuler rolls smoothly but rapidly into a steep left bank. I push the throttles forward to keep from falling behind on the whip-lashing outside of the turn. Joe confirms that we are turning over the I.P., and Grif and I, as per procedure, set the engines up to combat power—props to 2,400 rpm; manifold pressure to 40 inches; mixture controls from auto lean to rich; fuel boost pumps on, oil-cooler and engine-cowl flaps reset. When we roll out of the turn, we have once more nearly reversed our direction of flight. We're on the bomb run. The Bendorf railroad bridge is three minutes dead ahead.

I catch occasional glimpses of the lead bombardier at his station in Schuler's plexiglass nose frantically working at his Norden bombsight, checking figures and more figures—true air speed, bomb-drag coefficient, drift angle, density altitude, absolute altitude, and so on and on. The target, though still some miles ahead, will very shortly come into periscopic view under the crosshairs of the eyepiece, and if the bombsight has been properly set up, the target image will stay there after the bombardier switches into its automatic mode. When the Norden automatically releases Schuler's bombs, Joe and the other bombardiers in the box will release theirs with a manual drop switch.

Our props are slightly out of synch. They are making a beating, surging rumble we would normally find intolerable, but Grif doesn't bother to adjust them. At this moment, we couldn't care less about such niggling niceties of airmanship.

Schuler's bomb bay doors start unfolding, and Joe reports that he's opening ours. The hissing slipstream grows louder as the doors swing down and out to expose ten, yellow-ringed, 500-pound demolition bombs hanging malevolently on their gleaming chrome shackles.

Our drop speed is 270 mph, and the target, now five miles dead ahead, is just over a minute away, locked now presumably under the crosshairs of Norden. The bombardier's work is done. The tracking mechanism, with its stabilizing gyroscopes and timing devices, is running on automatic now, and the bombardier, peering through his eyepiece, is a mere observer monitoring the target image under the crosshairs. If it doesn't hold its proper place, he'll shut the Norden down and order a return to the I.P. for another run.

I adjust the airplane trim to compensate for the destabilizing effect of the open doors. During the turn over the I.P., we got very little ground fire, but it abruptly starts again, coming in surges, filling the sky around us with globs of greasy black smoke. We overrun patches of it drifting in eddies and swirls, and our cockpit fills with the pungent odor of burned cordite. No evasive action is possible now. I keep my eyes on Schuler's wing and try not to think about the flak (impossible). Joe is on the intercom saying that we're 20 seconds from the drop and that he's arming the bombs. He throws the arming switch and the bomb shackles jerk out the safety wires. The bombs are hot and the 20 seconds are an eternity. Finally Schuler's bombs are out. They fall lazily, seeming motionless for the first second for two, then they smoothly accelerate downward out of sight, speeding toward the Bendorf bridge. Joe squeezes his drop switch, and the airplane starts to balloon upward as it's suddenly relieved of its tremendous weight of bombs. I damp the ballooning with hard forward pressure on the yoke, and Joe calls, "bombs away" just as Schuler rolls abruptly into a steep diving right turn. I'm suddenly below him, banked steeply, looking up at him at the end of my sharply raised left wing. I'm on the slow inside of the turn, and I have to pull my throttles almost completely closed to keep from overshooting him. Joe's distant voice reports that the bomb bay doors are closed. We now roll violently left, and as my position swiftly shifts from the inside to the outside of the turn, I jam the throttles forward to hold my position on Schuler and to keep from being overrun by the number-six man directly behind me. We head due north toward Freilingen, picking up speed in a shallow dive, to get out of Koblenz defense perimeter as soon as possible. We're soon out of the worst flak. We get random bursts here and there, too low or high or wide to matter. Just south of Neuwied, we make a wide left turn for home, eyes peeled for fighters.

We loosen the formation a bit, thankful to be out of the flak and free of the killing labor and tension of the bomb run. Laacherlak, west of Neuwied, slides by blue and serene to our right, but no one comments. I ask Callery and Day, who had the clearest view of the target area after the drop, if we hit anything, and they assure me that we took the bridge clean out.

"High-box fell long, sir," Day says, "but we walked our drop right through it."

"It was a shack, sir," Callery adds confidently.

"Sure," Grif says. He's thinking that bomb strikes always look good from altitude. Boiling smoke, fire, and lifting debris can create false impressions of awesome destruction. We won't know for sure how much damage we did until the photo rec planes gets their pictures and the lab distributes the strike photos later in the day.

Grif points to a single airplane drifting back from high-box. The feathered right propeller is motionless. We can see that he dropped out of position six in the second flight of high-box, but we don't know who it is. Grif says he thinks it's a 555th crew. I check my briefing sheet and see that the emergency alternate fields are Florennes, southeast of Charleroi, Belgium, and Laon-Athies, near Reims. He'll have to make one or the other or go down in enemy territory, or at best, territory still being fought over. A combat-rigged B-26, even without a bomb load, couldn't stay in the air indefinitely with only one engine. This crew would eventually go down, voluntarily or not. I ask Joe to check his chart and figure distance, bearing, and time from our present position to Florennes. "Florennes is just over a 100 miles, mag heading 268," he says. "At best single-engine speed they're about 45 minutes out." I figure roughly that if they're not losing altitude at more than 150 feet per minute, they might make it. But it will be close. He'll be on the wrong side of the combat line for a while yet, and there is always the possibility—horrible thought—of his being picked off by a prowling German fighter. The wounded airplane drifts behind us, heading due west, for Florennes, we presume, and after he disappears from our view in the cockpit, Day and Callery follow him until he is a mere speck in the wide unfriendly German skies.

Grif has been fiddling with the communications receiver, anticipating the lifting of radio silence when we cross the combat line north of Luxembourg. We're at 7,000 feet now, slowly descending. Now we're listening to the voice of the mission leader, Captain Meyer, code named Crackling Green. "Crackling Green leader to Crackling Green. Open formation approved. Piss call and candy bars." Formations scatter for open space like nervous goldfish, and for the first time since takeoff, nearly three hours before, I can look at something besides Schuler's ever-threatening right wing. We strip off the armored clothing and grab for the ARTs, the Airman Relief Tubes. (Under the stress of a bomb run, kidneys work harder than brains.) Joe crawls back through the tunnel from the nose and tosses around candy bars, which we bolt down like starving wolves, three or four bites to the bar. Spirits rise. Radio chatter is as thick as Koblenz flak.

307

Crackling Green is soon talking to the tower at Beaumont-sur-Oise. The French countryside is familiar and good to look at. Grif is flying the airplane now, and he slowly begins to tighten on our flight leader when the base appears on the horizon. In no time at all, we're peeling out of our slots for the runway at Beaumont-sur-Oise. One of the best sounds in all the world is the cheerful "chirk" of tires kissing a solid runway after a combat mission.

We get word about the crippled B-26 while we're unloading at the hardstand. It's Second Lieutenant Albert Young of the 555th. He hasn't shown at either Florennes or Laon-Athies. No other information is available.

We drag through the formality of debriefing, where we're supposed to describe anything we saw in enemy territory that might be useful to intelligence. I give my standard response that the only thing I saw was my flight leader's wing, which was, in fact, very true. Then we head for our tents and collapse on our cots. We sometimes slept 11 or 12 hours after a combat mission.

Did you ever learn what happened to Young and his crew?

Oh, yes. A week or so after the mission, Lieutenant Colonel Peter B. Greene, our squadron commander, got a report from Young. He and his crew bailed out that day in eastern Belgium near La Roche-en-Ardenne. Their airplane crashed in a wooded area about three miles from where they came down in their chutes. They managed to get together somehow after they got on the ground, and late that same afternoon were taken in by a British infantry patrol unit. They eventually made their way to an air force base at Charleroi. A week or so later were back at Beaumont-sur-Oise, not quite as good as ever, but good enough, considering what could have happened to them.

Did they fly combat again?

Yes. They finished out the war in the 386th. Young himself played a prominent role in our June 1945, war with the RAF.

War with the RAF? With the British?

Yes. It's not well known that the 386th Bomb Group, United States Air Force, then at St. Trond flying A-26s fought a brief, but ferocious war, with an RAF Mosquito group based near Ostend, Belgium, on the English Channel. The war lasted three terrible days.

Really? What was that all about?

Insults, wounded national pride. At noon on June 14, 1945, just as we were setting down to a nice peaceful post-war lunch, seven restless, irresponsible, impudent RAF Mosquito pilots launched an unprovoked, zero-altitude surprise buzz-job on our base. We retaliated the next day. That's how it started. It was awful. The loss in American tents, British beach umbrellas and English Channel pleasure boats, not to mention RAF prestige and self-respect, was terrible. But that's a long story. Another time, maybe.

DAN BROWNE
An American in the RAF

Dan Browne is a witness to history as few are. As an American, he flew for the Royal Air Force during Normandy and later during the Battle of the Bulge. He was there to help locate downed pilots in the desert as they returned from attacking the oil fields at Ploesti. He flew cover for Johnny Johnson, the celebrated British flier. The consummate fighter pilot himself with more than 250 sorties, Dan shows an air of confidence—and humor—as he speaks, but also a sense of fatalism—as if war was a game that people were dealt, like cards.

Browne was born January 16, 1921 in Denville, New Jersey. As the war came along, he quit his job in 1940 and went to Montreal where he joined the Royal Canadian Air Force. Finishing first in his class, he was shipped off to England, landing in Liverpool on Christmas Eve 1941. He had served in combat with the RAF for only ten months when he received command of a squadron—something relatively rare. Dan attributes it this way, "I could always bring my people back home. I think I can say that I had the best record of not losing pilots during an attack." Dan left the military in 1945. He attended the University of Florida where he received his law degree and worked for one year as a special attorney for the Bureau of Internal Revenue. Later, he directed his own 92 person law firm. Active in civic affairs in Tampa, he served as chairman of the hospital authority and worked in local politics.

Did people think there was anything unusual about you, an American, flying for the Royal Canadian Air Force?

Yes, people said I was crazy. "What the hell are you going to do that for?" I said, "Look, this war is going to take over the whole world. I'm going to go over now." I wanted to get my wings, so I got them in Canada. The key thing was that I couldn't be accepted in the U.S.A. as a pilot because I hadn't completed college, which you needed in those days. I had only two years of college at New York University.

How did you get interested in flying?

I remember being absolutely thrilled about Lindbergh. In 1927, when I was six years old, my father tried to take me to meet him. There was a colossal gridlock because people had come from all over with the same idea in mind. We got within about five miles. Several years later, I saved all my money and went over to Hanover, New Jersey and paid five dollars for an airplane ride. At the time we were living in Florham Park, New Jersey.

Was your dad a frustrated wanna-be flier?

Oh, yes, everybody was a frustrated wanna-be fighter pilot.

After training, I was commissioned as an officer in the Royal Canadian Air Force. I had 30 days leave, then returned to Halifax. We loaded onto the *Leticia*, just as word of Pearl Harbor came through. Talk about a stroke of lightning. That electrified the whole world and especially our continent. Of course, Canada was already at war.

On the way over, a 109-knot wind caught us off Iceland. I was up in the crow's nest on sub watch and you cannot imagine the waves. They were incredible—100 feet high. I would look up at a 40 degree angle and thought we were going straight to the bottom. I was more frightened then than any other time during the war. The nose of the ship would be 20 feet underwater. When the propellers came out of the water, the propellers would shudder. A friend of mine, First Officer Wylie said, "Dan, you better get down now, because it's getting dark." I asked him to string a rope, which would give me a chance to survive, at least. They strung it and I came down. I jumped the last 20 feet, and several sailors came out and grabbed me and took me below deck.

We disembarked at Liverpool, and later, we ended up on the *Viceroy of India* and went to Gibraltar. The day after leaving Gibraltar a Focke-Wulfe Kurier came over the ship. The navy fired and missed it by a mile. We teased those guys about that. Then the next day the Kurier came over again. Anticipating an attack, we went on lifeboat alert. At about four in the afternoon, we heard this harrump-harrump. It turned out the German subs had hit two of the ships in our convoy with torpedoes. The ships broke away from the convoy and ended up grounding themselves in the Canary Islands.

We went to Freetown, South Africa, got fuel and left again. We were getting anxious. A little Norwegian whale fisherman who was with us, said one day, "We're very near land."

He got us all excited. We said, "Where? Where?"

He said, "Right down there. He pointed to the bottom of the ocean."

One day in Madagascar, after refueling at Cape Town, we got the Vichy French general and his beautiful daughter to join us on the ship. Later, I was on patrol on the ship with a sergeant and two corporals with machine guns, when we heard a scuffle. I sent one man down one side of a corridor; another down the other. Suddenly, we saw some French people carrying two rolls of carpet on their shoulders. They screamed at us to get out of the way. We had the machine guns aimed at them and I said, "Open those rugs." I pointed to the rugs. Finally, they opened them and there were the Vichy French general and his beautiful daughter, each wrapped in rugs. They were going to throw them overboard.

We finally landed in Suez, then in Abadan, in what is today Iran. I went on a mission with a guy from New Zealand in a Vicker's Valencia, a gigantic biplane. We picked up ten British generals and flew to Cairo. When crossing the desert from Baghdad, I looked down and could see a Ju 88 bombing the oil tanks at Haifa on the coast of Israel. The pilot saw us but fortunately for us decided to get out of there. He must have thought we had fighters coming behind us. If he had only attacked us, he would have gotten all those generals, and the only weapon on board was my .38 pistol!

I raised hell with the authorities, saying I wanted to go back to England and fly. So finally, the RAF put me on a boat back. I had longed to get into aerial combat. I landed in the Portsmouth area and went to London, then operational training, where I flew Spitfires for the first time.

When was your first contact with the Germans there?

My first contact with the Germans was on a flight when we'd hear from control, "There are 200 Huns coming up over Abbeville." Then they would add, "There are another couple of hundred plus coming over Liel. There are more coming over Cambrai." At the time we only had two squadrons of 12. The Germans figured they were going to beat the hell out of us. This is where I got to appreciate the mettle of Johnny Johnson, who would become Britain's great hero with 38 kills. I was flying with him and suddenly he headed due east. It seemed stupid to me with all those planes out there. Then we climbed to about 39,000 feet where the Germans couldn't reach us. After awhile he said, "Okay, Greycap, we're going home." We made a big sweep to the west. The Germans who were 3,000 to 5,000 feet below us could not get any higher. So they pulled up in the air and started firing at us. We could see their tracers, but that caused their airplanes to stall and they spun out. Then we heard, "All right, Greycap, down, down, down." And I want to tell you my anus started shrinking at that point. Once we dove for the English Channel, the Germans couldn't reach us. That approach settled strategy for the future, because we knew we could get up above the Germans. Several times I saved myself that way.

Johnny Johnson and I escorted the first B-17 bombers that went out to the marshaling yard at Rouen, on the Seine. On another escort mission, we had been told at a certain location to let the B-17s go on because of fuel supply. But the Germans were just ahead of the B-17s and when we turned around, they swept in. The B-17s were losing engines, on fire. Parachutes were falling all over the place; planes burning and going down. We cried when we saw that. Those were all our people.

The American general called up the RAF and said, "What the hell are you doing? We've got our planes going and you can't take your Spitfires out." But it was a fuel problem. The Americans then took some Spitfires to Akron to figure out what they could do regarding fuel. The Spitfires arrived back in Britain not long after. Someone asked how the Americans had gotten the planes back so fast. The American said, "We flew them here from Akron." That was a demonstration. The increased fuel capacity pissed us off, because then the RAF decided we pilots were better suited to ground attack.

What was your closest call?

Several times I thought I'd had it. Once I came down and saw this gun post, which I was nowhere near. I put my nose down ever farther and as I went over, I saw these 40 mm guns going Puu Puu Puu. Then I heard the shells go off, but my wing must have gone through as the German cannon recycled. Fortunately, I got out of that one. At times your prop isn't six inches off the ground.

Another time in March 1945, I was on dusk patrol over the Elbe River. I could see this convoy starting to move, so I went down on the lead truck. I told the second section to hit the tail end of the convoy. I thought it routine. I was at 800 feet, going about 420 miles per hour indicated and had two 20 mm cannons and four 50 mm machine guns. The air was stable as I caught the truck. I pressed the trigger and suddenly a huge white ball burst out and lit up the whole countryside. The convoy just blew right up. I was so low that I couldn't do much of anything. I just shut my eyes and went right through the burst. I got a terrific jar but came out the other side. I must have just passed the real burst of energy as it exploded and then went up to around 1,500 feet. I thanked God for that Spitfire. It was a sturdy plane.

Near the Elbe another time, I looked off in the distance and saw three German staff cars with German flags flying on the fenders. I thought, "You arrogant bastards." I knew I couldn't attack right then, since I needed to get trimmed right—get the gravity balls centered, so I wouldn't slip or skid. I watched to see where the cars went in the town. In an instant, I saw them swing around and disappear into a garage and the garage door closed. I told the rest of the guys—I was squadron commander—I said, "Give me a little time and make sure you watch exactly where I am placing my bullets. I saw three German staff cars go in there. Let's give them a reception." I dropped down and went right down the street and poured a load into that garage door. We had about 18 seconds of ammo, and I gave them about a five-second burst before I had to break off. Then the other guys came down and peppered the place. I always figured it was a German command office and I've often wondered what they thought when all this shit was coming in. I was charmed. I was only hit three or four times with flak, and it went through the skin of the airplane and out the other side.

Do you remember losing anyone in particular?

No, but you felt sorry for everybody. Every two weeks we used to go to the Brookwood Cemetery and see where our buddies were buried, have a little service for them, and then come back. When you consider that I did so much ground attack, it's remarkable that I am still alive. We went straight down the gun barrels. How the hell any of us got through the war, I don't know. They especially tried to kill us—the leaders.

We did rail interdiction in the Ruhr. Bomber command would hit the railroad centers that connected the marshaling yards. We became expert at dropping those bombs. We would cut the tracks in maybe three places. It could take a week to fix what we did in five minutes. Over the course of the war, based on my camera footage, I got twelve locomotives. I once got six locomotives in one day.

There was this little fellow named Frank, an intelligence officer. When he would come over with a clipboard after we landed from a sortie, we knew we were in trouble. He would say, "Group, just sent word you're going to do low-level interdiction in the Ruhr." The Ruhr to us meant low-level bombing and straffing. In that area the map was solid red, which meant a dense concentration of anti-aircraft fire. This time Johnnie and I had some scotch to fortify us for the mission. We knew we would probably lose a couple of guys. In the briefing Johnny had said, "If anything happens to me, Squadron Leader Browne will take over." That night one of our fliers went to the padre concerned about our drinking. He said, "Padre, I think that commander Johnny Johnson and Squadron Leader Browne are too intoxicated to fly." The padre put his arm around the guy and said, "Son, you stick to those two guys and you'll finish the tour."

Any aerial battles?

A couple. Most of the time I did top cover for Johnson. One memorable time, I was with Johnny when he took two squadrons into Eindhoven, Holland. He said, "Danny, I want you to take off and be at 39,000 feet and loiter." Eindhoven was the deepest penetration in 1943. You'd hear the fight going on, then I heard, "Danny, are you there?"

I'd reply, "Roger."

He'd say, "Okay, what are your angels? Are you making smoke? What's your course?"

I said, "I'm steering 25 degrees."

He said, "Okay, I'll be going right under you in about five minutes. Keep up there and drop on those bastards." Endearing terms. I could see him coming and a lot of shooting still going on. He had the squadron pulled tight together and they went under me by about a hundred feet. I immediately turned and broke right and went down. The Germans all turned and went down. They did not want to stay up there and fight with a Spitfire, because they knew the advantage of that Merlin 61 engine.

That makes it hard to make aerial kills if the enemy won't fight you.

That's right. We used to do what we called "a ranger." One by one we would do a turn around the Eiffel Tower. The French would all wave at us. It was fun to come diving out of the sky and then go around the tower.

One time Johnny got caught under a pattern of lethal density. There were a bunch of German airfields south of the Seine River. We would swing out and try to catch somebody. This time Johnny was right on the deck. And he got caught. The Germans put a sheet of fire around him that was solid red—incredible density. They probably thought they had him. I guess he thought they had him. I was up top for cover. I said, "What the fuck are you doing?" He said, "Go fuck yourself." At that point he went right down below the poplar trees, so the Germans couldn't shoot at him. Here he

317

was coming down the Champs Elysee. I said, "There's a big statue up ahead. You better get your ass out of there." Then I saw the Spitfire of his rising straight up, smoke coming out of the exhaust stacks. A close call.

You also flew at Normandy for the RAF.

Yes, Air Marshall Johnson was ordered to form an elite fighter wing to cover the beaches of Normandy. He asked me to be in command of one of the squadrons. We learned the date of invasion 48 hours in advance, so we had some time for planning. Our wing arrived over the beaches at h-hour minus 30, just as the boats were launching off the armada. I thought, "What a thing! Here I am in front stage center of the greatest epic that's ever occurred." Below, there were 6,000 to 7,000 boats, all kinds of planes diving in there, the navy shelling.

We were instructed to provide air cover to prevent German aircraft from coming in. The ceiling was low. We were up at 1,800 feet flying back and forth. I was in the Eighty-Third Group of the Second Tactical Air Force. The American fliers had gone inland in an effort to keep the Germans planes on the ground. We had all sorts of things to know. We were briefed every morning on where the troops were and how far they had gotten. We knew where the ships were that were coming in on the channels and we provided cover. When we were told there was a strong point, we took the strong point out. Then we'd range far afield, attacking targets of opportunity.

Did anybody shoot at you?

Nobody shot that day. But we learned not to go near any boats. If you came close to a boat, somebody shot at you.

Allied boats?

Yes. I was shot at a dozen times by Allied boats. Don't forget, those fellows down there were just as scared as anyone could be. I think they might have been given orders if a plane came close, not to let it identify itself, just kill it.

The Americans were stalled on the beach at Normandy, so at one point someone in the Eighty-Third Group called the Americans and said, "Is there anything we can do to help you?" There was a long pause that lasted maybe four or five minutes. Then the answer came back, "When we want help, we will ask for it."

My friend Jimmy Johnson told me that story. It was unfortunate because we had flown over the coast at Normandy scores of times and could have gone into the cliffs and poured our ammo into those slits that were maybe 14 feet high—where the Germans controlled the guns. A bullet would have ricocheted around in there and killed people.

One day while patrolling over Normandy, it was quiet so I got permission to range down south. I went way down to Nantes on the Loire River. Suddenly, I spotted about 50 of these giant German howitzers coming north on the highway to Nantes. I climbed back up to about 12,000 or 14,000 feet and decided I'd better break radio silence. I notified the Eight-Third Group of what I'd seen. Someone said, "Roger," then chopped me right off the air. Later, our fliers came down and took care of the howitzers.

I had already flown 175 sorties before D-day, crossing the English Channel. We were only supposed to do 50, then take a rest. But I never was interested in a rest. I just kept on going. One day the group captain said, "Damn it Browne, you're going to go home and take a break." I said, "Look, I'm an American. I came over here to help you. I want to be in the invasion." So he said, "All right, you can stay for the invasion." Then, later, on June 30, he said, "Get your ass out of this damn place, or I'm going to send you home in chains." I went down to the beach and caught an American ship and had treats like ice cream and fresh eggs. It was unbelievable. Then I went home on the Queen Mary.

Later, I was in a movie theater in Fort Myers, Florida when I saw my old squadron. They were over in Arnhem and Nijmegen. My guys were right up there on the screen! Immediately, I went out and called the Air Ministry in Ottawa and told them who I was. They identified me quickly, then said, "What do you want?"

I said, "I want to go back to England."

They said, "You want to do what? Are you crazy?"

The Air Ministry called me back and asked if I could be in New York the next day. "If you can, your papers will be ready there."

I caught a plane out of Tampa and got to New York and went back across on the *Queen Elizabeth*.

That was 1944. When I returned I got command of another fighter squadron—421st Squadron. Later, during the Battle of the Bulge, the weather was bad so we couldn't fly. Finally though, when the weather lifted, we caught the Germans pulling out of the woods. I'm telling you we tore the shit out of them. Of course, the Battle of the Bulge was Hitler's last gasp.

Ever feel any mixed pride? After all, you were an American flying for the RAF.

I was an American, I had Canada on my shoulders. Yet the very first American troops that came over were slovenly, untrained. The British said, "So this is the vaunted American Army?" Then Truman formed the Truman Committee and tightened up discipline and things changed. The military police would haul a drunk off. Discipline was different. One day I was in the RAF Club near Buckingham Palace. I heard something and went outside and here came the Eighty-Second or Eighty-First Airborne marching down Piccadilly. My throat just swelled up with pride, because each one of those guys was going full-tilt, their heels hitting the pavement in unison, their guns all the same elevation. At the time the British were stunned. Even greater than that, the next day or so I saw this majestic formation and heard this enormous roar and the ground shook. It was a thousand B-17s passing over London, heading down the Thames to attack targets in Europe. You just can't imagine it today. After that, the Brits knew what the Americans had. That's one of the moments I can still visualize.

How would you like to be remembered?

Johnny Johnson said he was proud of being part of the forces that defeated the forces of evil. I felt the same way. I felt like a little tiny person until the Invasion at Normandy.

George Tweedy during World War II.

GEORGE TWEEDY
Photographing the War

George Tweedy was in college at San Diego State, taking a pre-med course, when he ran into a friend with whom he had attended school and played football while attending Hoover High School in San Diego. The friend was now an Air Corps meteorologist. He said to George, "You ought to come up here and get in the Army Air Corps." George's friend took him in to see his first sergeant. George explains, "I guess the first sergeant thought I was all right, because he said that one of his men was being discharged in about three weeks, and he said he thought he could re-enlist me directly into the squadron." The military had a 200 name waiting list, which included a lot of one and two-year college people who wanted to join the Army Air Corps. Still, George got a call about four weeks later. First, he had to gain a discharge from the National Guard, which he did. Then he enlisted directly into the squadron, saying "I do" at about 9 o'clock in the morning. At noon he was on guard. The date was March 16, 1936. A year later, he was transferred to the Sixth Photo Lab, Second Observation Squadron, Nichols Field, Philippines, then to the Eighty-second Observation Squadron as an aerial photographer. In 1939, he attended basic navigation and Air Corps fundamentals, then returned to the Eighty-second Observational Squadron, then to the Thirty-fifth Pursuit Group for assignment to the Eighteenth Pursuit Squadron. In January 1941, he was transferred to the Second Photo Mapping Squadron, in Alaska. In 1942, he was mapping in Central and South America. After a stint at Talara, Peru, at the U.S. Army Air Corps Patrol

Base, he was ordered to return to the U.S. because inspections revealed major fatigue cracks in tail assemblies of all three aircraft. During this time he and the other crew were required to wear parachutes at all times when in the air. In October 1943, George was assigned as commanding officer in charge of 252 men and four officers for transport to Britain. A month later, he joined the 386th Bomb Group of the Ninth Air Force as group photo officer. He was assigned in 1944 to the 409th Bomb Group, again as group photo officer. The following year he returned to the United States and served with the Twelfth Photo Reconnaissance Squadron. Over the next 16 years, George served in various positions from counter intelligence to photography, retiring from the military in 1961 as a major. Born in Mena, Arkansas in 1915, George today makes his home in Eastern Washington, near Spokane, where he first soloed in a power aircraft.

Tell me about your solo.

I soloed in 1942 at Felts Field in Spokane. I had soloed in a glider while I was in high school—a secondary type. I flew the first time in 1922, over at Rockwell Field, which was on North Island in San Diego Bay—a part of Coronado Island. One of our neighbors, Louis Gregg, was a lieutenant and instructor pilot during World War I. In the demobilization after the war, the military kept him on as a civilian. Louis flew, but he never learned to drive an automobile. He didn't have an automobile. Once in awhile on Saturday, he had to do some business at Rockwell Field, so Dad would take him to do that. In exchange, he would take Dad up for a short flight with the excuse that it was a maintenance flight. This one Saturday I was with Dad and when we got over there and Louis had finished his business, he said, "Do you want to go up for a little while, Jim?"

And Dad said, "What are you going to do with Melvin, in the back seat here?"

Louis said, "You can hold him on your lap." So that was my first time in an airplane. It was a DH-4 DeHaviland with a big, WWI-type Liberty 12-cylinder engine.

What else do you remember of that?

I remember sitting in my dad's lap. I didn't have a pair of goggles. The air was coming around and hitting me in the face. We were in the back seat, with an open cockpit and all that.

Were you frightened?

No. Oh, I never was frightened until my first mission over France and Germany when I saw all that flak come up alongside of me. I said, "What in the hell am I doing in this airplane?" I was flying with the 386th Bomb Group in B-26s, as an aerial photo officer. I wasn't on flight status. I had a K17 camera, which is a big 7-by-9 plate-size aerial camera with a 200 foot magazine, hand-held. I tucked it up tight against me. I had a flak vest on, and I was sitting on one. That was quite an experience. We went down to the western portion of France, and you would think you could walk on that flak. I wasn't scared, exactly. I was too crazy to be scared. The funny thing was that I didn't have to be on that mission. I didn't ask where we were going, I just went over and got in the plane. I was flying a number-two plane of the first box. It was quite an experience. I did four missions.

Then the 409th Bomb Group, an A-20 type group, arrived and was assigned up north to Saffron Walden, up toward Cambridge, England. One day a photo officer there, who was flying in light bombardment aircraft, went on a mission. On takeoff, a P-51 went slashing through the formation and hit the box leader, and took them all to the ground and killed them all. The bombs didn't explode at first. The plane caught fire and when an English woman came running out to help, the bombs exploded and killed her. After that, they were having problems with photo coverage. Soon I was asked if I wanted to go to the 409th to assist in good photo coverage; I said I would. Of course, that was just a nice way of them saying, "You will go anyway."

The first thing I did was to report to the group commander. He said, "I'm glad to see you here." Then he added, "No more flying. I see your records. You've been flying but you're not going to fly any more in this outfit because we've already lost one photo officer." So that stopped my flying. In total, we had 21 men in the photo department, including the lab chief and me. We sent out combat camera teams and always had at least one man on a flight. I had five of the photo men on flight status. Today only one of those five is still alive. He is Hank Currin in North Carolina.

What was the toughest thing about doing aerial photography?

In combat you had to plan what you were going to do, because the minute you dropped those bombs the bomb bay doors would close, so you had to rack the camera around and get out of there fast. The reason for a photographer was in case coverage with the automatic, mounted camera didn't work. Then he could do the job.

When I got to the base, maintenance (electrical) personnel would run an electrical line up to the pilot's compartment. Right alongside of his throttle quadrant stood a toggle switch that operated the camera. A lot of times, because the pilot wanted to get the devil out of there, he'd forget to turn the switch on and wouldn't get any photo coverage. I went over to the Eighth Air Force at Burtenwood Repair Depot and got some pressure-operated switches, which were put in. That worked fairly well, except that when you had it set for 12,000 feet and the weather forced you to go a little lower—maybe to 10,000 feet, there were problems. Flying lower might result in more ground space between exposures and possible missed bomb strikes. On the other hand, the higher you flew, the less time, or interval between film exposures. At briefing, the bombing altitude was listed on the field order, so the camera intervalometers were set for that altitude.

Did you ever send a photographer out to fly a mission who got killed?

No, I didn't, but there were close calls. One day an A-20 was all prepared and loaded, sitting on the hard stand ready to go with the bomb bay doors open. The plane had four 500-pound GPs in the bomb bay and two 250-pound GPs on each wing tip. A young fellow named Gordon McMahon, who had worked for Eastman Kodak before the war and was now in our unit, had just installed a camera in the A-20. Everything was ready, so Mac asked the crew chief, "Is it clear that I can turn the master switch on?" The crew chief checked everything and said, "You can turn the master switch on." Mac reached over and turned on the switch. As soon as he did we heard thud, thud, thud, thud. It was the bombs releasing. They came right out and hit the hard stand underneath the plane. Mac made one gigantic leap out of the cockpit, landed on the wing, then jumped to the ground. The last thing we knew he was about a hundred yards away, running down the flight line. Do you know that it took two years for him to stop stuttering? That is a fact. Oh, we kidded him later on, even after the war was over. We would have our reunions and we'd say, "It's nice to see you, Mac. You don't stutter any more." McMahon is deceased now.

What exactly happened?

It was a short circuit. The electricians checked it, but somehow there was a short circuit. So when you turned the master switch on, it automatically energized the bomb release, and it dropped the bombs.

327

But none of them went off?

No. The nose and the tail end have a fuse in each one, and they have a spinner on it. That spinner starts going as soon as the bomb hits the air outside of the bomb bay. As soon as that spinner spins off, the bomb is alive. You'd have to get rid of the British bombs by dropping them with the safe wires still installed. And they'd blow every time. Even dropped safe, we killed more fish in the English Channel. The bombs were loaded with RDX, a very sensitive explosive.

What photograph are you most proud of?

I don't know. I started flying over at March Field. I went to the line and started crewing a P-12 Boeing fighter. We had two of these fighters there. The others were the P-26 Boeing. It had a high camel's back behind the pilot. One time I wanted to get a ride in this B-10B that belonged to the base. They were going to go up to Sacramento Air Depot. So I rode along in the "meat can," which was named that because if you cracked up in the nose, you were meat. The plane had a single .50 caliber machine gun in a turret-like location, which you had to swing around manually to shoot. Anyway, coming in, the plane blew a tire on touch down. I was tossed back through that canvas curtain into the bomb bay. I was in the hospital overnight. Luckily, it didn't hurt me too bad.

When the Seventy-third Attack Squadron got their A-17s, we did maneuvers out at Dry Lake. We would do gunnery. There were P-26s from the Second Pursuit up at Michigan Field. We were flying out of the county airport in Merced and made a morning attack. We were having a dogfight with a P-26. In the A-17s, located in between the pilot and the gunner, you had a compartment where there were 20 individual chutes that you could put 30-pound anti-personnel bombs in. On the wing tips were tanks that could carry different types of gas. The pilot could drop those. Anyway, one day several of us sneaked in there just when everybody was having breakfast and made the attack. General Westover and Hap Arnold were there and they got tear gassed by this other plane. After that, one of the planes went down. I don't know the reason, but it had a forced landing on a nearby dry lake. All of the planes were loaded with imitation gas (limewater), but what happened was that someone accidentally put tear gas in one tank. The military police brought the pilot back and he and his gunner did KP for the officers and the enlisted men for the rest of the time.

On December 14, 1937, I think it was, the USS *Panay*, a United States Navy boat was sunk by the Japanese fighters. We had two or three of these flat-bottomed riverboats there in Chinese waters on the Yangtze River, one of which was attacked. An international newsreel photographer, Norman Alley, managed to use his camera and photograph the Japanese planes. The water was so shallow, so that most of the upper part of the ship was still out of the water when it was sunk. Anyway, Alley got to the Philippines, where he delivered the film to the photo department at Nichols Field. There, staff sergeants Woody Wilson, Taylor Ford and I helped process it, and make a negative and a hostage print. The next day we got that film on the Pan Am Clipper for the U.S. We made the hostage print, because if word got out that the attack had been covered by photography, people feared that the Japanese might attack the Clipper. Fortunately, the film arrived safely in the States. But we thought we were going to be at war right then.

So finally, tell me about how you got into World War II?

I was mapping at the beginning of WWII. First, we were mapping the proposed location of the Alcan Highway before it was built in 1941. We finished up there in 1942. We would go into Fort Nelson where we had to tie the planes down because of high winds. We were flying A-29 Lockheed Hudsons and in 1942 switched to Beechcraft F-2s. We operated at 20,000 feet, doing aerial photography and had three cameras and each took a 20 mile strip. Once you took a picture, you put them together. Then you had it from the horizon to the horizon—right straight across as you flew. We got a lot of distortion on the wing prints, but you still needed to use them for control. Then the photo was put into a three-dimension situation. An engineer in the Twenty-ninth Army Engineers in Portland would figure contours and all that.

After World War II started, we worked in northern Canada all the way up to the Arctic Ocean and over in Alaska. At the time we had no maps of that country at all. They had mapped a little strip going from Great Falls right to Edmonton to Dawson Creek and over to Fort Nelson, Lower Post, Watson Lake and White Horse, but it was just a very narrow strip. The rest of the region was yellow, for unexplored territory. Between Fort Nelson and Lower Post there was a lake called Wolf Lake and another called Wolf Junior. The two places were only supposed to be a short distance off of the flag route. We discovered one was about 70 miles and another was about 100 miles north of that. That's how far off the map people were.

Why was that?

Back then they made maps by the plain table method. The maps were drawn by hand. Someone would get on a hill and look out and start sketching. Then you get this trapper who'd come along and he'd say, "Ah, there's a lake up here somewhere." The mapmaker would say, "Can you show me where it is on this sketch?" and he'd say, "Oh, it's about here." Obviously, when the map is about 100 miles off, one can get lost very easily.

Any problems flying up there?

No, except that living conditions were bad. We had C-rations and no baths. We had to make our own coffee on a one-man stove. We mapped during the summer in northern Canada and the winter in South America . . .in Peru and Bolivia, specifically to establish the lines between the two countries. We mapped the area, but so much of the time we couldn't do any flying because of clouds—especially at 20,000 feet. We were staying in Talara, Peru, where the U.S. Army Air Corps had a patrol base. The military was flying a lot of sub patrol out of there. At the time, Chile had not broken relations with the Axis. They had more Germans there than you could shake a stick at. Chile was using German aircraft, including Folkers, and the pilots were wearing German-type uniforms and helmets. When we had to refuel, the rules said that we couldn't leave our airplane and go to town. If we went into Santiago, we had to go in civilian clothes. If we were in uniform, we would be interned.

I was a master sergeant and came back from South America in May 1943. When I arrived home, I found a letter for me in the Felts Field mailbox. The envelope was a post-office envelope and had more marks on it, indicating it had been there awhile and handled a lot. Inside of the first envelope was a War Department envelope. I opened it up. It said, "You have been assigned a commission number and you will immediately notify so-and-so at Gravely Point, Maryland, within 15 days where you'll go on active duty as a commissioned officer." So I thought, okay. My C.O. in the Second Mapping Squadron, Colonel Brown, had been after me for months to go to OCS [Officer Command School]. Every time he'd see me he'd say, "George, are you going to OCS?" and I'd say, "No, Sir. I'm not going to go play soldier. To heck with it." But then the military gave me a commission. One day I was a master sergeant, making $116 a month and getting my uniforms for free, and the next day I find myself a second lieutenant, making $120 a month and I had to buy my uniforms [laughs].

That was barely break-even?

Yeah. Army regulations decreed you could not serve in the organization as an officer where you served as an enlisted man. I was commissioned the June 1, but stayed until about July 8 or 9 when I was assigned as base photo officer at Walla Walla Air Force Base. I stayed there until October and I received orders to take over as commanding officer of a provisional squadron of 250 men and four officers being sent to England as replacements.

Our four officers were brand new. They had attended Yale Communications School and didn't know their what-cha-ma-call-it from a hole in the ground. All they knew was radio. I had 252 men and I think another four supply sergeants. I told the supply sergeants what we had to get done and what equipment we needed when we got to Camp Miles Standish in Massachusetts. So one of the supply sergeants—a tech sergeant, named Collier, said, "What do you need?" I said, "I want typewriters because we've got to go through requisitions to get as much clothing and everything else here." I looked at Collier and thought he must be a pretty good scrounger from the way he acted. I said, "How about a jeep, Collier? We need transportation." Two hours later I had a jeep. And when we left Walla Walla, I put it right on the train with us.

Where did he get the jeep?

I didn't ask him. You don't ask a man where he scrounges [laughs].

I always took care of my men, though. When we had POM—preparation for movement—completed, the military gave me permission to give the men that lived on the western side of Mississippi five-day leaves and anybody on the eastern side three-day passes. That balanced it out. My men needed to get aircraft travel priorities so they went into the travel department in Hyannisport. I had all the forms made out for them to get A-1 priority to fly. At the time I noticed a couple of men standing around. I didn't know who they were. Then one of them came over to me and said, "Lieutenant, we're stymied here. We got leave orders but we can't get any aircraft travel out of here." I said, "Where are your officers?" They said, "They don't want to talk to us. They've got their other problems." I thought for a minute and realized there always was a public stenographer in places like this. I looked around and there one was just sitting there by her typewriter. I said to the lady, "Do you know how to make travel priority vouchers?" She said, "Oh, yes." I told her I had five of them made up for priority. I

331

said, "Use their names and I'll sign it and put me down as commander." The vouchers did not say who I was commanding. I signed and that was that.

When the war was over, we were at Lyon, France. We got word that we were going to go to Camp Lucky Strike and stage there for return to the States. But first we had to take all of our equipment, all of our cameras, all of the generators and everything and get them in first class shape. We had three jeeps and a one-ton that had to be taken over for maintenance. All of this stuff was going to be given to the French. That didn't go over very well, because we didn't like the French. I still don't like the French, but they made wonderful bread. The French stole us blind over there. The U.S. Army Transportation Corps had a pipeline coming from Cherbourg all the way up to Paris, and the French would drill hoses and get gasoline. Pipeline crews would chase them out and plug it, but before we could get down the road a half a mile, they'd be drilling more holes. All of the area had been German occupied area; so most likely the French were so used to stealing from them that they just carried on the practice.

I had five Speed Graphics cameras there—as well as the cameras of the K-21, K-24, and K-17 types. I said to my lab chief, "Sergeant, I'm going to go up to headquarters." I had the Speed Graphic cameras lying there and I said, "I don't expect to see them when I come back." He said, "Okay, Sir." Sure enough, when I came back a couple of hours later, the cameras were not there. I didn't see them again. When we got to Antwerp to go aboard a liberty ship, I was certifying officer in charge of making sure that no illegal equipment came aboard with the troops. You know I had to shut my eyes all the time. I would rather some of those men have those cameras than the French. I am safe, though, for there's a statute of limitation on that now [laughs].

Victory in Europe, VE night, was the most dangerous night of the war. I normally stayed in a small officer's tent in the back of the film lab; however, VE night was the only night that I spent in a slit trench, because that night the men went wild firing ammunition. We had .50 caliber machine guns all around the airfield for defense. They fired all of them. At one point, a plane was coming back from England and they darn near shot them out of the sky. Oh, they were just going crazy. Every flare that they had in those ships they shot. The next morning I had two holes in my little officer's tent.

They weren't intentional?

No, no, they were just shooting. Remember when you're shooting something up, it's got to come down. It still makes a hole coming down. That was the most dangerous night.

Did you fly the plane sometimes?

I assisted. When Colonel Brown assigned me to Aircraft Navigation while I was a staff sergeant, I completed a course in basic aircraft navigation. As a crew we had nine planes—three flights of Lockheed Hudsons. About that time we received eight navigators right out of school. The colonel called me into his office and said, "George, I am going to take you out of Photo and put you on a crew as a navigator because we are short a navigator. Don't let your pilot get lost." So I did photo mapping navigation up in the glass nose, but sometimes I'd sit beside the pilot in the cockpit. Lockheed Hudsons only carried one pilot, who sat in the left seat. The navigator sat in the right seat, commonly called "the idiot seat." The navigator assisted the pilot by operating the flaps and landing gear. When the pilot had to relieve himself, I would hold the aircraft on a straight and narrow course. Also, I would hold onto the throttles if it was bumpy taking off. For example, the pilot would put his hand on the throttles, and I would block his hand so it could not regress back. Overall, though, I got a few hours in flying time.

Tell me about the Philippine experience.

It was a different lifestyle. You didn't work in the afternoons. You went to work at 6:45 A.M. First you got up in the morning. First call 5:50 A.M. Reveille sounded at 6:00 A.M. You always slept in open-air barracks. No such thing as rooms. You had big open bays. You had your wall locker behind, and at the end of your bunk, you had a footlocker on a stand and then the shoes underneath. And you would have a mosquito bar, because you had mosquitoes there. The bunk boy took care of your bed. You sent your clothes out to the laundry by him. He brought them in, made sure they were stamped with your serial number and put away in your footlocker ready for inspection. He knew more about the inspection order because he'd been doing it for years. Those jobs passed on from father to son. Also, at the barbershop you could get a hair cut for ten centavos, which was five cents American and five centavos for a shave. The barber was probably 45 years old. His father had been barber there back in World War I. You didn't have to do anything, including shining your shoes. A shoeshine boy took care of that. You did make sure that if you wore a pair of shoes one morning that in the afternoon you would wear a different pair, because you'd get mold in that moist climate.

What was your biggest adventure over there?

You were allowed once a year two weeks TDY [temporary duty] to visit points of military interest, as long as you had a corporal and no more than five of you went at once. The military would give you a reconnaissance car and your gas and all your food and you'd all go over to Luzon. You had to write a report when you came back, which included where you went, the condition of the road, the bridges, the width of the bridges, what their construction was, etc. I went on trips for two years, and we went places where some of the natives had never seen an automobile. During that time, the natives had carts drawn by tiny horses. The first vehicle we had was practically a brand new Chevrolet. It had the window space but no windows. We pulled along a trailer with a 50 gallon drum of gasoline on it, in case we had problems finding gas. At one time, we went on a ferry, made completely of bamboo lashed together. We pushed that car on it and took it right across the river.

334

Was there ever any time you were really pressured to get a picture out?

We did that all the time over in Europe during World War II because all strike photos had real important targets.

Had they hit the target?

It would be a hot mission. We may have lost a couple of planes. They would want to go back and hit the target again if the mission failed to destroy the target. They needed the photos, so they could find out if the mission had been successful. So the film was processed and printed and then the photo interpreters examined the prints and did a bomb damage assessment (BDA) to prove whether the target was destroyed or not.

Any regrets?

No, I have no regrets. Think what you're going to do and you won't have any regrets later on. That's about the best philosophy I can give. I might have done things differently if I could have figured a way.

Have photographers been given the credit for WWII duty that they deserve?

Run-of-the-mill photo men received very little credit for the important work they accomplished. Photographers of the news media type received the publicity and credit, because they were in the public eye. Most of my men didn't want credit. They just wanted the war to get over so they could go home.

335

WILLIAM S. BARKSDALE
Hump Pilot

Colonel William S. Barksdale, Jr., was a flier's flier. As commander of the 130th Air Base Unit at Jorhat, India, he oversaw the Hump Operation, flying the snowcapped Himalayas in India, Burma, and China before moving to Calcutta to continue the operation there. Barksdale endeared himself to his men by flying the Hump himself, not just administering.

After the Second World War while stationed at Washington International Airport, he worked with the Special Flying Unit that flew the moguls of government and handled the president's airplane. He was commander of the unit and met President Truman and flew actor Spencer Tracy across the country once for a speaking engagement. Then he went to Wright-Patterson for two years of technical training—primarily physics and mathematics, and worked for the Atomic Energy Commission.

In 1955, General Tunner, Colonel Barksdale's old boss from the Hump pilot days, brought him to Europe where he operated a base of airplanes in France, hauling cargo to supply the many United States bases in France, Germany, and the Mediterranean. Later he became head of the Air Force Photographic and Charting Unit in Orlando. On his wall is a painting on velvet that the Vietnam group presented to him. It reads: "Every man a tiger," and shows a dowdy, pussycat of a tiger, with the caption underneath: "Presented to the number one tiger of them all by the Six-hundredth Photo Squadron."

This reddish-haired, friendly, slightly round man is a native of Charlotte County, Virginia, which he explains "is 700 miles southeast of Chicago."

He told me he always wanted to be a pilot. "Why, I don't know," he said. "Kids grab onto things."

He went to work out of Virginia Tech in a final assembly line in Linden, New Jersey, building Pontiacs and Oldsmobiles, and when they laid off everyone to get ready for the new models, he left and never went back. He went instead to the United States Air Force Flying School, Randolph Field, San Antonio, Texas.

Did you ever see Japanese Zeros across the Hump?

Well, you know Irv, I've often wondered about that. The first trip up over there—of course, I was biting the parachute the whole time—we did see some planes that the guy said were Zeros. But I have no way of knowing if they were or not, because by the time that I arrived over there, Stillwell and company and the Flying Tigers had done their job very well. Most of the Zeros were gone from Burma. Now I'm talking about from June 1944 on, you see. I was actually in the Hump Operation in the Assam valley for a year, then went down to the Hump Operations in Calcutta, where General Tunner had his headquarters.

What was General Tunner like?

General Tunner was a great guy and a real driver—he believed in doing things. He kept cracking on them. I suppose the most demonstrative thing that he did, while over there, took place along toward the end of the operation—before the war was over in September, I believe, in Europe. He decided to have a drive—a one day, 24 hour drive to see how much he could deliver. It was a major effort by all of his Assam bases and other bases in India—flying across the Himalayas into places in China. It was a plan to fly as much as you could—not dropping any safety standards whatsoever, and everybody got into this thing. You'd see an airplane roll up in China and pull off to the ramp. The fliers didn't just move away and let the crews based there unload the plane—they helped get the stuff off the airplanes, went back and got another load. But that 24 hour period delivered 5,000 tons across the Himalayas in those airplanes. We were still flying a few Gooney Birds, but very few.

What other planes did you have?

At that time it was the Curtiss-Wright C-46. We had three wings of the cargo-version of the B-24s, called C-87s. I had a base of 50 of those, and two wings of the Douglas C-54. Anyway, but let me say, the 5,000 ton day was a great accomplishment in those days. Of course, by the time the Berlin Airlift came around, the airlift was dominated by C-54s and a few other types of airplanes.

Why did he put on this massive effort?

General Tunner was an originator—he was pushing air power and particularly the air-cargo side of the thing. He had come out of the Ferry Division, which delivered all the airplanes to the Allies in 1943 and 1944 and then went to India as boss of the Hump Operation.

What was the hardest thing about administering the Hump Operation?

I think the hardest part of it for me was keeping the troops motivated to fly the Hump. It wasn't a simple operation. At one time there was a rule that weather was not a factor—you went regardless of weather. And to maintain the morale of the troops until they had completed 75 or 100 missions—particularly after they got nearly there, you know. There was a tremendous urge to then be suddenly done with it—and out of this came some problems with morale.

What sort of things did you do to get them going—if it was needed?

I think the best thing I did was to do my share of flying. There'd been some who had been critical of past performances by some of the people in the administrative section. So I think that to fly my share of night missions and other missions—along with the gang— had more impact than practically anything that I did there. In fact, I remember one of the guys, who had been having some trouble, saying, "Well, finally, we got a commander that flies"—which meant a lot to me.

I think I did 30 or 35 missions across the Hump during the time I was commander of the base there. And then there were many trips within the command—inside of India.

What was your worst discipline situation?

The pilots who refused to fly the Hump were the worst thing. I'm not sure I want to talk about that, because it's one of those darn unpleasant things that's not supposed to happen, but it did, and the consequences were not good for the parties involved.

That wasn't that widespread, was it?

Mostly the guys were ready to go without any problem. Most of them were the greatest kids you can imagine—they were over there doing their job. They knew they were doing their share—absolutely no problem.

What difficulties did safety officers have over there?

Weather was the primary one. You know, we were getting pilots that had very little flying time—300-400 hours, which is a very marginal amount, particularly for the conditions.

China had very few lights. You know, flying over the United States you can see lights all the time, unless it's bad weather, but China had no such horizons, so the dangers at the Hump were often at the terminal in China—as well as the Hump itself. In both China and India the pilots coming in had no orientation. Unless you glued yourself to the instruments, you wouldn't be able to guarantee yourself you were going to make it. We lost an awful lot of pilots. In fact, I lost my operations officer in China.

Do you know what happened?

No, except that the weather was bad at the time—and 500 feet visibility was considered great, you know. But the details I don't remember. He was going to Ch'eng- 'tu.

What did you think when that happened? Did that set you back?

It sure did. He was one of my favorite guys. I had promoted him to the operations job in Jorhat, up in the Assam Valley, because he was one of my outstanding pilots. It made me think, "Well, this is no child's play. If this guy can't make it, some of these other guys with three hundred to four hundred hours were sure in an awful lot of trouble." Even though we spent an awful lot of time looking at the weather, forecasting the weather, there were still those incidents.

Did it ever get you really down?

No, it didn't. I never got the feeling—I can't explain it; I think I'm human—of despair. But it certainly would get you down, particularly if you went to see the scene of an accident, which I did every chance I had, because I wanted to write letters to the families.

I remember one of those things crashed off the end of the runway, and I got there in time to see this thing still burning, and the guys in it were cooked, literally cooked. How do you explain the feelings? I don't know. But I did write to the families, and they wrote back, and we corresponded for a short time. There's nothing that you can do about it, except do the best you can with the weather, the pilots and the equipment that you've got, and demand as tight a performance of all personnel as possible, especially including safety in flying and pilot training.

341

Had you ever heard of the Hump when you were assigned there? Did you know what it was?

Not very much. I was at Long Beach, flying airplanes all over to United States air bases and our Allies. Then I was assigned from Long Beach to Homestead Air Base to run the special air training school—Air Transport Pilots in the Air Transport Command. We gave them airline-type training there. Well, I'd been there for about six months when General Tunner, chief of the Ferrying Division assigned me to that cold place, Great Falls, Montana. There was a ferrying base up there. So anyway, I said, "Okay, boss man, when do you want me there?" He told me "ASAP," so I collected my family and started on the road to Great Falls, Montana. I told him I'd go by my home in Virginia and spend the night. When I got to my home, there was a message to call General Tunner, so I did. And when I did, he said, "Willy, where were you goin'?"

I said I was going to Great Falls. He said, "You're now going to India" [laughs]. Just like that!

He said, "Come by and see me. I want to see you tomorrow morning." I was out in the boondocks in Virginia, where my family lived, but I got there the next morning by plane. I think he gave me a week with my family.

Any stories about instrument flying over there?

There was a guy named Dick Morgan, a friend of mine. He was at the Ferrying Division out in Long beach the same time I was, and I remember hearing him say, in talking to General Tunner, "General, these guys are coming out of here—they haven't even 1,000 hours flying time." Well, that was amusing to me because we ended up with pilots flying bombers over England before the war was over with no more than 300 hours. But anyway, I was assigned to Jorhat Air Base up in the Assam Valley in India, and after I'd been there about six months, Dick Morgan, who was assigned to command a C-54 base over there, came up to my base for me to give him an orientation trip across the Hump. Well, this was the time of year when the monsoon season is approaching, and you get ferocious winds blowing east to west across the Hump. On the day Dick Morgan came up there, it was one of those days. We flew over, on an uneventful trip, on one of my C-87s with a load of cargo. On the way back to Jorhat, we ran into 100 mile-per-hour headwinds, so you could look down at the ground and not notice much apparent progress. We had taken on enough fuel and emergency reserve to get back—and we needed it. We had to take some special maneuvers into Jorhat to make sure we got on the ground with any reserve at all.

Dick was totally strange to the radios and the checkpoints and navigation schemes that we used at that time. It turned out that I had to change my course and let down between a range of mountains, trusting entirely on the radio signals. Sometimes the Japanese had been known to alter the direction of the radio beams, so as to run you into a mountain, but we didn't have much of a choice—we were totally in the soup at this time. I said, "Dick, I'm going to have to go over here and let down between these two ranges of mountains—I don't have the fuel reserves to go in over the base and do normal procedures." So Dick was sitting over there—biting his parachute the whole time. I would have been too. Dick had more flying time and fully appreciated the hazards. When we landed, he looked over at me with an ear-to-ear grin and said, "Willy, you fly a *fine* airplane!" Then we went off to the club for a good drink.

Any examples of problems resulting from limited training or inexperience?

The pilots were coming out of flying training with not as much experience as you would like. The military was pushing for more and more pilots. Sometimes, while at Long Beach, they'd arrive with only 100 hours total time, and we'd have to check them out in the types of planes we were delivering at the time.

The Lockheed Hudson was one of those types, and it had landing problems. Because it was relatively short, its directional stability after landing wasn't too good. So we had difficulty convincing the student pilots that it was absolutely essential to pounce on that rudder immediately on landing and maintain strict forward control or face the possibility of a fiery crash. One kid was a little nervous— he was probably a good kid for the situation he found himself in— but he had heard all these stories. So I took him up to convince him, among other things, that the Hudson was what we called "a rudder airplane," especially on landing.

343

Well, we went up to altitude, and I demonstrated the stall and how you could control it. I was sitting in the right-hand cockpit, and the guy I was checking was sitting on the left side in the pilot's seat. So, when I demonstrated a stall, I said, "Please observe that I'm using the ailerons almost not at all. I keep it level with the rudder. And when I do use the ailerons, I feed it in very slowly." I asked him if he understood. He said he did. So I said, "Okay, you've got the wheel now—go ahead and ease back on the throttle until it starts to stall, then bring it out." So what does he do—the exact opposite. As soon as he stalls, he throws the aileron way over, and the plane immediately went into a spin—just like that. So I grabbed the wheel and pushed it forward as quickly as I could, to gain speed, and recovered in nice time. But this was a good example of too little experience. The question might better be, "How did so many of them survive?"

Any communication problems—cultural problems—over there?

They hold the cow sacred in India and, as a consequence, they don't push them around much. Cows walk about the streets of Calcutta quite freely—and anywhere else they want to go. Well, they were running around my runway, and this can be very hazardous to an airplane. The airplane would kill them, but it would also kill the airplane, even be deadly too. So I got upset about it and called the local town chief and said, in effect, "Get your cows off my runway today or I'm going to start shootin' them at nightfall. You take your choice—but do it, because my airplanes are in serious danger." Man, that caused me more headaches than almost anything I did, because I was unaware at the time that they were sacred. I soon got a call from our headquarters in Calcutta that I would not, under any circumstances, shoot any cows. My reply was, "Wait a minute. What am I going to do about these cattle on the runway?" And he said, "I don't know what you're going to do, but that's your problem," and so went the war.

So what did you do?

The townspeople cooperated quite well is what happened. They were very upset at my attitude. I could have had a better approach, I'll admit. But the Indians did cooperate. And I can't remember very many instances after that a cow was on the runway, day or night.

I can remember an old mule I saw once that was hit by a Model-T Ford, and it knocked the radiator off that Model-T Ford, back against the windshield. The mule survived well with nary a scratch, just a slight limp for a day or two, but the Model-T never flew again [laughs].

Along toward the end of the war, when General Weidemeyer was given the job to begin a western attack on the Japanese, we were given the job of hauling 1,500 mules over the Hump to aid in land transport of his war supplies in China. That was the basic reason for the Hump Operation—to carry munitions, fuel, bombs, whatever, to all United States forces in China, including Chennault's Flying Tigers. The B-29s would fly from India, refuel, and continue to Japan or short of Japan, or bomb them in China—it was the western front.

But one of the things they figured they'd have to have over there to get through some of the roads of China were good ole Arkansas mules. The job, in a nutshell, was hauling fifteen hundred mules into China from Myitkyina—one of the pickup points. We flew these mules into Kunming, then flew them from there into Luliang in southern China, where they were picked up by the army forces and used.

These were flown over the Hump by Gooney Birds, the fond nickname for the old C-47s. We carried three or four mules per airplane. None of the planes were made for, or equipped for, carrying mules. So these Gooney Birds ended up in the salvage yard after the operation. There's no way you can keep a mule from relieving himself in the airplane. Urine and aluminum don't mix well. The uric acid ate right through the skin of the airplane.

345

Did you have any heroes over there?

Any time that a crew went across the Hump during the monsoon season—with unpredictable bad weather, high winds, and heavy rains—and came back and lived to tell the story, they were pretty much heroes—all of them.

Donald Hillman during World War II.

DONALD HILLMAN
An Amazing Escape

One afternoon, driving by Moffat Field a few miles south of Stanford University, Donald Hillman saw several Army Air Corps pursuit planes. When the pilot took a break from flying, Donald was there to chat with him. Later after graduation from college, he remembered the flyboys at Moffat and applied for both the navy and the army for flight training. The army responded first.

In October 1940, he was sworn in at McChord Field. A stop or so later, he was at Randolph Field for basic flight training, to Barksdale Field, for advanced, and to Craig Field in Selma, Alabama, which it turned out was still under construction. He was then sent to Elgin Field on the Gulf of Florida.

When his course was completed, he returned to Craig Field for graduation. At the graduation-time dance held in the Selma Country Club, he met a girl named Lloyd, whom he would later marry. Once while flying an AT-6 to the airfield in Tallahassee, home of then Florida State College for Women, Donald arranged to pick up Lloyd at the fringe of the airfield. He brought a flight suit, which she climbed into, and the two headed for Jacksonville. On the way, they ran into a navy pilot in an SNJ, who came alongside and rocked his wings, indicating a dogfight challenge. They played at dogfighting and when the navy pilot came alongside, Lloyd pulled off her helmet, revealing her long hair—all of this to the chagrin of the adversary. Luckily, Donald wasn't reported.

After graduation, he instructed at Craig, a valuable experience, he says, in furthering his flying skills and habits. Finally, in May 1943, he was assigned to Richmond, Virginia, as group operations officer in a newly activated fighter group. In early December, the group proceeded to Camp Kilmer, New Jersey, and boarded the *Queen Elizabeth* with fourteen thousand other troops and headed off to war. *Queen Elizabeth* zigzagged across the ocean, since it had no convoy depending as well on its 32-knot cruising speed.

Six days later, Hillman and the others disembarked in Gourock, Scotland, and boarded trains for their new base in Gosfield in East Anglia. Initially assigned to escort the Eighth Air Force, he would later fly with the Ninth Air Force, where he did dive-bombing and strafing. He became an ace in the war, shooting down five planes, damaging one, and destroying two on the ground. He was shot down October 7, 1944, but made a remarkable escape.

After the war, Colonel Hillman joined the pioneer jet fighter group, the First Fighter Group. He joined the Strategic Air Command in 1950 and retired in 1962 as a B-52 wing commander.

348

You flew 145 fighter bomber missions. That's a lot.

Yes. I think the average was around 75.

Did you start to get nervous at any point, fear your luck might have run out?

No, I really didn't. In fact, the day I was shot down, I was discussing that point with my ground executive, Lieutenant Colonel Clyde "Fearless" Fuller, an older fellow, who'd served in World War I. We were sitting outside the operations tent, and he said he thought I should quit flying combat, that I'd flown enough. He said that the odds were going against me. I said, on the contrary, that I felt each time I flew a mission I was more experienced and knew more how to conduct a mission. I told him I thought my odds were better each time I went. Four hours later this discussion would haunt me.

Describe a tough mission you took early on.

Many were difficult, but several stand out in my mind. On one mission I heard another squadron was in trouble with enemy aircraft, so I led my flight over in that direction. I spotted a Focke-Wulf 190 flying along low to the ground. I identified it as a long-nose 190, a later version that had a jumbo engine in it. It was a rather fast airplane. I proceeded to dive down on its tail, but I didn't get within close enough range. I followed it east and occasionally got off a burst, hoping I'd get lucky with a long shot, but to no avail. I had been concentrating on this 190 and broke the rule that you should be aware of what was going on around you. When I finally did look around, I saw three 109s queuing up and diving down on my tail from an off-angle, so I had to turn off the 190 and turn right into the 109s. That was all I could do. The group of us went 'round and 'round, three 109s and myself. By now everybody was flying right on the ground. I would close in on the last 109 and get a shot off. This went on for awhile. Finally, I got a good burst on their number three man and watched him burn and his canopy fly off. He couldn't bail out because of his close proximity to the ground. Then I tried to get number two. As I passed over the airdrome at Chartres, I spotted a Ju 52 below. I dipped my nose and sprayed the plane, but soon realized it was only a dummy. There was firing coming from below but nothing hit me. I managed to get a good shot at the number two man, and his plane began to smoke. He crashed in the woods not far from the airdrome. Then I looked around and noticed number one was gone. The group did well, destroying 13 enemy aircraft and losing only one. But that encounter was still a pretty close call for me.

Another big challenge?

The next toughest mission, probably just as tough, or tougher, was what we called an armed reconnaissance mission where we didn't have a particular target, but we just went out looking for targets of opportunity. On the mission itself, we didn't find anything particular, but suddenly I looked down and saw a German staff car, a sedan convertible with several people in it, cruising along, in occupied France. So I thought, "Well, the mission's about over. We'll have to return soon because of low fuel. Why not?" So I decided to drop my bomb on the staff car, which was headed towards a bridge. I dove down and released my bomb. I tried to time it so that the staff car was on the bridge, and it worked out right. I could see the car was destroyed. However, when I pulled up, I saw a whole bunch of large pine trees sticking out right up ahead of me on the hill. I pulled back as hard as I could on the stick, but I still hit the top of one of the trees. I was going up at a steep angle. The top of the tree—about six feet of it—stuck in my wing at midspan. My plane, a P-47, immediately rolled to the left due to the loss of lift and the extra drag. Then it went into a steep diving spiral. I put the ailerons hard over to correct but without effect. I saw the ground coming up on me fast. At the time I remember very clearly the thoughts that went through my mind. First, that it was a real stupid thing to do. I also thought that now I was going to find out what it was like to be killed, because it was obvious that I couldn't straighten the plane out. At the last moment of desperation, I kicked as hard as I could on the right rudder, because the ailerons weren't having any effect. Slowly, the left wing picked up, and then I could get the nose up, though I barely managed to clear the ground. When I got it straightened out, I was able to climb out a few feet. Although I still wasn't able to get much altitude, I took the long, slow flight back across the English Channel. The P-47 was a tough-built plane. The plane held on all right, and when I got back to the base, I still had the length of this French pine sticking in the wing.

Another time, based in Reims, I had a day off and decided to fly back to England to visit my brother who was a flight surgeon in a fighter group there. I was flying across the Channel to France to rejoin my group. As I crossed the Channel, I thought of all the missions we had flown out of East Anglia over this same route and how we were always at very high altitude, say 30,000 feet, because there was a lot of flak as we came upon the coast. Instead, this time I was flying low, heading into the coast near Amsterdam, and thinking this will be fun being able to see the sights. I hadn't been this low, going across the Dutch coast before. I was at 500 feet, looking around, and all of a sudden the sky filled up with intense light and medium flak. I pulled the plane off and avoided the flak, without getting hit. Still, I wondered why in the world I was getting shot at there. As soon as I landed at the base, I went to see an intelligence officer in this tent, and he gave me an explanation. He said that General Montgomery's troops had come up the coast, but that they bypassed several of the hotspots. Montgomery was in a hurry, and he left a few isolated places. Apparently, I flew across one of the places, and it was heavily defended. So I almost got shot down on my day off [laughs]. Actually, I was upset about that.

Any crazy stuff you guys pulled?

It was customary to give a pilot a two-ounce shot of whiskey—what we called sortie whiskey—after a mission, during the intelligence briefing. My squadron agreed we wouldn't do that, but would save it up for a big party one day, when we were all off operations. This occurred early in the game, before the invasion, and while we were escorting Eighth Air Force bombers at high altitude. Finally, one day an ops order came telling us we were off operations for 36 hours, and we could stand down. So we got all the sortie whiskey and proceeded to have a big bash. The guys really had a time. Finally, the party quieted down, and we all went to bed. We were living in Quonset huts in Gosfield over in East Anglia. To our surprise, the next morning the operations sergeant came along and shook me.

351

He said, "Major Hillman (I was major at the time), you've got a briefing at seven o'clock for a duel mission. First penetration. Then you'll come back and refuel and escort the fliers on withdrawal."

I said, "There's been some mistake. We have orders to stand down."

He said, "No, that's been changed."

So I got up and started thinking, "How could I get the 12 guys together that had the least to drink and were in the best shape?" I made my selection of the 12, and we took off and made our mission rendezvous.

We got up to 30,000 feet. We were on oxygen, and of course, the airplanes were not pressurized. It was cold. The guys were generally in pretty bad shape, but we stuck it out. We got back on the ground after escorting to the end of our fuel range. As soon as I, and several other pilots, had pulled our planes off the runway in a secluded place, we proceeded to lose our breakfasts. Then we had to pull ourselves together again and take off for our withdrawal mission.

One of our flight leaders, John Murphy, had been scheduled for temporary duty to a fighter group in Italy. He left that same morning by airlift. By the time he got there, he was experiencing severe stomach pains—besides a terrible hangover. He went to the station hospital where he spent the night. By morning he realized all his discomfort had come not from the booze, but from trying to top me in sit-ups.

Who was the biggest character you met over there?

Bob Coffee was senior to me. When I was squadron commander, he was the deputy group commander. Coffee was quite well qualified for the term "daredevil." He was a dashing, handsome guy and a very good pilot. But he was in the war for one purpose. That was to build up his record of kills. In fact, he would often jeopardize his wingman. During the war he lost a couple of them by his method of taking off by himself and just ignoring his wingman, who often wasn't a good enough pilot to stay with him.

On day, Bob got shot down on a strafing run on an airdrome in France. He crash-landed there in occupied France, but about six weeks later, he managed to get back through the lines with the help of the French Underground and rejoined our group. By then, I was deputy commander. Bob proceeded to take our new group commander out, and he almost lost him. Shortly after, he got back and started flying again (he'd done about five missions), and he ran into an overwhelming number of enemy airplanes. In the melee he got shot up, but he managed to get back to base. He came in to me, and his face was white and he was shaking. He said, "Don, don't ever schedule me to fly again. No matter what I say, don't put me on another mission." And he went home shortly thereafter. In 1948, he was elected to Congress from Pennsylvania, but was killed when he crashed a P-80 in Albuquerque.

Late in September 1944, I led a flight of 12 planes on a dive-bombing mission on a marshaling yard in Dusseldorf. We were stationed in Belgium and were east of the Rhine on a fighter sweep. One of the wingmen spotted a bunch of planes flying along. They were very distant. I called the controller. I asked him, "Do you have any enemy aircraft in that area?" He said, "No, they're all friendlies." I noticed they made it across the break in the overcast and knew that Dusseldorf was there. I knew if they were enemy aircraft, they'd get no flak; otherwise they would. I was still curious. We headed generally in that direction.

One of the sharp-eyed flight commanders said, "They're all Tiffies," which was what we called Typhoons. There was a group of Canadian Typhoons nearby, but I kept going. As I got closer, I recognized them as German planes—about 40 or more of them—109s and 190s. They were flying three abreast, separated in altitude by about 500 feet. I told everybody to drop their fuel tanks and said, "Let's go in on them." We were in a good position—above them and coming out of the sun. We apparently were not seen by the enemy. Still, the trouble was that I only had eight airplanes.

Group Commander Ray Stecker, a West Pointer and friend of mine, whom I would need, led another flight of four planes. By way of background, I had a standing bet with Colonel Stecker of 20,000 francs for each enemy aircraft destroyed. I owed him a lot of francs from playing plenty of gin rummy. So when I saw all these planes, I called Ray and told him what we'd spotted, and told him to come on down. At that time Ray's top cover flight was several thousand feet higher and he had not sighted the enemy.

The first enemy I picked up went into a diving left turn. I had too much speed to stay on his tail, so I pulled up with my wingman following and picked out another target. There were plenty there because 16 more joined in the fracas. The next 190 I chased, I stayed with. I took a deflection shot at 45 degrees, but hadn't led him enough. I pulled inside of his turn until he just disappeared under my nose cowling and let loose a long burst. I let up on the turn and could see him going down in flames. Suddenly, I saw the canopy flip off and the pilot bail out.

I called to Stecker and told him he owed me 20,000 francs. I heard the words, "Where are you, Red Leader?" I answered him, "North of Dusseldorf at 12,000 feet." I heard my number four man say that five FW 190s were taking turns firing on him and furthermore, that his engine was cutting out. I dove down, but couldn't find him. Above me 190s and 109s were tangling with our P-47s. The enemy tried to split-S toward the deck, right in the middle of Dusseldorf to draw us into heavy AA [Anti-Aircraft].

Reaching 10,000 feet with my wingman, I saw eight 109s circling just under the clouds at 15,000 feet. We firewalled the throttle, kicked in the water injection, and climbed to 15,000 feet to intercept. They never saw us. I shot one down, as did my wingman. I called Stecker. "You owe me twenty thousand more francs."

"You dog, where are you?" Stecker replied.

"South of the city at 5,000 feet," I responded.

We shot down 12 enemy planes during the mission and only lost one. And Stecker never arrived for the scrap. The 40,000 francs paid off my debt to him, but he has forever after accused me of giving him misleading information, so he couldn't get into the fight, (which clearly is not the case).

Let's talk about the flight where you were shot down.

It happened on a dive-bombing mission on a German fighter base near Cologne. After we bombed, we made a fighter sweep east of the Rhine River, where we'd experienced increased enemy fighter activity. In the dive-bombing we experienced some minor flak damage. Just after that, we saw two Me-109s at low altitude circling what appeared to be a farm field. I had the squadron stay at altitude, while my wingman and I went to investigate. It was clear they were going to land there. We began our attack.

The 109 pilots didn't see us, and as we were lining up to fire, an intense barrage of flak came up. There was also a lot of automatic weapons fire close to the ground. The place was too heavily defended, so we broke off our attack. We hit the deck and flew away. As we began to climb to altitude and got up to about 10,000 feet, I smelled something that smelled like an electrical short circuit. I continued climbing to about twelve thousand feet before crossing over the Rhine. Suddenly, flame burst out in the nose of the plane. I had no option but to jettison the canopy, loosen my safety belt, roll over, and drop out. The airplane blew up just after I got out.

Strangely enough, I felt a great sense of peace as I parachuted down. Everything was quiet, and I felt relaxed. It was as if all the built-up stress of the war was being relieved. For me, it seemed the war was over. That was it. Then I could hear single shots, and I realized that people on the ground were shooting at me. I saw civilians running toward my projected landing spot. On the other side, I saw Luftwaffe troops running toward me from a flak installation. I slipped my parachute, and tried to glide towards the troops, whom I hoped would protect me. As I landed and got out of the parachute, the troops surrounded me. One farmer broke through the ring of soldiers and struck me on the back with a pitchfork handle. He was pushed away by the troops. I'm certain that if the soldiers hadn't been there, I would have been killed.

Where'd you go then?

I was marched back to the flak installation. It consisted of open pits with 40-mm guns in them. I spent the afternoon watching them take pot shots at our fighters.

Did anyone get hit?

No, I saw none. Later, a truck brought me to the Cologne airdrome, a place we had dive-bombed that day. They took me immediately to the officer's mess. There, the Ju 88 Nightfighter Squadron was located. The German pilots and I did what fighter pilots and fliers anywhere do: we told war stories. To my surprise, several of them spoke excellent English.

They seemed amazed that after shooting down so many American planes, the U.S. still came back in full strength, that they seemed to actually be increasing. The Germans asked, "Where the hell do you get all the airplanes?" They explained to me that they had two secret weapons they expected to be operational shortly. Those would win the war for them. At about that point, the squadron commander "liberated" my leather flight jacket and put his own rank and serial number on it.

The next morning two guards took me to Cologne and onto a train for Frankfurt am Main where the Luftwaffe Interrogation Center was. At the interrogation center I spent four weeks in solitary. They interrogated me once or twice a day. The food was meager: coffee made of burnt barley stems and bread, soup for lunch, same for supper as breakfast. My interrogator was Second Lieutenant Ulrich Haussmann, a former photojournalist. We became well acquainted during the month there. Occasionally, he took me to the radio communications center, where I could follow the progress of the air battles. I believe this was, in part, to impress me with the extent of their intelligence. I remember one day Ulrich came racing into my room. He excitedly said, "We got Zemke!" After the war I learned that he was right, that our top fighter leader who was also a second-generation German-American, had spin in on instruments and bailed out. This was big news.

Next, I was sent to Oberursel, where they gathered a cross-section of POWs to try to find out their political thinking. These accommodations were relatively first class. My interrogator there was Herr Boininghouse. He would take me for a walk once or twice a day in the countryside. He claimed that the U.S. was politically naïve, that our real enemy was the Soviet Union. I spent five days there and then went to Dulag Luft, at Wetzlar.

The camp was run by Charles Stark, a U.S. Air Force POW, of course under the direction of the Germans. I spent five days there and then was back on a train, ending up at Sagan in east Germany at the South Camp of Stalag Luft III, which was well organized under direction of Colonel "Rojo" Goodrich, the senior American officer.

356

Is this the famous camp?

Yes, this is the one Hollywood depicted in *The Great Escape*. Before I got there, the prisoners actually built three underground tunnels, named Tom, Dick, and Harry. The food was bad, but I had lots of company [laughs]. I was in a group of about ten senior officers. We all messed together, throwing our rations together for meals. The food was supplemented by the Red Cross. The Luftwaffe was responsible for U.S. Air Force prisoners. They were quite proper in complying with the provisions of the Geneva Convention. For example, I was never subjected to physical mistreatment or threatened during interrogation.

There were 1,500 Air Corps officers there. I worked with the escape committee and was amazed to see every skill required for making an escape had been identified and activated from the group of us. We had tailors, forgers, metal workers, toolmakers, photographers, you name it. On the downside, the escape effort had been set back several months earlier when 50 of those recaptured from The Great Escape had been executed. There were signs that showed the pictures of the 50-man grave. They read, ". . . Escape is no longer a sport."

I enjoyed getting to know my fellow U.S. officers. During this time, we discussed the post-war air force, how it should be separated and how there should be an Air Force Academy. We even discussed what the new uniforms should look like. A lot of what we discussed turned out pretty much that way.

So these plans were actually used?

Oh, you bet. These guys were instrumental in it.

How'd you escape from the camp?

That's a long story. On January 29, 1945, we were watching a prisoner production of *You Can't Take it With You*. The play was interrupted by Colonel McNickle, who said he'd received orders from the German commandant to begin evacuating the camp in two hours. The reason was that the Russians were advancing, and the Germans didn't want us to be liberated by the Russians. When we started out marching at 10:00 P.M., the weather was miserable. It was cold and windy and minus ten degrees Fahrenheit. There was no shelter from the wind. We'd stop for ten minutes or so every two hours. We marched through the night. At one point, when the wind was taking its toll, I began chuckling. The guy next to me, Jim Luper, asked me what the matter was. I think he thought I was going crazy. I told him I had created this mental image of warmth and luxury. I was lying in a hot tub at the Claridge Hotel with a scotch and soda beside me.

357

The next day around noon we stopped in a small town called Priebus. They split us up and we stayed in barns, town hall, and church. Wagons distributed rations to us. The next morning we continued on, until we stopped in Muskau for the night. The next day we reached Spremburg, the rail center, where we were loaded into freight cars on the way to Mooseburg. They put us 60 men to the 40-man car. We had to sit in shifts and only were let out in the snow to relieve ourselves once a day.

At Mooseburg, they sent us immediately through the delousing showers. Mooseburg was huge—a camp of 15,000 POWs of every rank. There the buildings were dirty and full of vermin and lice. Things were kind of grim.

Major Hank Mills, of the Fourth Fighter Group and Eagle Squadron, and I felt it possible to escape. Because the Geneva Convention forbade officers from working, we had to become enlisted men. It took awhile for us to negotiate and connive for identities of enlisted men. Once we had the new identities, we went into Munich on the work gang to further scope things out. Finally, one night we hid in the railyard where we were working. We dug in and remained there. The men covered for us during the head count by slipping people up and back during roll call.

How'd you keep from getting caught?

We traveled at night and hid in the forests during the day. One day, when we had situated ourselves in the forest, we heard some noise coming from a nearby village. We looked over and saw a column of men dressed in prison garb with the Star of David sewn on their shirts. It wasn't until later that we realized they were not civilian convicts, but were headed for the death camps. We had traveled for five days toward the western front, when we were caught trying to get water from a farm well by a bunch of volksturmers—members of the people's land army. Escapees were getting shot, so we told them we'd just been shot down and were trying to evade capture. They took us to the nearest prison camp, not far from there. As we entered the interrogation room, whom should I see but Lieutenant Haussmann, whom I knew in Frankfurt.

Haussmann recognized me right away. He said, "What are you trying to pull, Hillman?" I answered, "Ulrich, you know that Germany is losing the war. You'd better look ahead to what's coming when Germany surrenders and you better start making plans." Later that night, Ulrich came into our cell. He said, "Just what did you have in mind?" I told him if he'd help us back to the front lines, I would help him after the war ended. He said he'd think about it. The next day we walked around in the village and talked.

What convinced you that you could trust him?

It was a pleasant little village. I saw them building up fortifications. I said, "You guys are going to fight against the tank columns going through here."

He said, "Yes."

I said, "You're just going to destroy the village, as well as this prison camp. They'll encounter resistance, then sit back and shell the area." We had about 75 prisoners there in the prison.

I said, "I know our intelligence officials aren't aware of the camp, so it looks to me like we should somehow get word out about it. He brought the idea to the company commandant, about saving the village as well as the American prisoners, and they agreed. That's how we got out of there.

So we set out on foot, supposedly being transferred to another camp. Before we left, we listened to the BBC to determine where the spearheads were going. Because there were prisoners, Ulrich was given another guard, Sergeant Walt Hanneman. This time it was easier. When we needed food, instead of stealing, Ulrich would go to a farmhouse, show his ID, and get what was needed. Sometimes after the farmer's children had gone to bed, we'd listen to the BBC for further information.

One morning very early, we woke up to the sound of gunfire. It turned out to be an American tank column that was encountering resistance at a nearby village. The four of us raced into a nearby forest. At the edge we could see the tank column, maybe one-half mile away. We got down on our hands and knees and crawled slowly through the tall grass, toward the column. We feared we might not be recognized.

When we got to about 300 yards from the column, Hank and I stood up, put on our U.S. flight caps with our rank insignia, and placed our hands over our heads. We called out to the column. Luckily, they realized we were Americans and didn't shoot. Walt and Ulrich turned over their pistols and came along as our prisoners.

Ever have any nightmares afterwards?

It's hard to describe, but my wife tells me I have. I don't have them anymore. She said I did for years.

Do you think if you'd have had a slightly different personality, you'd have fared less well?

I think so. I saw this film on a fighter pilot not long ago. He let the casualties and deaths of his friends get to him. I didn't. You couldn't. I was amazed at him. I think it was atypical. I've always had a lot of confidence in myself and that helped, too. I had pretty savvy parents who instilled that in me.

What happened to the other guard?

Neither Ulrich nor I have heard from him since 1945.

You had a lot of clever excuses and did quite a bit of planning. Did you think of most of that on the spot, or did you have these things planned ahead of time?

We planned and prepared for the first escape carefully but played it by ear from then on.

Much later you flew over Russia, didn't you?

In March 1993, the story broke about this. Thirty-seven American fliers were shot down over Russia. Since the security lid has been lifted, I can talk about one of the first of those flights.

In the fall 1952, I was directed by Major General Frank Armstrong to accompany him to Strategic Air Command [SAC] headquarters. At the time, I was deputy commander of the 306th Bomb Wing, the first and only B-47 wing in the air force. We were briefed by General Curtis Le May. Intelligence reports indicated that the USSR was constructing a number of air bases on the Siberian peninsula. These were suited for bomber operations. No aircraft existed for performing the aerial photography needed, so the people at Wright Field had been directed to modify the B-47 with proper camera equipment.

This was a secret, wasn't it?

Yes, the mission had the highest security classification. At SAC, only General Le May, his director of operations, Major General Montgomery, and the director of intelligence, Brigadier General Jim Walsh, had detailed knowledge of the mission. Back at MacDill, I began the planning in strictest security. In fact, because of security restrictions, I spent many long hours in my office, behind locked doors doing the planning. We were to stage out of Eileson Air Force Base, Alaska. To improve chances for a successful mission, a primary B-47 and a back up were designated. The primary would penetrate while the back up would orbit outside and north of Siberia as a communications relay, prepared to take over the mission if the primary was forced to abort. Intelligence indicated that a MIG regiment was stationed in the target area, and that anti-aircraft artillery could be expected. We directed our defensive measures in terms of the following: tactics, surprise, aircraft performance, electronic counter-measures, as well as the B-47s tailguns. Two KC-97 tankers were set up to transport the necessary men to Eileson and to aerial refuel both B-47s on the mission. At this point the rest of the flight crews were given the mission and its plan.

Because this was the first cold war overflight of the USSR, it was necessary to brief President Truman and obtain the go-ahead for the mission. Truman didn't hesitate a bit on it.

Did your wife know?

At the Officer's Club social a few nights before takeoff from MacDill, General Armstrong took my wife Lloyd, aside and said, "I feel like I'm sending Don on a mission like sending Christ to calvary." Still Lloyd had no knowledge of the flight or the nature of the mission. She was puzzled by the comment, and there was little I could do to allay her fears.

We flew to Rapid City Air Base to help maintain cover for the mission. We had company because the B-47 was quite a novelty. For example, Brigadier General Dick Ellsworth asked for a ride. We strapped him in a rear seat, the copilot position, and the copilot rode in the aisle. After running the checklist, we started down the runway. A third of the way down, we realized that the flaps were fully retracted. Somehow in the mixed crew configuration, we'd missed them. That meant trouble, for without flaps, the takeoff run would have meant a fast and disastrous run off the end of the runway. We couldn't abort at that point, so I pulled down the flap handle. I watched the flap indicator creep down—slowly, very slowly. We made it, but we used up a lot of runway.

Our next stop was Eileson. The two KC-97s took off, followed by the two B-47s an hour later. We rendezvoused in Nome and took on more fuel. Pat Fleming, the back up, went to the communications area, and my aircraft headed to the penetration point. I went west to the top of Wrangel Island, some 100 miles off the north coast of Siberia. From there, the course was southwest to the point of penetration about 500 miles into the Soviet Union. When making landfall, we turned southeast. That might make it appear as though we were a friendly aircraft coming from western USSR.

At this point we had burned our fuel down and were light enough to be flying above 40,000 feet, well above normal cruise speed. We went to our photo points when instruments showed we were being tracked by enemy radar. We knew that MiGs were in the area, so the copilot, sitting in the rear seat, was on the lookout. Suddenly, he called out that he saw enemy aircraft climbing up below us. Fortunately, the MiGs never got within range, largely because of our speed and altitude. The element of surprise had worked.

So then you headed home?

Yes, we finished the photo runs on the last site. It was well after dark when we touched down at Eileson. Pat landed a few minutes later. Our camera crew took the film to the photo lab to make duplicates prior to air shipment to the States. The fun part of this was the next day, intelligence sources learned that the Soviet regional commander had been replaced and that a second MIG regiment was being transferred into the area. Finally, six months later, I was assigned to SAC headquarters on a normal rotation. One day I was called down to General Le May's office. When I arrived he came around the desk and pinned a Distinguished Flying Cross on me. He saw how puzzled I was, and when he did, he flashed this very slight (also very rare) smile, and said, "It's secret."

Going back to the escape, did you become very good friends later with Ulrich?

There's quite a large German contingent in Seattle. We keep a distant relationship. I see him for lunch about once a year. He felt heavily criticized by those Germans who still think the war's going on—the real, old-type German people. They looked down on Ulrich for helping me escape.

This escape story is an amazing story. What's the most amazing thing to you about it?

A couple of things are. One is that we were able to pull it off. Two, that Ulrich and I were able to carry out our agreement that if he would help me, I'd help him. After I got him out of prison camp, he went back to his wife in Innsbruck, Austria. I sent care packages there, and in 1948, I flew into Munich on a mission, so I got a car and drove up to see him. He said, "This is a bad place to raise kids." He felt the educational opportunities were limited and the economy was poor. It was an occupied city then. "Could you help me get to the U.S.?" I told him I'd try if it was possible. When I left, Ulrich insisted on driving me as far as Garmisch, where we spent the night in a hotel. Later, I checked with the State Department. I told them the story, and they said, "If you'll make sure he's not on welfare, we'll let him in."

363

What did Ulrich do over here?

He went into the sportswear business. His children both got degrees. His daughter got a degree in art, his son a degree in engineering from the University of Washington and later went to work as an engineer for Boeing.

What are you proudest of?

I can look back on the war with a lot of satisfaction on what I accomplished. I do a lot of retrospection. I feel good about what I did in the war. I feel I did at least my share for the country and the guys that were depending on me. I guess that's it.

BOB SCHIMANSKI
"No Good-byes, No Regrets."

When the government started the Civilian Pilot Training program (CPT) at Felts Field in Spokane, Washington, Bob Schimanski joined the second class of students in July 1940. He was 18. After completing the class and receiving his private pilot's license, he applied for Army Air Corps cadet training. At that time, Bob had only one year of college and the military wouldn't accept him. After the war started and the entrance regulations changed, he joined the Air Corps at Geiger Field, on July 23, 1942, and became an aviation cadet. He went through basic in Garden City, Kansas, and advanced at Eagle Pass, Texas, where he got his wings and a commission. Next, he went to Harrick Neck, Georgia, for fighter training, where he flew P-40s, and thereafter started flying P-51s.

Bob flew 70 missions over Europe with the 357th Fighter Squadron. He became an ace, making ten kills, and received the Distinguished Flying Cross, 17 Air Medals and Seven Battle Stars, as well as the Presidential Unit Citation.

We sit down in lawn chairs on his spacious patio, overlooking a golf course in the South Hill section of Spokane, Washington, as this distinguished flier speaks frankly about his war years.

Any unusual things happen during training?

Since I already had a private pilot's license, I was a little bit advanced. Frankly, training was easy for me, easier than the others. There was a huge washout rate of pilots. But I already knew I could fly, so really I was a better-than-average pilot. But as far as anything unusual, not particularly.

How do you attribute it? Do you think you had a natural aptitude for it?

Flying single-engine airplanes, you've got to have good coordination. I did have darn good coordination. I was a good pilot. I worked hard at it, studied at it, and I became a darn good pilot. I had a lot of compliments.

I've had people tell me that they sometimes got tougher tasks because the instructors knew that they were advanced.

No, not particularly. In fact, I'd say that a lot of the people admired me because I, obviously, was a little bit better than they. For example, I was exceptionally good at aerial gunnery. As soon as I got down there, I knew how to fly and I knew how to fight, so I knew I was a darn good fighter pilot. It came easy to me, both flying and then the aerial gunnery.

You mention that people had a lot of respect for you. Do you remember anybody that kind of followed you around in training?

Oh, no. I can't say that. Thirty-four of us graduated out of fighter training and we all went over to England. I flew 70 missions in England. When I finished, there were only six of us still flying, out of the 34. A real tough washout rate.

Washed out?

They were killed, missing in action or weather.

Do you remember the toughest loss you sustained?

On my last mission, number 70, six of us were going to finish our tours. It was March 24, 1945—the day the Allies jumped across the Rhine, so it was a big mission. We divided the group into two halves. The first half patrolled for four or five hours and was done. At that point the second half went over. I was in the second half. I remember taking off, and as we entered into Germany, we talked to the first group of pilots and asked them if there was any action.

They said no, that it was real quiet there. There was a little ground strafing, but nothing much had happened. So we went in there, 12 of us in my squadron, and ran into 16 M-109s right off the bat.

This was my last mission, and frankly it was the first time I was actually a little bit reluctant to get into combat. Someone said, "Let's go," and down I went. We tangled with these 16, 109s and shot down 14. Then we kept patrolling along. I'd gotten my last victory in my 70th mission. So then we started back home and, of course, I'm feeling pretty good. The War is practically over for me. I'm done with combat. And I started buzzing the field and to show off, and the tower called me and said, "Schimanski, quit it. Don't do it."

Nobody had ever told me not to maneuver and show off, but the tower persisted. And so, finally, I reluctantly quit. As soon as I landed, the tower said, "Otto Jenkins, who was on the last mission, did what you are doing, and he crashed and killed himself." So it was a traumatic experience for me to get my last victory on my last mission, and then I find out that this friend, whom I knew well, was killed. All he had to do was set that airplane down and the war was over for him.

How did it happen? What exactly did he do?

He was buzzing the field and crashed near the runway.

How did that impact you?

I had seen so many people who died and were missing, what was one more tragedy? It really had no impact on me. We never had funerals or memorial services for pilots, but on this particular occasion, Otto was buried at Cambridge Cemetery in Cambridge, England. The war was over for me, but I went to the funeral. That day they buried 26 airmen, all at the same time—full military honors. If anything had an impact on me it was that funeral. It was dramatic: 26 coffins all lined up, all draped with the American flag. They were from different groups and as each man's group was called forward, we all stepped forward. Then they played taps and fired a 21 gun salute. It was just a dramatic funeral. It was a moving experience for me.

Shortly thereafter, I got on a boat from South Hampton for home. It took 11 days to get across the ocean. The troopship that left right before us was sunk by German U-boats. That's how close I came to not making it back to the United States. Finally, on May 2, we entered New York Harbor. It was a beautiful day and I'd never been in the New York Harbor. As we entered the harbor, on the loudspeaker system they announced that Germany had capitulated and was laying down their arms and would be surrendering shortly. Just at that moment, we passed the Statue of Liberty and the American flag. And again, it was a tremendous experience for me— entering the harbor, seeing the flag, and remembering my friends and everything. It was truly a dramatic.

Did you ever feel like you wished you'd been able to be there to help someone?

No. I can't say any particular loss had any effect on me. We didn't have large, catastrophic losses. We had no 10 or 20 losses in a mission. It was a daily thing of one or two being missing, and this was not unusual. You just got used to it. Whether it was a good friend or a casual friend, he was gone. There was a replacement—a new pilot and a new airplane the next day. And life went on. For me, I didn't experience any traumatic losses of friends. I was kind of numb to it.

Did you ever have nightmares afterwards?

Never. I slept beautifully over there. I killed a lot of Germans, and it never bothered me one iota that I had killed a person. In fact, the first time I actually was in combat, I was flying wing with my squadron commander, and we ran into four German aircraft. We paired off and we shot down two of them. I was elated. I wanted to make sure this man never flew another airplane. When the battle was all over, we flew back and it was just like a Hollywood story, flying back home in the sunset. I felt absolutely great. So, I never felt any loss or any traumatic experiences of killing people. No.

Did some of your friends have problems with it?

Yes. You bet. I have a calendar, a chart of my squadron. It shows what happened to 90 pilots in about 18 months of combat. Out of 90 people, 42 were killed in action or missing in action. Seventeen of them were transferred out. They were a liability—inadequate as fighter pilots. Our group's policy was, as soon as you realize that you had a pilot who wasn't contributing, the person was transferred out. So 17 out of the 90 were transferred out. Not all pilots are good fighter pilots—good combat pilots. There's no question about it. Overall, we had an excellent squadron, an excellent group. We did a tremendous job. But there were failures.

You shot down how many planes?

I was credited with ten.

Can you talk about some of those ten kills?

The most difficult was March 2, 1945. That's the day before my birthday. We went on a mission deep into Germany and a lot of German fighters showed up. We started hassling and fighting. I remember one flight of P-51s from another group started after a 109 and thought they'd hit him and knocked him down. A lot of times when you fire and hit an airplane, the plane will snap roll, high-speed snap roll, and go down. And, this guy did. For some reason or other, I followed him down. We met below overcast, at about 500 feet, head on. This guy was the best German pilot I've ever run into. In fact, for a little bit, when we first started the engagement, he got the better of me. I just couldn't believe that anybody could fly an airplane better than I could, but he was. I hung in there with him, determined that either he or I was going to go down. I was going to stay with this guy forever.

About that time, one of my wingmen, Dale Carver, came along. Carver was a young kid, the youngest ace in the air force. As I kept the German pilot in a tight turn, Carver started making passes at him and hit him. We both knocked the German pilot down, and he crashed into the ground. It was the most traumatic experience had with anyone I engaged.

Because this guy was so good?

He was so good. I had met somebody that was just about as good as I, and he gave me a real hassle. Oddly then, a few years ago, one of the British air magazines, and I forget the name of it now, wrote a story about this engagement, called *A Day in March*. A historian from my group stayed over there in Germany during the occupation and met with a German historian from fighter groups in Germany. He had heard about my engagement with this particular pilot, so the two historians studied the records of my group and determined who this German pilot was that was killed. And so many years later, for the first time, I learned the name of the person I was engaged with and killed.

Do you remember what the name is?

Yes. I still have the name; it's Ault. And, I have the magazine. This was quite an experience, to see magazine many, many years later.

How did that impact on you?

I had the impression that perhaps I should try to contact his family. I thought about it; I have a German background, myself. My grandparents both came from Germany, so I have somewhat of an attachment to Germany. I did think about contacting his family and telling them my experience and how I felt about it and everything, but I never did that. I neglected to do it.

What would you have told them? What would you say?

Our group had a philosophy that said, "There are no good-byes and there are no regrets." This applied to us pilots who were flying. When we lost somebody, there were no good-byes and no regrets, no funerals, and no ceremonies. You're just gone. If I had written to this family, I would have said the same thing to them, "I have no regrets. There were no good-byes. I had no animosity toward him. It was a war. He did his best, and two of us killed him."

And he was very good.

He was damn good.

Why was he so good? What was he doing to you?

A lot of times, particularly at low altitudes, when you start fighting you're in tight circles. Frankly, he was out-turning me. He was getting onto my tail rather than letting me onto his tail so that I could shoot at him. He was shooting at me. You get used to having somebody shoot at you. It never particularly bothered me. I never got horribly worried, but it is an uncomfortable feeling. But this guy was shooting me, and I wasn't shooting at him. I was just determined I was going to stay there until he or I went down. Unfortunately, it was him. And again, I made sure when he went down that he crashed and that man never flew another airplane. He was dead.

One of our better pilots, Bud Anderson, has a philosophy for fighter pilots. Many times you're asked what makes a good fighter pilot. You've got to be a good pilot and you've got to be aggressive. His story was that you have got to take them down to the ground. And this man, Ault, I wanted to take him down to the ground. I had to finish him. I didn't want him to ever fly an airplane again.

371

Tell me another episode that stands out.

In November, I remember that we were going on a mission to Berlin. We were at about 18,000 feet and saw a bunch of German fighters there as well as our own planes. I started making a pass at one guy and pulled six and a half Gs while firing. On the pass, I hit his right wing and cut the wing off. It was an excellent feeling to see that happen.

We did very little strafing, though we did strafe some trains. What the pilot would do then was to go after the lead engine. In fact, the most dangerous job in Germany was to be an engineer on a train with bullets ricocheting around in that train car. In all, I strafed about a half dozen trains.

One day we were going along and saw a train with probably 20 passenger cars going along the side of a hill. We went down and started strafing this particular train. It turned out it was loaded with troops. I imagine there were 2,000 German troops on this troop train. I tell you it was a traumatic experience to see these men trying to get out of the train. They were jumping out doors and windows, crawling around. I made two passes at that train with maybe about 1,000 rounds of ammunition each time. I imagine that day I killed maybe 200 German troops on that train. Didn't bother me.

Besides, I was not the only one. Twenty others were strafing the other 20 trains. So, that day, easily 1,000 or 2,000 German troops were killed—perhaps, in a matter of ten minutes. It doesn't take very long.

What was some fancy flying you did, something maybe that you did for show?

I'll tell you two experiences. I have flown into compressibility three times. Compressibility is just under the speed of sound. A P-51 could get up to, somebody says 89 percent and somebody says 92 percent of the speed of sound. When you get to that level, you get into compressibility. I did that once in combat, and then just horsing around. To do this, I would be in a steep dive. Anyway, one time the air conditions were such that my canopy froze over, and suddenly I'm in compressibility in a dive and I'm on instruments. This is an unusual experience. Another time I was up at 25,000 feet over the base, and was just showing off, horsing around, and I went into a tremendous high-speed dive down to about 500 feet. I got into compressibility and I ruptured my left eardrum and it hurt like heck. I pulled that airplane straight up to get back up to altitude, to get out of this situation. With the P-51, you could put on full power and go straight up—to 18,000 feet. So it was kind of an unusual experience. I still have the ruptured eardrum. I've lost hearing of high tones in the left ear. It's my only damage or injury from the war.

We had tremendous, terrible weather in England. I was a darn good pilot, but I will say I probably wasn't the best instrument pilot. I knew how to fly instruments, but I wasn't as comfortable flying instruments as I was doing other things. One day the entire group went out on a mission. It was terrible weather when we took off. We got to Augsburg, Germany, escorting bomber, and we ran into German jets. We started chasing those jets all over the sky, and our group shot down a couple of the jets. I never got close enough to one to be able to fire my guns, but I used up a lot of gas chasing them all over the sky, as did a lot of other pilots.

After that, a lot of the pilots decided they didn't have enough gas to get home, and so they started trying to find auxiliary fields or any airport where they could set down. They had a lot of trouble. I elected to come back home. Part of my squadron came home with me. I remember flying along at about 25,000 feet on top of the overcast, and as I looked down, I could see a hole in overcast and through it, the French coastline. So I thought, I will come back home across the English Channel. I dove down, and everybody came with me. I got down there and we started across the Channel at about 200 feet. As we came back, we started getting lower and lower, and I got down to 50 feet. All of a sudden, I looked up ahead, and it was completely closed in. I was right down to the water. I said to the fellows I was flying with, "I'm going on instruments at 50 feet, and if you want to stick with me, fine. If you want to go in yourself, go on." Most of them stuck with me. So I climbed to about 250 feet on instruments and called to our base for a heading. The only navigational aid we had on getting home was to call the base and have them give us a heading to our own base. I called in to our tower and told them I wanted a heading. They got on the air and told me that the base was closed and that I was to return to the continent. I told them that I didn't have enough gas to go back over there, and that I was coming to England. I said, "Give me a heading to any other base in England."

The voice said, "England is socked in. There are no bases open in England. You're to return to the continent."

And I said, "I'm not going back to the continent. I can't make it. I can't ditch in the Channel."

With a P-51 you cannot ditch in water. With the air-scoop underneath, when you hit the water, you'll nose down and kill yourself. So, I decided that I was not going to do that, and I was not going to the continent. Instead, I was going to land in England. I called in and said, "I don't know who closed the base, but as the commanding pilot of this squadron, I order the base to be reopened, immediately, and to have fire trucks at the beginning of the runway." Usually, what they would do was have a truck go sit at the beginning of the runway and then as the plane came over, the men would fire flares into the sky for the pilot to see, so as to determine where the beginning of the runway was.

I told them, "Get those fire trucks down there because I'm coming in." So they gave me a heading, and I came in over the base and sure enough I saw the flares. I was now at 250 feet on instruments with other planes on my wings. I decided then to make a single needle-whip turn to the left. If ever a good single needle-whip turn was needed, this was that day. I flew an extra-long, downwind leg of probably a couple of miles—to make sure that I would have time to line up. I then made another single needle-whip turn, 180 degrees, and asked for a heading to the base. Fortunately, I was right on. I had made two perfect single needle-whip turns. I then cut the throttle to probably 20 inches—half flaps and lowered my landing gear. I couldn't see a darn thing. Solid on instruments, I started lowering, and at 150 feet I still couldn't see anything. At that point, I told the other pilots that I was going in and that if I didn't make it, they were to climb to 1,000 or 1,500, and make sure they were over land before bailing out.

Anyway, I kept coming down and at about 75 feet I could see straight down but with limited visibility. I couldn't see anything ahead. I kept going, and suddenly I saw the end of the runway. I pulled flaps, cut the throttle, and set that airplane down. I told the pilots with me, "When you touch down, don't drop your tails. Keep running down the runway because you've got people coming in behind you." Number one was on the left of the runway; number two was on the right, etc. When I got down there on the ground, it was so foggy I could hardly taxi that airplane, but everybody made it. When I got back there, there was my old crew chief waiting for me. I had brought the airplane home once more.

What did he say to you?

His was a quiet guy. Normally he didn't have too much to say and sometimes, I regret that I didn't have too much to say to him. I thought an awful lot of the guy. He was just as conscientious as you could possibly be. He'd been with the group a long time. He'd lost two pilots and two P-51s before I came there. Now I come along, a brand new second lieutenant—a hotshot pilot ready to go in a brand new airplane. He's got to contend with me. And frankly, he thought the world of me. Since the war, I've kept in touch with him. We probably have a closer relationship now; I knew how sincere he was about that airplane. If everything was not perfect, he wouldn't let me get in the plane. I had to fly something else. He made sure that airplane was perfect and ready to go. I took care of it for him. I flew 70 missions, and I never had a bullet hole or a dent or flak, nothing, in that airplane.

That sounds almost impossible. You were in a lot of combat.

You bet. I was in combat on 16 different occasions, sometimes with me leading, sometimes with me as a wingman.

What do you think happened to a lot of the lost WWII fliers?

The number one killer as far as P-51 pilots was engine trouble. Of course, most of the time you were over enemy territory and so you go down in enemy territory. The second-biggest cause was weather. And again, you're over there in Germany. The third cause of death is enemy action.

Very few pilots died in England. My friend died there in England. He killed himself. But, that's unusual. One other horrible accident we had was when we were coming across the channel in bad weather and four airplanes flew into the White Cliffs of Dover. Everyone was killed.

375

The White Cliffs of Dover, huh?

Yes. On instruments, couldn't see anything, and ran right into it.

Did you know those guys?

Yes.

And they were good pilots?

Yes. I left the group in April 1945, a month before the War was over. But after the War was over, my group went into occupation at an old German base around Munich. There was nothing to do but fly an airplane and fool around. The men were flying all over Europe—down in the Riviera and Nice. Just having a ball. But one day someone took—I think it was a P-47—and crashed in the Alps. Sixteen guys were killed. What a horrible way to die after fighting a war.

It sort of makes you reflective, though, doesn't it? Have you reflected on why, obviously you had great skills, but still do you think somebody was helping you through this?

Sometimes I almost thought so. For some reason or other, I thought perhaps I was one that wasn't going to die. I felt that. There was no religion over there in our group; in fact, I would assume in most of the groups. We had a chaplain. I knew his name, but I'd never talked to him. Of course, we were over in England—Sunday morning there were no religious services. If there was a God or any religion, it was you in yourself. We didn't pray together. This business of pilots praying is a Hollywood story, I think. Nothing like that ever happened that I saw. I'm not the absolutely most religious person in the world, but I admit this: I individually prayed a few times. I have only one prayer. Let me explain something first; I was a young replacement pilot who advanced rapidly. On my 15th mission I think it was, I was a flight leader. On about the 35th mission I was leading a squadron. I was a young kid, and I suddenly realized that as a leader, I had the tremendous responsibility of taking care of the guys flying with me. For instance, this time I mentioned when we came in on instruments, those guys with me put their lives in my hands—just no doubt about it. They trusted me, implicitly. In combat situations, guys that are with you are putting their lives in your hands. They were with me and I realized this.

I wasn't a professional soldier. Heck, I was just a civilian that got caught up in the war. Suddenly, here I am over there leading a bunch of guys. It didn't bother me. In fact, I enjoyed leading. I wasn't afraid, but I just had a silent prayer: that I wouldn't fail and that I wouldn't fail those with me. Pilots make mistakes. You can make some horrible, big mistakes when you're up there at 30,000 feet, and it doesn't make a darn bit of difference. But once in a while, in critical situations, you can't make even a tiny mistake. When I was flying that airplane at 250 feet on instruments, believe me there was no room for any mistake. And so, I prayed that I wouldn't make a mistake. I felt that lives were entrusted to me and I was going to do the best I could, and I didn't want to make a mistake. That was my only prayer.

KATHERINE "KADDY" STEELE
WASP Pilot

Katherine "Kaddy" Steele has been a pioneering WWII flier, a chicken farmer, and an academic. Nicknamed "Kaddy" when her sister had trouble pronouncing the word Katherine, the name stuck.

Born in Marquette, Michigan, she graduated from Northern Michigan University in 1940. That same year, she had joined the Civilian Pilot Training Program (CPT), where she received her private pilot rating, after which she joined the Army Air Corps and became part of the Women's Airforce Service Pilots (WASP), training at Sacramento at B-25 Transition, and at Biggs Field, El Paso, as part of a Tow Target Squadron, where she remained until deactivation. "Kaddy" has flown a variety of planes:

PT-19, BT-13, AT-6, UC-78, A-24 (SBD),

A-25 (SB2C) AT-7, AT-11, C-45, B-25, B-26, P-47

Her duties included tow target, simulated strafing (with the sun at the pilot's back, diving to buzz troops and gunnery), searchlight missions, flying at night without navigation, radar tracking, low-altitude night missions, laying smoke screens at low altitude, and occasional ferrying.

At the end of 1944, the military deactivated her. Katherine would continue to blaze trails after that. After the WASP years, she went to the Middle East where she was farm production manager at a poultry farm and hatchery in Beirut, Lebanon. She received both her master's degree in 1965 and her doctorate in 1969, from the

University of Florida. After a stint as an adjunct professor at the University of Florida, she took a job at Florida Atlantic University for four years, then returned to an administration position at the University of Florida, retiring in 1986. "Kaddy" has also been an acrobatic pilot, control chief tower at Bartow, Florida, and a flight instructor.

She is still active in the WASP organization, where she says her deepest friendships still endure. Of them she says, "It's a camaraderie that I don't think you can get anyplace else. After all these years, we're as tight as ticks. I see my WASP friends at the meetings and correspond with them. We're very, very tight." A member of Women in Military Aviators, Experimental Aircraft Association, P-47 Thunderbolt Pilot's Association and Women in Aviation, International, this bright and lively veteran served as chair of the "2000 and Beyond" committee of the WASP.

Tell me about your solo flight.

I had only seen two airplanes in my life before I got involved the Civilian Pilot Training Program (CPT). In fact, I didn't take it to learn to fly. I only took it because I needed two credits in Physical Education to permit me to graduate that August. Dr. Harold Bottom, who was in charge of the program, asked me to take it because they allowed one woman for every ten men. He felt sure that I would be able to succeed because I was athletic and he thought that my coordination would be okay. Then the first time I flew, I was hooked. At the time, we flew a side-by-side Taylorcraft. For my solo, Sig Wilson, my instructor, just got out of the plane after my eight hours of dual instruction and said, "Go around the field." I did and thought it was very exhilarating. I had a lot of confidence in myself at that time, I guess. I didn't think it was any big deal. I mean I wasn't particularly nervous or upset.

Where do you think you got your confidence?

I got it from my mother, who was a nurse and a very strong, confident woman. My father died when I was 13 from a ruptured appendix. It was right in the worst part of the Depression, in 1932. My mother went to work and raised us and sent us both through college. She was born in Sweden and came to this country when she was 18 years old with her six-year-old sister and her nine-year-old brother. She didn't speak a word of English. They came to stay with her older sister, who lived in Omaha, Nebraska. Tragically, the day my mother arrived in the United States, her older sister died of a heart attack. That meant my mother was on her own from then on. She was just a very, very strong person and she just convinced us at a very early age that we could do whatever we wanted to do if we just worked at it hard enough. And I believed her.

The only reason we weren't on relief was because my mother was working. She was very capable; she really was. When I went to the WASP, I was 24 years old and did not have much flying time—maybe about 75 hours. But it never entered my mind that I was going to wash out. I just did whatever I was supposed to do and I guess I did it well enough. There were 161 in my class and only 58 graduated. After we finished at Sweetwater and got our wings, I was sent with 19 others out to Mather Field in Sacramento, California for B-25 Transition School. We were there for almost four months. I didn't have any trouble with that one, either.

381

Did you run into any tough instructors, or instructors who seemed anti-female?

When I first went to Sweetwater in that primary program, I had trouble with my first instructor. A civilian contract company under the direction of the army ran the field. We had all the army personnel there, but the instructors were civilians. We got instruction from the civilians and check rides by the army pilots. It was not that my first instructor was anti-female, but that I just could not understand him. I had never been south of Chicago in my life and this man was from Corpus Christi, Texas. I didn't think he was speaking English. A gentleman that I knew at the Detroit airport just before I came down to Texas, one of the flight commanders, called me in at the end of the first week and said, "Why are you doing so badly? Your instructor isn't giving you good grades at all." I said, "I don't know what he's talking about. He tells me to do something and I don't have any idea what it is that I'm supposed to do." So the flight commander gave me a change of instructor immediately. Incidentally, the new flight instructor was from New Jersey and I understood him perfectly. That kind of an accent was closer to what I was used to listening to than that Texas accent.

I know that many of the WASP had a lot of trouble with regard to the reaction of some men; however, I can say that all the time that I was in, I never had anything but real good relationships with the guys.

What's the worst story you ever heard concerning the mistreatment of WASP?

There's so much rumor and misinformation about it; I don't know how much is true. I was in Class 43-7. Camp Stewart, near Savannah, had women from earlier classes who had problems. The military sent these women down there, and I think one of the problems was that the people at the base didn't know that they were coming; they just sort of arrived. This threw all the men there into a flap because they didn't know what to do with them. It was a Tow Target Squadron and the men were very much opposed to having them there. The commanding officer opposed it too so, of course, everybody in the chain-of-command did. Not only were the women treated badly, but also some of the women thought that the airplanes were being sabotaged. One woman was killed. They didn't do an awful lot of investigating at the time. When they finally investigated the incident, they never really came up with any satisfactory explanation. It was then that Jackie Cochran came down and jerked them all out of there. Three of the girls that were at our field at El Paso also had been at Stewart. They said that even the enlisted men on the flight line treated them badly. I know that few of them had overt hostility. It was mostly covert: just being ignored or not considered or given the worst assignments. On the other hand, I was very lucky. I can't believe it. Our commanding officer, Major Richard Aikens, loved us all. He had been at Ascension Island, in the middle of the Atlantic for about two and a half years. When he returned and they made him commanding officer of this Buckeye Squadron with 27 women, he thought he'd died and gone to heaven. He was really wonderful to us. He really was.

Give an example of how he went out of the way for you?

I guess he must have been responsible for it, because before Aikens came we had a major who ignored the girls, and would always give them the least enjoyable assignments. The girls would get the trainers to fly or be assigned to rather dumb jobs. But when Aikens came, he made it very equal. We got to fly all the best airplanes, just like the men did. We alone didn't get the best planes, but they were on the line so when we did the rotation, we could fly them. The men didn't seem to object to that.

Aikens just treated us like we were equal, which was what we thought we were. He didn't want to alienate the men either, so he didn't show partiality to us necessarily. He had the idea that our jobs were rather boring and we had to have a chance to do something that wasn't quite so boring. From Friday night until Monday morning, he let us take any airplane on the line that was flyable and go as far as we could go as long as we got back. Consequentially, we had these wonderful cross-country flights to Los Angeles or to Dallas or to New Orleans.

383

Give me a typical day in your life as a WASP.

Our missions changed every day. Sometimes we had a lot of night flying. The squadron flying personnel was divided into three flights: flights one, two and three. We had required missions from 6 A.M. until noon; from noon until six in the evening; from six in the evening until midnight. We would rotate through that schedule. For an early morning mission, you had to be down there at six o'clock, and sometimes before six, because we were flying gassing missions that meant we had to take off before dawn. When we had to fly gassing missions, it had to be calm air, because they didn't want the gas to be sweeping away from the troops before they had a chance to complete their practice. So gassing missions were those early morning flights. If your mission didn't start until about nine o'clock, then maybe you were towing the sleeve in a single-engine SBD— the Army called them A-24s—but they were really navy planes. You would be towing a sleeve for 50-mm guns on the ground. All of our flying was for anti-aircraft. The sleeves had 2,000 of feet cable on them, but we used to call up and say, "I'm pulling, not pushing it! You're shooting too close to the airplane." Sometimes we'd come back with bullet holes. It didn't happen to me, but it did happen to other pilots. We also flew targets for the 47-mm guns, but that was at higher altitude. There, they used a twin-engine airplane because they had to have a bigger sleeve and they had to let the sleeve out through the bomb bay doors with a winch on it, which allowed them to winch it back in—and winch it out, too.

We flew night missions endlessly. Sometimes we had to fly night missions for radar tracking two weeks in a row. The radar tracking missions were connected to the searchlight training. We had to fly at higher altitude because the radar was tracking our aircraft and sending the information—our position—to the searchlights. We were flying Twin Beachcraft for that. The plane had a service ceiling of about 19,000 feet, though were usually flying between 16,000 and 19,000 feet. Usually there would be four airplanes separated by 1,000 feet. We would fly prescribed courses where we were constantly crossing each other. We flew with no lights on and faced some danger.

384

Describe a close call.

I can't describe one because you never knew what the close calls were. You couldn't see anybody. We were constantly saying, "What's your altitude? What's your altitude?" The two guys in the middle, especially, had somebody on top and on the bottom. The preferred place to be was either on the top or on the bottom, because if you were on the bottom you could drop down 1,000 feet, and if you were on the top you could go up 1,000 feet. We always drew straws to see who was going to get those middle spots—because nobody wanted to get stuck there all the time. It was very, very tense and nerve-racking. They were four-hour missions. It was all instrument flying. We just had to sit there and grind it out.

Did you lose any women?

We only lost one woman in our base, and unfortunately we never got a chance to know her very well because she was in a later class. She was only there about two weeks before she was killed. She mistook the dive flaps for the wing flaps and the plane just went right in on takeoff. It's terribly upsetting, even though we didn't know her very well. Another crash on base proved to be even more depressing to us. We were a very small squadron on the end of an RTU B-24 base. RT stands for "re-training"—for replacing troops that had already been to combat. The base had 152 B-24s and each B-24 had a crew of ten. Just west of the airport in El Paso, there's a mountain that's about 5,000 feet. You have that T-setting that you would fly, which was to the northwest. Each time, the pilots would be reminded in a briefing of the mountain. We would hear, "Make your first turn at 700 feet to avoid the mountain because you have not got enough altitude to go over it after that point." Month after month we all remembered that. During the winter months, when we got a lot of wind out of the northwest, one of the B-24s took off and went right into the mountain; never turned, never made any attempt to turn. It just went right into the mountain and killed all ten men aboard and so the military suspended flying. They shut down until everybody could try to get over the shock. They resumed flying and two nights later, another plane hit the mountain. We had three airplanes in less than two weeks that hit that mountain. They never had the funerals on base. Rather, they sent home all the bodies.

How did people grieve?

We were in shock. Unfortunately, most of the grieving took place at the bar at the Officers' Club. When I look back on it, I'm much more perceptive than I was when I was there, because I was too young to understand what was really going on. When you think of it, these are 19-23 years-old. We didn't have counselors that would talk to you like they do now. But, nobody wanted to talk about it. They didn't want to mention it. And they just sort of tried to act as though it didn't happen. Even among us women, who didn't even know these guys, we did the same thing. We didn't mention it, either.

Do you think that's one of the reasons that people from WWII sometimes have chosen not to talk about the war experience?

I think that probably had something to do with it. But my theory about why military people, not only in World War II, but in other situations—maybe even in peace time—find it very difficult to talk to civilians is because civilians don't understand at all what it's like to be in the military. All the people, who've been in the military and will talk about it, will talk about it in the language and the vocabulary that we used. We used terms like TDY [Temporary Duty]. These are expressions that we know about. We know exactly what they mean. I find when I talk to someone who is really a raw civilian, I have to do so much explaining. I don't think it makes any difference whether you're in the infantry or the air force.

It may ruin the story if you have to stop before the punch line to explain?

386

Now that we WASP have become living legends, everybody wants everything talked about. I always tell people that there is nothing in civilian life that prepares you for the military. There's just nothing that I can think of with the exception of incarceration in a minimum-security prison. It's not like going away to college. It's not like going to summer camp. Because, really, your entire life is regulated. They tell you what to wear. They tell you when to wear it. They tell you where to sleep. They tell you where to eat. They tell you where to work. They tell you how to get there. There is nothing in civilian life that prepares you for that, because you really don't have any self-reliance. You don't have to figure anything out. They give you a manual to follow for every operation that you do. And you better damn well do it that way. I mean, don't be creative, if you want to stay in the military. It was said, "There's a right way, a wrong way, and the army way."

Was there ever a time that you departed from regulations?

There were a couple of times, but I certainly didn't let anybody know.

I did something when I was in training. We came to the cross-country part of our training we thought most of us were going to go in the Ferry Command—so we got a lot of cross-country time. At first, they would give us a prescribed course to fly. We would fly to maybe three different points on the map. We weren't supposed to land. We'd fly over these points and we had to radio in, report to the station, and go onto the next one, and so on until we got back to the base. We were flying BT-13s, which was a basic trainer with fixed gear.

After coming to Texas from Michigan where I had a lot of things to orient myself with such as Lake Superior, I found Texas looked like just a big flat piece of land where everything looked the same. I couldn't find anything. For example, there were very few trees and nothing that stood out to help you keep track of where you were. (That's what I like about Florida. You can't get lost in Florida because there's water on both sides.) But Texas looked too much the same to me.

If you had a forced landing, you were supposed to land and leave the airplane there and then go call the base, which would send somebody out to pick up both you and the airplane. That was a very strict regulation. Once I went out on this cross-country flight and at about the second check point, I got a little confused and had no idea where I was. I knew I was going in the right general direction, but I couldn't tell exactly where I was from anything on the ground. I didn't want to go down and buzz the town so I could find the water tower and read the town's name off of it. I feared the local people might catch the license number on my plane and turn me in. Finally, I looked down and I saw a little grass strip with two runways, which looked to be about 2,000 feet long. Someone had burned the grass. There was one tree off to the side of the end of one runway and a man who was plowing a field nearby. There weren't any buildings or other people around but a town was within about two or three miles of it.

I decided I needed to know the name of that town because if I found this out, I could figure out the rest. So I thought to myself: I don't want to wait until I run out of gas to find out where I am. And now that I've still got enough gas to get to where I'm supposed to be, the best thing to do would be to land, even though I knew I was not supposed to do that. I took a chance and I went in and landed. I thought to myself: If I crack this thing up on landing, I'll tell them I had a forced landing, and if I crack it up on takeoff, I'll tell them that I tried to get in and missed the field. I had this all figured out in my head. A nice lie I had. I went in and I landed. I was in a hurry because I didn't want the people behind me to come by and see the airplane on that field, so I parked over by the trees. I ran over with a map in my hand to the man on the tractor. When he saw it was a woman, the poor man nearly fainted. I said to him, "Where am I?" That's a nice leading question to ask this poor fellow.

And he said, "What do you mean, where are you? Don't you know where you are?"

I said, "No, I don't. What's the name of that town over there?"

And he said, "That's Breckenridge."

I said, "Thank you." And I turned around and ran back to the airplane and jumped in it and quickly took off.

I never told a soul about that, because I would have been washed out for it. That was a very bad "no-no." Regulations made a lot of sense because at that time, we were not really proficient enough to be making those kinds of landings and takeoffs. If it had been at an operating airport, it probably would have been a little bit better, but to land in the middle of a field like that was ridiculous.

388

Tell me a story that illustrates the courage of the WASP.

I think the courageous part of the thing was that we did our job. We did it well, and we didn't cause anybody any trouble. We did exactly what we were supposed to do when we were supposed to do it. Women, especially my generation of women, were better at mundane, repetitive jobs, because that is what women were raised to do; to make the bed every morning, to feed the family, to do the washing, those kinds of things. I think there's a truth to that, although that wasn't my particular background. I wasn't married and I didn't have those kinds of responsibilities, but I was raised like all women of my generation. That was what women did. I'm not so sure how good we would have been in combat then. Everybody says, "Oh well, we could have done that too," but I'm not so sure about that because in combat every day is a new day. It takes a tremendous amount of guts to get in there and get your head shot off. But to do the kinds of things that we did: the training of navigators, the training of bombardiers—those are the worst jobs in the world. And so is flight training. It's the same thing, over and over again. And the tow-target business was the same thing. Ferry command pilots had much more excitement than we did. I don't know if there was any bravery connected with it, but at least they went different places and saw different things. I think it takes silent courage to do something when you have to do it over and over and over again. We didn't have to do what we did. We could have quit, which is more than the men could have done. If it got too much for us, we could have quit. And some women did; not very many, at least for that reason. Women did resign for other reasons. Sometimes it was personal.

Ann Darr, another WASP, told me about a WASP who was killed, and the women had to take a collection to send her body back.

That was at Davis Monter. There were 38 who were killed. That's the only one that I know of where that commanding officer wouldn't send the body back. And I have no idea why. When that woman was killed on our base, our commanding officer sent the body back, and he sent one of the WAFS [Women's Auxiliary Ferryng Squadron] along with the body to meet the family and try to console them about what happened. I don't think that there was anybody that got into that program that couldn't have made it if they'd had enough time. The problem with that kind of a program—not just that program, but anything that happened during the war—everything was accelerated. They had to get everybody through in the shortest amount of time that they could. The men told me the same thing about male cadets who washed out. If they'd only given the person enough time, things would have been different. I had been an instructor myself and I know that's true, almost anybody can learn it. I used to say I could teach a cow to fly if I could get it in the cockpit. The instructors would tell us how to do something once, demonstrate it and then we would try to execute the maneuver. Most of the time, unless the effort was so bad that it wasn't even close, they would allow us to do it again. More often than not, they did it once and then they'd send you up solo and say, "Now, practice that." So you'd go up and, if you hadn't done it exactly right the first time, you probably were practicing it wrong to begin with. Then, they'd check ride you and they'd say, "Well, you didn't do it right." At that point, you were out of the program.

389

You have taught, so you know what learning theory is all about. Everybody doesn't learn at the same rate. You had to be really quick to get it the first time. I found out when I was being instructed that sometimes if you asked your instructors at the time if they would demonstrate something again, they would. But most of us were so damn scared of their instructors. It wasn't that the instructors bullied. Somehow we all got the idea that unless we said nothing but "Yes, sir!" we were going to get washed out anyway. One of the things that may be indicative of that is that nobody I know of in that whole program ever got washed out for on-ground school. We were tested two or three times a week on our ground school work. There was a lot of geometry for that navigation. Some of the girls were not very good in math and the geometry was a little sticky if you hadn't had it. I'd already gone through college so I guess I had a little more education than some.

Were there any complexities in terms of men and women working together?

The men just accepted us as guys. I don't mean so much in the military, because in the military we were separated. When we were in El Paso, for instance, we didn't fraternize with any of the men in our squadron. There were 4 ,000 men on that field, and 27 women, so we did not have to look for companionship. The base had a wonderful Officer's Club, which had a big swimming pool and a bar. As a girl, you just picked somebody you wanted to be friendly with. If somebody put a hit on you and you did not like it, you could say, "Bug off!" I think all this stuff that is going on now in the military, especially in the enlisted ranks, is because men are using their rank and position to intimidate women. They should be bashed for that. During WWII, if our commanding officer had demanded sexual favors, I don't know what we would have done. Of course, we had a net. If anything detrimental came up, we could call on Jackie Cochran. She had tremendous clout. If we told her, "These guys are giving us a bad time," the guys would hear about it, not from her, but from someplace at the top.

What has flying meant to you?

I don't think that this applies just to me, but I think for anyone in my generation involved in WWII, that it was probably the highlight of his/her life. It was such a turning point. It was more important than the other things we use as benchmarks, such as graduating from college and getting married. But to go through the experience of something of the magnitude of WWII and to be actually involved in it and maybe contribute, is something—although I get very annoyed when somebody calls me a patriot.

Why?

I did not do what I did for patriotic reasons. I did it because I wanted to fly airplanes. I was just fortunate to have a war.

But you're not an anti-patriot?

Oh, no. I'm not an anti-patriot. I think the concept of patriotism is very good. The people I think are patriots are the ones who lead exemplary lives as civilians. They do their job, raise their kids, vote. I think that's what a real patriot is.

391

How would you like to be remembered?

I can't think of any particular way. I hope they don't forget me completely. I don't know. I never thought of that. I think I would would like to be remembered as someone who was very good at making a commitment. Once I started to do something, I did it. If I didn't think I could do it, I wouldn't even start. I think the other thing I like to be remembered for is as someone who had the confidence to do and accomplish whatever she started out to do. I never quit on anything. I never quit on my marriage. I never quit on my educational objectives. I never quit on my flying objectives. If I decided to do it, I did it. I think that is something I wish more parents would stress with their children. It just seems to me that people don't make commitments like they used to. Maybe there is a generation gap, I don't know. Maybe that's not so important, but it was important to me.

Raymond "Hap" Halloran in 1946.

RAYMOND "HAP" HALLORAN
A POW in Japan

As with other seminal events, like the assassination of John F. Kennedy, people tend to remember where they were or what they were doing at the time the event happened. It's not hard for Raymond "Hap" Halloran to remember what he was doing when the Japanese bombed Pearl Harbor. He was playing golf. At first word, however, Halloran didn't realize what the bombing meant, but when he did, he decided to go up to Wright-Patterson Field at Dayton, Ohio, and sign up for the Air Corps. That trip led to bombing over Japan, incarceration as a POW, and 39 years of nightmares and tortured memories until he was finally able to confront the past. All of which he speaks of in this interview.

Halloran was born near Cincinnati, one of five boys, in a family with a loving mother and father. Of modest means, the family of seven lived in a two-bedroom home. He attended Catholic schools, earned money by caddying on the golf course, and would sometimes sleep on the golf course in the cool sand of the sandtraps with his head on the edge of the slope of green, where he would occasionally see what he thought were airmail planes going north to Cleveland.

Hap remembers the first B-29 he saw, in Salinas, Kansas, after completion of training. They had formed a B-29 crew and were training in B-17s and B-24s. "That morning when I saw the first B-29 was absolutely exciting and exhilarating. A magnificent silver bomber. Long-range. Pressurized. With remote control guns.

Everything in the world you would dream about. The plane was designed for high-altitude, long-range missions in the Pacific."

Halloran has become well known in recent years from appearing on Dan Rather's CBS documentary, *Victory in the Pacific*, NBC's *Nagasaki*, as well as Nightline and numerous other shows commemorating the anniversary of the end of World War II.

What was your job on the B-29?

I was a navigator and a bombardier. To qualify for a B-29 crew, you had to have a dual rating, in case one of us was killed on a long-range mission.

Where'd you fly from in the Pacific?

We flew out of Saipan, an island in the central Pacific, which was about 100 miles from Guam. The targets were mainland Japanese cities about 1,500 miles to Tokyo.

On the way up, we went a little more leisurely—in loose formation. At a certain designated point, we would start climbing before hitting the coastline. The weather was rough. In fact, between Saipan and Japan was some of the roughest weather and weather fronts in the world. To give an example, in May, 40 or more P-51s left from Iwo Jima en route to Tokyo and ran into severe weather. Twenty-seven went down after midair collisions.

After we left the target, each plane was on its own. We were trying to hit a four-by-ten island (Saipan) with the help of minimum navigational equipment radar, no Loran. The Japanese held Iwo Jima, so we couldn't turn on the radios or they would have homed in on us. So, going back home, we used celestial navigation. We'd stay up on top of the clouds, if necessary, to get star shots. This meant you were doing some of the most demanding work in the world—celestial navigation—when you were most tired, after about 10-12 hours in the air. (The trip itself was about 15 1/2 hours from wheels up to wheels down.) If you missed the island on the way home, you ditched because you only had about 20 minutes of fuel reserve. We lost quite a few B-29s because of lack of fuel.

You flew past Iwo Jima? Did you ever get spotted?

We didn't, but others did. I did bomb Iwo Jima once, but the first time over we didn't have a good bomb run. We were at about 20,000 feet. So I said, "Let's loop it back and go into the wind." However, on the way back we got hit with a lot of flak. That was enough of that.

Describe when you got hit over Japan.

It was on my fourth mission that I was shot down. First, we entered Japan over Hamamatsu. We went north quite a ways because there was a heavy wind coming off of Russia. We didn't know exactly what it was, but it was running about 180 to 200 miles per hour. Today, they identify that "wind" as the jet stream on all weather maps. So we're up there going north, and start to do a turn to go to Tokyo. As we do, the wind blows us, and we find ourselves crabbing 25-35 degrees to try to make it. That is not an effective bomb run. Later, we revised bomb run procedures to increase our accuracy.

395

The intelligence briefing that morning was that, at our altitude of 32,000 thousand there would be no fighters. They said there'd be flak, but it would be very light and probably not at our altitude. "Have a good mission. Get one for me." So shortly after we got inland and made our turn to the right of Mount Fujiyama, we found the flak very heavy. (Intelligence wasn't at fault. We just didn't have good information about Japan. Understandable.)

Shortly after that, even as the flak was coming up—contrary to the European theater or any other theater—the Japanese fighters came up through the flak and came right at us. Documents in the archives now show that on January 27, 1945, over the Tokyo area and west of there, and east on the way out, there were over 300 Japanese fighter planes. We B-29s were strung out, and the total of 300 fighters made over 900 fighter attacks. During the attacks, part of their procedure was to do direct rams against the B-29s. They were very successful with that.

Our target that day was #357 Nakajuma Aircraft—Tokyo. We saw two twin-engines coming at us from about eleven o'clock at 34,000 feet. We swung around. Then they made a pass at us from one o'clock. They cut loose on us with the guns. We could see the fire coming out of the cannons and guns, and it hit the nose of our B-29 and blew a large segment out.

On the one hit, we lost the generator power, controls, and two engines, and radio contact. It had been 70 degrees above zero in the plane (we were pressurized) and, when the nose blew out, the temperature immediately went to 58 degrees below zero—that's a 128 degree change. We were on fire, smoking, dead in the air. We tried to make it out to the submarines that were just off shore. There were some brave guys doing that stuff out there, but we couldn't make it. We knew then that we had to bail out, but we couldn't get word to the guys in the back to do so, because we had no radio communication within or outside the plane. We had a brave crew member, radioman Guy Knobel, who took off his chute and went through a 40 foot tunnel to go the back section and tell our gunners and radar people to bail out.

It was a sad sight to see our squadron's planes pulling away. The tailgunner was dead in the plane. He was 21 1/2. The gunners were ages 19, 18, 18; radar was 18. The average age of the crew was 21. Once the guys in the back were informed, we prepared to bail out, but we couldn't get out. Up front, the nose wheel, which folds up into the escape hatch, blocked our exit. We started to get hit by a dozen single-engine fighters. Finally, we said, "Let's give it a try through the bomb bay." The bombs couldn't be released, so we got in between the bombs and the side of the plane. Once halfway out in the air, we were sucked out. As to why we didn't get blown out of the plane earlier with the depressurization, I do not know. We sucked oxygen and put on jackets before bailing out. We looked down and saw Tokyo below. I was freezing to death, lacked oxygen, and saw some adversaries in the air, so I elected to fall free, down to between 3,000 and 4,000 feet off the ground, above Tokyo, northeast—a 23-24,000 foot free fall.

You didn't pass out or anything?

I didn't. I prayed to God.

How many guys didn't make it?

Six people didn't come home from the war.

Were you watched coming down?

Yes, at low altitude, after the chutes opened, three Zeros made a pass at me, and I thought that was the end. In fact, they came in so close that the prop wash sucked me into a pendulum action, probably 40 feet off center. They came back, and I waved to them as best I could—I was in bad shape. Then they came back a third time and were very close. I saw the lead pilot kind of nod, smile, and take off. Perhaps that's the comradeship between fliers, or perhaps they were too close to the ground to do what they might have done at high altitude. I'd rather credit them with being good people.

I could see the crowd below—it looked like thousands of them, following the flow of the chute. I hit ground at the end of one of those pendulum swings, and it really, hurt.

Describe your capture.

I had left my .45 pistol in the plane. It wasn't by design; it was fortunate. It seemed like of the people who did survive, none of them had their .45s with them when they hit the ground. Anyway, the people in the back of the attacking mob ran over the ones in the front. The crowd gave me severe, severe beatings with clubs, rocks, stones, feet, etc. In fact, it was seven days before I could get my mouth open—except for water. I was in terrible shape.

When I was being beaten, I saw a little opening in the crowd. Some Japanese soldiers came, who turned out to be their Kempei-tai secret police. They put their guns, which looked like lugers, to my head. They proceeded to cut up my chute and beat the hell out of me with their rifle butts. They beat me on my head, body, and all over. Then they blindfolded me, tied my hands behind my back, and my feet together. After tying my hands and feet together behind my back, the four of them picked me up and threw me on what looked like a coal truck, and we drove off.

You didn't think you would make it out alive?

That's correct.

Where'd they take you?

I don't know. First I went to an airstrip; I think it was Matsudo. You figure these things out later. There were about ten soldiers with bayonets on their rifles and a couple of interrogators. They tied me to a chair because I was in such bad shape I kept falling over. Next, they beat me with a rifle in the chest, knocked me over, set me up, knocked me over, set me up, etc. This continued. I hurt; I was ready to die. Then fighter pilots came down from the mission that day and came in. I might admit none of them touched me. Fortunately, my captors found about ten packs of gum in one of the pockets of my summer flying suit. The pilots thought that was about the greatest thing that had ever happened to them. They fought over the Dentine packs.

I was then taken on a truck, and it stopped at what could be construed as a shopping center. All the bindings were taken off. They had to hold me up because I was in such terrible shape. At that location there were thousands of civilians. "This is a B-29 flier. Do not fear them. Look at this one." I ended up later at this place, Kempei-tai, I now know was a torture prison, adjacent to the north moat of the emperor's palace. More beatings, more interrogations. I was put in a cage with a couple of Japanese people.

What size was the cage?

The cage was four-by-five feet. It was extremely crowded. At first, I thought the two Japanese in there were there to kill me. I was five or six days there with them.

Did you ever find out who the other prisoners were?

No, one guy indicated he had invented a six-engine bomber that was going to take off from a carrier and bomb New York City. The other fellow looked to me like a kindly minister. I was screaming from pain, and I wanted some medical treatment. I couldn't control it. The Japanese don't like noise, ever, ever, ever. You didn't work codes or tap the wall with your fingers. If you did, you were taken out and terminated. So I knew this, but I couldn't help it. I was in such pain. One day a doctor came in to my cell. He spoke perfect English. He had with him a mean-looking officer. At Kempei-Tai, they had mean people. They were brutes. The doctor said, "I understand you're in pain. We have some relief." He had a tube, eight to ten inches long, maybe one inch in diameter, with green fluid in it. He said, "This will help you." I had a sixth sense about what they were there to do—kill me. So I pleaded. I said, "Please, I know I've been noisy, but give me one week. I'll do everything I can." I said, "If you won't do it for me, do it for my mother and father and my four brothers. I don't want to let them down. They're expecting me home." Anyhow, you do see some good in people, for the doctor, after talking to the officer, said, "Good luck," and the two left. The officer with him obviously was not very happy.

Can you describe the mean officer?

No, sir, I wouldn't describe him if I knew it. No purpose.

After six days, I was moved to a horse stall. They were like cages in a wooden stable, adjacent to the Kempei-Tai main building. There was no heat, no toilet, no bed—nothing but a very dim light lit occasionally to verify that I was still alive. A POW was the lowest form of life, and the Japanese treated us accordingly. I had to sign a statement the first night captured that I had killed their civilians by indiscriminate bombing. I was therefore guilty of murder. In it I agreed to waive all Geneva Convention rules, etc. I know what the form said now, though I didn't the night I signed it. Even if I had known, I would have signed it anyway, since I had a pistol at both of my temples.

So the statement was in Japanese?

Yes, three pages worth. I couldn't hold the pen because my hands were frozen, but they put the pen in my hand and scribbled my signature.

What next?

On March 10, I was in the horse stall at about 1 A.M. I had no watch or calendar, so how do you keep track of time? After all, there's no difference between day or night in a black, solitary cage. How you keep track is through the guards and shifts and every third day or so, you get a confirmed fresh start. "Today it's

Wednesday. I'm on the noon to three o'clock shift." Obviously, some of the guards had some compassion—maybe about two percent of them. Anyway, on March 10, I heard the sound of multi-engine planes at low level, coming over my place near the emperor's palace. I thought, "Where in the hell did the Japanese get all these multi-engine planes?" Then the bombs started to drop. I realized they were our planes. That went on for about three hours, as far as I can estimate. It was terrifying!

An anti-aircraft gun sat outside the stable and, when it started to shoot, the whole stable would move three, four, five, six inches vertical. I was half-cuffed, hands and feet, just bouncing around in the cell. It got so bad the guards left, because they didn't want to die in the fire as it moved closer. While I couldn't see out directly, I could see the red sky through this little black drape in the back. There were pieces of debris flying through the air and hitting the stables. The wind got up to maybe 60, 70, 80 miles per hour—a firestorm. The next morning when the guard returned at 9 A.M.— three hours late, he spoke from out of the dark and told me what had happened the previous night. He said, "As I came to work, there were dead people stacked two, three, four, five deep in the streets, trying to cross the Sumida River. There were people trying to go west, people trying to go east, who had collided in the middle. They were all cooked down to their bones." He said, "I regret to advise you that it was announced at the staff meeting this morning, that as a result of the fire raid last night, the B-29 people will be executed this morning."

Nineteen days after the fire raid, I was moved to the Ueno Zoo in Tokyo, and I still felt I was going to be killed at any time. Occasionally, somebody (a B-29er) would be taken out of a cage stall and never return. On this one day, I was taken out, and I thought that was it—the final trip for me also. At that time I was having trouble walking, so they just pulled me through the courtyard. I was blindfolded with a blanket over my head. There was snow out there in February or March. I now know where the zoo was. I was back there this year. They put me in a lion's cage with big, metal bars up front. The place had a rear entry way, leading out to the walking area for the animals. All my clothes were taken from me, and it was very cold. I hadn't washed, I hadn't any water, I hadn't had a haircut. I had a beard. I looked terrible. I was covered with running bed bug, lice, and flea sores. When you fell asleep, the sores would stick to the clothes and when you awoke, you would tear them all apart. They tied me up to the bars, and I think it was a scheduled plan to have civilians come by and look at me, naked in the cage. The purpose for the visits apparently was that they hated the B-29 guys. "Look before you. There's one of the crew members." It was a disgrace, but I tried to maintain my dignity. That lasted two days. It was a low point in my life.

I was taken on another truck to a place called Omori, on the southwest part of Tokyo along the bay. For the first time, there I saw other Americans. I saw some insignias that looked like Air Corps people. We were standing but leaned against each other. It wasn't until they started roll call that I realized the person I was leaning against was E.G. Smith, who was our aircraft commander on the plane. We had been next to each other for at least 20 minutes and didn't recognize each other.

Describe liberation day.

On August 15 over there, I was out in a garden working. Don't really picture this as a garden. These were just all these homes, all burned down—debris for miles and miles. We would try to move some of the junk and pile it up, and then put in gardens. We were never allowed to eat any crops. For fertilizer, we would go out and scoop up buckets out of the toilets and put it on the crops. Amoebic dysentery was rampant as was beriberi, yellow jaundice, malnutrition, open sores, etc.

Once before, on August 7, a guard came out and said, "Campa, go back. Campa, go back." He was very excited. An angry crowd of civilians had gathered. That would have been about atomic bomb time, though we prisoners knew nothing about it. Anyway, the civilians around there had learned to live with us, if on the other hand, a B-29 was shot down that day, these people would kill anyone who came down in a parachute. Fortunately, we managed to get by the civilians and back to camp.

Regarding the end of the war on August 15, 1945, a Japanese colonel told us, "The sphere for greater prosperity in East Asia has temporarily come to a halt. However, you are still prisoners of war and you will follow all rules or you will be executed when you fail." This was the first time we were called POWs. Part of the stipulation for the agreement to stop the war was to provide and identify the POW camps, which were never identified before that. We had been bombed and strafed regularly, with planes coming in at 400 feet. You'd just lie there and hope you didn't get hit.

On this particular day, when we painted, we painted our POW identification on our roofs. We also painted, "Pappy Boyington is here." On a rooftop. In about five days, some SB-2Cs flew over, dropped packs of cigarettes, and sent a message to "hang in there." Then later on, some B-29s came over and dropped 55 gallon drums with supplies in them, affixed to parachutes. But 70 percent of the time, the parachutes didn't work right and the drums crashed in the camp or in the water. We were out digging chocolate and shaving cream out of the ground. The drums also contained medicine and some clothes. Our B-29 guys came back to help their buddies and other POWs.

On August 29, 1945, we saw some landing craft coming in. I believe we were the first camp on the mainland liberated. The navy craft came in with Commander Stassen in charge and picked us up. They took us out to the hospital ship, *Benevolence*, in Tokyo Bay. That was August 29 at 3:30 P.M.

Any recollections about life on the ship, or your arrival there?

We took off all our infested clothes and took showers. I remember beds with clean sheets. Compassion. Food, food, food. Showers. Admiral Halsey visited me. I was near the Missouri when the treaty was signed on September 2, 1945, and will always remember the "Show of Power" flyover. It must have included almost 1,000 planes, including almost 500 B-29s. I stood at the rail and cried.

How'd you learn about the big bomb?

There was a guard who said something like, "Big blue light. Big blue light. Bad, bad, bad. Domi, Domi, Domi." That's about all we knew about it. We had no idea about the atomic bomb.

What did you feel when the day of liberation came?

It was a great feeling. My greatest day ever. Even after August 15, we thought we'd be executed. The orders were out. Now they're public information. They read that in the event of an invasion, at the very first sign, every prisoner in every camp would be executed. In the documents, they point out choices. They could gas you; they could behead you; they could shoot you; they could drown you.

What about the revisionists' views of World War II?

These are a bunch of suspect people, who can't find a real job and don't have a real profession, so they sit around and try to talk/write profoundly. I haven't met one of them who's been in combat. I have asked them directly, "What would you do if you were a prisoner like I was and were going to be executed? Knowing that, would you have the atomic bomb dropped?" I think all this revisionism is a damn waste of time. There's no reason to go back 50 years, second-guess, and say what we should have done then. The football game is over—whether we passed or punted is unimportant. I know the veterans and the people who did fight are totally fed up with these sanctimonious historical revisionists.

403

What's your feeling about the Japanese today?

I have many, many Japanese friends over there. Their culture is different from ours, but I can understand why they do things differently after long years of living different lives from ours. I've had their leading ace fighter pilot, Saburo Sakai, over to my home to play golf. His daughter married an American soldier, and I am kind of mentor to her on behalf of her father. Also, I met the guy who shot us down, Isamu Kashiioe, whose name was determined after a lot of study. He and I are friends now. He lives in Niigata, which was one of the atomic bomb's alternate targets. Looking back, when we dropped the bombs, they were all impersonal. So what do I think of the Japanese today? I've visited all their major cities, all their major schools and temples. I'm totally at ease and get along very well with them. I judge them as individuals. Maybe that's triggered by the fact that I had nightmares for thirty-nine years and had to go back to Japan and be in control. I did that with help from Ambassador Mike Mansfield. I did some favors for our government at the time. But there are certain Kempei-tai personnel who should have been executed for the treatment accorded POWs.

Describe your first trip back.

It was in 1984. I went alone. After you have nightmares all those years, when you check into a hotel, you have to explain to them ahead of time that if someone hears noise in room 110, it's okay, you're not being killed. In fact, I've never slept at a private home because it was too hard to tell my hosts, "Tonight I might break some windows or knock down some doors."

The nightmares were pretty severe and affected family life, so I thought if I went back and gained control, it would help. I had a room on the top floor to the Palace Hotel, across from the emperor's palace. From there I could look down on the palace. I also walked around it. I met some of my former guards, one of whom, Kaneyuki Kobayashi, I had arranged to come to this country to study English at the University of Illinois in 1957, because he was a good person.

The thing is that my visit back there worked. Once I was in control and viewed the people as individuals and did not say, "They're Japanese and that automatically makes them bad," I came out in pretty good shape. Maybe I was selfish, but it worked.

Do you still have nightmares?

No sir.

What was the worst moment of your capture?

Oh hell, a thousand of them. Every day. I never genuinely expected to live to come home.

JOHN W. CARSON
The Life of a Military Man

John W. Carson had seen articles in *Mechanics Illustrated* about the tech sergeant aerial gunner, so he enlisted in the Army Air Corps right out of high school. From swearing his oath at Philadelphia, he headed to Biloxi, Mississippi, for basic training and then to Chicago for radio school at the Stevens Hotel. After that he went to Tyndall Field in Pensacola for gunnery training, and then on to Blythe, California in the Mohave Desert for training.

John had a twin brother who flew. In his zealousness to join his brother in B-26s, he wrote to General Hap Arnold. It didn't take long for John to find out that sergeants shouldn't have the audacity to write to generals. He explains, "I soon found myself in front of the base C.O. and the next day I was assigned to Flight Officer George Levchek's B-17 as an assistant radio operator, not as a radio operator." At that time all the other first radio operators made technical officer; Carson remained a staff sergeant.

John's most harrowing experience occurred aboard a B-17 over Europe, when his plane was torn apart and he took a 10,000 plunge in the body of the plane. Through the years of war and loss, John's powerful and close relationship with his twin brother, also a flier, sustained him.

Following World War II, Carson went to Officer's Candidate School after reenlisting in 1947. He served tours of duty in both Korea and Vietnam. In Vietnam, he headed a thousand-man communications squadron. This modest Pennsylvanian, who makes it clear he doesn't want to be considered a "hotshot" retired a lieutenant colonel in 1970, to a world of motorcycles, not flight.

You often flew unescorted missions, didn't you?

Yes, in August 1943, we started flying. We had come in as replacements for the Second Bomb Group. I remember the first mission I went on. When the Germans began shooting at us, I absolutely went blind for a matter of seconds. I was terrified, of course, but I got over it. But yes, most of the flights then were unescorted. You had to battle your way in and your way out. It was pretty tough. Usually, if we did have an escort it was short-lived, because the escort aircraft didn't have the fuel or capacity to go with us if we went very deep into a territory.

One time flying out of North Africa, supporting the troops in Italy at the Salerno Beach Invasion, we lost an engine. The pilot elected to stay with the formation, so we went in and dropped our bombs. On the way back, we were over the coast with darkness setting in, and we lost another engine. That meant two engines out on one side. As we came in to land, a plane cut us out of the traffic pattern. At that point we lost a third engine. We were near Tunis in North Africa, and I looked out of the radio hatch and saw these adobe buildings that the Arabs had, quite low. The crew, except for the two pilots, got into crash position in the radio room. We crash-landed, but the pilot did a beautiful job of getting us in at night. Though we had a small fire, we had no explosion, and everyone got out of it okay, with but a few bruises. The two pilots, both six-footers, managed to climb out the cockpit windows, though I don't know how they could have. In the incident the plane had broken apart where the lower ball turret was attached. We were happy to be in one piece, but disappointed because the aircraft we had brought from the United States was ruined.

I might add that flying out of North Africa our runways were dirt, and it was not infrequent that we were forced to use nearly all of the strip to get off. This condition became worse whenever it rained and the strips were muddy. It is an incredible and real tribute to the pilots that, with very few flying hours experience, they did so well.

I remember the first mission of the newly formed Fifteenth Air Force over Weiner Newstadt. It was a joint effort of B-24s and B-17s and one hell of a battle. Fighters picked us up before the target and stayed with us all through the target, despite the heavy flak they had to contend with. We had a hole in number one prop and the induction shot out on number two. Ahead of us were the B-24s. One crew had bailed out and were swinging in the air between us and a wave of twenty-seven German fighters. It was a frightening moment because we dared not fire for fear of hitting the guys parachuting down. On that flight I was tail gunner, and they blew the hell out of my gun cover. The cover was right behind me. I kept thinking I might have to keep the door loose and go out. Fortunately, we were able to continue on and landed on the island of Sicily, where we were scheduled to refuel. As I look back, I believe I truly had an angel on my shoulder the whole time. We were badly shot up and had to lie around for six or seven days waiting for an engine and a prop.

While on the ground, some of the army troops treated us like we were kings, giving us a concoction of medical alcohol and lemon extract mixed with sugar and water. Two cups, and you were stiff. Since the army guys were so nice, the pilot, Captain Philip K. Devine, decided he would give 17 of them a ride when he went up to slow-time his new engine. Devine was a pilot who liked to buzz things. This time he picked a local whorehouse. I swear there must have been 25 or more guys in line at the couple of brothels, so we buzzed that. During his pull-out, he got a little busy when the prop ran out of control and he had to feather it. Finally, when we left Sicily for North Africa, he gave us a ride home right down at ocean level.

Another time, when I was flying as radio operator, we went into Greece from Italy. We had moved up to Italy on December 7, 1943. We were lead aircraft again, and the fighters jumped us. The fighters took the wing tip off and blew holes in the tail end. When a 20-mm hit an aircraft laterally, it would really put a hole in the skin. That usually meant a tear three or four inches wide and eighteen inches long. This time, not only was the plane full of holes, I thought I'd been hit. What happened was that I had a parachute bag in the ready room that somehow had some red paint on it. When the gunner sprinkled machine-gun bullets right up the back of my armor-plated chair, I spotted this red through the dust and smoke inside the plane. I started feeling all over myself. I told the pilot, "I think I'm hit." Then I had to say, "I'm all right." You feel kind of foolish. On the way back, an escort of P-38s came up. We were out of formation, and we were getting beaten up quite bad. As a result of all this, our airplane was vibrating wildly. Then I heard a voice on the radio from the P-38 next to us. He was saying to the pilot, "Gee, Dave, it doesn't look very good over there." We all heard this. It sure is encouraging to hear negative remarks in a time like that.

But you made it back.

That time we did, but another time we had real fireworks and weren't so lucky. We were the lead aircraft, flying at 21,500 feet, and going to Aloyses Airdrome in Athens, Greece. As we entered the target area, the plane went on the I.P.—the indicated point—which is where the bombardier essentially takes over control of the aircraft. There can be no evasive action taken now—you're straight and level as the bombardier takes aim.

I could see the heavy flak—88-mm anti-aircraft—coming up on the tail. I heard the pilot say to Lloyd Haefs, the bombardier, "How you doin,' Lloyd?" And Lloyd said, "Gonna let them go any second." Just then we took a hit under the aircraft in the area of the bomb bay. When that happened, I had my hands on the door handle. The radio operator's duty when bombs were dropped was to open the bomb bay door and take a look, to insure that all the bombs had cleared. You don't want ordinance hanging up there. When we took that hit, I turned around and had nothing but the door handle in my hand. I grabbed my mike to report damage. The aircraft just seemed to roll over and went into a dive—engines wide open and screaming. I could see someone wrestling around in back of me. I got my feet tangled in the machine gun in the radio hatch. The gun was on a ring and it slid out; the configuration was probably three feet in diameter with the gun in the center. So anyway, I got tangled up in this. I was trapped, astraddle the gun, with my feet hanging out in the slipstream. The plane had been blown in half, and I could see the mountains out the back. I strained to get my feet free, but I couldn't. Then I decided to try to faint, but I couldn't. I thought if I could faint I wouldn't feel anything when we crashed. Strangely, I didn't panic, but I knew it was over. I said to myself, "Well, piss on it—I'm going to die." The next thing I said was, "Please, God, I don't want to go to hell." I was quite serious about it. As with most young troops, I had led quite a riotous life. The next moment something gave me the strength to extricate myself, and I went out of the plane where it was broken in half. How the hell I did it, or where I got the strength, I don't know. I know I kicked free and pulled my ripcord. This occurred at about 10,000 or 11,000 feet, and I could only see one other guy with a parachute. Flak was exploding above us; bombs below us from the target. When I spilled the parachute, which in those days meant about a 24 foot canopy, the chute started to swing, you know the kind of oscillating back and forth they'd do. That movement caused me to vomit. So here I was vomiting and bleeding all over myself, as I drifted down.

As I got near the ground, I was looking right at it—not at the horizon, which you should. (No one really taught us how to jump in those days.) Suddenly, I struck the ground as if it were a ton of bricks. No sooner had I landed, when two German soldiers collared me and took me prisoner.

Was there only one other person who survived the explosion?

411

I'd seen the one chute I mentioned, but didn't know at the time that five of us had escaped the aircraft—we lost the other five. I found out that Caputo, who was in the tail, landed in the tail and was killed instantly. I knew one guy in the prison camp who had actually crashed while still inside the tail of his plane, and had somehow lived, but he experienced terrible headaches all the time. As for our survivors, the waist gunner broke his leg. The ball-turret gunner was lucky enough to have his chute fall in his lap the moment we were hit, so he was able to parachute down. His name was Crawford and he was captured too. In fact, he and I were incarcerated together. Another crew member, named Horner, was an Indian, and he evaded. Right now, I believe Haefs, the bombardier, and I are today the only ones alive from that flight.

I was a POW for 16 months, part of which was nasty. We were headed from the interrogation center at Frankfurt to a camp in East Prussia, when I suddenly had acute appendicitis. The Germans put me in a German military hospital, where they removed my appendix. The hospital was anything but a sterile environment, so about six days later, the incision became abcessed. When that happened, the doctors took a couple of hooks with handles on it and opened it up. I had the advantage of no painkiller at this time—

though I had a spinal the first time. I'm sure had there been medication, they would have given it to me. Today I have a scar that's about eight inches long and maybe about one-half inch wide in some places. Fortunately, it's never given me any real trouble, but I remember in 1945 when I was no longer in the service, I would see loose pieces of suture and would pull them out.

They put me in a British hospital prison at Thorne, Poland, which was used for Australians, British, and New Zealanders. I was the only American in the place. The people there had been in the Black Watch and included people captured at Dunkirk. I was treated quite well there. After that, they held me in a camp in East Prussia.

In July 1944, they moved us down to Gross Tyrhous, because the Russian front was closing in on us. The Germans put some 2,000 of us in a coal ship, in the hold. From above, the prisoners looked like fish worms down in there. I headed down and got as far as the prop shaft, and hung there on the ladder. I stayed there for three days. I didn't want to go down there in that mass of people, because if something had happened, I figured I'd never make it out.

When we got off the ship at Stettin, a group of young German marines met us. The group included a captain who hated the world. At that time we were handcuffed together and forced to march. I happened to be handcuffed to a kid named Murray Adler, a Jewish boy from New York. (Recently, I contacted Adler. He's alive, the father of five sons, and is retired from the airlines.) The next morning we were still handcuffed and made to hit the road and run three or four kilometers. The Germans had troops located in the woods in case we broke ranks. The troops used fixed bayonets and German shepherds, and we outran those bastards, though some prisoners fell and were bitten by the dogs. Early on, I had told Adler that we should get in the center, and that would provide a little protection, which it did.

We marched from February 1945 to April 1945, back and forth away from the Russians, in one of the most severe winters Europe had had in a long while. It was bitter cold, with snow and slush. You'd walk maybe 20 miles a day and then would find a barn to sleep in. We ate little—a couple of slices of bread a day. You'd always eat some, but save the rest until you got some more. You couldn't afford to eat everything—you had to save. I had two GI blankets, which I tied together with shoestrings. During that time, I never took my shoes off. I carried a new pair of shoes, but I never took my old ones off for 57 days. Then, when those half wore out, I put the new ones on and traded the old ones for some bread from a native. I knew if I'd taken my shoes off, I wouldn't have gotten them back on in the morning—my feet were so swollen.

What helped you survive as a POW? Was it anger?

No, it wasn't anger. I used to dream about coming home to my wife and having a house and kids. We would dream of businesses we'd start, of food we'd eat—a lot about food.

Talk about your brother.

My brother's nickname was "Wingding." In the prison camp, guys would come up to me, and because we were twins, think I was my brother. "When did they get you, Wingding?" they'd say.

When we were liberated, I talked the folks at Camp Lucky Strike into saying I was all right. They sent me to London, where I met Adele Astaire, Fred Astaire's sister. She cared about doing things for the troops and was a gracious lady, a friend to everybody. It turned out that Adele knew my brother, and she brought us together on VE night. What a reunion! When my brother and I saw one another, we just kind of ran together and hugged and hugged. The moment was indescribable. It turned out that my brother had volunteered for another tour when he thought I had been killed. He was going to avenge my loss. There were all these emotions, the emotions of seeing him, knowing that we were free, that the war was over, and that we had survived. Also, being a twin is special. In the past as kids, even though we used to fight each other all the time (he was bigger than I was), he used to always look out for me.

That night he took me out to the Windmill Theatre in the Piccadilly Circus. There I met a woman, Valerie Ware of 39 Marlowe Drive, North Chears, London. I'll never forget her or her address. There was no hanky-panky. She was a nice girl and a good singer, a lady.

During the war, my mother thought I was dead. So did my wife at the time. I had married this sweet young thing from Chicago, a secretary, named Dorothy Spinka. We met at a roller skating rink.

413

She was 18 and I was 19, and we were in love. She came up to Rapid City, where I was doing phase training on gunnery, and we got married about a week before I got shipped out.

Later, when I got back to the States, I first saw Dorothy's mother. She was crying and carrying on. I said, "I'm all right."

Then I saw Dorothy. She said, "I've got something to tell you."

I think, "What the hell's this?" You know, after the war experience, you're pretty hardened, then she lays it on me.

She says, "I got married again when you were reported killed."

And her mother pipes in, "It was her old high school sweetheart. He's in the navy."

I said, "You could at least give me time to get rigor mortis." (A little foxhole humor.) When we went over to her house, I noticed she had my clothes all packed in a cardboard suitcase. I got teed off. I said, "First, you get my clothes in a decent suitcase, then get me a compartment on a Pullman going to Fort Myers, Florida, and I'll leave town."

So I went home to Fort Myers and cried on my mother's shoulder. My mother had been widowed at age 22. My father had been gassed in World War I. He died of consumption. Mother never remarried. In fact, her whole life was dedicated to my brother and me. She was a great lady. So after arriving in Fort Myers. I found that she had skimped on ration stamps so she could serve me up a steak. Sadly, I couldn't eat it.

When my son was killed in Vietnam, I was on my way to Vietnam. I went in and saw the Marine Corps general, and he arranged to have my son's remains expedited to the States. So I flew back to the States. The air force general gave me his aide to accompany me. At the funeral my brother and I were in uniform. There was a closed coffin because my son was killed by a mine. So my brother and I just walked up to the box and saluted. That's about what it was like when the two of us had met in England. Just deep emotion. My son was a hell of a marine.

Leo Haynes (front row third from the left) in 1944.

LEO HAYNES
A Decision Made Easy

"The military decided for me," Leo Haynes says. He was 24 years old at the time and received a low draft number—he was number ten. A native of Spokane, Washington, he went out to Geiger Field, where he passed the test for the air corps. He trained in Santa Ana and Bakersfield, California. After a year and a half of schooling, he graduated and went home for a short leave. Then, his crew formed in Bend, Oregon and began training in the B-17s. During WWII, he flew 31 missions as navigator with the 390th Bomb Group. Leo was 26 years old at the time he joined the flight crew, which meant that age-wise he just made the limit.

Did anything quirky happen during training?

They sent us up at night to get the pilots used to night flying, but we never flew a mission at night. The bombardiers got practice that way, as did I as a navigator. The bombardiers dropped flour sacks on the bombing ranges in northern Oregon. The B-17s were new to the pilots, and one night the pilots got frisky. They would raise the front end of the aircraft up and then flop the airplane over. That put you up against the ceiling because the crew would become weightless. They did this several times. All at once, they had trouble. The pilot went too far and lost control. We were floating around in the nose of the plane. The gunners in the back were doing the same, having a good time. We had no idea how close we came to the end.

What did you say when you realized it was such a close call?

We were quite upset. We were all friends, but at the time we did not know how close the pilot was to losing control. The incident lasted probably 15 minutes.

Did anything else unusual happen during training?

The B-17s were new to all of us. We would go out over the ocean for gunnery practice. We had a couple of guns in the nose. The gunners in the back got their practice. One day they sent us out and said to the navigators, "We don't want you to do any navigating. We have told the pilots to fly the plane and keep track of where they are and to bring everyone back safely. We do not want you to give them any help." We went out over the ocean and shot targets for a while. The unit consisted of eight to ten planes. When the planes returned, they didn't head toward the base. I knew because I was the navigator. They were heading down toward California. We went past Mount Lassen, and finally the pilot called me out and said, "Leo, you know where we are?"

I said, "Sure, I know where we are."

He said, "Gee, we are lost. How do you get back to base?"

I told him how to get back to base. We missed our arrival time by quite a bit. We were getting messages from the base, wanting to know what had happened to us. When we arrived, one of the officers gave us a bad time about our navigating. We were navigating, but we were told not to tell the pilots where they were. The pilots were supposed to be learning to navigate on their own. We got heck for it anyway.

Did you take to navigating easily?

I took a math course in high school. Math always came easy to me. I think I was a pretty good navigator.

Was there a time you were navigating when things didn't work out?

On our sixth mission, we were flying out over the channel, when the number three engine blew. If a pilot is quick enough, he has a button that he can push to feather the prop. In all the excitement, they did not get the button pushed fast enough. The prop was just wind-milling out there. We turned around to return to base. The prop was getting looser and looser. Sparks were flying. The wing was catching on fire. We had a full load of gas in the wings—2,800 gallons. The plane was shaking terribly. We knew we had to get out then, or we might never get out, so we bailed out. I landed on a tall English apartment house and my parachute caught on the chimney. There I was dangling over the edge of the building.

In training I was told that when you land, you must be relaxed and keep your feet together. That way you take the jolt without being stiff. I did all these things but I didn't expect to land on a steep roof. When I landed, all my weight was on my left leg, which hurt. I was lying there on the steep roof, yet enjoying the fact that there was something under me.

I became aware of a lot of noise on the ground. I was up about two floors on this roof. I looked down and saw English people. They had no idea who we were, Germans or Americans. At that point, I unbuckled my chute and slid down the roof. I was taken to the police station and by the time we arrived there a good share of the crew was there. My leg hurt, but I thought it was just a sprain. It turned out it was broken. I spent a couple of months in the hospital. I found out that when the tail gunner, Sergeant Bernard E. Jensen, landed, he was knocked out. Then a young English lady he had never seen before kissed him back into consciousness. He said afterwards, "For a few seconds, I thought I dropped into heaven."

When I got back, my pilot was gone and the crew had been disbursed. I was to be assigned to another crew. Finally, they asked me if I would be interested in being a navigator for a lead crew. I told him that I would like to do that for two reasons, you get better planes and a lot better care. I got a good pilot. He loved flying.

You mentioned you lost your pilot.

He had been on a mission. The plane had dropped its bombs and was on its way back. They were being shot at. A piece of flak came right up between the legs of the pilot and hit him in his crotch. It tore him up. They placed him on the walkway between the pilot's compartment and the nose, where the navigator and bombardier hang out. The engineer, who was a big Texan, came down. He took care of the pilot as best he could and attempted to stop the bleeding. The plane was still under attack by the German air force. Next, a bullet came through the side of the plane and hit the engineer in the ankle. He lost his foot as a result of that. They had two wounded men there.

By this time the plane had fallen out of the formation. When you are alone, you are in trouble. The Germans loved that. The copilot flew the airplane: he didn't have much experience, but he got back to the base. He shot off the red flares indicating that he had wounded aboard and was told to go ahead and land. As he approached for landing, someone cut him off. He was authorized to land but he couldn't. He tried to pull the plane up but he couldn't get any power. He forgot to turn on the booster. He was flying but couldn't gain any altitude. The people in the tower were watching him. They figured that he was done for sure. He finally realized what was wrong and turned on the booster. It gave them enough power to make his landing, and when they landed, the pilot was dead.

What's it like to lose a pilot?

They broke up the crew. The crew would then be used as fill-ins. Cooper, who was the copilot who landed the plane, became a copilot on another plane. They offered him a pilot's position, but he turned them down. He didn't want to be the head pilot. He completed his missions and got home all right. I believe that most of the crew got home okay as well, outside of Tex, who had his foot shot off. He and the pilot were the only two that didn't finish their tours. Anyway, I returned from the hospital and was put on a lead crew. I was happy to have the responsibility.

I ended up flying thirty-one missions. A tour consisted of twenty-five; after twenty-five, you could go home. While I was in the hospital with my broken leg, the number of missions in a tour was raised to thirty. At that time, Hitler was building big concrete abutments in France all along the Channel. The military raised the total to thirty because many of the men were getting in two or three missions per day. There was one crew, the pilot was only eighteen years old, and his entire crew was younger than he was. They got a couple of missions each day and in thirty days, they had finished their tour. That woke up the air force and from that point on, they required thirty missions.

When you're in the lead crew, you don't fly missions every day. You don't fly every other day. You fly probably once every week to ten days. So it takes you months to get through. Then they raised the rate to thirty-five. I was losing ground. The more missions I flew, the farther I was behind.

Were you pretty frustrated?

It didn't make me feel real good, but you are in the service and you do what they tell you to do. Finally, someone realized how long it was taking the lead crews to finish up a tour while others were finishing in a few months. The lead crews were putting in twice the time. The morale was deteriorating on the lead crews, although we didn't feel it in the crew I was in. I never heard anybody complain about the length of time.

They cut back to 30 missions. By that time I had thirty-one, and I was done, I thought. Some general had the last word. He said everyone else on the crew could go home, but that I had to do one more mission. Nobody could figure it out except him. We asked the squadron commander and he said I should be through. Eventually they got everything worked out and I came home in November 1944. I flew two missions in 1943 and the rest in 1944. Coming home on the ship, we got word about the Battle of the Bulge.

I understand you flew a shuttle into Russia. When did that happen?

It happened shortly after D-day. It was June 21, 1944, when we took off on a mission to knock out a refinery at Ruhland, Germany. Then we proceeded to Russia. On the way we flew over Warsaw at low altitude and saw the terrific damage there. Then we flew to Mirgorod. We knew where we were going because we had been briefed. We were shocked and wondered why we were chosen for this mission. Unable to locate an airfield among the rolling hills, the landing was rather precarious to put it mildly, but everything worked out all right. We were the lead crew, and were not given specific instructions about what we'd have to do when we arrived. We had to pack our B-4 bags and take our dress uniforms as well as our flight equipment, which we wore. We had no idea what was expected of us. Would we have to go to a meeting or dinner? We took a lot of stuff that we didn't need. I had a friend I went to high school with at Rogers High School in Spokane, Washington. He was on the ground crew. I used to see him once in a while and we would chat. Next thing I knew he had disappeared from the base in England. I asked the men who worked with him about his whereabouts. I wanted to know what happened to him. They said they didn't know. They said that about twenty guys were removed from the base. They didn't know where they went or why they went.

When we landed in Russia, Russians surrounded the plane. We had a lot more bags than usual. I was going to remove them from the nose of the plane when someone on the ground said, "Can I help you, sir?" I said, "Sure you can." I was rather surprised to hear an English-speaking voice. I looked down and there was Matt Subadin, the ground crew guy who had disappeared. He and the crew had been secretly sent there to prepare the field and the quarters. It was a shock and a surprise to see him.

We were put up in a barn for quarters. They did not have regular quarters at Mirgorad. The Germans would send reconnaissance planes over and would observe the landing field and then head back to report. At about midnight one night, several German bombers showed up and bombed the Poltava Airfield from low altitude and destroyed every B-17 sitting there—58 planes, I believe. A horrible, frightening sight. They had also littered the airfield with anti-personnel bombs.

The American officers had wanted to send a P-52 after the German observation plane and shoot it down before it could report us, but the Russian officers wouldn't permit it. Why? I don't know. What to do now? Too few planes left to continue as planned. The planes that were left flew about one hundred fifty miles south to the Zaporoze Airfield and stayed overnight, then came back north each morning and parked. They would sit on the damaged airfield during the day, so the Germans would see us. Then we would fly back down to Zaporoze later in the day. The Germans never did find us, thank God. Anyway, this hiding went on for about a week before we got word to complete the mission to bomb Drohobycz Oil Refinery in Romania and continue the mission into Foggia, Italy, where there was an American air base. We stayed at Foggia for about one week and flew one mission with the Fifteenth Air Force. Much of the time we swam in the Mediterranean Sea. Our headquarters was a horse stable—flies and all. One July 5, we completed the third leg of our shuttle: Italy to our base, but it was not without incident.

On the way we bombed the marshaling yard at Beziers, France, then noticed we were low on gas. We doubted we could make it across the English Channel. We planned to crash land on Omaha Beach, but we saw it was covered with broken-down equipment from the D-day Invasion landing. Our only hope was to get across the channel and find a spot to land. We crossed and were looking for an airport that showed on our maps, but even at treetop level, vision was not good. Fortunately, someone at a small, grass airport realized we were in trouble and started to fire up red flares. We landed there at what was a British fighter-plane base. We had about thirty gallons of gas out of twenty-eight hundred gallons. The British gave us enough gas to return to our home base.

What are you thinking while you are bouncing back and forth in Russia trying to avoid the Germans?

It was rather comical. We knew that they didn't know where we were. What were we to do? We didn't make the decisions. The brass makes the decisions and they didn't know what to do. We were not aware of all the problems. We were getting a kick out of the whole situation.

We were living with Russians, who were poorer than church mice and didn't have enough food. That area had been fought over twice, once when the Germans were attacking Russia and then when the Russians got on the offensive. The Russians had regained the territory and now it was in trouble again. The buildings were all bombed out. We slept under the planes at night. The Russians were great. They fed us even though they did not have enough food for themselves. We ate mostly borsht soup. To this day, I would never order it, because of my experience. Also, the Russians served us black bread with straw in it, not just grain, but straw that you could see.

The Russians admired us. They communicated as well as they could with us. They had many questions about our uniforms and our planes—most from eight to ten-year-old children. There was a community compound there, which was something like a small amphitheater with concrete on the bottom. It had survived the two battles over there. Steps surrounded this thing. The Russians would come down in the evenings with their musical instruments. They would play and the women danced with the fliers. You wouldn't even know that there was a war going on. I cannot say enough about the Russians I met. They changed my opinion of the Russians.

Tell me more about the cat and mouse games you played.

We knew that every day we got fuel was another day we escaped detection. That gave us confidence. The best place to hide was just under the plane. I don't know why we just didn't sleep in the plane. The airfield was not being used at that time. It wasn't built for B-17s; it was pretty hard to land there and even more precarious to take off. One time we landed and were taxiing when a wheel went through the concrete. It made quite a hole. We had somehow to get the plane out of there, so we got shovels and jacked it up. We put a block under it and got her out. The field was not fit to land on.

Tell me more about Italy.

The first night, we were put up in an old stable. We slept under the stars after that. We picked cherries, sunbathed, slept in our planes until an alert when we went into the tall wet weeds.

What is your fondest memory?

You meet a lot of people and make a lot of friends. You are all alike, pulling for each other. You play softball, read, and play poker. We played in the barracks. I was pretty lucky. I used to make a few bucks each month and I'd send it to my wife to put in the bank. In fact, I used to make about one hundred dollars extra per week. That was pretty good money in those days. When I got home I figured I would have a pretty good nest egg to do something with. I asked my wife how much money we had in the bank, and she told me none. That really shocked me. She told me that she paid off the house. It made me feel pretty good. We had paid three thousand dollars for the house. I had a lucky streak.

DICK WIDDICOMBE
A Different Kind of Aircraft

Dick Widdicombe is considered by many to be the dean of blimp, or lighter-than-air pilots. This slender, balding veteran of more than 20,000 hours of flying is a genial type—but definitely his own man.

Widdicombe was born on December 5, 1918, in lower New York State, not far from the military academy at West Point. This small-town boy would become the envy of people all over as he piloted the most majestic of aircraft across America and Europe.

After joining the navy in 1937, Dick went to sea, then three years later joined lighter-than-air. He went back to sea again on destroyer escort for the last year of the war. He attended George Washington University while still in the navy, then Navy Line School, then went back to flying airships in Squadron ZP-4 off the East Coast of the United States.

He was one of the persons who helped develop in-flight refueling, using a high-speed pump. He and his colleagues would lower a winch wire from the back end of the ship, pick up the hose from the tanker or carrier, and haul it up through the fitting. They would then pump fuel aboard at 200 gallons per minute.

In 1950, Dick went to Pensacola and flight training, then to Hutchinson, Kansas, for advanced training and patrol plane training. He flew P-2V Neptune patrol bombers at Whidbey Island Naval Base, Washington. Then once again, he returned to lighter-than-air—this time as a test pilot in airship testing and development. He went to Akron, Ohio and monitored the contractors' building of the ZPG-3W airship. He brought the 3W to Lakehurst, New Jersey, site of the famous *Hindenburg* crash, and tested it there. The military era of lighter-than-air was drawing to a close because, as Dick says, "The powers that be thought it was not capable of handling the modern atomic submarine, which was true—but it was also true that nothing else could either." So, realizing the die was cast, he decided to change jobs and went to Alaska, flying search-and-rescue missions.

Widdicombe retired in 1964 from the navy, then went to work for Goodyear Airships, flying out of Miami. Next, he was out to the West Coast as chief pilot of the *Columbia* airship for Goodyear, where he stayed four years until 1971. From there he went to Europe to start the European Blimp as chief pilot. Another position followed as manager of airship operations in Europe. During that time he also served as a fill-in pilot and flew blimps right up to his retirement in 1983. Since that time he has been a consultant and test pilot to several airship companies, including USLTA, American Blimp Corporation, and Aerotek.

Dick, who is unique in that he has flown the smallest blimp (50,000 cubic feet) and the largest (1,500,000 cubic feet) says, "I don't care what it is, I'll fly anything from a free balloon, to a glider, to and airship or airplane."

You flew navy airships in World War II. How did you get into that?

I enlisted in the navy as a seaman in 1937 and went to sea the next two and a half years. I became a quartermaster on the USS *Chester*, based in Long Beach. I used to stand watches on the bridge and at sea and on the quarterdeck, when we were at port. There was an officer by the name of Henry Eppes. He was a lieutenant junior grade at that time. He had come from Lakehurst, where he had just gone through navy lighter-than-air training. At that time it was common for lighter-than-air officers to rotate from airships to sea. They were not dual qualified, as we became later on. Anyway, Eppes and I used to night watch—especially the midwatch—pretty slow, even at sea, unless we were actually engaged in maneuvers or something. We got to talking about airships, and there was a book in the ship's library called *What about the Airship?* by Admiral

Rosendahl, a commander then, who was also the driving force behind lighter-than-air from then on. That was in 1939.

Henry Eppes, by the way, is my longest continuing shipmate from my navy days. We've served together on numerous occasions, and I consider him to be one of the finest examples of what a naval officer should be. He's been my mentor and inspiration over all of these years.

So you became interested in lighter-than-air.

Yes, I became interested in this lighter-than-air business, and as things often happen, fate lends a hand. The Bureau of Navigation, which was the old carry-over from the sailing ship days—it later became the Bureau of Naval Personnel—sent out a circular letter throughout the fleet and asked for volunteers to go to lighter-than-air school in Lakehurst. This was for crewmen. I answered the call, and as fate would have it, volunteers sometimes get what they volunteer for. In June 1940, I arrived at Lakehurst, New Jersey and started through lighter-than-air school with 45 other guys.

429

How many guys made it through?

I think all of us did. There was a pretty stiff selection process to get to go, plus you had to be recommended by the shipboard officers. We all came from the same fleet—every single one of us. Among them was another sailor who became a lifetime friend and shipmate, C.C. Moore.

Any anecdotes about training there?

Actually, we just had two instructors—two chief petty officers. They were from the rigid airship days.

The schooling was a flat six months. It was half classroom and half practical. At that time, Lakehurst was a very small station. There were only about a couple of hundred people on the whole station, and about five or six old airships there.

The airship was at a pretty low ebb at that time. In fact, what we were involved with was rebuilding. A lot of the people were anticipating World War II, and my class—and the class before it—were at the beginning of the build-up of airships.

As far as anecdotes, a lot of these men had served on the airships *Akron* and the *Macon* and even on the *Shenandoah*, and back to the early 1920s, which was the birth of navy airships.

Did any of them remember the Hindenburg?

I remember one of them who did—a man named Sheridan. He was on what was called a stern line. He recounted how, when the *Hindenburg* blew, it was drifting somewhat sideways, and off course, they ran for their lives because they were right underneath it. He said, "It seemed to me like the doggone ship was chasing me." He was one of the navy men that went back into the flaming wreckage and helped haul people out.

Have you ever heard that Herb Morrison recording of the WLS broadcast, where he actually announced the downing of the Hindenburg?

I'll say I have. Actually, we realized that hydrogen was a very dangerous thing. Morrison did quite a job—it was emotional. The blowing up of the *Hindenburg* was sort of a curse to lighter-than-air. It was so dramatic. As air disasters go, it's peanuts by some of today's standards, but it's always been an albatross around lighter-than-air. No matter how much you'd tell people the *Hindenburg* was filled with hydrogen—and we don't use hydrogen—and so on. It's amazing, and that film gets shown every year. No one throws rocks at Morrison. He was doing his job, but we sure as hell wish it had never happened.

Then you flew lighter-than-air in the navy. Where were you flying?

As the build-up was going on, I finished training. Then they extended it for six months. I started in June 1940, finished it in June 1941, and was sent to the flight division there at Lakehurst. We had the old TC-13 and TC-14, which were taken over from the army, when they finally got out of airships and they were handed over to the navy. We had one old airship—the K-1 that was an experimental ship. The K-2 was first of the class that became the prototype for the entire fleet of airships that were used during World War II. It was what you could call our first modern airship.

Can you give a brief explanation of each of those airships and how they differed?

The TC-13 and TC-14 were roughly 350,000 cubic feet, which is getting up to a decent size for a patrol airship. They had a lower fin arrangement, which was kind of like an inverted Y because airships at that time were taking off like an airplane.

The K-2 was designed by a famous yacht designer named Burgess. It was given to the Goodyear Aircraft Corporation, as it was called then. The K-2 type was the real workhorse of World War II. They were about 425,000 cubic feet. They started out with Wright engines, and then they switched to Pratt-Whitney R-1340s, which was a stock engine used by both services for all kinds of aircraft.

431

These airships had a nine-man crew. They later developed it to where we carried radar and other detection devices, depth charges, and a .50 caliber machine gun. They were really well equipped to escort convoys and hunt for submarines.

Where did you work?

I worked as a crewman—as a rigger who worked on the hull airship envelope and all of its attachments. I was also a flight crewman. Up until the outbreak of the war—Pearl Harbor—we were just working up for war. Our people had developed their first tactics for escorting convoys and anti-submarine warfare. We also developed what we called the expeditionary mast, which was just a stick mast. We could move it around from place to place. For example, we would go to Cape Cod and put up a stick mast and operate there for a couple of months.

What was that?

It was just a mast that could be put up very quickly. It had guide wires to hold it up. You can put one up and down in about an hour. In fact the Goodyear fleet and all the little airships in service today use the same thing.

Were you being followed on the ground by people?

Yeah, usually what we would do is we would send out a crew. In fact, I was on some of the early crews. I can remember going down to Cape May, New Jersey one summer. We dug the postholes for the anchors and put the mast up. Then we'd have a ship come down that day or a day later. We'd have a few old trailer-like vehicles we'd stay in. As the war developed we went all the way from Bar Harbor, Maine, to Rio de Janeiro. Most all of the crews had shipped to them the regular triangle mobile mast with a tractor. Ninety percent of all operations took place from them.

432 The mast was triangular, a steel structure, and it was mounted on dual rubber tires at each corner. It had a tongue on the lead corner that swiveled, and you would hook a tractor to it. You could haul it around wherever you wanted to. A ship might land out in the middle of a landing area, and the mobile mast would come steaming out there with a man on a tractor pulling it. He would pull up in front of the ship, and a cable from the nose of the ship would be threaded through the top of the mast. We had a winch on the mast—a little gasoline engine and drum head—and we would haul in the cable and just throw it over the winch head and winch the nose of the ship right into the mast and secure it.

You were basically covering a lot of coastline during the war.

Yeah, we covered all the coastal convoys out to about two hundred miles out to sea—all the way from Maine down to the Caribbean and around the Panama Canal and South America. There was a lot of important cargo. Crude, for example, came up from Venezuela, and there was bauxite. The biggest thing airships did during the war was we escorted 59,000 merchant vessels without a single loss.

What would you do while you were escorting one when you observed a problem?

Mainly, our purpose was to keep subs down and away from convoys. I had only one incident personally where I know we drove down a German submarine. We were escorting a coast convoy in the early months of 1942. We were just off the Delaware Capes with about eight ships in the convoy. We sighted a German submarine that surfaced about five or six miles upwind from us. So, of course, we immediately turned toward him. He saw us and crash-dived. It was blowing real hard—about a 30 knot wind—and there was no visible evidence. We dropped a couple of depth charges to let him know damn good and well we knew he was there. We had no real chance of finding him—we didn't have any detection devices—no radar at that time. That came along a few months later. At any rate, we drove him down, which did the trick, because there was no way underneath the water he could ever get into an attack position. The convoy went on into the Delaware Bay. That happened lots of times. Submarines were really very, very leery of blimps because blimps could stick around. Airplanes could only stay for a limited amount of time. When a blimp sighted a submarine, that was it for him. The submarine would steer clear.

433

So the blimps had an important impact on the war, you think?

Absolutely. Eventually, we went over to the Strait of Gibralter. The Germans were traveling these straits constantly, and we set up what we called a barrier. We flew back and forth across the straights continuously—a distance of 24 miles. We had a "magnetic airborne detector." Whenever a submarine—or anything metallic—was under the water, it would disturb the magnetic field, and we would detect this. Once we set up the barrier, we stopped the German subs. This was toward the end of the war. Our biggest handicap was that we were not transatlantic. We couldn't take conveys all the way across the ocean.

Why couldn't you escort a convoy across?

Airships weren't big enough and didn't have enough range and endurance. You would have to have a ship about three or four times as big to have been able to carry enough fuel.

Could you do that today?

Modern airships could, if they built them. For instance, the ZPG-3W, which was a million and a half cubic feet, could have done it. But they came along much later.

Give me a problem you found in the early days, when you were flying?

When I say "early days," I mean from 1940 to 1945. The ships went out on long, long flights. Sometimes they were out up to 20 to 24 hours. I've been on a 27 hour flight, and that's a long time in the "K" class wartime size of airship.

One of the chief problems was that—even though we took off heavy, about 2,400 pounds heavy—we would burn up so much fuel during the long flight that we'd come back in very, very light—statically light. We didn't like to valve helium because it was expensive. So we had a heck of a time driving the blimp down to the ground crew, who would then just get a hold of the lines and mule-haul the ship down.

The airship would be upwards to 2,000 statically light. You can just imagine men getting hold of two major handling lines, and trying to snub that ship in. I can remember being out there at night, and the pilots would make eight, nine, ten passes. We'd make jokes like, "Looks like we're going to have to shoot this guy down—if we're ever going to get him down." We'd get dragged all over the landing mat, mule-hauling this doggone airship in. But, you know, we'd always finally prevail and get them in.

I used to be a line runner, which, of course, was when I was young and fast—in those days. When the lines first came in to be handled, the line runners would grab the lines and then run up toward the main group of men, who would then get on the lines and try to bring the ship in. I can remember taking big giant steps when the lines would just be down on the ground and the ship moving forward about the speed of a running man. I'd be taking 20 foot jumps on the end of this line. Of course, lots of times, we'd have to let go. Guys would get knocked on their fanny and all.

Anyone ever get hurt badly?

I remember one ship came in, and the guy in the car party grabbed the railing of the car. When the ship got low enough, the car party would grab the railing to get weight on the ship and haul the ship in. The ship got away from us, and one guy failed to let go. He went up about 20 feet and when he did let go, he came down on his backside and was really hurt badly.

How safe is a blimp?

Oh, hell, safe as can be. The Goodyear Blimp fleet has been operating from the late 1920s and the early 1930s to the present, and they have never scratched a passenger. They have carried well over a million people. The only thing that ever made airships dangerous at all was when they used hydrogen. The *Hindenburg* was the last one to be filled with that. The U.S. Navy dropped hydrogen in about 1922 or 1923 when they had the *Shenandoah*. It was first filled with hydrogen and then it was exhausted from it, then it was filled with helium from then on.

What sort of strange things happen with blimps?

Gosh, more whales have been bombed. Weather too, could be a factor. We flew in some ferocious weather during the war. There were very few days in the war that we didn't go out on a mission. On the East Coast, particularly in wintertime, we had very bad weather, when cold fronts would come through. I would really be miserable.

I can remember experiencing negative Gs in an airship, which is very rare. We were out escorting a convoy when a cold, frontal passage came through. It had about 30 - 35 knots of wind, gusting to 45. The air was very turbulent. I can remember sitting at the navigation table. In those days we used parallel rules and dividers, which are so ancient now—and we were getting so many up and down vertical currents that more than once, I would be suspended over the table—my dividers and rulers in space with me. Then we would slam down with a hell of a jolt. You know, you would be literally floating there.

Did that make you feel like you'd had enough of blimps?

Well, actually, no. When you're young, things like that are kind of prosaic—you just take it as it comes. The navy blimps were extremely rugged aircraft. Once airborne they were virtually indestructible. One thing about a blimp is they bend rather than break. In severe weather, I have practically seen the tail back there bending a little bit from the force. We weathered near-hurricane conditions in them. On the ground, that's another story—they can be very tough to handle.

What's the hardest thing about working back and forth between lighter-than-air and heavier-than-air?

There wasn't any. That's one of the funny things about it. After the war, when I was in Airship Test and Development, when I did all my flight test work for the navy, I used to fly an airplane—an AD Skyraider. I'd fly to Akron to do some business that day and fly back. I've literally gone from an airplane to an airship the same day and started flying it. You know, you just never think of it. I think if you're an aviator, an aviator is an aviator, is an aviator.

Now, I can remember one time I was flying and I thought, "God, this is just like an airship." I was flying an SNJ trainer—it was out at Barron Field in Alabama. I was coming around in what they called the field carrier landing practice pattern. The SNJ came around the pattern, pretty slow—at around 65 knots. I came around over a big, sandy area—during July it was hotter than the hubs of hell—and there was a big thermal over that sandy area. In an airplane a thermal is a vertical current of air that is fast and abrupt, whereas in an airship it's a long, slow motion. Anyway, as I came around in the plane, it just ballooned up. That happened because I was going so slow and it was a fairly light airplane, and it was a very strong, vertical movement of air. Just for a moment I thought the feeling was just like an airship. Then, I went on with the landing and never thought two cents about it. Only occasionally, when I was in one kind, I thought of the other. There are quite a few differences in flying them.

What are the main differences?

Airplanes are obviously faster; things happen quicker; they respond to control inputs much much quicker. Those are the principle differences.

You tested blimps. Tell me about that.

I spent four years in Airship Test and Development. I did some test work for Goodyear—including work on one we developed there from the standard airship that Goodyear was using when I joined. It was called the GZ-19 and was about 156,000 cubic feet. We then went to the GZ-20, which is a 200,000 cubic-feet airship.

Blimps get certified, don't they? How does that work?

Yes. Well, it works just like it works for an airplane now.

Actually, that's what I've done since leaving Goodyear. I left in June 1984. Since then, I've been a consultant and test pilot for these new, little outfits—American Blimp Corporation, out of Seattle, and USLTA in Tillamook, Oregon. They're both running ships through certification right now.

Is certification a lengthy experience?

I can tell you it's a big job going through FAA certification. The FAA will let you do almost anything as long as you don't try to sell it commercially. Once you want to sell it commercially, then you have to go through the whole ballgame, and it's a big, long process.

Anything out of the ordinary happen in certifications you've seen?

When Jim Thiele (designer and builder) and I were flight-testing the A-50 in Phoenix, there was a situation involving the ballonet.

A ballonet is an air compartment made of flexible fabric and what it does, is it takes the place of expansion and contraction of the helium. As the helium expands, you let air out of this air compartment through an air valve. When it's contracting you pump air into the air compartment—so you are never varying the helium. You are just pumping air in and out.

Anyway, we went up to a couple of thousand feet and started back down. But we found we were unable to maintain pressure, so we leveled off. What was happening is the air was getting trapped behind the exit. Jim crawled back into the ballonet and cleared it manually—he just pushed the fabric away from the opening. So we landed, and he went into town and bought one of those laundry baskets, made of plastic—the ones with holes. He took that and brought it in and just placed it over the air inlet, so when the fabric fell down around it, the air couldn't get trapped. He did that for about $20 or less. Of course, you know the FAA would never buy anything like that, so he engineered a good fix for it. It shows you what you can do if you aren't constrained by a lot of technicalities.

438

What are the prime differences—or advantages—of airships from airplanes?

Well, it's different. An airplane can fly fast as something with a low drag, and it can get around very shiftily, but its endurance is relatively limited. It also takes a hell of a lot of energy to fly an airplane—you use a lot of fuel. With a blimp, because it's being lifted by helium, all you have to do is push it forward; you don't have to hold it up. All you need to use the engines for is to move it. Now, because it's a high-drag vehicle, you can't move it fast, but you can use a very small amount of energy to go 60 miles per hour for a long time. Because of this, airships have long endurance, and they can carry a big load. There are instances where that's a big advantage and also the cost can be considerably less.

Did you ever crash one?

Ah, yes, but it was a malfunction. This happened about 1958, I guess. It had an electrical control system, and I was coming in for a landing. I wasn't actually at the controls—I had a guy in for instruction. Anyway, he pushed over and I was expecting him to take the control out. All of a sudden we were blasting right for the ground. I was sitting next to him, and I could see him—he was yanking like the devil on the yoke, but it wasn't moving—it was frozen forward. What had happened is that one of the electrical control wires into the control column broke, and the whole system froze right where it was. By then we yanked off the power, but we went in, crunched the landing gear, and were stuck nose into the ground. We were on the heavy side, so I decided to stay on the ground rather than free the balloon off again. A lot of people came and took the ship in hand and put it in a hangar, but that was malfunction more than anything.

What was the most scared you've ever been?

The most scared I've ever been has been in airplanes, but I can remember one time having some anxious moments in an airship. I was going down the coast of South America during the war, ferrying a ship from one point to the next. About halfway through the 600 mile flight, we hit really strong winds and I was down to twelve miles per hour ground speed for five hours, just dragging along. I was beginning to wonder if I was ever going to make it. Toward sunset the winds eased off. We started picking up speed and, first thing you know, I was up to 50, 60, and I steamed on in to Maceio, Brazil, way late at night. I did get there. That was kind of anxious.

I crashed once in South America, then again...when I was ferrying.

What happened?

We hit dense fog just north of Rio and ran into a small mountain that was not on the chart. It was a crash. I mean, it was a wipeout.

Was anyone killed?

Nobody was killed. We hit into a sloping , jungle-covered island called Cabo Frio, just north of Rio at about two o'clock in the morning. I was knocked out, and one guy had his foot torn up; another guy had his scalp laid open. There were nine of us. Everybody else was fine.

439

It was one of the weirdest sensations I ever had. I came to, and the rest of the crew had already gotten out, and the chief pilot, Joe Bartoff—I was his copilot—had just sent someone back in to find me. I was the only one missing after they mustered back there. When I came to, I remember scrambling down the flooring and the decking of the ship. It was all kind of jumbled up, and I remember I appeared at the entrance door of the ship and looked out. Of course, it was dark, but they had flashlights, and I could see these guys on the ground.

The last thing I was conscious of was in normal flight. It was so hard to take in what in God's name had happened. The crew members got me down and saw I was cut all around the face. Apparently, I was at the navagation table, and the sudden deceleration threw me forward in the ship—all the way up in the nose. (They took ground wood out of the corner of my eye.) No one will ever know, though, because nobody found me up there in the front of the airship. I staggered to the back of the ship, and I didn't know where I was. Then, they patched me up, and Oh God! I'll never forget those open wounds. Of course, the big fear down in that part of the country was always infection.

What did you use?

We used sulfanilamide; that was the first wonder drug. It's a kind of yellow powder. They sprinkled this in all my wounds to keep me from having infection. Then, Joe Bartoff and two of the crew made their way to the bottom of the island. They fell in ravines. There were wild pigs. It turned out to be Cabo Frio. It seems we hit at the 250 foot level—the mountain was 1,092 feet high. I can remember all those details, vividly. We carried machetes just for jungle incidents like this. Imagine modern aircraft running around, carrying a couple of machetes. They turned out to be very useful.

The crew got down, and there were some fishermen coming out of the village of Cabo Frio, which is on the mainland. The men managed to get the attention of the fishermen, and those fishermen really saved our butts. They came to the top of the mountain, where the rest of us were. We had two big pipe bunks in the ship, and we yanked one of them out and laid the guy with the torn foot on it. These natives took the machetes and literally hacked our way down the island. It was so thick that there was one place where they had to turn this kid on the bunk—his name was Jones—almost on edge to get him through. That's how narrow the path would get. We got down to the bottom at about four o'clock in the afternoon, and the local doctor came out in a motor boat. He took us all in to this little clinic.

The doctor had been trained in France. He was really very good, but his equipment was very austere—and there was very little of it. He cleaned me up. I'll never forget: he sewed me up all around my face with catgut and a curved needle—without any anesthetic.

The air force sent out a great big powerful truck—four-wheel drive—and they hauled all of us from this little fishing village. The French doctor probably saved my butt, except he put more sulfa dust into me. I got into Rio and the air force doctor put more sulfa on me. I ended up with a hell of a case of sulfanilamide poisoning. It took about two months to work its way out of my system.

How about flying in Europe? Were there any logistical problems?

Oh, what a hassle. When we first went to Europe, no one had flown a blimp over there except for this one German. He flew just inside Germany.

Goodyear put the ship together in Cardington, England, and then we had to get permits to fly all over Europe. We finally got it all straightened out at the higher levels, but you still have to cross borders and go through customs. Most customs people are good. We would go from one airport to another, and there would be a local customs guy, who would come up and check passports and stuff like that. But the ground crews, which had big vehicles full of parts and equipment, would have to cross the borders and would be in with all the rest of the trucks, and it would be a big hassle for them sometimes.

The one good thing about being in public relations is that the department would have all these souvenirs and stuff they would hand out to the public and passengers: bracelets and pins, pencils and key rings—I don't know what all. So the crew would start handing out souvenirs, and pretty soon they were best friends with the people in customs, and we'd zip through customs.

Actually the first one or two years were really tough, because every time we had a border to cross, it was a brand-new deal. But we got to making the run regularly and we got to be like the birds flying north in the summer and south in the winter, because we would go up from Rome, we'd go through Italy, across the Mediterranean, through France, through the Rhone Valley, and spread off either into France or into Germany. It got to be a milk run—a very enjoyable one.

Any other difficult experience that stands out in your mind?

Many years after the war, I was coming down from Kiel, Germany, to Kassel. The flight started out all right. I was with Fred Gebhardt, a German pilot that I was training. God, we really ran into some still winds and rough air. It was so rough that Fred, the student, couldn't really cope with it, so I had to fly the last three or four hours by myself. I mean, that ship just bucked around and roamed all over the sky. We finally slugged our way into Kassel and landed. I've never really thought, "I'm not going to make it." I've had some hairy times in airplanes. But with a blimp, you just get to where you have a tremendous amount of confidence. They can usually outlast the weather.

442

They're so forgiving. You have a lot of time in one and, if you keep your wits about you, you can get out of almost any kind of scrape. I think the closest call we've had in a Goodyear flight was when some guys got caught in a thunderstorm up around Albany. They got blown way up into the air and lost a lot of helium, which scared the living hell out of them. They finally worked their way out of the thunderstorm, got back down, and landed.

What was the most mystical experience you've had while flying?

The gray whales make a run up the West Coast every January, February, and March, and a whale society got wind of us. So we flew up toward Catalina, looking at whales, and I thought the people were going to jump out of the ship. We saw lots of whales. God, they are majestic. We saw the whales in groups of six and eight, and sometimes they would be solitary. And, you could see mothers with their young.

I'm not the most mystical type of person, but I tell you, the most emotional experiences were during cross-country, because a lot of times you are seeing new terrain.

Have you flown any celebrities?

There was a real big one, when I first joined the Goodyear organization. I had been flying for years, but I had little time with Goodyear. The chief pilot there was Dean Mealey—a hell of a guy. He was considered by many to be the greatest airship pilot ever. He was the test pilot for the ZPG-3W for Goodyear, when I was still in the navy. I was the navy representative for flight testing for the 3W, and we flew together lots then.

Time went by, and here I was out of the navy and Dean was chief pilot for the little old *Mayflower* down in Miami. I think this was my first summer on tour. We went in to York, Pennsylvania. I was in charge of the ground crew; Dean was flying. I was setting up the mast, and a fellow named Chelsy Brothers, one of the crewmen, says, "Look over there, General Eisenhower, president of the U.S." I looked and saw Eisenhower getting out of this plane. So just out of the blue, Chelsy says, "I'm going over to ask if he wants a ride." I said, "That's a good idea. You got the guts—go ahead, Chelsy."

Eisenhower was quite a guy—interested in everything. In fact, he had been a pilot in some small way. So Chelsy came running over and says, "Yeah, he'll go for a ride." I said, "Oh, God." I called Dean up on the radio, and while we were putting the mast up, Dean continued to fly around. We all lined up real fast. Dean came in for a landing—we put the general on board and away he flew.

What about some other big events you have covered?

Goodyear has covered many big events—sporting, fairs, papal visits, air shows—you name it. One of the big ones was the royal wedding of Prince Charles and Princess Diana in London. Fred Gebhardt— the student of five years before on the Kiel to Kassel flight—had risen to chief pilot of the *Europa*, and covered most of it with a TV camera on board. I covered the royal couples' departure on the railroad train from central London. We chased the train until it pulled out of sight. I was manager of Goodyear blimp *Europa* then.

What's the hardest thing about covering sporting events?

If there is no wind—and a lot of times there isn't—it's hard to hold stationary at a particular location, because once you stop, you don't have any air flow over the control surfaces. You are just kind of flopping around up there. It takes a lot of judicious changing of trim and using the engine discreetly to hold your position, because thermals are moving you up and down. I can remember covering golf matches at Torre Pines near San Diego. I used to like to try to get in real tight for pictures. It wouldn't make any noise, because I was within maybe 300 - 400 yards of the golfers, off to one side. I can remember watching the par-three hole, watching the ball leave the tee, ride up and go onto the green. Most of the time, you are so doggone busy up there you don't see a heck of a lot and others say, "Oh, you've got the best seat in the house." Well, yes and no.

I've been inside of the Indianapolis 500, right inside the infield. You could hear those guys screaming around the track. If you didn't have a radio or something, you didn't know who was leading. We finally got a little TV monitor in the ship, so we could tell what the hell was going on.

What's the biggest event you've covered?

In one sense, I think covering the World Cup Soccer in Europe is one of the biggest. I've covered the Rose Bowl, but I'll tell you one event that was really meaningful to me was during the war. I escorted the *Queen Mary* out of New York Harbor, when it was shoving off for Europe. All we had to do was get them out to the swept channel and cover the ship about 100 miles or so out to sea. Then the old ship rumbled along on its own. It could really move—at maybe 30 knots.

Of course, I did that during World War II. When the old *Queen* was finally through its service, they sold it to the Port of Long Beach. So they sailed the *Queen* down around Cape Horn, because they couldn't get through the Panama Canal, and came up to Long Beach Harbor.

The day of its arrival was a big to-do. I said, "Boy, I'm going to cover that one with the ship, because I remember the *Queen* from the war."

I was then chief pilot for the airship Columbia. So I covered the *Queen*. There were more yachts that day than I've ever seen in my life.

How'd it make you feel, looking down on that?

It was a nostalgic feeling—I must tell you.

How about any reflections—parting shots?

There's nothing else like flying. It's just something. Once I got into it, I never looked back. I'd never want to do anything else.

I've learned from old-timers, and I've passed it along to the newcomers. I get a lot of satisfaction out of that. There aren't very many blimp pilots, and I've had a hand in training a lot of them.

The funny thing was, when I retired from Goodyear, I was sure that was it. That was the end. I would never fly again and all that crap. So the guys gave me a big going-away and retirement party. I was on my way back to Akron then. And, hell, I got a big retirement party from my crew at Mannheim, Germany. Then I got one from the lighter-than-air people in Rome and in Akron, then I got one from my PR department. I had four retirement parties!

Since I left Goodyear, I've been doing all this consulting work, and I've flown two different airships, the Aerotek/USLTA 138S out of Tillamook and A-50s and A-60s for American Blimp Corporation. Then I went down to Mexico on a consulting job. I'm still at it! Old pilots never give up—they just fly off into the wild blue yonder.

445

Bill Heath (left) during World War II.

BILL HEATH
An Enlisted Pilot

Bill Heath enlisted in the navy in 1939 and following boot camp was assigned to a World War I destroyer, the USS *Clemson*. He ended up in Panama after a transfer from the ship over to base radio in San Juan, Puerto Rico, where he got a chance to fly as radio man third class in a squadron that was flying PBYs. While there, he applied for flight training, and around Thanksgiving 1941, received orders to report to Pensacola for flight school. Because the war had started, he completed, he says, "one of the fastest flight courses ever given by anybody—instrument training, formation flying, navigation, and bombardier training, celestial and dead reckoning in seven months." I asked him what was it like being an enlisted pilot.

"Being an enlisted pilot was an unusual thing. Once when I was flying into Alameda—at the time we didn't have hard hats; we'd just wear our white hat or a baseball cap—I landed and the guy puts chocks under my wheels, and I climbed down wearing my white hat and dungarees. He stood there, looking all around. I said, "Who are you looking for?"

He says, "The pilot."

I said, "I'm the pilot."

He said, "No, I'm looking for the pilot."

He wouldn't believe me. So I said, "He's in the back seat." (There was a bag of sand back there for ballast.) The guy then climbed up on the wing and looked in there. He finally realized that I was the pilot, so I said, "Okay, are you going to give me the yellow sheet to sign, so I can go get a cup of coffee" [laughs]. That sort of thing happened a lot.

We were in Fort Lyautey, French Morroco, North Africa, and were flying down to Bathhurst at night. I was navigating the flight. Our briefing officer told us to stay away from the Canary Islands, a Spanish territory, which was very hostile toward Americans. It was a long flight down—maybe ten hours over water. No lights on the shore. About 2 A.M. I wanted to shoot a star fix with the octant. I grabbed one of the crew to record the time when I said "mark." While I was getting the octant lined up on a star, I saw a streaking light passing through the lens. I asked the timekeeper if he had seen it. He said, "no." I tried again, and again I saw the streaking white light. Still the timekeeper didn't see it. All of a sudden, about half a mile to the rear, there was a blast that was obviously anti-aircraft fire. I realized those streaks I was seeing were tracer bullets. I told my comrade: "I know exactly where we are. Let's get out of here!" Of course, it had to be Canary Islands."

448

How early did you get interested in flight?

I can remember when I was a kid. I lived in Bayonne, New Jersey. I used to go to Carney. They built destroyers there. I always wanted to go in the navy, maybe because my father was in the navy in World War I. We'd go to see those little old destroyers they were building, but I realized I preferred planes. I was never a brilliant student, but I tried hard—barely maintained average. Still, the only time I ever skipped school was when I went to Newark Airport to see the *Gee Bee*.

After flight school, July 1942, the squadron I was assigned to was in Alameda, California, and was picked to be equipped with some top-secret equipment that would pick up submarines under water. There wasn't anything on the West Coast we could do with the equipment, so they sent us to the East Coast. Then they told us to pack our white uniform for about a two-month stay. This was around May 1943. Guess what? We ended up in Iceland. It was all secret stuff we couldn't even tell our families about, and we didn't go back home for two years.

We went to Iceland, then to Wales. Flying down there, I saw a bit of action: Germans flying out of France and trying to intercept us in the Bay of Biscay. Our standard patrol would be out of Pembroke dock down to landfall on Spain, back to a point off France we called Junker's Junction. They called it this because of the Ju 88s. They came out from the Brest Peninsula, which gave them a rather short trip to intercept our north-south route. On my fourth trip, which was a three-plane sweep, we were flying a rather loose formation, going down. However, going back the weather had turned sour, so we tightened the formation. When we were in the vicinity of Junker's Junction, the plane on our right, which was the one closest to France, sent a coded message saying they were under air attack. We immediately dropped down under the clouds to join them. The clouds were breaking up, and everything seemed quiet. We and the P-boat stayed and searched the area until gasoline required us to leave. This was the first engagement in World War II of the United States Navy and the Luftwaffe. Three days later a British sea-going tug rescued the three crew from that plane, which had been shot down. Our guys were credited with four Jus. Not bad for the old 110-knot fighter.

Then they sent us to Africa where we flew the Straits of Gibralter. That's where we sank three submarines. They were coming from the Atlantic into the Mediterranean. We just flew a fence—a two and one-half mile fence between Africa and Spain.

449

Any problem picking the subs up?

No, every sub we picked up, we sank. Flying the fence, our highest elevation would be 100 feet above the water. The cold water from the Atlantic going under the warm water from the Mediterranean prevented the British from picking them up with their destroyers. We received a commendation for this, because during the year and a half, we did what we did without losing a single airplane in the straits. In other areas we lost 12 aircraft and 35 crewmen. I was in two of the lost aircraft.

We had two planes out there all the time, but not at night. They sent over some blimps who'd do the honors at night. On one occasion the weather people told us they expected fog in the morning. We got in our planes and stayed overnight in Gibralter, then went out early in the morning. We'd get to our station about seven. We always had two planes out who'd try to stay 180 degrees apart. One of our airplanes picked up a signal a little after 8 a.m. We got the signal. There was a button right on the yoke. We pressed that button, and the smoke lights would be fired out of the tail hatch. We marked our contacts with float lights. Two on initial contact, and one on each individual contact, thus giving us a path to follow on the fourth contact. Thirty retro-rockets would be fired off at the same speed the aircraft was going forward. An intervalometer would fire three rows of ten bombs.

We were among the first to have sonobuoys, which was a long tube of electronics with an antenna on it. When it hit the water, it would drop a hearing device that could detect underwater sound and we could tell if we got a hit or not. This time we had lost the location of the doggone sub three times. Then we'd pick them up again. The fourth time around, we dropped our bombs and the other plane dropped his. We each got three hits. Then when the sub surfaced, the British came up and let them have it with the hedgehog rockets.

The first sub we sank, we had the same thing happen: we'd lose them, then pick them up again. One time British ships were dropping those markers down there. The Americans told the British to get the hell out of there, so they could do their job. They backed off, and the Americans went in and got a couple of hits. Next, the British went in and shot the sub. I wasn't there at this time, but apparently the sub came up, and when it did the bow came up high; the stern was still kind of low. About that time, a British Corvette and an American PV-2 each made a pass on them. The poor bastards were trying to get out of the submarine, not knowing they were already sunk. Just then, the British ship blew the tail end off the other British Corvette.

We were the only units in the world to have the equipment I mentioned; we were the first navy squadron to get radar, the first to get sonobuoys, and the first navy squadron to engage the Luftwaffe. Also, the first submarine we sank was the first one ever sunk without making first a visual sighting.

Did your sinking the subs affect things?

The area admiral commended us by saying that VP-63 turned the Mediterranean into an Allied lake. In fact, the Germans didn't sink another Allied ship in the Med during the rest of the war. I know this saved many a GI who got to Italy from North Africa. They stopped sending subs through after that. We still kept our planes up there, though. One story here: the French had earlier doubted our ability to hit subs in Gibralter. As a consequence, we invited them to send one of their subs through. We knew about what time they were coming because we didn't want to think they were a German sub and actually sink them. I was flying that day, and we picked them up. We only dropped a practice depth charge. Practice depth charges weren't very big, but they were equipped with a shotgun shell, so if they hit the sub, they made a big bang. We sure gave them a welcome. After that, one of our guys says, "Let's go down about ten miles and do it again." So we did [laughs].

What's the funniest thing that happened when flying after the war?

451

While instructing students one night in Corpus Christi, Texas—and when flying saucers were a hot item—I was sitting in the left seat coaching a cadet through night landings, when the tower directed us to leave the traffic pattern for about fifteen minutes. We climbed to about 1,500 feet on a southeast course, which took us toward the Gulf, which was very dark—no moon. The cadet was making a shallow turn when I saw a light. It appeared to be slightly below us and moving. I asked the cadet if he had seen it. He said he had. I told him to hold a steady course, which he did, but the light still seemed to be moving. I called the tower to confirm if he had any traffic in our area. He gave me a negative. Finally, I took the controls and went right for it. It was farther away than I thought, and now I was thinking UFO. We finally got to it and discovered it to be the gas burning off an oil well. We all got a good laugh at that one.

WILLIAM H. HOLLOMAN III

Tuskegee Airman

On his 18th birthday, William H. Holloman III applied to the Army Air Corps for the pilot training program. The date was August 21, 1942. He would later graduate as a second lieutenant pilot from Tuskegee Army Air Field, Alabama, where he became one of the Tuskegee Airmen, a group of World War II African-American fliers whose work has been largely overlooked until recently.

In the interview, Holloman talks about the indignities of racial intolerance. Naively or not, he felt race had not been an issue to any great extent growing up in a sheltered environment in St. Louis, unconscious of the racism that existed throughout the city. He would find things different almost from the moment he stepped on a train headed for training at Keesler Army Air Field in Biloxi, Mississippi. Holloman has served as a pilot in three wars—World War II, Korea, and Vietnam. He flew P-40s, P-47s and P-51s during WWII and after the war was over, he stayed in the Air Corps until 1947. From there, he attended St. Louis University in engineering for a year before returning to the Army Air Corps as a fighter pilot with his old unit, the 332nd Fighter Group, which later became a separate branch of the U.S. Air Force.

The appeal of the academy struck again in 1950 and he returned to school at the University of California at Berkeley to study architecture. It was while he was at UC that he had a reserve assignment with SAC [Special Agent in Command] that led to his recall due to the Korean Conflict. He still had a knee problem which got him out of fighters in the first place, thus preventing him from getting into a tactical fighter unit. Instead, he was assigned to MATS with various duties as pilot for medical evacuation and air rescue in Korea. It was during this period that he became the first Black helicopter pilot in the air force.

After the Korean War, he sought his fortune as a commercial pilot. Many companies, in answering letters, said he was qualified and wanted to interview him. But, when they interviewed him and saw the color of his skin, there were plenty of excuses. He sued and won a judgment in one such situation.

Over the next couple of years, he had jobs in helicopter training and then crop dusting in Central America, which led to an offer to go to work as a pilot for Pacific Western Airlines in Vancouver, British Columbia. It didn't take long to make his decision; he didn't even ask how much money he would be making.

As an expert in aircraft accident investigations, safety, and standards, he was sought by army aviation for service in Vietnam as early as 1963. Already having 15 years of active military service in the army, air force, and army again, he said he would go to Vietnam, but only if they would keep him for five years so he would qualify for retirement. An arrangement was worked out by late 1966 and he joined a new unit for deployment to Vietnam. After 13 months in Vietnam, 1967-68, he was assigned to USAREUR where he retired in 1972.

Despite a myriad of setbacks, William H. Holloman III seems sanguine about it all, a tribute to his courage and full confidence.

What was your earliest interest in flight?

I had a neighbor, whose name I believe was Bonnet, who was a kind of big brother to his own younger brother and those of us his age. In the mid 1930s, he taught us how to build model airplanes, some history of aviation, and often told us stories about World War I war planes, the early barnstormers, and of course, the feats of Charles Lindbergh and his solo Transatlantic flight. It was exciting.

How did you view a flight career as a Black man? Did you look at it as a difficult thing to do?

I don't think I saw any real obstacles in my desires to fly. It just seemed like it would be fun and exciting to soar like the eagles. I used to go out to Lambert, St. Louis's airport just to watch airplanes. Back in those days, if you didn't make bus connections, you had a long wait or had to walk the last two miles to the airport. I was always too impatient to wait, so I walked. I spent considerable time just walking around watching people working on planes and asking questions. I finally talked my way into a job there around 1937.

What was that?

One guy paid me ten cents an hour to clean up around the hangar, wash airplanes and do other simple tasks. That was big bucks back then, and I was happy being able to touch those little planes. The job came about from my continually asking him for a ride in a plane. He had told me that it would cost four or five dollars. Of course, I told him I didn't have that kind of money. I figured if I asked my parents for money for something like that, they would think I was crazy and laugh at me. You know people were still living in the lean years of the 1929 crash. At any rate, I saved money from my newspaper route and what I was making in the hangar working for these guys. The first time I got in an aircraft I was charged a day's work just to sit there for about 15 minutes. I must have been the joke of the hangar.

455

Do you remember your first flight there?

Oh, yeah! It was an open cockpit bi-wing aircraft. I don't remember the type of aircraft, but it was a real thrill. The pilot pointed out landmarks as we flew over the area and did all kinds of maneuvers I would come to learn in later years. The first time I went up I felt like my heart was going to go right through the top of my head. I hung onto the aircraft for dear life and prayed I would get back on the ground, in one piece. Yet once we were on the ground I was ready to go again.

It changed your life?

It changed my life. But, what's interesting is the fact that I must have gone three more years before I got into another airplane. Finally in 1940, a friend of mine told me how he had been up in an airplane. He said, "Come over to Illinois and you can go up for four dollars." His older brother, also a flying enthusiast, accompanied us to Park Air Field in Illinois, which was later to become Park Air College during World War II.

What did you ride in?

It was an Aeronca, which was a two-seater. We were in the air for about 30 or 40 minutes. I sat next to the pilot and handled the controls. I didn't think I'd ever learn to fly because I was having difficulty just keeping the plane straight. I was almost 16 years old and as a result of that ride, I joined the Civil Air Patrol (CAP). This was the period where I first became cognizant of the racial issue. My CAP unit was the only one to which the Black cadets, referred to then as Negroes, were assigned.

What did you learn while in the CAP?

We studied basic ground school subjects such as aerodynamics, aircraft mechanics, meteorology and navigation.

Do you remember anything unique about your instructor?

No, except that when he left during the Battle of Britain, we heard that he had gone to Canada to join the Royal Canadian Air Force. A number of the older fellows in the unit followed the same procedure. In fact in 1941, I had written to the Royal Canadian Air Force inquiring about their qualifications. I had heard that a person could join there at 17 and that high school graduates met their educational requirements. However, I think my main reason for inquiring was that Canada was involved in the war in Europe, and there was something exciting about being a fighter pilot. I couldn't even drive, but flying never seemed dangerous to me. So, in a way, he apparently planted the seed about the possibilities of flying in Canada.

What did your parents think about flying?

My father had been the first to take my brothers and me to Lambert Field to see an air show in the early 1930s, so I know he had some curiosity about flight. He had an interest in looking at planes, but to fly in one, that was out of the question. I often attempted to talk him into going for a ride with me, but he always had a reason for putting it off. Now, my mother was another matter. When I finally told her about my second flight out of Park in Illinois, she went through the roof.

What did she say?

It would be simpler to tell you what she didn't say. She said, "Those things can fall out of the sky and kill you." When I was leaving for combat in World War II, she said, "Remember to fly low and not too fast." They both had different reactions when I got the papers back from Canada.

457

What was that?

My mother wasn't about to sign any papers. There was no discussion. I was just a child and she was not going to let me pull a stupid stunt like going to war to get killed trying to show off.

Your father wouldn't sign them, either?

I think up until high school, I had been giving my parents trouble in school. My father made the comment that my attention span was too short for me to learn how to fly an airplane. He also led me to believe that he did not think I was smart enough—he somewhat ridiculed me about my desire.

What did he say?

Well, he just said, "You don't have what it takes to fly"—or something to that effect. He challenged me. He said, "You don't have the intelligence." He also commented that he had never seen a Negro pilot—that he didn't know if there were any. I told him that I did know two Black pilots, that my squadron leader in the CAP was a pilot as was his replacement.

That was a pretty valuable piece of information for you to give him.

Yes. He even met my second squadron leader when he came by my school to attempt to interest some other boys in flying in late December 1941 or early 1942. He had been in the neighborhood, so he used the opportunity to talk to a half-dozen kids there, but only one, Doug Seals, joined the CAP squadron. Anyway, I lived right down the street from school, so as he was walking back to the catch the street car, I spotted my dad coming home from work and introduced them. They talked for a while and my dad thanked him for working with me and the other kids, and I believe my dad invited him to the American Legion, Tom Powell Post. So, my father really wasn't disinterested. He said years later, after I came back from the war, that he had prodded me into doing something in which I showed some interest by taking the negative approach and telling me that I didn't have the ability. His prodding prompted me to say to myself, "I'll show you."

458

He used to tell the guys at the Legion that had it not been for him, I wouldn't have had the determination to make it. He was very proud of that fact. When I first graduated from flight school and came home—the first day—he took me down to the Legion to show me off to his buddies.

Had he served in the military?

Yes, he had seen service with the 93rd Infantry Division in France during World War I. You know, our city produced a large number of Black airmen during the war. I remember James McCullin, whose mother ran the candy store right on the corner from our school, was the first to sign up for pilot training in St. Louis, Missouri. Another pilot I knew well was Wendell Pruitt, who had completed pilot training before I went in. His brother, Luther, who lived a few doors from us, worked with my cousin. Wendell looked sharp in that uniform, and I was determined to be just like him.

What was the hardest transition to the Tuskegee Institute, when you got there?

My ignorance of racial practices in the south. When I left St. Louis, there were four of us that left together for Keesler Field, Biloxi, Mississippi, on the train. It was a Pullman car and we were in a four-person parlor. We had the freedom of the train from St. Louis to Evansville, Indiana. When the train left Evansville, the conductor came in and told us we had to move to the coach car up front. We explained that our tickets were for this parlor compartment to Mobile, Alabama, and that we had been paid for by the government. John Squires told him we were not going to move. There was much discussion on the matter, and after intervention by some army official, we were permitted to stay put. Sometime after the matter was settled, and before reaching Nashville, Tennessee, we all went to the dining car to eat, as we had done from St. Louis to Evansville. Were refused service. Again, it was pointed out that we had government paid meal tickets and were entitled to eat. At this point, we were told we would have to wait until colored passengers were served. When we returned again, there was this curtain up which they sat us behind for our meal. It was very degrading. We felt apprehension and fear. I told myself anything was worth going through to get an opportunity to fly. After our meal, we were told to stay in our parlor. As I recall, when we arrived at Nashville, Tennessee, the conductor attempted to move us to the Jim Crow car again, and even called for the military police (MP) to force us to move, but they left us there until the next morning at which time they took the Pullman car off the train and informed us that there was no space in the remaining Pullman cars. We were forced to move to the Jim Crow car for Blacks in coach, but were still permitted to go to the dining car, with its curtain, for our meals. I think one of the more depressing things about the whole incident was that our uniforms were nice, clean and neatly pressed when we left St. Louis. We were very proud of the way we looked and that we were embarking on a venture to serve our country. In that Jim Crow car, right behind the engine, believe me it was hot. The windows open and the soot from that engine blew into the car. By the time we got off the train in Biloxi, we looked like death warmed over. You couldn't tell what color those uniforms were. You must understand, here we were, four 18 years-old, and for the first time in our lives we were far away from our parents, friends and home. The excitement of being near military aircraft and the joy of future dreams somewhat offset the disgust and anger of a racist system that required young Black Americans to endure such treatment. At any rate, the trucks picked us up and took us to Keesler Field, Mississippi, where we spent the next three or four weeks.

Do you remember anything unusual about being at Tuskegee?

We were all young kids—many had no college education—which requires us to go through one semester of college at Tuskegee Institute—now Tuskegee University—to prepare us for the strenuous training ahead. We went to school all day and studied half the night for about two months. We were in a college environment, yet we were controlled. By this I mean we had to march everywhere we went, to and from class and mess. There were only military students of a single class in each course or classroom. No other college students from the university. They didn't give us very much free time. There was at least one girl there whom I knew from St. Louis. She provided an introductory link to other female students on campus.

Any funny stories about trying to see her or any other girl or any outrageous punishment for trying to see girls?

Nothing that I can remember off the top of my head. We were free after Saturday's inspection until bed check on Sunday, so we had plenty of time to attend movies, dances, church, and other social interactions. You must understand, we were there to learn and failure to comply meant being eliminated from the program. I have heard stories of fellows in the girls' dorm and about others slipping out all night, but I have no direct knowledge of such conduct.

Did you have any friends that didn't make it? It was a demanding experience.

Someone was leaving all the time for failure to keep up with the academic pace or the inability to adjust to the discipline demanded of military personnel. Of the members that were eventually in our

CTD class—there were six from St. Louis—only Fischer didn't make it to pre-flight. He remained at the Institute after our class left to begin our first phase of training at Tuskegee Army Air Field. My closest friend was washed back in primary, so the remaining four graduated and went on to fly combat in Italy. You must understand we were so submerged in our own survival and completing the course that we had little time to worry or help people outside our class.

You flew in three wars. Is there anything that sticks out in your mind from World War II?

I think most of us were excited about getting into combat. We were a cocky group, all under 21, and thinking we were the best pilots in the world, able to out-fly any enemy pilot. We felt this after having just completed nearly 130 hours in the P-47. I think probably one of the most disappointing things we had to learn was that our commander wouldn't let us go off chasing German planes. Our early missions were bomber escorts and we had to stay with our bombers unless they were attacked by German fighters. Even if we sighted German fighters out there and wanted to go after them, our instructions, in no uncertain terms, were that unless the planes attacked the bombers, we were to leave them alone. If you consider the tactics involved, those planes were probably sitting out there to lure us away and leave the bombers uncovered, so they could have another group of fighters, not seen by us, ready to attack the unprotected bombers. At that time, some pilots may have been somewhat unhappy about not being able to go after those planes, but sticking to mission plans paid off in saved bombers in the long run. Years later, after some research had been conducted, we found out that our fighter group had the distinction of never losing a bomber to enemy aircraft. That, as the records have revealed, was quite a feat.

461

What other accomplishments of the Tuskegee Airmen stand out in your mind?

I remember Easter Sunday 1945. The Red Tails, flying the North American P-51, shot down 13 German fighters while losing only one. And the pilot of the plane we lost, after bailing out, was home by dinner. I think the unique thing about this was that they confirmed 13 that day, and then went out the next day and shot down 12 more. I thought that was a record, but in doing my research on our unit, I discovered that the Ninety-Ninth Fighter Squadron had matched that some time prior to my arrival in combat. I think another mission of note was when we covered the Fifth Bomb Wing's B-17s on the raid to Berlin, which was the longest raid for the Fifteenth Air Force. This mission taxed our P-51 fighters to the limit of their range, though we had 110 gallon, external fuel tanks.

The job of 332nd Fighter Group was to escort the bombers to a point southwest of Berlin where they would be picked up by another fighter group that would escort them over the target. That group was late, and the Red Tails were directed to stay with the bombers for their run over the target. On that particular raid the Red Tails shot down three German jet fighters. That was significant since the numbers I have indicated that the Fifteenth Air Force's five fighter groups destroyed eight German jet fighters during the war. The 332nd accounted for three on a single mission.

What frightened you the most?

At first, it was the flak. In fact, the Germans threw that stuff up like people throwing rice at a wedding—it was so thick. Our tactic was to change direction and altitude continually so their guns could not get a fix on our planes. Frequently, planes returned to base with holes from those guns—it seemed like part of a day's mission. I think probably the most frightened I had been was when we were on a fighter sweep in central Germany near Nuremberg. We had spotted this convoy on a road below, moving in the right direction. Our mission was to take out all traffic moving south—highway, rail, and barge. Anyway, we spotted a convoy of three large trucks with trailers, traveling along with four or five smaller trucks, moving southeast. We spread out, lined up on them and dropped down to attack. As we were going in at tree-top level, the sides of the big trailers dropped away, revealing their big guns. We kept boring in— we didn't have much choice at this point. (I often think of that and compare it to the experience of the 302nd when they were attacking the destroyer.) We couldn't turn because we would expose the underside of our aircraft to the guns. We continued the pass, firing away. I guess I was maybe 20 or 30 feet above their guns when I flew over them, firing like crazy. One shell put a large hole in my left wing, while another blew away part of one of the blades of my prop. The shell that went through my left wing was a cannon shell of some type and must have been equipped with a delayed fuse, because it didn't explode when it hit the aircraft. It just made a big hole, but it exploded some 50 - 100 feet above me. Shrapnel fell on me, inflicting my plane with additional holes.

My gosh, that stuff raining down could have knocked you out of the air?

I guess so, but it was over in a second. I started screaming, "I'm hit! I'm hit! I'm hit!", while reaching for altitude. As I climbed, I slid the canopy back preparing to bail out. By the time I had reached 700 or 800 feet, I was ready to jump. By then, the aircraft was shaking as if it was going to come apart any second. I stood up in the seat to bail out, but I guess I got chicken at that point, because I said to myself, "This is a good aircraft. This thing is still flying—maybe I can put some distance between here and being a prisoner of war." So, I sat back down, strapped myself back in and kept climbing. By the time I got to 5,000 feet, I was headed south and feeling a little better about my situation. I remember one of my buddies escorting me home—there were three other aircraft with me. They said I was flying so fast they were having a hard time keeping up with me. They could see my plane vibrating and kept warning me, "If you don't slow down that thing is going to come apart" [laughs].

What did you say?

I said, "I'm just trying to get over the Alps." I was trying to get as much altitude as possible. You have to realize that I was in this situation for the better part of two hours. A lot of things go through your mind in that time. The aircraft was very unstable and I kept looking out there at that gaping hole in my wing. I prayed a lot. I continued to move the controls checking the aircraft's

463

maneuverability. Every time I moved the controls rapidly, it began to shutter and I would lose some control. I soon learned to make maneuvers very gingerly. By the time I got to 17,000 feet and over the Alps, I could see the Adriatic Sea and our British rescue people giving us radar vectors. Then I began to calm down and assess my situation and plan for what might be a crash landing at home base. When I arrived home, I was able to get the gear down and locked, and with the crash crew standing by, I landed without incident.

I think one of the amazing things is that our mechanics and crew chiefs were so proficient, thorough, and creative, which always gave me great confidence when I climbed into my plane. After I had landed, they pulled that P-51 into a revetment, assessed the damage and said it could be repaired. They replaced the left wing, put on a new prop, patched all the holes, and had it ready to fly the next morning. You know, we had superb crew chiefs and maintenance personnel. The work they did getting my aircraft back in the air was just one example of the abilities and teamwork demonstrated by Black airmen. General Hap Arnold, Air Corps Chief of Staff, had reported to the War Department that Blacks would never be able to do the maintenance work to keep the proposed Black pilots in the air. Their accomplishments and the success of our unit have certainly proven him wrong. By the way, the rest of the flight destroyed those guns and knocked out the trucks.

What other memory stands out about the war?

We had been on stand down for a couple of days, preparing to move to a new location further north, near Cattolica. We knew something was developing, but we didn't know what. Of course, mind you, I was not flying anyway. I had been injured in a motorcycle accident and was temporarily off flight status. Since I could not fly and I felt somewhat adventuresome, another pilot and I, really out of curiosity, acquired a jeep to drive up to the new location. After scouting that site and hearing that the German forces had been pushed some 200 or 300 hundred miles further north and were retreating rapidly, we decided to continue on northwest. We somehow managed to pass through our lines and after scrounging some gas we ended up near Bologna about 2 P.M. As we were driving down the street, we noticed there were no Americans or American vehicles; we saw German vehicles instead. We concluded they were vehicles taken over by American forces. After deciding to see if we could get something to eat, we parked the jeep in front of what appeared to be a hotel, got out to walk into the place and these German officers came walking out. They saluted us and we saluted them back. You can imagine our surprise. Why, here we are still at war with them. They got into their command car and drove off. Within the next 48 hours, peace would be declared and maybe they already knew something we didn't. I don't know, but I can tell you, seeing a German officer face-to-face kind of left my heart in my mouth, and I began to shake. We got back into our jeep and made tracks back to where we belonged. Something else we discussed was, what if they had drawn their weapons and attempted to fire at us?

You weren't unarmed?

465

No, we always carried our .45. The point is that we had gone beyond the point where we had permission to go, and where we found ourselves in an embarrassing situation without orders or anything. So, as I said, we climbed back into our jeep and got the heck out of there. While going back to Ramitelli, we were stopped twice and questioned each time. We managed to convince the military police patrolling the roads that we were on a special mission, enabling them to allow us to continue back to our own base.

Any other incidents of racial intolerance that you witnessed?

There were not many connected with the performance of our military duties. Once overseas, I think everyone concentrated on the prosecution of the war. To avoid incidents similar to on the train, when I left Jefferson Barracks as a young 18 year old, I did everything possible to keep from using public transportation. I became aware of how much racial tension existed—how much segregation meant to people in certain parts of the country. Whether my parents brainwashed us or over protected us in St. Louis is difficult to say. There was considerable subtle segregation in the city. I recall that we couldn't go to certain theaters. This wasn't earth-shaking since most people just went to neighborhood theaters because of cost and distance. While concentrating on winning the war, I directed my efforts towards being respected as an American and sharing in the full citizenship that White Americans enjoyed. I tried to be the best I could. It took years for me to realize we Blacks had a long uphill battle. That brings me to a couple of incidents that occurred after the armed forces were integrated. One story I remember, was while I was at Keesler and had become an instructor pilot in the B-25. One of the pilots that had come there to school had been assigned to me for transition into the B-25. When he came in and we met, he excused himself and went to see the training officer and never returned. I understand he told operations that he wasn't going to fly with any "niggers." He insisted that they assign him another instructor pilot. The officer I admired—I think his name was Owens—was the operations officer, and as I have been led to believe, told our racist pilot he had been assigned to fly with a pilot and if he wanted to fly, he had to fly as assigned. This pilot still refused. A month and a half went by and they took his flight pay away; another month went by and his flight pay was taken away again. By the third month, his need for this back pay overpowered his disrespect for Black pilots. So, he kind of tucked that tail of his between his legs and said, "Okay, I'll fly with any pilot I'm assigned to." He needed 12 hours of flying time, and I believe he flew them all with me. Another incident at Keesler that sticks in my mind happened in 1950. It involved the officers' swimming pool. Integration had worked well under General Lawrence during my first year there and as the result of his leadership he had been moved to Lackland Air Force Base, Texas. In the minds of most Black officers and airmen there at Keesler, the new commander was not as forceful in applying the intent of President Truman's integration order. As a matter of fact, he set about to establish policies that were a setback from the previous year. This new policy was an attempt to re-segregate the officers' swimming pool, under the guise that he believed that Black military people would prefer to spend their leisure time together. To achieve that, he had converted one of the NCO [non-commissioned officers] pools for the use of Blacks. He then issued an order that Black officers could no longer use the designed officers' pool. This order brought outrage from many officers—both Black and White—who set about to test the commanding general's (CG) order. Our plan was that mixed groups with their wives or girlfriends would appear at the officers' pool in shifts, to test this admittance policy. I was one of three Black officers in the first group. I believe the other two were Theopolis Johnson, now of Los Angeles, and Fred Hutchens, of Atlanta. When we approached the entrance to the pool, a very large sergeant blocked our path to prevent entry. Very politely, he said, "Sir, Negro officers are to use the other pool," referring to the pool designated for use by all Black personnel, regardless of rank. My response was, "Sergeant, move aside or I will have you court-martialed, and have your superior send someone here that outranks a captain to issue that order." He stepped aside and we went about our business. Sometime later, three staff cars arrived, one containing the CG, from which a number of senior officers got out and stood looking, talking and taking notes. At this point, I decided to be a show-off. Not being much of swimmer, I climbed the ladder to the high diving board and began bouncing up and down. As I was looking around and saying to myself, I'll show you, my foot slipped and I found myself in mid-air heading for the water. Needless to say, going through my gyrations on the way down, I ended up parallel to the water and hit on my back. The pain was unbearable; however, we did manage to reintegrate one facility on base. There was never any mention of the incident again. I could go on, but after 42 years the system is working, not perfect, but working.

What was the toughest transition from WWII to flying in Korea?

I don't think there was any tough transition. You make adjustments each day to changing situations and conditions, to assignments and missions. In later 1948, I had gotten out of fighters, flying P-47s, and was flying B-25s at Keesler AFB. In 1950, I was assigned to a SAC unit at Fairfield-Suisun AFB, California (later Travis AFB), flying B-50s. I didn't like SAC and, of course, we were involved in Korea at that time. SAC crews were always flying off on extended missions and some may even have been to Korea. I figured if I had to go to Korea, I had to get back into fighters. I didn't have any interest in bomber tactics. I mean, something that sits up there and lets the enemy shoot at it was not for me. And of course, by 1950, our jet fighters were faster and more maneuverable, which seemed

467

more exciting and thrilling to fly. Another thing, I never liked flying over water. I never had a great liking for any water I could not stand up in, or drink from a glass, especially after my diving board escapade at Keesler. When I was flying in MAC and we would pass the Golden Gate Bridge and the Farallon Islands going to Hawaii, I had problems dealing with all that water. I remember the first time I flew to Hawaii, that island looked so very small. It gets larger and larger each time I go out there.

What sort of special tricks did you guys use to do as the Tuskegee fliers?

I can't say it was special, but like most pilots we took great pride in our ability to fly aircraft. One of the more demanding aspects was formation flying. We would fly formations so tight that if the wind velocity was not too strong, a person could get out and walk from one end of one aircraft to another. We prided ourselves in how well we could tuck it in. I remember one time when practicing formation, I was on my buddy's wing, so tight, that he said, "Bill, your prop's going to hit my wing in a minute. Why don't you slide it back a little bit?" But I kept sticking it right up in there. So, later to get even, someone decided on the next flight that it would be my turn to lead. We got up in the air and they began to pull in real tight. You see, when you are in the lead aircraft, you can get the picture of what it is like and how critical the maneuvers are with the other aircraft pulled in real tight. I would try to speed up or turn or something like that, but they had their wings tucked up under my wings so tightly I couldn't escape. If I had tried, I could've touched the other planes' wings. Those formations required excellent reflexes, good hand-eye coordination, and teamwork.

So they got even?

I would say they did and they scared the hell out of me in the process.

Anything else like that you remember?

Well, yes, there are many others. One in particular occurred in Italy after the war ended. As I may have pointed out, the P-51 was the finest piston-engine aircraft ever built, and the easiest to fly, even upside down. Anyway, one of my comrades—who later went on to excel as an air force officer and commander—and I often flew in the same flight, would do low level passes over other Allied airfields. You could call into their control tower and request permission to buzz their field. In most cases, they would approve the request with the stipulation "make it good." So this particular day we were doing our little show over one of our B-17 bomb group bases, low, in a nice tucked-in formation. We thought we were looking good, but the control tower operator called on the radio and said, "You call that a buzz job? Our B-17s will do better than that." The remark kind of ticked us off, so we requested a rerun to show them. We came back across the field the next time, not more than 20 feet off the ground. John said, "Everyone tuck in real tight," and when I looked out at my wingman, he was upside down. Twenty feet off the ground! One mistake and you're dead. With the P-51, you could push forward on the stick when upside down and the aircraft would actually climb, and that is what he did to get enough clearance to roll back over. The tower operator screamed, "Oh, my God! He's going to crash." But Sam was good, and he was always testing the limits of the aircraft. As I said, he just held his position in the formation across the field, pushed the stick forward, climbed a little bit, up maybe 20 feet and rolled back over. The tower operator said, "That was a great buzz job."

469

What was life like when you got back after the war was over?

Many of us were sent back to Tuskegee after WWII. They really didn't know what to do with all the Black pilots they had produced. Both the 332nd Fighter Group and the 477th Medium Bombardment Group had been deactivated in favor of a composite group, made up of two squadrons from each group at Godman Field, Kentucky. This reduced the personnel requirements for fully qualified crews considerably. In keeping with the "separate, but equal status for Negroes," by sending the surplus back to Tuskegee, the War Department, had created another monster. While some were lucky enough to get assignments as instructors, the remainder became assistant to the assistant to the assistant. In other words, multiple people were doing the same job. Even though some outranked and were more qualified than their White counterparts, they were denied the opportunity under existing policy. With so many attempting to do the same job and trying to keep up their flying proficiency in the few aircraft allocated, there was considerable free time.

I remember how angry I became years later looking at some of my old slides and thinking that the War Department had sunk to a new low in human degradation when I would see a slide of George S. "Spanky" Roberts. Roberts was the first Black American selected for pilot training; the first squadron commander of the Ninety-Ninth fighter squadron; former deputy group commander and Group Commander of the 332nd Fighter Group. He had all of the credentials and demonstrated leadership for a key position, but suffered without a meaningful job. He was just one example of gross misuse of qualified military people. At any rate, the situation created new problems at Tuskegee Institute, where in their war preparation days, our military people were busy training and didn't have the time for social interaction. Now, it seemed they had more than necessary. We were now combat veterans—we had no studies to consume our time—we had no pressure on us, therefore one could devote his attention to personal pursuits, namely the girls in school. This was very disruptive to the university academic atmosphere, and Dr. Patterson, who was responsible for bringing the pilot training program to Tuskegee, finally went to Washington, D.C. and, using his influence, requested that the base be closed.

You stated that the people at Tuskegee University requested that the air field be closed and the airmen moved to a new location. How long did you remain there?

Once the aviation cadet program was concluded they began moving people to the new home of the Black air force at Lockbourne Army Air Field (later Lockbourne Air Force Base) near Columbus, Ohio. I remained at Tuskegee AAF until late August 1946, with a small contingent, to ferry out all of the aircraft and close the base. I was then transferred to Lockbourne AAF and reassigned to the Ninety-Ninth Fighter Squadron, again flying the P-47, until I left the service in January 1947, to attend St. Louis University.

This was just one of many breaks you had from the air force?

Yes. In September 1947, when I wanted to put in two weeks of active duty in the reserves, and since the Air Corps still operated under their "separate but equal" segregated military force concept, I was able to perform that duty at Lockbourne AAF with my old group. This time, however, I was attached to the 100th Fighter Squadron for training. There were a number of us shipped in from all over the country. It was like a homecoming, except that there were so many of us I was able to get only two flights in the P-47. It was while there for those two weeks that I found out that so many of us left the service that the group was now undermanned and that they would welcome anyone that wanted to come back in. I took the papers back to St. Louis with me and completed them so I could return to the service at the end of the next semester. Colonel Davis, later to become the first Black general in the United States Air Force and retired as a lieutenant general, told me on one of his trips to St. Louis that I should give him my application and that he would attach his letter of recommendation to it before it was sent to Washington. I went on active duty in the spring 1948 and was assigned to the 301st Fighter Squadron, again flying the P-47, until I was selected to be one of the early pilots to integrate the air force later that year. I was sent to Keesler Air Force Base, Mississippi, which was the same Keesler Army Air Field I discussed earlier, then under army control. One thing I would like to say about Colonel Davis, and I am not sure it was by design, is that as we left Lockbourne, they made sure we were qualified in the type of aircraft at our new assignment, whenever possible. That made our new transition to the environment in an integrated air force much simpler.

But, you were not to stay in the air force for the remainder of your career?

No. After the swimming pool incident, conditions at Keesler became somewhat strained. I began to think that Black military people would never be given the opportunity or acceptance that President Harry S. Truman's integration order intended. In early 1950, I was one of many selected for non-flying status as part of a budget cutback. It was my opinion that the action was in retaliation to my

471

defiance to General Mayo's swimming pool order of the previous year. I complained to the Department of the Air Force at the Pentagon, but to no avail. I believed that I was a good pilot and, by virtue of my instructor pilot ratings in two types of aircraft, I should have remained on flying status. I had no desire to stay in the air force in a non-flying position. I applied for release from active duty, to the University of California at Berkeley that fall, and headed west. When I arrived in Berkeley, I searched for a reserve assignment at Fairfield-Suisun Air Force Base—now Travis Air Force Base— while awaiting the start of the fall term. I secured an assignment in the SAC Bomb Wing, flying the B-50 and the B-36. The units in those days had little or no use for the reservist and getting flying time was hard, if you were not part of the "in" group. My problem was even more difficult being a Black captain. One day I was on base performing my active duty for training when I ran into Captain Paulus Taylor at lunch. He had been a personnel officer at Lockbourne. During our conversation, I had told him that I was dissatisfied with the problems I was having working my way into a B-50 crew. Some three or four days later, he called me at home and asked me if I would like an assignment in the MATS group he was personnel officer for. That assignment involved flying the C-47 (DC3), C-54 (DC4), and the C-97. I was qualified in the C-47 and because of their shortage of crews in the C-54 and my amount of flying time, I could expect to be checked out in that aircraft in the very near future. This appealed to me since I had planned to test the commercial market in the future. The assignment was beautiful. Every time I was available I could call in and get training days, and was soon checked out in the C-47, then started my checkout in the C-54. It was great. I was flying all over the country and to Hawaii. In October, I received orders for recall to active duty. My wife and I had just had our first child and the semester at UC would not end until mid January, so I requested a deferment until then.

The operations officer for the 1704th was transferred to Japan just as I reported for duty and I inherited his job. You can imagine the height of our nostalgia as many old friends came through on their way to the Far East. Colonel Davis, Captains Chris Newman, Hugh White, Lieutenants James Harvey, Edward Drummond, and Exum were just a few of the Tuskegee Airmen to pass through. I had my first experience in Korea and the Far East when I was sent over on temporary duty in the summer 1951. We provided air evacuation for our wounded troops out of Korea and back to Japan where they were evaluated for treatment and, where necessary, for evacuation back to the U.S. In 1952, I was assigned to flight service at Hamilton AFB, California, which did not require a family move at once. Our job there was to approve military flights out of any airfield not having their own clearing authority. While in assignment, I submitted my third request for helicopter training and, in the spring 1953, became the first Black helicopter pilot in the United States Air Force. This was a real experience and quite exciting to fly a machine with no visible means of support. I became very intrigued with the capabilities of this up-and-coming means of air maneuverability and flew one on every opportunity I could get, until I left the Air Force again at the end of the year.

So, at this point, you attempted to break into commercial aviation?

Yes, but this was not the first time as I had sent out resumes and many applications while in school at the University of California. However, with my new endorsement in helicopters, I believed my prospects of obtaining a position in the career I loved so intensely were much more promising. But, the U.S. aviation industry was not yet ready to accept a Black flyer. By this time in my life, I had acquired nearly 2,000 hours in fighters, bombers, various multi-engine transport aircraft, and helicopters, and yet my experience could not overcome racism. One day, while walking in downtown San Francisco, I ran into Major Charles Bussey, who had been one of the Tuskegee Airmen who remained in the Army when the two services split. At the time, he was on the aviation staff at the Presidio of San Francisco. We had lunch together, and during our reminiscing, he pointed out that the army was high on helicopters and said that if I wanted to continue flying them, I should transfer over to the army, since I had been unable to get a reserve assignment with the Fourth Air Rescue Squadron at Hamilton AFB. The idea had merit and after some investigation, I made the service switch in 1954. The one problem was the army would not accept me as a qualified pilot. In order to acquire my army pilot's wings, I was required to attend helicopter flight school again at Fort Sill,

Oklahoma. I had more helicopter time than my flight instructor. I truly believe that had I been White they would have made the transfer based on my record and given me the necessary field training to become proficient in army field operations. After all, I was already qualified in the H-19 (Sikorsky S-55).

I remember my first flight in the army trainer. This young second lieutenant, whose name I chose to forget many years ago, took me out for that indoctrination ride and after demonstrating the basic maneuvers, instructed me to take the controls and not to be afraid—he was right there with me. I handled the aircraft as smoothly as any pilot. This prompted him to ask if I had any bootleg time. My response to him was I had none. Throughout the flight, as he demonstrated maneuvers and instructed me to perform them, he would asked me the same question again. Each time I gave the same answer. I knew I was getting to him, but I was angry with the treatment I was getting after flying in two wars. He finally concluded the flight, and I believe made an unusual report in my flight folder. The next day he decided to put me through some more advanced maneuvers by demonstrating auto-rotations. This is a maneuver where you cut the power and make an emergency landing into a small field. In this case, for safety reasons, they always used one of their emergency fields. After going back up he requested that I attempt the same maneuver and not worry, because he was right there to help if I made a mistake. As I came around and chopped the power, I was really getting my jollies. We approached the ground, I did not start to level the helicopter as he had done in his demonstration. Instead, I had decided to make the landing as we did in the air force. As he nervously reached for the controls, I shouted, "Get your hands off those controls." I must have shocked the hell out of him because he froze for a moment and by the time he recovered, I was successfully on the ground. He sat there stunned for what seemed like eternity before he collected himself and asked me the same question he had asked so many times. "Mister, I am going to ask you for the last time, where did you get your bootleg time?" My response was the same as before, "I have no bootleg time." In disgust, he directed me to take us back to the main field where I parked and shut down the helicopter. He walked off without another word. As I returned to the ready room quite pleased with myself, I was approached by a sergeant, who directed me to report to the commandant. I walked in and smartly saluted as he told me to stand at ease. The commandant then proceeded to explain to me that the honor of pilot and officer in the army was based on truth and he was giving me one last chance to come clean and explain where I had acquired my bootleg time. My response was "Sir, I have no bootleg time."

"Well, where did you learn to fly like that?"

"In the air force, sir."

"So you do have some illegal time?"

My response, "No, sir, I do not." Oh, was I enjoying this!

His next request was "Mister, please explain yourself."

"Sir, I was an air force pilot for over 11 years and flew H-19s in air rescue and I came into the army because of my interest in helicopters." He began to turn red. His next question inquired as to why I had not given him this information before.

"Sir, you asked about bootleg time and all of my time is duly logged in my form five, which I have been trying to convince the army was legitimate for over three months." If I was to continue in my vocation as a pilot, I had to play the army game. But after I arrived, I decided to show how stupid this racism game had been. With shock, disbelief or whatever was going through his mind, he directed me to bring my flight records to him as proof—which I did. The next day when I reported to the flight line, I was again summoned and instructed to report to the school headquarters for further evaluation. I spent the next two days taking tests and, after the results were in, the school was instructed to graduate me with the next class. Since one had just graduated I had to wait another four weeks. I had many confrontations before leaving the army in 1957 with undertones of racism that could not be proven conclusively.

Was this when you began your next quest to break into commercial aviation?

Yes, but this time I had done my homework before leaving the service. I had already secured a position with Allied Helicopters, Tulsa, Oklahoma, spraying bananas in Central America and had believed this was going to be the beginning of a great future. That was not to be the case. The companies we were under contract to spray for Standard Fruit and United Fruit, both of which had policies against socializing with the local people and when I came along they forbade their people from socializing with me, so I was like a person that wasn't there, except when working.

How long did you stay there?

Not very long, just three weeks. I was just a replacement pilot. When I returned to Los Angeles for Christmas break, a friend and fellow Tuskegee Airman, Alvin Harrison, stopped by on his way back to Canada with his wife and my sister-in-law, Willer Mae, and talked me into helping him drive up. The trip turned out to be very advantageous to me, and began another chapter in my flying career. While there, I was introduced to some of the pilots at Pacific Western Airlines during one of their holiday cocktail parties. It was after I returned to Allied Helicopters in Tulsa that I received a call, at work, from the chief pilot of Pacific Western, asking if I would like to come to work for them. I was due to depart for Central America within a couple of days and did not relish the idea of the conditions down there, so after considering the pay reduction for a few minutes, I accepted the offer and was off to a new life in Canada. For the first time in my life I was treated like a person and not some second class citizen as I had been in the United States. The flying was exciting, the country was beautiful, and the people were, what I sometimes considered, overly friendly. With ideal working, social, and community conditions, I had found peace of mind and home.

476

Yet you were to return to the U.S. Army as a pilot once again. How did that come about?

I remained in the reserves and traveled to Seattle and San Francisco once a month for training. In 1959, I was promoted to major in the reserves, which resulted in my having to relinquish my assignment in the aviation unit to which I was assigned. With 15 years of active duty and a little over three years to qualify for reserve retirement at age 60, I decided to train when I could, through various schools. I also found out that my flying time with the airline counted for retirement points. I attended a number of schools, and by 1965, I held all of the top ratings in army aviation. It was then that I was asked if I would return to active duty to serve in Vietnam. I had been selected to attend the Command and Staff College at Fort Leavenworth, Kansas. After completing that school and taking a short Christmas break, I reported for duty at Fort Hood, Texas, as Aviation Safety and Standards Officers for the 268th Aviation Battalion in January 1967. The unit departed for Vietnam in the spring. I later moved to Saigon with the same job for the First Aviation Brigade. After 13 months in Vietnam, I requested and received the same assignment in Germany. In Vietnam, the majority of my time involved investigating causes for our downed aircraft and aircraft accidents; in Europe, my major task was instrument training, check rides and standards. I enjoyed teaching people the finer points in their flying technique. I demanded the best from them and took special pride in my own ability to demonstrate. I have heard that I have been referred to as the "Black Baron" because I demanded perfection. Whatever name the White pilots gave me, I felt that, after over 17,000 flying hours of which 12,000 was in helicopters, I have made a major contribution to aviation and gained some respect for Blacks in the age of flight.

STEWART ROSS GRAHAM
Tales From the Coast Guard

At eighty-one, Stewart Ross Graham is still active and maintains five acres of land in rural Maine. He still does carpentry, and has a machine shop, which he takes pride in. Aside from his quiet, modest demeanor, Graham is one exceptional flier, with more than his share of United States Coast Guard helicopter "firsts:"

- first night air-sea helicopter rescue
- first rescue of a helicopter crash
- first to be photographed hovering over the Statue of Liberty
- first ice survey
- first autopilot test
- first airmail flight in a helicopter
- first Coast Guard ferry
- first cross-country flight in a helicopter

Of all these firsts—and more—I asked him of what he was most proud. He was most proud of being invited to join the Coast Guard Aviation Hall of Fame, and of having a building named for him in Elizabeth City, North Carolina, the commander Stewart Ross Graham Performance Systems Building. The statement accompanying the naming of the building summed up his remarkable life of flying, "Your foresight, initiative, and persistence are largely responsible for the current application of helicopters in Coast Guard missions today."

How did you get into flying?

When I was a young boy, I lived close to Valley Stream Airport on Long Island, New York. That was during the early years of flight—around 1927 or 1928. I was always interested in the planes and could tell each plane that came in. Just by the sound of the engine, I could identify them. I would use my bicycle and go over there and actually help them wing-walk planes off the mat into the hangars. After awhile there, these pilots began to recognize me. Before I knew it, they gave me a rag to wipe up the engine oil around the cowlings so I'd give them a hand cleaning. Those experiences more or less inspired me. Now that little airport is John F. Kennedy International Airport.

Was there anybody that showed a great deal of special interest in you as a child?

There was a fellow by the name of Roger Q. Williams who later, after Lindbergh flew the ocean, flew it in a Belanca aircraft. He used to come and go at Valley Stream Airport quite frequently. At one particular time they held a contest there, which he and his backers actually sponsored. I was about 12 or 13 years old. The contest consisted of building a model of any particular kind of airplane and writing an essay on it. I was already a model maker and had already built solid and flying models. Anyway, I entered the contest and scored enough to win first prize. The first prize involved the opportunity to get up to a solo stage with Roger Q. Williams as the pilot instructor. After I'd won, I was told to proceed to New York and get a flight physical from a doctor that used to do all the aviators' flight physicals. I passed that with flying colors. About a month later Roger Q. Williams contacted me and said he'd be ready for a first instruction, but first he had to contact the FAA to make sure there weren't any things that would restrict me. According to FAA you had to be 16; I was only 13. So I had a few years to wait. The contest people gave me an option to receive money in lieu of the training, or to wait a few years until I was 16. Conferring with my mother and father, I decided it would be best to pursue my education. These were Depression times, too. So we elected to use the money. It was about $5,000, which was quite a bit in those days

Let's talk about your solo and how you finally learned to fly.

When I was around 18, I put in my request to enlist in the Coast Guard. These were trying times, in the 1930s. There wasn't anything going on as far as good jobs go. I graduated from high school, and the fellows I was involved with all went down and requested to enlist in the Coast Guard. The request went through, but then we didn't hear anything from them for several months. All of sudden, I get a telegram telling me to proceed to the Coast Guard district office at Bay Shore, Long Island. At the end of the telegram it said, "Bring working clothes." None of us knew anything about the Coast Guard. We knew something about the Army, Navy, and Marines, We didn't know what working clothes were. The only kind of working clothes we had in those days were farmers' overalls, with a bib in front and pockets all over. Anyway, we went down and enlisted.

I was stationed at a Coast Guard surf station out on Long Island, at a place called Smith Point where my job was to patrol the beach and to try to protect the sailing vessels in inclement weather. When the vessels were coming in from overseas in those days, there were two places where they would head: the New Jersey coast or the Long Island coast. We'd patrol the beach with all kinds of signal flares. Day or night, when visibility was restricted from fog, snow, or sleet, we'd still have to walk that seven miles.

481

I did that until I got transferred to a bigger station, which was on a place called Georgica in East Hampton, Long Island. I was a surfman, which was the lowest rate at that particular time in the Coast Guard. In order to get promoted you had to take correspondence courses and get a high enough grade to be considered for promotion. I took a motor machinist-mate course, out of New London. After a year's time, I passed the course. Then six months later, I was promoted to second class motor machinist mate in charge of all the motorized equipment. I did that at that local station for two years and later was transferred to a larger station at a place called Long Beach—which is close to New York—where I was the number two man, maintaining equipment.

I did that for a couple of years until our Coast Guard headquarters came out with a bulletin in 1940, requesting any enlisted man interested in aviation submit their request by way of official channels. That was the genesis, I guess, of me going into Coast Guard aviation.

My request went through, but I found out later that the Coast Guard only wanted 20 enlisted men to participate in this particular training program. Then it turned out that out of the 20, all they actually wanted was ten.

The elimination training program was inaugurated down in Charleston, South Carolina at a little Coast Guard air station. They didn't have any runways—just an open field. They had three or four operating aircraft and two training aircraft, one of which was a Philadelphia-made N3N navy trainer. That's what I trained in. Anyway, I passed and graduated from that particular end of it.

Making it or not was a constant worry, because it was all competition in between the other fellows. I was one of the ten that was chosen to be further trained down in Pensacola with the navy, the marines, and of course the Coast Guard. I graduated from Pensacola and my first assignment was Floyd Bennett Field in Brooklyn, New York, where I flew Hall aluminum flying boats, which were a twin-engine biplane seaplane. This was before the war started. At the time we were flying what were called routine patrols out to sea, local patrols involving search and rescue.

Do you remember the first patrol that wasn't really routine?

This was during the war, actually. I was out in a Widgen, which was a Grumman amphibian. Because the plane was small, we could only carry one 350-pound depth charge. This time it was just myself as pilot, and a radio operator. Our job was to look for submarines, because there was a lot of sinking going on all along the New Jersey and Long Island coast.

I was just coming off of patrol still about 20 miles off shore and I came across this Norwegian freighter coming in from overseas. Our job was to fly alongside of it, identify it to see what flags it was flying, if possible to try to get the name of it, and determine whether she was deep in the water or whether she was coming in light.

I had just let go of the plane's controls, gotten my clipboard and was putting down all of the information that I obtained, when the starboard engine quit. I was maybe about only 100 feet off the water then. These little amphibians weren't noted for single-engine performance. Furthermore, this was during the winter, cold as hell, rough water, and we were heading for Davy Jones' Locker. So without even thinking, I jettisoned the 350-pound depth charge I was carrying. Lucky enough, it was at the end of the patrol, but I still had a limited amount of fuel left that would hopefully last the 20 odd miles home. I fire-walled the good engine, which was the port engine and I was just able to kiss off the crest of the waves, bouncing from one to the other. Then I gave a small amount of flaps, which increased my lift. Instead of bouncing off the waves, I was able to just fly above them and gradually gained a little altitude. In the meantime, the radio operator was sending in all kinds of SOS distress calls. Of course, I was busy trying to keep flying and stay above stalling speed. Eventually, I got up to maybe about 75 or 100 feet and reached land. I got landing permission to land at my own discretion at Floyd Bennett, which I did.

I understood that I was the first—out of nine mishaps which they considered was engine trouble—that ever made it back. Consequently, Grumman took that engine and analyzed what took place. They found that the crankshaft had snapped. Incidentally, on the way back, I could look out the side window and see a piston hanging out alongside of the cowlings. There was oil all over the place. Grumman found out that these engines were susceptible to failure because of the way they had the bearings honed. The fix was to shot-peen blast the sharp right angles on the crankshaft. Afterwards, they cut that section of the crankshaft off from the failed engine and presented it to me as a memento. The skipper of the base said, "When that good propeller has seen its day, I'll see to it that you get the propeller." I forgot all about it. In the meantime, I got transferred down to Elizabeth City. I had been there for about a week, and all of a sudden, a plane comes down from Floyd Bennett Field with that propeller, which they presented it to me. I've had it ever since. This past year, I presented it to the Owl's Head Transportation Museum up in Owl's Head, Maine. They have it on prominent display up there now, with the parts of the crankshaft that went haywire.

Talk about your solo flight in a helicopter.

On October 20, 1943, I actually can recall the words from my instructor, which then was Commander Frank Erickson. He said, "Stu, you're safe to solo." With only a few hours of solo time himself, he stepped out of a YR-4 helicopter. He waited a safe distance away behind a tree, which was located near the Sikorsky factory in Bridgeport, Connecticut. I pulled into shaky hover and watched Frank give me a thumbs up sign. I smiled nervously and pushed forward, making a few circles around the meadow. Then I landed. That made me Coast Guard Helicopter pilot number two. At that time I only had a total of three and one-half flight hours in a helicopter. Actually, it was an extraordinary way to graduate. There were no written tests, no diploma, no certificate, and no curriculum to follow thereafter.

So then you were just a bona fide helicopter pilot?

Yeah. I was just set free to penetrate the unknown with an unleashed, unreliable, underpowered, vibrating, revolutionary type of flying machine.

484

What was the weirdest thing about that flying machine in those days?

Of course, I had to teach myself, just as Frank did a few months earlier. He didn't have anything to go by, either. Then he and I had to fly the first helicopter ferry flight to Floyd Bennett Field. We were hesitant in considering this venture because the first aircraft weren't too reliable.

Previously, Frank had lost a tail rotor blade as he was coming into a landing while he was being checked out with a British helicopter. Then an army pilot actually lost a main rotor blade in a landing approach. He recovered, but the first two operation helicopters were nothing but a bunch of junk by that time. So was our confidence for this trip. Nevertheless, we were determined to ferry that machine back to Floyd Bennett Air Station.

We left Sikorsky's factory and stayed close to the Long Island Sound shoreline, but eventually we had to cross that large body of water before reaching New York. As we started across, we had a big decision to make on whether we should fly high and take a chance of auto-rotating to the shore if the engine conked out, or to fly low in case the machine started disintegrating in flight. That's how confident we were. We had no life rafts or parachutes and little faith in the engine or the helicopter. Anyway, we decided to fly low over the water and tried to stay close to as many boats on the sound as we could. Of course, we figured if we had to splash, help would be nearby. Crossing was actually uneventful after that, and the flight to Floyd Bennett was without incident.

What was the most extreme reaction you got from people who saw that?

People were amazed, but they stayed a safe distance. They didn't want to have anything to do with it because the machine was so flimsy. These people looking at wings that would flap all over the place, just shook their heads and thought that we didn't have it all in our heads. It was hard to convince them, really. I demonstrated the helicopter to VIPs, which included a day-long demonstration at the U.S. Capitol Building in Washington, D.C. I flew some members of congress as passengers—the first time most in Washington even knew of the helicopter. Commander Erickson was attempting to sell the helicopter idea to anyone who'd listen. It wasn't easy. Even other Coast Guard pilots were not interested. I was looked upon as not having all my marbles and was ridiculed beyond belief by my fellow fliers. They told me I would jeopardize my well-being by flying such a contraption. Eventually, some of the ex-enlisted pilots would approach me in groups with questions concerning the helicopter. They seemed to not want to speak to me alone, as if they would be ridiculed by their peers.

One day Ensign Walter Bolton and I had flight duty at the air station. He had flown with me in the past on anti-submarine patrols in our fixed-wing aircraft. I convinced him to take a ride with me. As we flew, I felt the need to put him at ease. I endeavored to make the initial takeoff and forward flight as smooth as possible, so as to not frighten him too much. It wasn't long before I observed he was beginning to take interest in the control movements. I allowed him to follow me through holding the control stick as I made several landing approaches. After this, I demonstrated backward takeoffs into the wind; right and left turns over a spot on the ground; and flying sideways. He seemed amazed over the precise control I had over the machine. Convinced, he indicated his desire to be checked out. He became my first student, soloed, and received helicopter pilot designation number three.

Did you have some forced landings in helicopters?

I've had a few. The first one was when I was the lead instructor. Frank and I were the only two pilots and he was busy running the air station, doing all the paperwork and trying to promote the machine. As a consequence, I was free to instruct any of the other pilots. One time I was over at an auxiliary airport, which we used for training purposes, checking out somebody. One of our experimental HOS-type helicopters came over with two pilots to pick me up to put on a demonstration for some dignitaries that were coming into Floyd Bennett. After they picked me up, I was seated in the jump seat behind them. When we were about 200 or 300 feet in, en route to Floyd Bennett, the pilot yelled back to me. He said, "Stu, I can't control this thing. The controls are frozen."

I told him, "See if you can auto-rotate."

He said, "I can't even do that."

In the meantime, we were heading right for the water. When we did crash, the two other guys were thrown out through the front of the helicopter, and it started to sink. Meanwhile, I was pinned in the back. It was going under water and the only way out that I had was if I could kick the transom over my head out. To do that, I had to get on my back and actually physically kick the Plexiglas out.

I did, and as I was getting out, the machine started tipping over into the water. I had to swim out.

When I swam to shore and tried to get up, I couldn't. My back was injured. This was in December. It was cold as hell. It was on an isolated island, which we had swum to. Eventually, an ambulance came on the other side of the island. When the ambulance people got to me, they found I couldn't be moved without a stretcher, so they improvised some boards that they found washed up on the beach and they put me on these boards. They proceeded to the ambulance but soon found that they couldn't shut the ambulance door because these boards would be sticking out. Finally, they got me to a hospital. I was still on these boards. My face and eyes were all full of salt water and sand. When I got into a hospital room, the doctor looked me all over. He could tell right away that I had back trouble, so he says to the intern, "Go and get this gentleman a drink." About ten minutes later, the intern comes in with this shot full of whisky. I thought it was going to be water or some damn thing. Just enough to wet my whistle, I guess. That was my salvation.

I was eventually transferred over to a navy hospital. After about a month or so of recuperation I was back in service again. That was in 1944.

What was the Coast Guard like during war time? Was there a lot of pressure on you?

Yeah. Being an enlisted man, there was a lot of pressure flying during wartime because we weren't allowed to do anything with codes. All of our flying had to be done with an officer. The officers started complaining "Jimminy Christmas, these boys are just as good as we are. The enlisted guys are doing all the flying and we're the copilots." Headquarters then came out and instigated a rigorous program for enlisted pilots who wanted to qualify. This was similar to the Coast Guard Academy's acceptance. So all of us had to take these examinations. Eventually, a lot of us passed and a lot didn't. I was lucky enough to pass. Then we could fly ourselves and accept coded messages and decode them and be just like a regular officer. But they said, "Gee, they can't do that either when they're still at enlisted rate."

So we had to be promoted to ensign. To do that we had to take additional exams. Anyway, I passed that and became a chief, at first. From headquarters, they said, "promotion achieved: aviation pilot." I had to go to Abraham & Strauss in Brooklyn to get a chief's uniform made up for me. I did that within a week's time, but the uniform wasn't supposed to be ready for about two weeks. In a week, headquarters sent another message saying I'd been promoted to ensign. So one thing led to the other and I had to get a cancellation on the chief's uniform because now I had to get an ensign's uniform. Anyhow, that's how I became an officer.

I was involved in the first helicopter night mission. I have the citation here, [reads] "The citation says, 'First helicopter night rescue at sea. United States Coast Guard Aviation has accorded this honor. The president of the United States takes pleasure in presenting the

Distinguished Flying Cross to Lieutenant Commander Stewart Ross Graham, U.S. Coast Guard as set forth in the following citation: "For extraordinary achievement in aerial flight during the early morning of 19 of January 1955. This pilot with Coast Guard helicopter engaged in a rescue of three crew members from the fishing vessel Kimtoo, which had grounded southwest of Anna Maria Key, Florida, in the Gulf of Mexico. Proceeding to the scene, Lieutenant Commander Graham succeeded in locating the vessel by effectively using the helicopter's landing lights and due to the heavy seas and violent winds it was necessary that the survivors be rescued without delay. In spite of the fact that guy lines and rigging on the vessel could not be removed, Lieutenant Commander Graham, by his indomitable courage and determination in the face of unfavorable conditions of wind, sea, turbulence and darkness, successfully hovered and maneuvered his helicopter so that the rescue basket could be lowered into the maze of rigging on the deck of the stricken vessel and a survivor hoisted into the helicopter. This dangerous procedure was then twice repeated as the survivors were expertly evacuated from their position of extreme peril. Lieutenant Commander Graham's expert airmanship, dauntless valor, sound judgment and unwavering devotion to duty reflect the highest credit on himself and the United States Coast Guard'."

Give me another great rescue that you did.

Another time at Saint Pete, I was involved an air force refueling of a B-29. The plane caught fire with 11 people aboard. Right away the plane sent out an SOS, and we intercepted it at the air station. I proceeded out. This was in daylight and in fairly good weather. When I got in the general vicinity of the Everglades, the men were still coming down in the parachutes. That meant I was able to hover over and pick up some of them, but there were others that I couldn't get to. I had to use the basket to get two of these people up. Another flier was maybe about a mile from there. I landed where he was, to pick him up, but he was all blue and looked like his neck was broken. We got him into the cabin. He was probably dead when we picked him up. We brought him over to the air force base at MacDill and unloaded the other survivors. In the meantime we had another helicopter come out and pick up the rest of the guys. That was a fairly exciting deal because we were there before some of them even hit the ground.

Do you remember the greatest reception that you received from saving somebody?

That would be when the Sabena airliner crashed up in Newfoundland. I was down in Elizabeth City at the time. This was in September 1946, at night. The plane had crashed close to a mountain top in an inaccessible place. Nobody knew where they were for several days, until an American airliner was coming in on a good day and the pilot saw the remains of an aircraft. He called the tower to see if it was an old crash or whether it was a new one. The tower informed him that there was a C-54 missing fairly close by. So this American Airlines pilot swung around and went down lower and observed that there were survivors around this crash, which started immediate action. The Coast Guard got word at headquarters that the only means of retrieving these people was by helicopter, but the only helicopters available were at Floyd Bennett and at Elizabeth City where I was. The only way of getting the helicopters up there was to dismantle them and then put them all together again at the Gander, Newfoundland airport. One helicopter in New York was put aboard an Army Air Force C-54, dismantled. Another Army Air Force C-54 flew down to Elizabeth City and proceeded on with our dismantled helicopter.

490

We started out around midnight. We had two pilots, Captain Erickson and myself. Eventually we reached Gander and assembled the aircraft, which took most of the day. Towards evening we had gotten one of them airborne and proceeded to the site of the crash area. It was estimated that it was about 27 miles due west of Gander. When we got there, there were 18 survivors out of 44. Some of them were ambulatory, and some weren't.

By nightfall we'd picked up eight of them. Then it got too dark and too risky to continue. The next morning we had both helicopters in operation. We went back and forth to pick up these survivors, but it was a 27 mile trip there and 27 mile trip back, and we could only carry one survivor at a time. There was a lake about seven miles from the disaster scene, so we figured a Coast Guard PBY could land on that lake. Soon they sent a PBY there and it landed on the lake. That meant that the survivors we picked up were flown the seven miles to the lake. They'd use seven-man life rafts to paddle them out to the anchored PBY, which we did. That eliminated a long, drawn-out program of flying them one at a time, back and forth, 27 miles each way.

We concluded the operation in one day. On the following day, a representative from Sabena flew in from Belgium, and I flew him to the scene of the accident so he could make out his report on just what his findings were. That rescue was the first whereby the Coast Guard was involved in a rescue concerning civilian commercial aircraft.

The emotional point actually was when headquarters wanted us pilots back to Washington. The army aircraft flew us from Gander after the operation was all over. We left our helicopter in Argentia for search and rescue missions. When we arrived in Washington, D.C., we were greeted royally and brought up to the Capitol Building and the White House whereby we were introduced to the secretary of the treasury and several congressmen. We were given a royal welcome.

490

Give me another "first."

Let me look through my log book. On November 12, 1942, "Witness the first flight of the Sikorsky VS-300." That's when Sikorsky's test pilot was showing off the first helicopter. I found the demonstration so eventful and awe-inspiring. That's what inspired me to go into helicopters. I soloed after that.

I made the first airmail flight in a helicopter. This was to the outer banks of North Carolina, commemorating airmail week. John P. Daniels was the first airplane tragedy. He suffered broken ribs a short time after the Wright Brothers had done their third flights. He was trying to hold the plane, but got lifted 30 feet in the air and crashed. He'd been very leery of planes after that, but took a ride with me—his first since the crash. But, he was calm and collected throughout the flight.

In 1949, I did the first cross-country flight with a helicopter. The Coast Guard was accepting brand-new helicopters from

Sikorsky, but they had to get them to the West Coast. They figured it would take six months to send them by freight, what with having to take them apart, package them, send them, put them together, and test them. I was chosen to fly the first helicopter out as a pathfinder for future flights. I set out on a course for San Diego in March 1949, and got down as far as Monroe, Louisiana. The next day I took off in threatening weather and as I flew, I found myself going lower and lower, as the cloud cover came down. It was raining hard. I decided to follow the "iron compass," which is the railroad tracks. I did this until it was really getting rough and the rain was getting heavier. I decided to go back to Monroe. When I got back, I housed the helicopter for the night and retired. During the night a tornado went right through the path that I was heading on. The next day a hurricane followed the same path. I was glad that I had enough sense to turn around and come back [laughs]. The third day, when I did take off, I could see the devastation that had taken place. That experience gave me a hint not to press my luck.

491

IVON KLOHE

Putting the War in the Past

Ivon Klohe served in three wars: WWII, Korea, and Vietnam. In WWII, he flew the B-17 and the B-24 in the air war against Germany in several of its most famous bombing raids. In the October 24, 1943 issue of *Yank*, the army weekly, Sergeant Walter Peters writes: "Klohe headed the Fort northeast, hitting a straight course for the tall column of smoke 6000 feet high, which marked the target. At our level, and higher, flak blackened the sky. Roth was ready. It was only a matter of seconds before he released the bombs. Then came the flak, great black balls of it were all around us. It seemed almost impossible to escape the barrage. We weren't having fighter trouble now; our enemy was flak, and there was nothing we could do about it—except evasion action. Klohe did just that, beautifully. It seemed a miracle that we escaped."

Klohe is a tall, pleasant-faced man, almost gangly. His family history is an interesting one. His grandfather was of Welsh descent from Liverpool, England; his grandmother was from Queensland, Australia. His father was an innovative man, who patented among other things, an odometer for counting cans. Ivon grew up in Monterey, California, where he knew the Chinese man who would become immortalized in John Steinbeck's *Cannery Row*.

After the war, Ivon flew for Jim Ryder of Ryder Trucking and for Hal Du Pont of Du Pont Chemical. Today he still flies his own plane—a home-built. The WWII experiences are strong and weigh heavy on his mind. He says, "In all honesty I think I have put a lot of the war experiences on file like so many of my friends, who think they want to put some of that behind us."

How did you get into the military?

I learned to fly when I was in high school in Monterey, California, and had some great people supporting my interest. Of course, you've heard the story of the lad who hung around airports and polished a little fabric and swept a hangar or two. That was me. In addition, I had the pleasure of being a lifeguard at Fairmont, a resort on the Monterey Peninsula. I attended a pool that was one of the only saltwater pools on the West Coast. The owners of the resort were two brothers, one of whom had been a WWI pursuit pilot.

Did he ever let you off early to fly?

Oh yes, if I had a schedule. David was one of many military who did not glorify war. Many of us just wished to put the war behind us when we came home from WWII, and I think many of us felt very mixed emotions about raining bombs down.

494

Why?

We haven't talked about it, because of the carnage and destruction, although I can honestly say, having been in on staff duty in a group, that we made every effort to hit the aiming point. A lot of people think that the Norden bombsight was infallible, but it wasn't. The main reason wasn't in the synchronization, but rather because of the winds. There'd be pretty high winds at an altitude of 25,000-30,000 feet—particularly in the winter months if a jet stream blew in the area. At that time we didn't even know what jet streams were. Anyway, under certain conditions, you'd have a tremendous drift angle, and here you have a whole box of aircraft—or maybe three boxes of 18-21 aircraft per box, going toward the target. The winds sometimes would actually pull the bombs of all these aircraft off target and they could drift a long ways. Yet, at the same time, the bombsight was telling the bombardier that the crosshairs were synchronized on the target.

We'd get strike photos to see what we did, but who could know how many crew members—pilots and other crew members—suffered from hypoxia, or lack of oxygen. Remember the oxygen systems were not that sophisticated. Hypoxia comes in at around

10,000 feet, so if you fly above that you have to put a mask on. Now, I happen to live at 6,800 feet in the foothills of the Rocky Mountains, so I'm acclimatized some, but when you were flying in WWII, you were apt to feel the effects, which included some loss of coordination and diminished eyesight. I'm sure there were many cases where a bombardier was up in front of a B-17, looking out at a flak field and prepping the bombing system, and he would hyperventilate—or maybe have a hose come loose. As a result, he'd be breathing ambient air instead of oxygenated air. Then he suffered from hypoxia. Who knows how many accidents were caused, or how many bombs were dropped off target because of that?

Everybody handled the war differently. Many people would drink. After a mission the intelligence officers who did the debriefing would encourage you to have a snort of rotgut liquor. I was not a drinker. I don't think a lot of my contemporaries drank, but the idea was to loosen us up for the debriefing. In the final analysis, I think all of us had a little different approach to the tension and horror. When you had a B-17 blow up right off your wing and you knew those people and had just been to breakfast and debriefing with them, it was rough.

Through most of my career, I was group staff, so I wasn't as close to a lot of crew members as a lot of crews became, because I flew with a lot of different people. But for my relief, when the debriefings and other duties were over, I'd relax by hopping on a bicycle and going out in the country. That was my stress relief.

When we were training out of Glascow, Montana, Chuck Irving, my radio man, and I had one of our crew members commit suicide, and it changed both of our careers dramatically. We had taken off one evening on a night navigation training flight. As we were climbing to around 10,000 feet, I alerted the crew to the altitude and told them to go on oxygen. Then they would check in one at a time to confirm they were on oxygen. We continued to climb. As we went through that exercise, I knew that the aircraft was trimmed to climb. We didn't maintain a lot of pressure on our controls because our mission could last up to eight or ten hours, so we'd trim the aircraft to ease muscle tension. Suddenly, I felt the aircraft pitch down, which meant that the nose came back up again, meaning we were out of trim. As we checked, our tail gunner didn't report in, so I told one of the waist gunners, Heath, to go back and check on the tail gunner, Sergeant Jackson. Heath went back and reported in from the tail station that Jackson wasn't there. Putting two and two together, I realized that Jackson had opened the tail-gunner hatch to get out, and when he did, the hatch went down into the slipstream and acted as an elevator. It literally pushed the tail of the plane up. Heath reported that Jackson's parachute was still there—not a good sign. We knew then that he had committed suicide.

Was that loss one that wore heavy on you?

The trauma was just starting, really. We reported the incident to base and returned. The next morning at dawn my crew and I took off to try to retrace the route. Our navigator was Ed Grabowski from Green Point, New Jersey. Ed was an outstanding flier. His logbooks looked like those of a professional scribe, which in many ways he was. Anyway, Ed had documented our route, so we were able to fly it exactly as we had flown it. When we didn't see him, we elected to fly the route in reverse. Then we saw him. At the time, we were flying at several hundred feet, clearing all the terrain. It may have been grazing land, but it had a brown, fall look. From the air we saw the rancher approaching with a couple of dogs. He had driven close to Jackson's body. We flew back to base and returned in jeeps. I didn't approach the body any closer than 50 feet.

Years later, having taken a few psychology courses, I can now look back on other traumatic incidents and remember some things. I remember sitting in a funeral home with my father when my mother passed away. That was two weeks before my seventh birthday. I could hear my father stuttering. He was a big, powerful man. As I think back, I think that moment was something that had gone into my subconscious. Also, one of my classmates from Santa Fe, with whom I went through cadets, was killed in a crash out near Walla Walla, Washington. I escorted his body home. It seems you may handle things like this well, but some place it's being filed away. Then it surfaces. I know I was very shaken up by Jackson's passing. I think the fact that you've developed a rapport and a cohesion and rely on each other, that affects your response. You are buddies and then one day you lose him.

You said it changed your career?

It changed both Chuck's and my career, because who knows what goes on in the minds of our leaders. They live or die on statistics, so when someone commits suicide, for some reason the leaders feel it reflects on the leadership. We had a squadron commander whom I respected. Still, I don't know how much under the gun he was from the suicide incident. I was immediately transferred from the group. I wound up on the group staff as assistant group operations and training officer.

So they broke up the crew?

They broke up the crew. Looking back, I felt some guilt over the incident. I also felt that maybe I hadn't recognized his temperament. After all, Jackson did have a short fuse. He was inclined to blow his stack, which some do. Though he never blew his stack to me, he did get in a fight on the train between home and Glasgow, Montana. He was the only one of the men who got into a fight, which I knew because I was troop train commander. But, for a man to commit suicide was something else. My feelings were assuaged somewhat when I met his wife and she came out and told me that there'd been some mental problems in his family. Nevertheless, I still thought that if I'd known more about psychology, I might have been able to prevent it.

In March 1943, when the group was finally fairly well trained, and we were about to depart for overseas duty, we went down to pick up a new aircraft. We were what were referred to as a ferry crew. On these flights, stateside, we didn't need a bombardier or navigator. The aircraft we were flying was new and featured a new Norden bombsight, which was in a metal container, locked and chained to the fuselage. At the time the Norden bombsight was a top-secret device, protected so it would not get into enemy hands. In fact, the FBI had keys to the locks to them. Anyway, our instructions were that if we landed anyplace short of home plate, we were to call the FBI.

Before we took off, we had these army lads (remember we were Army Air Corps) with us. They had coats, but they didn't have the fleece-lined, heavy jackets that he had as a crew. We took off and it

497

was winter. We went up to 10,000 feet, in weather. We were flying along in the snow, picking up ice, east of Butte, Montana. Chuck, who was taking care of these lads who were back in the radio room, not up in the nose, suddenly called me and said that the army lads were getting frostbite. We were all trained in frostbite, so when he said that the guy's face was getting waxy looking, we knew it was serious. I said, "Chuck, get the strongest station you can pick up." At the time there was lightening flashing here and there. Still, Chuck managed to tune in Butte, Montana, which had a good signal. I asked the copilot if we had our geographic maps. Ed pulled out Butte, Montana, handed it to me, and I studied it and elected to make an approach. That was back when navigation and approaches were primitive. We looked at beams, but they would bend every time the lightening would flash in the thunderstorm. The conditions were rough with temperatures between 55 and 60 degrees below zero. A dry cold, but cold nonetheless.

We made contact with a lady controller and told her we needed an emergency landing, because we had two lads aboard that were getting frostbitten. From her we learned what the ceilings were—they were low—and we also requested the FBI. Also, I requested and fire truck and ambulance support. When we landed, they were all there, as well as several other vehicles. I think the mayor was there, too. It was a little unusual for Butte to have a four-engine bomber land.

The fire-department people were great. The men just threw the two lads over their shoulders and off they went in the ambulance. We went downtown to a restaurant and they gave us hot-buttered rums. Not having been a drinker, I was surprised that hot-buttered rum tasted pretty good. After that, they put us up in an old hotel and we listened to Ed Farrell, who was a real character, recite *Dangerous Dan McGrew.*

We had to keep the engines of the plane running, because of the temperatures and the need to dilute the mixture. The B-17 had the capability of pumping gasoline into the oil system to dilute the oil, which would help in starting. But the next morning it was so cold that those engines would barely turn over, and weren't about to start. We communicated with Spokane, and the people there sent us some auxiliary power and engine heaters. Toward the end of the next day, we were able to get the plane fired up and ready to go.

I don't know whether or not the military thought I needed to be watched because of my stability. I know when I lost friends, I could get pretty emotional. I'm still that way. And, as I say, I don't know whether it goes back to the loss of my mother and my buddy. I've had difficulty dealing with this sort of thing, although I've conducted graveside services, most recently for Chuck Irving, my radio man, but it's very disturbing to me.

Talk about how you handled the emotional stuff overseas.

On one of the bicycle trips out in the country in England, we found a place where royalty used to stay that had been converted to a temporary orphanage. The British had evacuated ten miles north from the North Sea and had moved the children inward to protect them. Anyway, I was not a smoker, so I used to trade my cigarette rations for candy rations. In fact, many of us used to give a lot of our candy rations to the youngsters. A Babe Ruth candy bar then was monster-size, so the staff at the hall would cut that into little half-inch pieces. I used to cycle out there once a month. Then some of my buddies began doing that, particularly men who had children at home. That was a nice interlude.

One of my favorite meals was fish and chips. The fish and chips were wrapped in newspaper and the newsprint would come off, but no big deal. It sure beat powdered eggs. The British were really hurting. Anyway, there was this one little boy I remember. He was dressed in a wool sweater about twice what it should have been over his little body and he was groveling around in potato peelings for food. That really grabbed me. You saw quite a bit of that sort of thing. People have no idea in the U.S. what the British went through.

Did any of your men get badly injured while flying?

I was very fortunate in that I had only two Purple Hearts, that is, two injured men on my tour. Once we took a rocket strike from a M-262. A tail gunner was hit. We weren't far from Bremen, near the Belgium coast. The rocket hit the tail assembly, and a piece of it when it blew, opened up his eyebrow. He was not hurt as seriously as he thought he was. It was a sight. Blood was coming down and then freezing over his face. He was okay, though.

There were lots of close ones. Once I came back from a mission and was handed a piece of flak from a parachute rigger. It was about four inches square and three and one-half inches long—hard enough to cut glass. It had markings on it, which identified it as part of an .88 shell, Germany's most popular weapon. They not only used them on tanks, but they aimed them skyward. Anyway, the rigger told me that he had taken that piece of flak out of my parachute. A shell had come through the fuselage right next to me and had missed my spine by probably no more than four and one-half inches. For years, I carried that around like a kind of souvenir paperweight. Finally, the children's mother decided there were too many holes in my pockets from the rough metal, because one day it disappeared.

The guys used to paint nose art on the airplanes with airbrushes, and the art was very life-like. Someone saw a picture of my betrothed, and asked me if they could put her picture as nose art on the plane. My betrothed was a long-legged, attractive girl, so the artist went about painting a likeness of her head and body. I was quite a prude, so I was amazed when I came out to the plane and saw my wife-to-be depicted bare-breasted. I said, "That's not going to pass muster"— in so many words. I said, "You're going to have to change that." It was a very, very close likeness of her. So the artist painted one of her arms across her bare breast; the other arm he extended out in front of her. He had her in a cowboy, red bandanna, which ladies used to wear as a halter. At the other end of the bandanna, tugging on it, was a cocker spaniel. Since the airplane was named Yank, it was pretty appropriate. My wife-to-be never knew she was revealed in the nude like that. Unfortunately, the aircraft crashed within a month or so after the Schweinfurt Raid. Anyway, somebody flew it back and did a belly landing, which pretty well wiped it out. Yank was well documented. I flew it in Schweinfurt and in eight other missions.

Was your father in the military?

Yes, he was. At 15 he joined the Marine Corps. He told them he was 16. He became part of Teddy Roosevelt's Great White Fleet and saw action in Cuba and the Philippines. He was in the Philippines when "Black Jack" Pershing was there. One story he told took place when they were in Boston, and he and a buddy slipped over the side of the ship, went into the city, and got drunk. When they came back to the ship, they had to climb across these big lines. He made it on, but his buddy didn't. So he ended up on guard duty, guarding his buddy [laughs]!

What are you proudest of in terms of the European Theater?

As training officer, I'd fly in the tail of the lead ship. I knew the positions of all the crews. We were on a common frequency, and I could identify everyone. I had identified one aircraft that was lagging behind, not anticipating the turn. A pilot had to anticipate because you don't get 6,500 pounds of aircraft going right unless you anticipate. In other words, when the lead says, "Left turn," if you're on the outside of the left turn, you'd better start getting some power, because the next thing he's going to say is, "Now," as he rolls into the turn. So I was in the tail and said to this guy, "See those four levers in your right hand. Use 'em." That's all I said. I got teased a little about that comment.

Flak was a worry, especially if you saw aircraft getting hit and spinning out. It was with mixed emotions when you saw people bail out. Our parachutes were white; theirs were a kind of brown color. So you would see the airplane spinning down and burning and your gunners were counting the parachutes—and bodies as they came out. A real horrible thing was to see the chute open out, but then see the body falling beyond it. In other words, the flier either fell out of his harness or didn't have it fastened on.

Probably the most horrible thing was to have an aircraft next to us take a hit and blow up. Now we'd have parts of aircraft, including propellers flying by, and bodies. Also, when you'd be flying in back of another formation, you'd pick up a lot of damage from the shells out of the ball turret. These shells weren't collected or saved. They went overboard. There was a lot of brass to a .50 caliber shell, and that could do an enormous amount of damage to propellers and the leading edges of wings. There were many things a pilot had to keep an eye out for.

After you'd done your missions, it was time to go home.

I started to talk about another tour in P-47s, but one of the generals knew I was engaged and he knew I loved the lady that would become my children's mother. He said, "You're going to be on the next boat home."

Were you sad?

You miss home, but at the same time you want to get the war over. I had committed to 28 flights and I had done a total of 31.

Remember the day you got home?

I got off the train in Monterey and met a first cousin for the first time. She was on the same train, and I didn't know it. Anyway, I got married shortly thereafter. See, I had put off marrying though my fiancee was pushing for it. Before I'd left, my father had said, "You may not come back."

502

Leonard Komor returning from World War II.

LEONARD KOMOR
Finding His Place in the War

Leonard Komor's grandfather moved to China in the late 1800s. An expert in Oriental art, the elder Komor traveled all over the country discovering valuable *objets d'art*. His son Paul—Leonard's father—was born and raised there and entered the import/export business, founding his own firm. Paul Komor exported such things as pig bristles (used at the time for paint brushes), pig and cow hides, and metal ingots. Paul and Adele Komor had two sons, Leonard A. Komor and Peter E. Komor. Leonard was born in 1917 and raised in Shanghai, China. Leonard chose to become an engineer. He graduated from Kaiser Wilhelm Schule in Shanghai, then went to the University of California, Berkeley, where he received his B.S. in Engineering. Returning to Shanghai, he went to work for an American-owned firm, Shanghai Power Company, as an engineer, but he could sense the possibility of war on the horizon. Determined to join the U.S. military (he was still a U.S. citizen), he left China.

Upon retiring from the military, he flew for Pan Am for six years, then became employed as an engineer for GTE in the Sylvania division. He stayed with them for thirty-odd years and retired in 1984.

How'd you get into the aviation cadets?

In anticipation of war, I resigned from the Shanghai Power Company and took a boat out of Manila on November 27, 1941, which was pretty close to the infamous December 7. The minute I hit the coast, I enlisted in the aviation cadets. I had a thing about the Japanese. I had seen them pushing foreigners around in Shanghai. They were brutal to the Chinese. I could see what was happening. I had to cross over into the Japanese section of Shanghai every morning to go to work at the power company.

I wasn't new to what was happening there. In 1937, before going to college, when the Japanese invaded Shanghai, they had used Shanghai International Settlement as a base of operations for their war on China. Because Shanghai was leased by the Chinese government to an international consortium of countries, including the U.S. and Japan, Shanghai had its own army. I was a member of the Shanghai Volunteer Corps, the Armored Car Company. You could have called it the Army of the International Settlement of Shanghai. Before I went off to college, I stood guard duty at the boundaries of the International Settlement, which was behind a barbed wire entanglement. The Japanese were on the other side of the entanglement, searching and brutalizing Chinese civilians. The war front itself was about five or six miles away. We could see Japanese planes bombing and the Chinese part of Shanghai on fire. Anyway, my duty was to see that the Japanese did not enter the International Settlement.

Pretty scary?

You bet, it was scary. When you have shells going overhead, it's bound to be. You had Chinese snipers around you, firing at the Japanese. It was like having a grandstand seat in a theater, watching a war in front of you in which you had no part and into which you could not intervene. But, you were in plenty of personal danger. You had the Japanese taking somebody and lining them up against the wall and shooting them.

You saw that?

Yes. If they caught a sniper, they would line them up. Also, another scary part was that we knew that any time the Japanese wanted, they could come in, and we wouldn't be able to stop them.

What was your first duty in the Army Air Corps?

During aviation cadet training I was involved in a mechanical breakdown on a night flight. Most aviation problems seem to occur either at night or when you are on instruments. Anyway, this breakdown had a major impact on my fervent wish to fly airforce missions in China and be in the vanguard of the liberation of Shanghai, and with it, of course, of my parents, who had been caught there by the war.

The procedure on landing was that the pilot and copilot would look out the window of the cockpit to look for wheels. The plane had a red light on the dash when the wheels were up. When we were on the down-wind leg, we'd look out the window and I'd say, "I got a wheel." The copilot would say to me, "I have a wheel." You'd look at the dash and at that point it's supposed to be two green lights. This time I looked, and we only had one. We tried several times to get the wheels downs, but no luck. Clearly, one wheel was not down, so I called the tower and said, "Mechanical Emergency." It happened to be Saturday night, so the engineering officer was at the Officer's Club. He came to the tower and said, "Okay, go back to the toolbox in the back of the plane." This was a twin-engine plane, an AT-17 we were flying. The copilot went back and announced the box was empty. When I told the engineering officer that, he said, "Then I can't help you. You're going to have to make a crash landing." I told the copilot, "Run this for awhile," and I went back to investigate. I listened and could hear a grinding noise when we hit the electric switch to put the wheels down. I noticed a plate in the plane that covered a hole of some kind in a bulkhead, which ran through and across the cabin. When he hit the switch, I realized the grinding noise was behind this plate. There was a fire ax mounted on the bulkhead. I took it and pried that plate off and there it was—a chain drive that operated the gears. The chain had jumped the sprocket. We turned off the electricity and very slowly my copilot hand cranked the gear, while I slipped the chain on. Lo and behold, when we put the wheels down, we got two green lights on. With the landing gear down, we came in for a landing. The crash crew was standing by. The only problem was that I hadn't put the chain on at exactly the right place, so when the plane lost flying speed, the left gear dropped about a foot and we

507

ground-looped and nicked the propeller, but we saved the airplane. Anyway, this anecdote went into my service record, along with the fact that I spoke Chinese.

When it comes time to graduate, this group of guys was going to B-29 school; these guys were going to B-24 school; these guys were going to P-38 school; and Lieutenant Leonard Komor is going to the Fortieth Service Group, 555th Service Squadron. I said, "What the hell is this?" When I got there, I found out. This involved training an all-Chinese unit.

What had happened was that Chiang Kai-shek, President of China, and President Roosevelt had met and decided it would be nice to send an all-Chinese group over to service General Chennault's Fourteenth Air Force, successors to the Flying Tigers. The problem was that the other officers and I were going to make airplane mechanics out of people who were mainly cooks and laundrymen, and do it in six months. That was the plan. You can imagine. I've got it in for the Japanese, and I want to fly in the China-Burma-India Theater (CBI Theater), but I'm stuck in Florida trying to teach these guys, many of whom spoke very little English. I learned later that the fact that I fixed the gear on the airplane and had an engineering degree, put the finger on me. The crazy thing was that half of the Chinese were not even citizens. In fact, every Friday we loaded up a C-47 and flew from Punta Gorda, Florida to Saint Petersburg, Florida, where a federal court judge administered the oath of citizenship on 30 or so Chinese.

What happened when you tried to teach them?

These guys were going to be mechanics. How do you explain to an individual who has absolutely no mechanical ability how an aircraft engine works? You'd explain that on a 50 hour check that the first thing you'd do was take the spark plugs out and replace them. You'd look out there, and half the people or more didn't know what the hell you were talking about. So the interpreter comes along and says to me, "They don't know what a spark plug is." So you'd have to go to the engine, take the plug out, and hold it up and say, "This is a spark plug." Can you imagine sending someone like that to service General Chennault's combat airplanes?

Obviously, to overhaul an engine, you have to take it off. We explained for some time how that was done, that you had to get an engine stand and hook the engine to this bridle, so you'd get the engine out without dropping it. The first airplane we turned them loose on, we had problems. Apparently, the sergeant who was supervising them had gone for coffee. So these two Chinese guys got under the engine and were holding it as another guy took the bolts off. They figured they could hold up the engine by hand. You can imagine what happened. The engine dropped to the ground, but they managed to get out from under it. These men were damned lucky they weren't killed. One guy broke his leg.

While I was instructing, I wrote letter after letter requesting an overseas transfer, but the letters kept coming back: "Request Denied." Finally, I got a transfer. They shipped me to Lalmaniritat, India, to the 1326th Air Transport Squadron as a pilot on a C-46. It is now six months later. I get a week of rest in Calcutta because I have had a certain number of CBI flights. The British had opened all their clubs to American officers, so I went to the Gymkhana Club. I'm sitting there with three buddies at the table, and I look over, and who the hell's sitting there but the executive officer of the Chinese unit from Florida. I'm sure it's the same guy. I go over and say, "Are you Major Wong?"

He says, "Yes."

He says, "Oh, you're Leonard Komor, the lieutenant who left us to go fly."

I said, "What are you doing here?"

He said, "Well, if you must know, we've been here for two and one-half months, sitting in camp outside Calcutta."

I said, "How come?"

He said, "General Chennault doesn't want us" [laughs].

You guys flew some tough missions.

Yes, we were known as the "pipe-eyed pipers." They would carve little airfields out of the jungle for us to do things like unload these 40 foot lengths of gasoline pipe to be used for the gas line they were building. The jungle on either side seemed just wide enough for the wings to fit in. We would stop and get unloaded, then get the hell out of there because the next airplane would be right behind us. We had one pilot who landed and got unloaded and headed back to India. He ran into a thunderstorm and got bounced out of the thunderstorm at about 18,000 feet on his back. By the time he pulled that plane out, he had exceeded the red line, which is the maximum speed a plane can fly without doing irreversible damage. So he returned to the Burma base, from which he had just taken off. The plane was a mess. Part of the right cowling was missing. The radial loop on the top of the plane had been bent flat. I was at the airport with my plane, and I could see that the top edge of the wing where it bolted on was slightly wrinkled. The wing tips turned out to have about one foot permanent set. The pilot and his copilot were very lucky to survive this. The airplane never flew again.

When that happened the two guys from the incident wouldn't fly back to India. They were ordered to fly, and they refused. Finally, they were shipped home on a six-by-six truck, down the Burma Road. But that is an example of the kind of weather conditions we flew in all the time.

Here's another story. To have a Zippo lighter was one of the "in" things in the service. For example, when the PX would get Zippo lighters in, if you were interested, you would have to draw a number out of a hat to get the opportunity to buy one.

On this particular night, I was flying out of Kunming, China, during the monsoon. The direction finder wasn't working because it was pointing to thunderstorms, not radio stations. I was taking 45 fighter pilots of the Fourteenth Air Force back home on rotation. You know there's nothing more haughty than a fighter pilot. The attitude is anyone else in the air force is really just a civilian in disguise. We flew with the Air Transport Command (ATC), and the fighter pilots used to say the initials stood for "Allergic to Combat." So these pilots get in and sure enough, they're giving us a hard time. Then we take off. I want to tell you something: they got a ride. The fighter pilot doesn't fly in stuff like this. Fighter pilots were generally a daylight operation—at least over China. Here we are at night, flying down through this absolutely terrible weather, with lightning all around, and severe up and down drafts. We get over to the other side of the Hump, and it seems as if we're through the worst of it, approaching the Assam Valley, where we plan to land. All of a sudden, one of the fighter pilots comes running up to

510

me. "Sir, your right engine is on fire," he says. My copilot looked out of the cockpit window there and saw a big cloud of what looked like black smoke coming out of that engine. What it actually was was oil, not smoke. Apparently, the oil line had broken from the jostling caused by the up and down drafts. I turned that engine off, and we declared an emergency. Now, we're coming in on one engine, on instruments, because it was cloudy and foggy. There wasn't a peep out of those guys back there. They all sat there. I managed to land the plane okay and we rolled to a stop at the end of the runway. Of course, I couldn't taxi because I only had one engine. If I had, it would have pulled me off the taxiway.

The captain in command of the 45 guys came up and said, "Lieutenant, that was one hell of a ride. You did one hell of a job. I'll never call anyone from the ATC, "Allergic to Combat" again. I want you to have a little memento of this trip. With that, he hands me this Zippo. I didn't smoke then, or now, but I took the lighter. I was drenched in perspiration; I was terrified, but that's how I got my Zippo lighter.

Most unpleasant things in aviation seem to happen at night. Here are two examples. One example was when I had just leveled off after taking off from Chabua for a flight over the Hump. We had a radio on-board called "Identification Friend or Foe" (IFF). This radio sent out coded messages, which when received by fighter planes of our air force, identified you as a friendly aircraft. This was especially important when they got Northrop Black Widow night fighters over there. They were supposed to shoot you down if you were not properly identified. Inside the radio was an explosive charge that you were supposed to set off manually to destroy the radio if you bailed out or landed in enemy territory. That way the Japanese wouldn't get to know the ID code for that period.

We had an explosion in the plane, and I gingerly tried the controls. They were still there, so I declared an emergency and returned to base. The "meatwagon" and fire engines were standing by for a crash landing. The plane rolled to a stop on the runway, and we got out as fast as we could. When nothing else happened, the mechanics made a careful inspection of the tail section. They found that the IFF apparently got tired of living back there and for some reason blew itself up. I never did find out why. I am sure, though, that the experience took a couple of years off my life.

The second example was when I had just taken off, had barely cleared the runway and had just retracted the gear, when there was this tremendous explosion in the back of the airplane. At least that is what it sounded like in the cockpit. There had been reports that Japanese saboteurs had infiltrated some of the bases and placed explosives in the tails of some of our aircraft. That is what I first thought when I heard the explosion. I declared an emergency, tested my control, and again found they all seemed to be working. I circled back and put the airplane down on the runway with all the emergency equipment standing by. The minute the plane lost flying speed and the tail dropped on the runway, I knew what the problem was. The tail wheel tire had blown up in the retracted position, which is what we heard. The explosion had blown open one of the tail wheel doors. Such was life flying in the low maintenance CBI Theater, which was the end of the air force supply line for parts and maintenance.

Earlier, when I had convinced the military for me to join the CBI Theater, I said in the letters that my folks lived in China, and that I hadn't seen them in four years. For all my folks knew, the ship that I had sailed out of Shanghai in, in 1941, had been sunk by the Japanese. The Japanese reported they had sunk it, though it was not true. I didn't know whether dad had been treated well by the Japanese. I told in the letter that I had a personal reason that I wanted to get into combat.

I was flying over Agra, India, when I saw a bunch of flares go up and explode ahead of me at a nearby air base. Suddenly, the statement came on Army Airways Communications (AACS), announcing that the U.S. had dropped a new device on Hiroshima and that it had wiped out the entire city. The rumor then was that this would cause the end of the war. I didn't know it was the atomic bomb—neither did the announcer. When I got back to home base, I went to Colonel Keppel, the base commander, and told him the same story I'd used to get out of Florida. I also said that with this new device there might be some activity in China, and as a Chinese-speaking individual, I would like to participate. He told me to go to air force headquarters in Calcutta and said, "Here's the name of a colonel, Colonel Ruppenthal, he'll probably have something going."

I went there and spoke to the colonel. He was very understanding, and he transferred me to a place called Tezgeon. I was assigned as a pilot to the Cannon Project. This took place around the middle of August, before the Japanese had surrendered on the battleship *Missouri*. They put us through briefings on going into Shanghai to take the surrender of the Japanese air base there, the Kiangnan Air base. The military planned to have about one hundred C-54s, with Chinese troops on board, to take over the airfield before the Chinese communists could.

Ours was to be the first plane to take off, ahead of the impressive number of C-54s, which had arrived to take part in the operation. It was September the fourth, two days after the signing of the surrender by the Japanese. We were to go in first to make sure that all was in order and that the Japanese were indeed going to turn the airport over to us. After a five hour flight, we landed there. I was copilot. Colonel Cannon was with us, with his staff. He was to take the surrender. As we rolled up to a stop before the administration building, we saw the whole Japanese command lined up there. They had their swords and their sidearms on them. The colonel got out with his adjutants, and I watched from the cockpit as I filled out flight reports. As I looked out, I saw our colonel and the Japanese general exchange a few words and then the Japanese general performed the symbolic act of surrender by handing over his sword to our colonel. As I watched this, I was furious with myself that I didn't even have a camera with me.

The colonel knew I was there because I wanted to look for my folks. In fact, he had said to me some time before, "Hey, you go ahead. Do what you want to. Just let me know daily where you are." So I got off the airplane. Remember, I was a first lieutenant—a pilot. I was dressed in my khakis, old and rumpled from having lived in the Burmese jungles for about a year. As I did, a Chinese interpreter and two Japanese officers greeted me. The Chinese man asked me what they could do for me. I said I wanted two cars.

During the briefing for the Cannon Project, when I had told Colonel Cannon why I wanted to go to Shanghai, he expressed a good deal of interest. He said, "Do you know anything at all about your folks?"

I said, "No, I don't. I don't even know if they are alive or have been eating well."

He said to me, "Why don't you go to the commissary and draw 50 pounds of training aides. Spell that f-o-o-d."

That's why I requested the two cars. In a short time they brought out a 1940 Cadillac and a 1940 La Salle. Since the Japanese were very short on gasoline, where the trunks should have been were charcoal burners, to make charcoal gas to run the cars' engines.

I knew the exact way to get to our house. We drove down roads on which Japanese infantry was still marching fully armed, but the Japanese imperial chrysanthemum protected us. We drove down Nanking Road, the main thoroughfare of the city, and as we passed the American YMCA, I saw a high school friend of mine standing at the curb. The street was jammed with Chinese civilians. I stopped the car, got out, took off my hat and called out, "Hey, Jim." He recognized me and came flying across the street and we embraced. It turned out he had just been released from a Japanese internment camp. We were immediately surrounded by mobs of Chinese, patting me on the back and tearing at my uniform. I was the first American soldier they had seen. The war was in fact over—it was not just a rumor. Anyway, it took us some time to get out of there because of the crowds, but we did and proceeded down Bubbling Well Road, Great Western Road, Columbia Road, and Amherst Avenue, on which my boyhood home stood.

When we got to the house, the two staff cars pulled up in front, I could see my father was looking out of the first story window, but he didn't respond. He later told me when he saw the staff cars drive up, he thought, "Oh no, they've come to get me again." He had been arrested and placed in confinement in a place called Bridge House. The Japanese claimed he was a spy and said he should confess, but he had nothing to confess. So my father's standing there, thinking that they're going to get him again. I climbed out of the black Cadillac and started to walk up the driveway. I had been anticipating this moment for so long. I was really concerned how my folks were, whether they had been mistreated. I even figured that the Japanese might have expropriated the house. On this day I could hardly contain my emotions. When my dad didn't respond to me, I thought it was because the military hat I was wearing covered my face. I had never worn a hat in civilian life.

I took my hat off and said, "Hello, Dad." I want you to know that moment was the defining moment of my military career. I could forgive anything the military had ever done to me—in the way of discipline, deprivation of liberty, anything—for that joyous moment. My father disappeared from the window. My mom had a visitor in the living room at that time. It turned out to be a woman who had gotten some people out of jail and concentration camps. My father ran to her, yelling, "Our son is here." My mother looked at him. Due to the fact he'd been so sick, my mother thought he'd flipped out. The front door was about three steps above the driveway level. My father came flying out of the front door, with my mother in hot pursuit. We all three embraced on the driveway where I stood riveted, too overcome with emotion to say anything. It's hard for me to put it into words. I looked them over for a few seconds. I felt pleased my mother was in good shape. My father looked okay, but was very thin. At that time I didn't know he had suffered like hell. Anyway, I'll say that moment was absolutely the high point.

So what did happen to your dad?

My brother told me that the Japanese claimed my dad was passing information about what was going on in Shanghai to intelligence sources. They wanted him to confess, so when he didn't, they beat the hell out of him with bamboo slats. They would beat him till he was raw. They would allow him to heal up, because he couldn't talk in that condition. On several occasions, according to my brother who was still over there, they beat our father beyond sensibility. My brother said when he came out of there, he was a shadow of a man. He never fully recovered.

VIOLET COWDEN
A Life's Passion

Violet Thurn Cowden saw a hawk and wanted to fly. Fly she did as a member of the pioneering WASP (Women's Airforce Service Pilots), doing the important task of ferrying planes during WWII. It was work such as hers that freed up pilots to fly in the many theaters of the war. Violet speaks of the pride and pain those women felt who sought to fly at that time.

Violet was born in a sod house on a farm in Bowdle, South Dakota, on October 1, 1916. She attended Spearfish Normal School and graduated in 1937. Four years later, she received her private pilot's license at the Spearfish Clyde Ice Airport. In August 1943, she received her silver wings from Sweetwater Training School, Sweetwater, Texas. She was a member of the class of 1943-1944. At Sweetwater and Love Field, Texas, she flew a variety of planes:

PT-I 9, BT-13, AT-6, UC-78, BT-15, AT-11,
C-45, B-18, PQ-14, A-245, P-40, P-51, P-39,
P-47, P-63

She is a member of the Aviation Hall of Fame in South Dakota. She has served as WASP organization president and vice president, and represented the airforce, cutting the ribbon for the dedication of the Women Veterans Memorial at Arlington Cemetery in 1997. She is active in Women in Aviation. A city activist, she still has time to work to save the environment. Married for 44 years, she and her husband Scott have one daughter, Kim and three wonderful grandchildren, Ferrin, Kiki and Quinn. An active and engaging speaker, this diminutive veteran speaks compellingly in her soft voice about the dedication and skill of America's female pilots, then and now.

Did anyone try to dissuade you from flying?

I used to tell my mom that I was going to fly and she would say, "Oh no, you wouldn't do that." She didn't say, "You shouldn't do that." She just said, "You wouldn't do that." It was always in the back of my mind that I would fly. One day, I was out at the airport. I was watching my girlfriend's boyfriend shoot landings and I looked over at her and said, "You know, I'm going to fly."

She said, "You're kidding."

I said, "No."

So I went up to Clyde Ice, who was running the airport and I said, "Clyde, I wanna learn to fly."

He said, "Come on, I think you'll make a dame good pilot. Let's go."

He showed me a few things and he said, "But you have to fly by the seat of your pants." Then he shot a couple of landings. The runway was gravel. He said, "If you can distinguish each stone, you better be down!" He was an excellent pilot. I learned to fly in the Black Hills of South Dakota in Spearfish Canyon. The cliffs run pretty close together. When we'd fly through there, he would turn the plane sideways and we'd just breeze right on through. We didn't kid while we were in the air. It was a serious business up in the air. On the ground, he was very friendly. No, the only thing that stuck in my memory was the damn good pilot' comment. He was very busy and was training many pilots at that time. That was 1940 or 1941. I had my private license by the time war was declared on December 7, 1941.

Do you remember your solo flight?

[Much enthusiasm] Oh, yes!! You aren't supposed to know the day that you solo in advance because if you knew then you would probably be nervous. The instructor pretty well knows that maybe the next time you come out that you will be soloing. One day when I went out to the airport, they were playing on the airport PA system, "I'll Never Smile Again" and "I'll Walk Alone." I said to Clyde, "I'm gonna solo today."

He said, "What makes you think so?"

I said, "Did you hear those songs they're playing?" Anyway, we went out and we shot a couple of landings. They kind of know that you are either on or off. Some days you have off days and couldn't make a good landing.

He said, "Now, I'm going to get out." He weighed about 150 or 160 pounds. He said, "It's gonna go up real fast. You'll also notice that when you come down, and you will need to correct for that because it will take you longer to get down."

Later, his son, Cecil, and I were stationed in Dallas, Texas. At that time, both his son and I were flying 51s. Clyde came down to see his son and I got to see him then. He said, "Boy, I really envy you. I taught you to fly and look what you're flying, when I'm still flying small planes." I didn't see him for maybe 50 years, and we had a reunion in Reno during an air show. Clyde was 100 years old and the air show was honoring him. They drove him around the stadium in a convertible giving his stats. It was like no time had passed.

Any unusual things happen during training?

When I give my presentations to the different organizations, like women's clubs, schools, or whatever, I tell them that when you have a dream and you want to follow your dream, sometimes it doesn't come easy. When I got my call, I took my physical and didn't pass my physical because I didn't weigh enough. I weighed 92 pounds and I was supposed to weigh 100 pounds. I told the doctor, "Give me a week and I'll gain the weight." He gave me a week and during that week I ate like crazy. I had heard that you were supposed to drink water and eat bananas to gain weight, so I did. On the day that I was supposed to take my physical, I drank an awful lot of water and I ate a lot of bananas and I weighed 100 pounds.

When I went there, I got on the scale and he said, "By God, you've made it. How did you do it?"

I said, "Look!" My stomach was extended like I was about five or six months pregnant.

He said, "That is the funniest thing I've ever seen. Do you mind if I call another doctor?"

I said, "Not until you sign this paper that I passed my physical."

You strike a tough bargain.

Also, when this woman whose husband was the movie producer—not Hal Roach, but somebody like that—she wanted me to go for an interview and she asked about my past experiences. She said, "How badly do you want to get into this program?" I said, "I really want to learn to fly the Army way. You know, if you ask me to scrub this house with a toothbrush, I would do it." She said, "You're in." When I got my orders to report to Sweetwater, they said there would be transportation at the airport. When I got there with a little suitcase, to this sordid Texas town of Sweetwater, there was a cattle truck pickup with two benches in the back. Two army fellows from Sweetwater arrived to pick me up. Being the girl, I was always having somebody open the door and being real nice to me, I just figured one of the guys would ride in the back and I would ride in the front with the driver. That didn't happen. They got in front and I crawled in the back with my little suitcase and bounced all the way to Sweetwater. When I saw the PT-19 flying over, it looked big compared to a Cub, I thought, "No way will I be able to cut the mustard here." I realized at that moment that I was in a different field. I was going to be competing against men and knew that I would have to hold my own. Nobody was going to open the door for me. It was up to me. It was a rude awakening. Then, to sleep in the barracks with six women and share a common bathroom that had four shower heads, with an additional six women in an adjoining barracks, I didn't think I was going to survive. A little cot with wire springs and a little thin mattress, a place to hang clothes that was maybe, not even two feet wide, with desks in the middle and a waste basket. That was it.

My focus was not to socialize. I didn't really make too many close friends and I studied like crazy. I held my own and I did everything I was supposed to do in the barracks. If it came time to clean up, I probably did more than my share. I was motivated to do the right thing. I had about 70 hours and a private pilot's license. I found out that some of these gals came in there with thousands of hours. I thought I would wash out competing against all this. I guess I had the desire to do a real good job, the best I could. Every day that I was in the program I thought, "I've had another day to fly." When I found out that some of these girls that had many hours washed out, I really didn't think I'd make it.

What was the greatest compliment you received about your flying?

I can't think of any one incident. Usually, when you had a check ride, they didn't say anything. That was the toughest. I know that some of the girls had instructors who said, "That was a good landing or that was a bad landing." My primary instructor was really tough. His name was Pace. I don't remember his first name. We called him "Ace" Pace. He would say, "Whatever gave you the idea that you could fly? That was the lousiest landing I ever had." Then he'd take the stick and whack it back and forth. He'd swear at you. It was really tough, really hard. He liked to fly upside down. Whenever we came in after practicing, he'd fly upside down. I used to keep money in my flight suit for Cokes. He'd fly upside down and the money would fly out. Once he said, "Boy, are you stupid. Why don't you put your Coke money somewhere else? You're just scattering money over the Texas prairie." I think that when the girls washed out, they didn't wash out because they weren't good pilots. I think they washed out because they couldn't put up with the lingo. I found out afterwards that they used the same lingo on the men. With instructions, almost anybody can fly. But how do you act under pressure? When you have lots of pressure, can you think? Can you do the right thing? I think that's probably what washed out a lot of the girls. They just weren't used to this type of treatment. It wasn't harassment. It was just the way they did it. Of course, at the time, we didn't know that. I found out afterwards.

521

I guess another experience that probably you might be interested in would be when I was taking my pursuit training. We had ten hours in the back of an AT-6. I was in a flight with three guys and myself. This instructor had never ridden with a woman before. He was always on the controls. He was flying all the time and wouldn't let me fly. Then the guys would say, "Well, how is she doing?" At that time, the men were so supportive. I needed a pillow to reach the rudders and things. Usually some guy in my flight would save pillows for me. They'd say, "How did she do today?"

He would say, "I don't know. I don't think she'll make it." Every day they'd ask and he'd say, "I don't know. I really don't think she's gonna make it." Then they'd tell me.

This one day, when we came in for a landing, he said, "That was a very poor landing." He critiqued the thing, the angle of the approach and all this.

I said, "You know something." I figured I was washing out anyway, so I followed with the statement "That was not my landing."

He said, "What do you mean?"

I said, "You have been on the stick the whole time. You haven't let me fly." The next day he said he would let me fly. When we came in, one of the guys came up and asked, "How did she do today?"

He said, "By God, if you guys could fly like that, I'd be happy."

On the day we graduated, a fellow came up to me and he said, "I want to thank you for what you did for me." Honestly, I couldn't remember ever seeing the guy's face before.

I said, "What did I do?"

He said, "You know, I was so afraid of flying the P-47. Every day I would call in sick. One day I was standing out there watching everybody taxiing by and you came by in the P-47 and all I saw was the top of your curly head and I thought by God, if she can do it, so can I."

I guess you never know when you're out there doing your thing that you are helping someone or influencing someone's life by what you do.

Did you have to fly some clunker planes?

I was in the best place that you could possibly ever be. I was at Love Field, Dallas, Texas. All the planes that we picked up were from the factory. We took them to training bases and to the point of debarkation. The only time we flew war-weary planes was when we were taking our pursuit training. A lot of those planes had been in battles and been misused. Those are the only planes that I flew that were in bad shape.

We would pick up a plane either in Long Beach or Dallas and we'd fly it to the East Coast and deliver it in Newark, New Jersey. Every evening we would have to send a telegram back to the base so that they would know where all the planes were. Once when I sent my telegram I said, "Delivered P-51 so and so, mother and child doing fine." When I got back to base, this one guy said it was about 4:00 A.M. when he was reading the messages and he had a good laugh over that. After we delivered our plane, they'd take us up to Buffalo, New Your and we would pick up a P-39 and fly it to Great Falls, Montana. From Great Falls, Montana a guy would pick it up and take it to Fairbanks, Alaska. There the Russian pilot would come over to pick it up. The weather during the winter was really touchy up in that area. Just before Boris Yeltsin took over leadership in Russia, about 40 WASPs went to Russia to meet the women Russian pilots. We met a fellow that had flown to Alaska to pick up the P-39s when we were there. The Russian women flew combat. They were called the "Night Witches" because they flew not a very much better plane than a souped-up Cub. They would tie a bomb on the bottom. The men would do the dogfighting during the day and then the women would fly their sorties. They were ten miles behind the line and they would go over and bomb the Germans so they couldn't sleep. Sometimes, they'd do ten sorties a night. These women were really something. They entertained us royally. The language barrier wasn't even there. When we came they had flowers for us and hugged us. They cared about their families and their grandchildren and their country. The love of country and the love of flying were apparent. They loved to sing and we loved to sing. It was just great.

We met about 25 of the "Night Witches." There are only nine still living. At the WASP Conference in Omaha in 1998, 220 WASPs were in attendance. A producer from Britain wanted to film 200 women pilots. He shot the scene for a documentary of women pilots.

How unusual was it to be a woman pilot when you were first flying?

Jacqueline Cochran didn't want publicity concerning the program for the simple reason that had they known that 38 women had lost their lives, they would have cancelled the program. We weren't supposed to say that we were pilots.

The first girl that was killed, her name was Jean Rawlinson. She was in my class. We went to her service. I can remember, I don't know who said it, but they said, "We're not going to shed a tear for her because she is going to be living in our hearts." No one shed a tear.

523

No one?

Not one. I didn't think that way, but I think some did think, "this could have been me." That didn't cross my mind. It never did. Hazel Ah Ying Lee, a Chinese girl in my class, was killed in a P-39. She and I had the same orders to fly P-39s to Great Falls, Montana. I was several stops behind her. This really bothered me. What happened was there were about umpteen people in this flight. There were a few girls. It was just before we were deactivated. I think it was her last orders. We were scattered all over the northern part to the United States because the weather was so bad. One guy was flying without a radio. He got a signal to land, and then they told her to pull up or something. Anyway, it was because he didn't have a radio and she did. He ran into her because he didn't have the communication. They were both trying to get down.

Did you feel any survivor's guilt?

Yes, I did, mostly because I was on the same flight. We all had the same orders. Her uncle was mayor of Chinatown in New York City. If we delivered into Newark, New Jersey, we would go to Chinatown and the mayor of Chinatown would treat us royally with Chinese dinners. Often times when we would meet her, she'd cook Chinese dinners for us. Being that she was of a different nationality, I think we kind of looked out after her. She was special.

Were there any other minority fliers in the women's program?

She was the only one that I knew of. There were no blacks.

Do you have any Jacqueline Cochran stories?

I have a couple. She was visiting the base. Our class was the first class of women in Sweetwater. The other three classes were trained in Houston. There were still men cadets on the field. As the classes came in, they phased out the men cadets. We weren't supposed to be with them. We were supposed to pretend they weren't there. On certain nights we could talk to the cadets at the PX. One time, Jacqueline Cochran was in the office. I was walking down to the PX [Post Exchange]. There was a cadet standing there and he whistled at me. I gave them a dirty look. They weren't supposed to do that. I didn't know that Jacqueline Cochran was standing at the window. She called me in. "You know," she said, "you're not supposed to be communicating with the cadets."

I said, "I didn't. All I did was look at them."

She said, "You're not supposed to even look at them."

That was my first experience with her. I met her many times after this, because he entertained the WASPs out at her ranch in Indio, California. Her bartender was Chuck Yeager. This one time, we were in her living room and we were singing songs and I was standing behind the davenport. I remember she came over and said, "You are so tiny. Had I known that, you would have never been flying."

What did you think?

What I thought in my head was maybe she wished she were that size.

How big was she?

She was not very much bigger than I. At that time I was almost 5'2." She was maybe about 5'4." I doubt if she was more than 5'5." The other time, we were checking in at Reno for a reunion and at that time her husband was quite ill with arthritis. He was bed-ridden for years. She came up in a motor home and had some parking arrangement made with the hotel. My 11 year-old daughter [Kim] was with me. I wanted her to meet Jackie Cochran.

Was she friendly to Kim?

Yes, she was nice. Jackie Cochran was a multi-faceted lady. She was wonderful. She was good. One time she flew a planeload of Christmas gifts to some families in Spain. She paid the way back for some of the girls, when they were killed. She bought wings for the first six or seven classes. She paid for them herself. She had whatever it took by way of money. Her husband, Odlum, was considered one of the 12 richest men in the world, at that time. She had the money and power, plus she had a gift of gustiness that got her talking to Hap Arnold and to Congress. She knew all these famous movie stars because her husband had Fox Studios or something like that at the time. She had an in with people, but she also had the ability to get things done. Without her, there never would have been a program.

Do you have a Nancy Love story?

No, I only saw her once. She was then the director of the ferrying division. Jackie Cochran was the director of training. She visited Love Field one time. I didn't even talk to her. I saw her at a glance and I knew she was there checking on how things were going. I was one of these eager beavers. I was so happy to fly. You were supposed to lay over for 24 hours. I never did. I would pick up some orders and clean clothes and be off the next day.

Did it ever get you in trouble?

No, because we worked seven days a week. I could sleep on the airlines where a lot of people couldn't. They would have to take time off. When we had the big push for the Normandy Invasion, they were saying how important it was to deliver as many planes as we possibly could. I never spent one night on the base for two weeks. I was on the road the whole time.

I don't know how many planes I delivered. I just picked up one plane and flew it. Came back, picked up orders and picked up another plane and away we went. I loved it. Let's put it this way, I wasn't doing anything that was hard. I was doing something that I loved.

What did you think when you had to quit?

It was the worst day of my life, one of them. I'll tell you what an eager beaver I was. I didn't even know we were being deactivated. I was so busy flying. I came in on Friday and we were deactivated on Saturday. People said they couldn't believe I didn't know. I was just too busy. I never was on base. I didn't hear the scuttlebutt. It was like the end of my life. I thought, "What am I going to do with the rest of my life?" I knew I didn't want to go back to teaching. Can you imagine, after doing what we were doing, then to go back to teaching little kids to read? It did not appeal to me at all.

Were you in a depressed state for awhile?

Really depressed, I went home and there was nothing to do so I went to Newark. There were a couple of WASPs living in New York City so I went there. I worked for Trans World Airlines (TWA) at the ticket counter for about a year. It just wasn't satisfying.

That must have been frustrating standing at the counter watching the pilots go by.

The only interesting thing was that I met Howard Hughes and many famous people. That I enjoyed. I don't know who owned TWA before Howard Hughes, but he bought TWA. His flight was from Dallas to New York, that was La Guardia Field at that time. He had Jinks Falkenburg with him. I remember how thrilled we were when he came in. Talk about a good-looking guy; he had everything. He was tall and handsome and kind of rugged. As far as checking in people, the only thing that interested me at all or was challenging to me was that I made it a point to memorize every passenger's name and identify them when they checked in. At that time there were 36 passengers on an airliner. If they came back again, I knew them. I could call them by name. That was kind of a mental game. That was the only really exciting thing.

527

Did you get any funny responses when you remembered them?

Oh, they loved it. They couldn't believe it. This one guy, he didn't want anybody to check him in except me. I would recognize his voice on the phone.

Do you have a photographic memory?

No, I don't. I have to work at it. I play mental games. After the WASPs, I went into the ceramic business. That was very challenging to me because I didn't know anything about it. All my life, whenever I get into anything, I go all out. When I learned to ski—before I flew—I drank, ate, and lived skiing. That was big stuff. When I got into flying, I did it full bore. Same way with the ceramic business. The mental game I played there: I kept the books.

I would try to remember the checks that I wrote. Just how many checks I wrote, the date. One time, a business auditor came. He started asking some questions. My answers boggled his mind. The other night, I wasn't sleeping so I named the presidents in order.

Ceramics? What did you do?

We made television lamps. When television was first coming in, there was a lamp that gave indirect light on top of the television. We also had ceramic classes. It was a fun business for about ten years, until I got pregnant and had a child. Then I went full bore on that. That's the way I am.

I just celebrated my 82nd birthday on October 1, 1999. I was born in Bowdle, South Dakota. When I think of my life, of how far and how much has happened, it is unbelievable. When I was born, my parents wanted to take me 14 miles to show me to their grandparents, in a horse and buggy. I had the experience of flying the fastest airplanes at the time. Now I know Eileen Collins, who is going to be the first woman pilot to fly the shuttle. She was commander about a year ago. I've met all these young, wonderful women: Michelle Johnson, who is the first woman commander at Travis Air Force Base. One her final dine-in she invited me to speak. We dedicated the WASP Statue at Colorado Springs. I was president the last two years of the WASP Organization. I sat next to Janet Reno at the dedication. I can't even describe what that experience has led my life through. I wouldn't have met all these wonderful people.

How do you feel about being a kind of mentor?

I feel good. I didn't really realize it until one time when we had a P-51 conference in Colorado Springs. We went to the Academy and this darling little blond girl came up and put her arms around me and said, "If it wouldn't have been for you, I wouldn't be here." The other day, we just returned from Omaha. We were flying along and I said to my husband, "Dad, they've got a woman captain." There are 600 women captains on United Airlines. When we landed, instead of getting off the plane, I went to the cockpit. I said, "Congratulations, I am so glad to see you in that seat." I introduced myself.

She said, "You broke the barrier for us and I want to thank you."

I said, "I want to thank you for being where you are and congratulations." That was a conversation just last Sunday.

You retired from the pottery business to become a homemaker. Did you ever fly again?

I just flew the Goodyear Blimp on May 5 of this year. I've always wanted to fly the Goodyear Blimp, not just to ride in it. The day that we went up, the pilot was going to marry the granddaughter of a WASP—a very good friend of mine, Lila Mann. Before we went up, I said, "Well, who is your copilot?" He said, "You're going to be my copilot." I thought that we would just go up, and he would put the earphones on me and let me listen to what was going on. When we got up he said, "Over here are the rudders. It works just like an airplane but instead of a stick, there is a wheel. If you want to go down, you put the wheel down." He was explaining all this. After he had leveled off (we took off at Carson and we were flying out toward the ocean), he said, "Would you like to fly?" I said, "Sure." I flew the blimp for about 15 minutes. It was wonderful. It was great. Also, I did a taut sky dive on my 76th birthday in Perris, California. This was one of my dreams that came true, because I had always wanted to make a jump. It was a great experience—much more than anyone could imagine.

Anything else? Any regrets?

No, I believe you have a choice. When you get up in the morning, you can be miserable or you can be happy. I try every day to do something nice for someone, help someone or give them a phone call or do something nice for my husband or grandchildren or friends. I have had a few very hard things in my life. Whenever those come along, I think, "What do I have to learn from this experience?" When it really comes down hard, I find that in the

529

long run, it was the best thing that happened to me, not the worst, because I learned from it.

What were some hard things?

I met the fellow in college that I thought was going to be my husband for the rest of my life. He was in the navy. I had every intention in the world of waiting for him to marry him. After he graduated from officers' school, I thought we would be married. Then I received a "Dear Jane" letter that was a true disappointment. I thought it was the worst thing that could happen to me. That's when I picked up my boots and said, "I'm going to serve my country." That was the best thing that ever happened to me, because look what it did to my life.

I have had a wonderful life, having had so many rich experiences in the service. I count my blessings by my friends and family. I love my grandchildren almost as much as my only daughter Kim. My parents were my role models. They believed in the golden rule, honesty, service and finding joy in whatever you do.

HOWARD MUCHOW
The Boy Who Would be Pilot

Howard Muchow has lived an aeronautical life. He served in both World War II and Korea, helped establish the South Dakota Civil Air Patrol, fathered the Experimental Aircraft Association, Chapter 806, and was inducted into the South Dakota Aviation Hall of Fame.

Howard's interest in aviation began at a young age. In grade school, he started to build model airplanes, such as the SC-5 Sopwith Camel from WWI. The plane, which featured a 12 inch wingspan, was powered by, of course, a rubber band. At about 12, Howard's interests turned to balloons—for he had learned to make hydrogen. He remembers absconding with an aluminum pot from his mother's kitchen, cutting it into small pieces, and putting the pieces in a small-necked bottle. He then added the necessary liquids. Lo and behold, he had come up with hydrogen. He fastened penny balloons to the neck of the bottle, included a message, and sent the package out into the ether. One time he received a message response from New Jersey, and later one from a hunter in Iowa. After that he built model airplanes, including gas-powered ones and condenser and coil-type ignitions. He waves his finger that he banged up from his experience with models, and marvels that he did not do serious damage to, or kill himself, by his fooling around with hydrogen.

Howard attended School of Mines in Rapid City, South Dakota, intending to be an aeronautical engineer, but in 1942 decided to enlist in the Army Air Corps:

"I can remember when I was a little boy, my parents went up for a ride in Clyde Ice's tri-motor airplane from an airport on 41st Street in Sioux Falls, South Dakota. My aunt was taking care of me when my father and mother flew. I cried my eyes out because I didn't think I would ever see them again. This set the interest in aviation in motion. Later, during college, wartime action was heating up. I decided with a friend of mine, Roger Gudahal, to enlist in the Army Air Force, in Minneapolis. We took the examination. I didn't have high hopes, because I had just had an operation for a hernia. My friend Roger Gudahal, was having trouble with his eyes, so he'd been eating carrots and drinking carrot juice to take the physical. At that time, if you got a certain grade point in taking the test, you could stay in college and you could take flying lessons in college and that's kind of what I wanted to do. Well, it turned out that we took the examination, Roger got first in it and I got second. On our way to the physical I thought I could still go back to college, because they couldn't possibly take me with my hernia. Wrong conclusion. I passed the physical with flying colors. My friend Roger passed the eye test in flying colors. He was so happy and elated that by the time he took the blood pressure test, he failed that, and never did get to go in the service, or fly. He ended up being an engineer and my career in the future was in the air force."

He never got to fly. I went on to Jefferson Barracks where we lived in the Pneumonia Gulch. They put me up in a pressure chamber and took us up to 25,000-30,000. Coming back down I had severe head pains. I started, literally, tearing out my hair. That's why I am bald. Then they had to take me gradually back up and it took quite a while for them to get me down, after which they pulled four teeth, thinking there were air pockets beneath the teeth. They later found out that I had a cold and my sinuses had clogged up. So I lost some of my teeth. I had sinus problems before, but since that time I haven't had sinus problems. After that I went to Washington University in St. Louis, where I met my wife-to-be on a blind date. She lived in California, and her grandfather turned out to be one of the first engineers in the Black Hills of South Dakota, so it's a small world. I mailed her an engagement ring [laughs] which she hasn't forgiven me for yet.

She didn't think that was too personal?

I guess not. While at Washington University we learned celestial navigation and other courses and had ten hours of flight time in a Cub. I happened to find my old flight book and there's a notation by the instructor pilot, about halfway through, which says, "A good pilot but too cocky."

I guess I was over confident. I wanted to whip that airplane around. I wanted to be coming in for a landing and slipping it in. I would do a loop or a roll or anything I could get away with. I loved it, and I thought I was a good pilot. Anyway, when I read the quotation that I was cocky to my wife, she said, "Well, they're right" [laughs]. You know a military pilot, but especially a fighter pilot, has to be that way. You have to be invincible. At 18 or 20, you feel that you are invincible, that nothing can happen to you. It will always happen to the other guy!

I went to primary training in Texas, where we flew the PT-19s and then from there we went on to the BT-13s. One thing I remember about our training in the BT-13 is my first night. I took off and looked up and found the whole side of the fuselage was on fire. Nobody had told me about those big exhausts coming out and that it was a natural thing [laughs]. Here I was flying with the canopy open and I looked down and said, "Oh, my God, I'm on fire!" I started to get worried. Then I noticed the fire was coming out of the exhaust; they should have told me about this.

We had two active runways running parallel. When you would turn on your base leg, you'd fly with landing lights on, and then all of a the sudden you saw landing lights coming toward you from the opposite direction, just before you turned on your final approach. You'd wonder if that son of a gun was going to keep coming at you when you made your final turn to come in and land. What an experience. After that, I reported back to Texas, then went to Lincoln, Nebraska, where our B-17 crew was formed. I was a second pilot of the crew. From there we went to Rapid City Air Base, Rapid City, South Dakota, my old college town. That's where our B-17 training was going to take place. At 21, I was the old man on the crew, and the only married person. I had some very interesting things happen in B-17 training. I replaced the ball- turret gunner and finally got my 6'1" frame into the ball turret; I had to cross my legs but I got the job done. The other time we flew cross country at night and headed towards Minot, North Dakota. We got mixed up in a big thunderhead and flew right into it. I remember dropping the nose, applying full power and going up tail first at 2000 feet a minute. I was wondering what was happening. I guess I didn't listen to that part of our lecture [laughs]. We got out of the storm and spent the night in Minot, North Dakota. We had just landed and taxied over to the parking area and started to shut off the engines when here comes seven or eight fighters, P-38s, P-47s. They buzzed the field and then rolled out and I thought, "Oh God, wouldn't that be fun. It turned out to be flyers that were running ferries up to Alaska to be picked up by the Russians. When they taxied by they took off their helmets and they were all gals [laughs].

WASPs?

Yes, the WASPs. It was years later that my tail gunner told me what a fantastic time they had that night, while the old married man was at home [laughs]. After that we went back to Lincoln and picked up a brand-new B-17 and took off for Bangor, Maine, and then went up to Goose Bay, Labrador. I don't know how we ever found the field up there. We ran into fog at Newfoundland, and were flying by our navigator's position on the nose, telling us when to pull up and down again, but we finally landed.

After a day or two we took off for Iceland or Greenland. I was flying over the Atlantic and after hearing hours and hours of the hum from the props, everyone was fast asleep—all of the sudden I woke up and I looked at my watch, and I thought, "God, we're about ten degrees off course and about 30 minutes late." We were on autopilot and I had gone to sleep. I thought I'd over-correct, fly back to get on course, which I did. We came over Greenland just like we were supposed to. Just then the navigator called me up and said, "How's that for navigation? But we are a few minutes late, I can't understand that." I laughed, I never did tell the crew what had happened. We thought we were going to keep this brand-new airplane, but when we got over to England, they took it away from us. We were sent to the 385th Heavy Bombardment group, 550th Squadron, Third Division of the Eighth Air Force. We arrived at the base completely confused, not knowing what the future would bring.

When we checked into our Quonset hut, nobody would even talk to us. They wouldn't even ask our names or where we were from. They ignored us. Then we went into training and went on our first mission. At the completion of a mission we got a shot of whiskey, to loosen us up I guess. Some of our crews were too young and they didn't want to drink, so I went back to the barracks with them. After that first experience, you don't know what the hell's happening. You just thank God you're back. Once we reached our quarters, out comes the Canadian Club. They all began to talk to us. But, you had to have that first mission before they'd do that. Later on, when we were in Quonset huts, that's the ones with the corrugated sides, I embellished the procedure. We'd ignore the crews, just as we had been ignored, until they'd come back from their first mission, but when they came back from their first mission we still wouldn't talk to them until they went to bed because they were so exhausted. We had small lights up in the ceiling of the Quonset huts. I would light a flare that filled the place with smoke. Then we'd take a stick and run it across the corrugated walls, yelling out "Gas." And all of us, except the new crews, would have our gas masks handy and they would tear their bags apart looking for their gas masks [laughs]. When they found out that it was all a big farce, we'd take them up to the Officer's Club for the rest of the indoctrination. The home base had three poplar trees as landmarks. One time we couldn't find our airport because of the fog and weather, but we landed at a neighboring B-17 base, not too far away. We found out that their shot of whiskey after the mission was twice as much as what we got at home, so we stayed there. After a while we walked down the highway singing our songs and calling to each other as if on the intercom. We were invincible.

On the 22nd mission, I came down with the shakes at night and somebody turned me in to the flight surgeon. He came down to the Quonset hut and grounded me. The rest of the crew went up on a mission, it was in March. None of us wanted to be grounded because it would break up the crew. I stayed home from that mission. Coming back at 1300 feet, *Mr. Lucky*, our airplane, had a midair collision, when a B-17 came up and cut off the tail of the airplane. I later was briefed on what had happened. They said the crew members were falling out without parachutes. The tail gunner, Joe Frank Jones, tried to bail out, but he couldn't because the door was jammed. He said the last thing he remembered was starting to light up a cigarette. The tail landed in Belgium. The people in Belgium got him out of the tail. He was bruised quite a bit, but nothing was broken. He came back to the base, but of course he didn't fly anymore. He did get his name in *Believe it or Not*, by Ripley and *Time* magazine.

So you lost friends?

Yes. They were more than friends after the crash. I was given pickup crews. I was first pilot then and given pickup crews to complete the missions. You had new people on every mission. You didn't even know their names. You just wanted to make damn sure they knew their jobs. They also were survivors from other crews.

I think by the time I had my 35 missions, I had a barracks bag filled with good luck charms. For instance, I wore the same uniform for over 35 missions and never had it cleaned. I always carried anything unusual that I had taken on the last mission, thinking it would help. I took a lot of photographs with an M. Foth Derby camera and later all the negatives were destroyed or lost.

What did you uniform look like at the end?

Kind of dirty and smelly!

I remember one B-17 that blew up on the ramp because of an oil and grease combination. I think it was down in Texas someplace. That always bothered me, so I would treat the oxygen and oil with a great deal of respect.

On one mission my radio operator said we'd been hit. I went into the bomb bay and saw that a piece of flak had gone through the bomb bay and knocked the tail fin off a 500 pound bomb. I went into the radio room and saw the third leg of the radio man's chair had collapsed. That's why he thought he was hit. When I saw that tail fin shot off, I couldn't understand why it didn't explode, because I had seen a picture of a B-17 where that had happened, and it wasn't anything but a mushroom cloud.

When I first started to fly combat, I told my crew chief that I was going to have four kids. A soothsayer had told me that. So when I was over there, the first thing I did was to have a piece of armor plate cut and put underneath my seat cushion to protect the family jewels. It was with me all the time.

Who was the soothsayer?

She was a fortuneteller in Long Beach. When I was a kid during the Depression, I saved a quarter just to have my palms read.

There's one thing that happened in flying combat and I'm sure it happened to everybody, but you would go through different phases of thought concerning living and dying. You'd be afraid and concerned, thinking that you were going to die. What was happening—you couldn't understand it. The next phase would be, you're gonna die anyway, so what the hell? You'd wonder why these thoughts would rise. Possibly it was when somebody had been killed or wounded, but you had to maintain an overall thought that you were invincible, that it wasn't going to happen to you. During this time, I can remember one phase I was going through. That I figured that if I'm going to get it, I'm going to get it. We were on a mission to Hamburg and I was flying at the time. I didn't put on my flak helmet or vest—the hell with it. Anyway, we were coming into Hamburg and there was a burst of flak off the copilot's side, and a piece of flak came in through the side of the airplane and hit my copilot in the gut. He had his flak vest on. The piece of flak ricocheted up, cutting the earphone wires on my helmet, then went up through the top of the cockpit roof. It cut the earphone wire right in two. I'll tell you something, old Howard, in ten seconds had his flak vest on and his flak helmet and was peeking through about a one inch crack. Later on, come to think of it, it's probably a good thing I didn't have the helmet on, because that flak might have just ricocheted around the inside of the helmet and done more damage.

Ernst Trexler during World War II.

ERNEST (JIM) TREXLER
Test Pilot

Jim Trexler has led a colorful life of flight. He once flew as copilot for Charles Lindbergh in a B-24 and worked closely with General Tunner, USAFE Commander. Overall, he has flown in 85 different types of military aircraft and several hundred civilian aircraft—all without an accident. During WWII, he completed two tours of duty, including serving as a test pilot.

Jim Trexler was born and raised on a 325-acre farm in North Carolina where his great flight adventure began. In July 1925, a Ford Tri-motor landed beside the highway. Jim and his dad saw it and hopped in their Model-T Ford truck and drove over to see it and in exchange for using their field, the pilot gave them a free ride. From that day forward, it was his dream to become a pilot.

Jim was 10 years old when the Depression hit in 1929. He took Piper Cub lessons at the Salisbury airport where he would pick apples and peaches and trade them to the airport manager for an occasional ride in a Cub. "That little yellow bird kept my dream alive," he says. In 1938 his parents were adamant he attend college, but they had no money. He soon found a job at a local funeral home where he lived and worked whenever he was needed, driving the ambulance or hearse, embalming, conducting funeral services and singing at some funerals. The job paid $20 a week, and with some borrowed money, Jim was able to attend Catawba College.

In his sophomore year, Jim and his good friend, Ralph White, met a senior, Ed Rector, who had similar dreams about flying as the two. All three wanted to join the Flying Tigers. Ed had passed his physical to obtain pilot training in the U.S. Army Air Corps and expected to be called even before his graduation from college—and he was. Meanwhile, Ralph and Jim decided to go through pilot training in the Army Air Corps. They received a scheduled physical appointment at Fort Bragg, North Carolina, a 125-mile drive. Ralph was skinny and underweight, so Jim fed him bananas and water during the entire trip—but he was rejected. Jim was accepted. Within a couple of months, he started primary training in Lakeland, Florida, where 50 percent of trainees washed out. His civilian instructor was Clem Whittenbeck, who was paralyzed from his knees down. Clem had to be helped into the cockpit of the Stearman PT-13. He was a famous stunt pilot whose teachings, Jim says, saved his life many times.

Jim was still enthused with the idea of becoming a Flying Tiger and worked extra-hard. At Gunter Field, Montgomery, Alabama, he flew the big Vultee BT-17. After three months of grueling training, he graduated from basic and went on to advanced school across town at Maxwell Field. At the end of school training—with fewer washouts and only a few days of written exams left before graduation day, a major advised Jim where he was going and what type of pilot he was selected to be—a fighter pilot. Jim nonetheless felt disappointment not to be able to join the Flying Tigers.

542

How much did you make when you first joined the military?

After graduation I earned big bucks $325 per month ($250 plus $75 flight pay).

I was checked out in the Bell Air Cobra P-39 and then in training for tight formation flying, night flying, gunnery and bombing and air-to-air dogfight. My air-to-ground gunnery (strafing) was up north at Oscoda. Our group had to share Oscoda with the First Pursuit Group.

What flight problems did you see in training?

We would follow the Pee Dee River enroute to their target. One time Buck Newman was in lead, and Sutton and I were wingmen. Sut and I saw wires across the Pee Dee, but Buck didn't. We both told Buck to pull up—but not in time. He flew right through the wires, knocking out electricity, denting the wings and knocking off the bombs (duds) and shackles but made it back to the base. For that, he was restricted to the tent in the pines and lost his room in town with me. One of the days while at Florence, each pilot could go on a one day, one night cross-country trip. I decided to take my flight to my hometown of Salisbury, North Carolina. I called and told my parents I'd fly over their home first and for them to pick me up at the airport for dinner together. I put on quite an acrobatic show over town, buzzed the funeral home where I lived and worked while in college. No one came out to wave, only later did I learn that a funeral was in progress. I landed safely on the airport's grassy strip, taxied in and stopped in front of the hangar, only to find the sheriff waiting for me. He and my dad were talking so he knew who the pilot was as he had caught me several times before for speeding. I howdied him and asked him to please guard the aircraft until I returned from dinner and later I would let him sit in the cockpit. He liked that, and I thought I had it made in the shade until I filed a flight plan to Charlotte. Upon arriving there around 10 P.M., a staff car met me and the driver advised me the Colonel of the Unit was waiting for me.

How'd you get caught?

The sheriff had reported me! Now, I thought, I'm in deep crap—what should I use as an excuse? After giving him all kinds of BS, he broke into a big laugh and said, "Son, I just wish I had done what you did. Now you be a good boy. Good luck—and I'm not going to report you to your commander." What a relief, but I had so much fun that any punishment would have been worth it. My hometown recruiting office was deluged with volunteers for pilot training after that. To this day, 49 years later, every time I go home, everyone remembers that day.

The next morning I arrived back in Florence and the Crazy 3, (Buck, Sut, and I) as we were called, after having previously demonstrated our proficiency in precision formation acrobatics, were scheduled for seven days to put on air shows at various locations for recruiting purposes. We were so elated that we went up that afternoon to practice more on formation take-offs, slow rolls, loops and chandelles, dog-fighting, etc. and just before landing, we decided to buzz the Colonel's office tent. Tower permission was granted, but the tower reported that the tent collapsed on the Colonel and his staff. Now we knew we were dead. Upon landing, we were told that the Colonel crawled out from under the tent, laughing. His laughing didn't last long, and he restricted all three of us. Buck was already restricted to living in tents until we left for home base, Selfridge.

Where did you go after you went through test pilot school?

After test pilot school, my first assignment was to the P-51 North American plant in Englewood, California. In addition to the normal air corps acceptance test flights, I took my flight orders from Wright Field, which took theirs from the Pentagon. We had many hours of special testing involving max takeoffs and climbs to 35,000 feet. We were loaded with ammo and bombs; all gunnery and bombing tests; max distances with many different power settings; cruise charts with and without external tanks; power diving speeds, stall speeds, and weights at combat altitudes, acrobatics; max air speeds to redline instruments max bomb loads with ammunition; writing of the dash-one pilot's manual; and numerous other tests. All of this required we work seven days a week.

This was at this same plant were the B-25 bomber was made. One of the pilots from the bomber branch at Wright Field was with me at this plant and was killed on a test flight during take-off. I then had three different aircraft at this plant, the P-51, A-36 and B-25. So now I was working day and night, eight days a week. I loved the work. While at this location, I did make one save, in a P-51 on a test flight to 35,000 feet. An oil line broke around the rudder pedals spraying hot, black oil all over the cockpit, covering my cloth helmet, oxygen mask, and goggles. I knew the engine would have to be shut down immediately, which meant that I was now in a heavy glider and I didn't have glider wings yet! I was around 50 miles from the plant airfield, so I figured if I kept the aircraft clean (gear and flaps up), I could dead stick it in. I had communications with the tower, which cleared all air traffic. My hydraulic pressure was holding due to the propeller windmilling. At 1,000 feet on final approach, dropped the gear and quarter flaps. I had 50 psi left for braking the aircraft. It turned out to be an almost normal landing except that my parachute got chewed some.

In those days, the aircraft cost $35,000. For the save, I was offered a company car and an apartment in the Hollywood Roosevelt Hotel for my duration at the plant—and I took it. I did all kinds of tests on the three aircraft—gunnery and bombing, writing procedures, etc. While in the Englewood area, I was requested by Wright Field to run test flights at the Douglas plant (A-20s), the Lockheed plant (P-38s), and later at the Boeing plant (B-17s and the XB-29). All had experimental aircraft to fly.

By now (1943-1944) the Army Air Corps test flight facilities had greatly expanded to the Eglin Field, Wright Patterson Field (up the road from Wright Field) and other locations in California, Arizona and New Mexico. The higher altitude aircraft were coming on line, and the pilots then had additional training in altitude chambers to learn the dangers of high altitude and how to cope with those dangers. At this time, Wright Field had the only high-altitude chamber, and all our test pilots and future high-altitude line pilots had chamber procedure to go through—once a year for line pilots and once a month for test pilots.

545

When we got most of the bugs worked out of one kind of aircraft, we were shifted to other experimental aircraft. From California plants, I was sent to the Douglas plant in Tulsa, Oklahoma where the A-26 contract had been accepted and the first three aircraft had been assembled, ready for testing. This was our first aircraft with laminar flow wings. We ran all of the preliminary tests, like taxi tests; high-speed to take off speed then braking tests; nose lift off; and finally takeoff, then cruise low and high-speed, normal and max-climb—and a dozen other tests carefully calculated, then brought the planes down for a complete inspection. All discrepancies were carefully studied, sometimes going back to the drawing board for better engineering. Douglas Aircraft had always made fine aircraft, the C-47, C-54, the old A-24 dive-bomber and now the A-26, to say nothing about their commercial aircraft. The beginning tests on this aircraft showed they were excellent and required very little maintenance. Testing at the plant went well.

Ever test guns?

Yes, as a matter of fact, I took one of the aircraft to Eglin Field for many other tests. One specific test involved firing of a 75 mm cannon installed in the nose with the spent shell to be automatically ejected under the cannoneers' bicycle seat into a large bag in the bomb bay. The spent shell missed its target and hit the cannoneer in a bad place. I immediately radioed for an ambulance to meet the plane, and after a doctor's inspection, had him airlifted to a hospital. The 75mm was never fired again from an A-26, but the 20 mm was used in a small number of A-26s. After its combat approval, I flew the first three via the southern route—Georgetown, Natal, Ascension Island (where a German sub shelled the airfield on one trip)—on to Dakar, then north along the coast of Portugal across the channel to our destination, Nuts Corner, Scotland. There, I spent a week instructing and checking out combat pilots and flew several missions with them. On my first trip over, my navigator and I had departed West Palm Beach, Florida. After we stopped in Georgetown, British Guinea, I was pre-flighting the bird, when I noticed my navigator taking on an additional bucket of water in addition to our emergency rations. I knew we had an awful lot of jungle to cross en route to Natal and figured it was a good idea. About an hour after takeoff, we had a bad oil leak and I feathered the prop. After a loss of oil pressure and an increase in the oil temperature, I returned to Georgetown, repaired the damaged line, and off we went again. By then, the weather was getting really bad, and about an hour later, we were on solid instruments and really fighting to keep the bird level. Out of the corner of my eye, I noticed my navigator reach down for the bucket of water. Then he splashed it all over me! I was surprised and mad as hell. I started to sock him, and he laughingly said, "Congratulations, you've just crossed the equator and this is the standard initiation for first timers." We were still bouncing all over the sky, but I started thinking how I could get even.

We were trucked up to a small French house on base and naturally we were about to burst, so we both hurried into the bathroom. I used the regular toilet. I said, "You can use that other thing." I knew what it was, he didn't. I thought, this if my chance to get even.

So, when he said, "How do you flush it?"

And I said, "You have to bend over and open that valve."

He did, and the water flushed all over him—and I said, "Congratulations. This is your initiation to the French bidet." The rest of the flight was without pranks and the A-26, in my opinion, was the Cadillac or Lincoln of the Air Corps. I had an engine shot by an Me 109 along the coast of Portugal—on another flight. The Marrakech pass in Africa was socked in, and I had to land on a sand strip until the pass opened the next morning.

Then came the A-25 Helldiver made by Curtis Wright at Lambert Field, St. Louis, Missouri, and the A-31/A-35 made by Vultee in Nashville, Tennessee. The A-25 was a large, single engine dive-bomber, tandem seat, with the gunner in the rear seat. The Navy used them on their carriers. The main objective at St. Louis was the testing of the XP-55, a single Allison engine with a pusher prop—the pilot sat ahead of the engine, the elevator was in front and a rudder on the end of each swept-back wing. It was a highly secretive aircraft; I could only fly it at night. Wright Field wanted it there, so it was disassembled and loaded into a trailer for the trip to Dayton. I thought very little of it as a fighter airplane; it was slightly faster than the P-40/P-38—not as fast as the P-51. Only one was made and I understand it will be in the new Dulles Air Museum.

At this time in the war, the German Studka dive-bomber that raised so much hell over France was being phased out, so our dive-bombers likewise were no longer needed. I believe that the A-31 and the A-35s were sold to South America, some of our A-25s were needed to pull gliders. The A-25s relieved the C-47s from towing the CG-4s for training, until they began misbehaving. Reports from the field had them stalling out—so Wright Field sent me out to several units in Texas and California to determine the cause. I could see the cause before I got close to the first one—the heavily loaded CG-4s were elongating the A-25 fuselage, and popping rivets. They were immediately grounded and I have no idea of the outcome.

I was then called back to Wright Field and advised that I would be the chief test pilot for the new P-47 Thunderbolt. I went to the Republic plant on Long Island for several days of ground school and a ground check out by their chief pilot and flew the first one to

547

Wright-Patterson where further testing would be accomplished. But before flight-testing was to start, I would be required to do special exercising to prep me for the high altitude work. Dr. Lovelace, our flight surgeon, went through several days of high-altitude chamber training with me. In fact, the last day of chamber training lasted eight hours with special exercising and emergency procedures. I wondered what in the hell I was getting myself into, going up to 50,000 feet. Without oxygen up there, one doesn't last long, maybe five to ten seconds.

The P-47 wasn't pressurized either.

No. An oxygen mask was required from ground up. In fact, during my special exercising prior to each flight, Dr. Lovelace kept me on pure oxygen, walking beside me hooked up to an oxygen bottle until hooked into the plane's oxygen system. Instrument readings were recorded every 2,000 feet to 30,000 feet. Then each 1,000 feet to the upper altitudes. There were weeks of tests, with altitude cross-country flights, simulated dogfights, acrobatics, emergency descents, climbs, stalls, tight turns, and recovery procedures—which helped our fighter pilots to establish air superiority over the much improved German fighters. This could be done with the P-51s and P-47s. The Pentagon was still calling for 50,000 feet recordings, which they never got, since my highest altitude in the P-47, if I recall, was slightly above 47,000 feet. I always wondered why these high altitude tests were so important, as most, if not all of our dogfights with the enemy were below 35,000 feet.

No G-suits and masks back then.

No, we had only a pair of coveralls, warm clothing, and a cloth headgear. We learned later that this high altitude information was needed as our breakthrough to jet aircraft which was but a short time away. Incidentally, the Lovelace Foundation was named after our flight surgeon. The only near-fatal accident that happened to me was in the 47. I was again trying for 50,000 feet. Our chief test pilot was in the Wright-Patterson control tower yelling for me to take it on up—and after repeated calls from me that every instrument was above the red lines. The tower kept insisting and I kept saying that the turbo-supercharger was way over its max rpms—and then it happened—it exploded. That meant a thousand pounds of weight located just in front of the tail wheel was gone. I wouldn't be able to live through a bailout at that altitude, since I had lost about everything except my oxygen system. I had no choice but to ride the plane straight down and try to gain some control prior to bail out. My last chance was to drop the gear, open the cowl flaps—all way above maximum air speeds. I managed to gain control at about 500 feet above the ground. I did a dead stick landing with the propeller tips digging up the ground due to loss of weight on the tail wheel.

When did you decide to leave the testing business?

In today's Air Force, a pilot can be checked out in only one aircraft—maybe two. While a test pilot, I've flown as many as 13 different types of aircraft in a single day.

After having been a test pilot for a little more than a year, I realized I was the only one still alive of the original 12. I told my commander that I was volunteering for a second combat tour where it was safe. He said, "Only if you will come back to testing."

I said, "I'd think about that." So I volunteered for a combat tour. I was assigned to go through the C-46 Dumbo Instrument school at Reno, Nevada. It certainly wasn't a fighter outfit where I wanted to practice my skills at protecting our B-17s and 24s in Europe. Soon, however, I was sweating under the instrument hood of the C-46 and the Link trainer at Reno—with a night off occasionally. After a month of instrument work, I was assigned to fly C-46s at Wheelus Field in Tripoli, Libya, close to where my first combat tour was. Before arriving there, I first had to go through another two-week instrument school at Marrakech, Morocco. After two more sweltering weeks "under the hood," I thought I was now a hot instrument pilot. I later found out that I needed every minute of that hood time flying over the mountains of North Africa to and from Casablanca and over the Hump into China. The worst weather in the world is over North Africa and the highest wind velocity in the world is over the Himalayas. There, one could be heading east but flying north. And it was dark at night with no ground lighting.

I finally arrived at Tripoli. With Rommel and his forces defeated and out of Africa, the pilots lived in the Grand Hotel. It wasn't grand, but it was a helluva lot better than the tent cities I've lived in. Our flights were from Tripoli to Casablanca, back to Tripoli, to Cairo, to Baghdad, Teheran, across several different routes in India and to numerous bases in China. During this time I saw some of my envied Flying Tiger pilots. Most of them had amassed quite a fortune at $1,500 per month along with $500 for each aircraft destroyed. I flew to the Mediterranean Islands, to Italy, to Spain, and to Turkey, and I felt a lot safer in old Dumbo that had been flown before than in a first-timer aircraft as a test pilot. During this tour, I managed to get a four-day rest and relaxation. My friend, Buck Newman, had crashed around there, so I spent time researching the approximate vicinity of where that might have been. Finally, I managed to get the rescue boat with scuba divers, and after spending several days diving in rather shallow (100 feet) water, they found his P-38 intact—identified by tail numbers, but found only a pair of winter flying boots in the cockpit.

What did you fly?

I flew the old C-46s. It was like old home week. I learned to love this ol' bird; it was built like a brick privey, but was short on boost for the flight controls. It took two men and a boy to fly through heavy storms. Our reserve unit assisted MATS, at that time, in delivering cargo and we flew U.S. and foreign flights. While a Reservist in 1948, we were now no longer in the U.S. Army Air Corps, but in the new command called United States Air Force. A major command of our own. We did not, however, relinquish our relations with the U.S. Army and we moved cargo and personnel for them and participated in parachute and equipment dropping with our C-46s and later the C-119 Boxcar, the first aircraft I had flown equipped with reversible pitch propellers, used mostly for short field landings as well as normal landings. The new USAF command structure provided for latitude in growth and development. I thought that by staying in the reserves that I could still retire at 50.

Then Korea?

Yes, what a surprise. I was recalled in 1950 for the Korean War and sent to Randolph Air Force Base for B-29 special training. I ended up flying for three months out of Okinawa during the Korean conflict. I then went back to Randolph for complete crew training with specially modified B-29s. I had previous testing experience in the XB-29, but I still went through the complete 13 man aircrew training school, and upon completion of this course, we were sent to Mountain Home AFB, Idaho, for specialized training for our cloak and dagger mission. While there, I became an instructor pilot to new crews, instrument flight instructor and examiner, and test pilot for our Wing. After a year of 30 hour long training missions, you must guess where our wing was sent—believe it or not—to Tripoli, Libya, again.

That's when you started your illustrious building career?

That's correct. Having been stationed there twice before, I was very acquainted with the housing situation. Dependents were allowed only if they had housing for them. Knowing this and knowing the very hot weather in summer and cold in winter, I stopped by Selfridge AFB when flying my B-29 and picked up a two-ton, reverse cycle air conditioner, hoping that I could use it. As I thought, very few apartments were available in Tripoli and our personnel were over-bidding each other in an attempt to obtain family housing. I asked permission from the base commander, Colonel Buck Anthis, to place three house trailers in a small trailer park, already on the base—one each for my copilot, my navigator, and myself. I also asked for permission to build an addition to each. With his permission granted, I scheduled a training flight to Molesworth AB, England, to be a future base for another wing. Upon our arrival, we immediately went into London, bought three of the longest trailers built in England—16 feet long, paid for them and the freight. The trailers arrived in Tripoli on Christmas day 1953.

551

HERMAN ERNST
Night Fighter

Herman Ernst had been attending the University of Chattanooga where he overheard stories of a new fighter plane, "The Black Widow." He was interested in fighters, so decided to pursue the possibility of flying the plane, and ended up doing so in the Night Fighter Program.

Herman then traveled to Arizona for gun re-training and then went to Florida for Night Fighter training at Orlando and Kissimmee. He soon was part of the 422nd Night Fighter Squadron. After the first of the year, he was sent to England. From then on he distinguished himself in the war in Europe as one of America's Aces.

Did anything unusual happen in training in Florida?

Yes, one thing happened. After I was assigned to the 42nd Squadron, we trained in P-70s and A-20s. A P-70 is a modified A-20, with radar. We only had four. Finally, we got four YP-61s, which were still kind of experimental. We had some factory tech reps getting the bugs out. On Christmas Eve 1943, I had flown a YP-61 for a couple of hours with my radar observer. We landed and switched airplanes with another team, which included Bob Elmore and his radar observer. This time I went up and flew his old A-20; he flew the YP-61. At the time I was coming down the coast at 10,000 feet, right over what is now Patrick Air Force Base and was then the Banana River Naval Air Station. I was clearing myself to make a turn and go back up the coast when something happened. Suddenly, I didn't have an airplane to fly, and what was left of it was falling. I bailed out. What had happened was that another airplane had run into me and taken off my right wing and engine and tail.

What were your first instincts when you were hit?

I tried to communicate with my radar man and another man I had in the back end of the plane, but I couldn't get through. I knew that I had to get out of there because the airplane wouldn't fly.

What tipped you off to what was happening?

After I got out I could see the other airplane spinning in and the debris of my airplane falling. The collision had knocked off the whole right wing, and it was flip-flopping down. It finally hit down there in Banana River. I was the only one that got out of the plane alive. My radar observer was Jimmie Londeree, with whom I had gone through Night Fighter training and another guy that was flying with us just for the ride was a corporal named Bolger were both lost. We learned that the airplane that hit me was from the training squadron. It seems that the pilot had seen the YP-61 behind me, and because the YP-61 was such a new airplane, he like everybody else was interested in it. Apparently, he was too busy looking at the P-61, and didn't see me in time. Certainly I didn't see him because I was looking in the other direction preparing myself for a turn. The pilot who hit me crashed into the river down and died, but his radar observer survived.

It turned out that because the radar observer had lost his pilot and I'd lost my radar observer, we teamed up and flew together. The radar observer was Eddie Kopsel, who flew with me during the entire war, completing 70 missions. My first mission was in England in July 1944.

The British wanted us to fly Mosquitoes because they thought it was a better airplane. Of course, we wanted to fly our P-61s because it was a metal airplane, not wooden. With a wooden airplane when you got hit you had a bunch of matchsticks left. We didn't like that idea. One time we ended up having a fly-off between the P-61 and a Mosquito. One of our boys, Lieutenant Doyle, flew the contest in the P-61 and out-performed the Mosquito in almost every way you could. After all, our plane could land shorter, take off shorter, climb faster and out-turn the Mosquito. Doyle did a good job of it.

On our first combat mission, we were chasing buzz bombs in the English Channel, which were heading toward London. On my first mission out, I was inexperienced and didn't know what in the world was going on. We were at 7,000 or 8,000 feet and the radar station over on the coast directed us to start our dive. In a dive would pick up a little extra speed, in case the buzz bomb was going too fast to stay with at a level flight. When the operator on the coast gave us the word: "Okay, start your dive," I picked up that little extra speed. At that time I was diving down steep and wide because I wanted to show that we could get the job done. Suddenly, I realized something had happened to the airplane. I tried to contact my radar observer, but couldn't understand him on the intercom. Suddenly, the airplane shook for a moment. Unable to contact my radar man and figure things out, I aborted and returned to base. When I landed, I found out what had happened, which was that when I had gotten in that power dive, the tail cone, located back behind my radar observer, had just disintegrated. It left him with a big hole behind him. Of course, that was what created the noise so that I could not understand him. The mechanics did not have another tail cone, so we bolted a flat piece of Plexiglas on the back end to close up the hole. That's the way we flew for a month, until we got a new tail cone.

The next night, we went out and started chasing buzz bombs and we shot one down. As far as I know, the first thing a P-61 shot down in England, was a buzz bomb, a V-1.

Do you think you were the first person to shoot a buzz bomb down with a P-61?

Yes, that was on the July 16, 1944. That's when we first started operating. From then on, we ran regular missions, chasing enemy aircraft or whatever. At night all you can see is the fire coming out the tail of these rocket engines. When you would start to approach it, you just see the jet off of that rocket engine. But you don't want to shoot them too close up because they'd blow up in your face. One of our men, Captain Spelis, the flight leader, learned that. He got too close and the bomb blew some of the control surfaces off his airplane. Up close a pilot could not see, because of the black smoke that was covering up the airplane. That incident showed us all that you don't get too close to those buzz bombs when you try to shoot them down.

So he escaped?

Oh, yes. He got back all right. That airplane was a very stable airplane.

Did it take your eyes awhile to get used to night flying?

We tried to keep our eyes out of bright lights before we took off, but later we probably did not pay much attention to that, because in a few minutes you'd get used to the dark. When we first started Night Fighter training, the military had us eating carrots, which was supposed to be good for our eyes. We didn't pay much attention to that later on either.

556

On July 30, we landed at France at a field designated A-15, which was on the north coast. This was after the invasion. There we did regular patrols, chasing German aircraft and sometimes would hit ground targets and so forth. The first dramatic episode there was when I shot down my first German aircraft, a Me-110. Also, we saw an FW-190 on that mission, but I didn't get to shoot it down. We simply chased it by radar. Of course, we had radar in our airplane. We followed after the ground control gave us a vector heading. Then my radar observer picked it up and he could tell me whether I was above or below or how fast I was catching up to it. I would get close enough to identify it. We had to identify everything by sight before we shot, because we couldn't depend on the IFF. Anyway, we got close enough and when I could identify it as a Me-110, I shot it down. When I shot down the JU 88 we intercepted it and almost had a collision with it before we shot it down. Then we began to chase this JU-87 and once we had identified it, we shot it down the same way. As for the near collision, I would guess we were 300 or 400 feet apart, maybe. It was close enough that I could see the plane and identify it at night. We swung away to avoid the collision.

On December 26 we shot down another plane. We got JU 88, very much the same way. We chased and intercepted it and shot it down. Then on December 29 we damaged a JU 88, but we don't think we shot it down.

Were you an Ace by then?

No, I wasn't an Ace until March 2. In 1945 I shot down three airplanes in one mission, two JU-87s and a Me-110, in about 16 minutes. The funny thing was that I wasn't supposed to fly that night. That was my 56 mission. That evening I had been in bed in my tent when a friend of mine, Bob Bollinder, from Operations sent a guy over. He woke us up and said, "They've got something going on out there tonight. If you all want to make another mission, you could fly again."

We wanted to complete our 70 missions so as to complete our tour of duty, so I decided to go. Several of us got up, went to Operations and went out with the next flights. That night, the Germans had more activity around the Rhine River than they had for some time. So when I reported to the ground radar station from the air, the radar operator said, "We're too busy. I can't take you. Just hold on for a few minutes." We started circling behind our lines. At one point, I looked down and saw that our boys were shooting at us, by mistake. So flew over on the German side. There, we weren't being shot at so hard. In a few minutes, ground radar called us and said, "Okay, are you guys ready to go to work?" We said, "Of course we are." The ground radar guy then gave us a vector and we headed for a Me-110. We got it. Then he gave us another vector for a JU-87.

Was there any fight involving the 110? Did the pilot see you?

If he knew we were there, he didn't shoot at us. He didn't indicate whether he knew we were there or not. Anyway, we got him and then we did the same thing with two more JU-87s. We intercepted them and shot them down. All that happened, I think the report shows, in about 16 or 18 minutes. Of course, our plane received some damage from our boys before we had flown over the line, but luckily it wasn't enough to keep us from operating. And we got those three on that mission.

How did you celebrate that night?

We just did the same old thing; we went back and went to bed.

No one gave you a little drink of booze?

Well, they would have. But I didn't drink. I didn't celebrate by drinking.

But you must have been pretty excited?

Of course I was. Of course, I always wondered if I had shot down some of my daddy's kin. When my dad was a young man, he came to the U.S. from Germany. He was the only one in his family to come over.

On New Year's Eve I intercepted a Me-110. It was about a minute after midnight. I called my radar observer and I identified myself and said, "We're going to get the first German of the new year, right now." So I pushed the button on my guns and started firing, but my guns popped just a few times and quit. I must have hit the other plane a little bit because his rear gunner started shooting at me. I pushed every switch and circuit breaker in that dog-gone airplane, but I couldn't get those guns to fire any more. I didn't want that plane to get away. I wanted badly to get him, but finally I had to let him go. In the meantime, he shot out the front end of my airplane. As a result, I did not have a nose wheel to land on. As we landed, there was ice and snow, so the darn plane ended up just sliding. Luckily, the landing didn't really didn't tear up anything much more.

What was the most frightened you were in the war?

Oh, I don't know. I guess that first mission, when that tail cone blew out and I didn't know what had happened. I guess I was about as frightened then as I had been on any of the missions, because I didn't know what was going on there for a few minutes.

What did your dad say about you your military tour of duty?

He understood the situation and knew that I was just doing my job. I don't know that it would have had anything to do with his family, but of course I don't know that. I have been over to Germany since the war and I've talked to some of the family members. But I never got too close to dates and times of things. I did for the simple reason that I hoped I hadn't done anything to them. Of course, I don't know. I talked to one of my cousins over there a few years ago, and he'd been on the Russian Front all of the time, so I didn't have to worry about him [laughs].

So how many planes did you shoot down, altogether?

Well, actually, I got six or eight. There were some that I didn't get credit for, or full credit for. For instance, on one of the 110's I shot down, the ground forces claimed that they thought they shot it down. I was up in the air with it and could see my strikes on it. At the time I thought I'd got it, but what the heck. As it turned out, the military gave the ground forces half-credit, so I was not able to get full-credit for it. That's all right. Those men need credit. They did a good job. I'd damaged some other planes, too, but sometimes you don't know how much you damage them, so you just can't claim them. Other times, you don't get confirmation, because they flew off somewhere, though they might have crashed.

559

Are any general misconceptions about Night Fighters and about what you did?

A lot of people don't know much about us because of the fact that we never got any pictures. You see, the "day boys," the day fliers, were able to take pictures all the time, but it was harder for us. We had our gun cameras loaded, but we didn't have infrared film that would take pictures at night. The only time we got a picture was when something would blow up in front of us and we got a silhouette. The camera was always rolling while we were shooting. Without pictures, we never got many stories or much publicity.

So, what else do people misunderstand or not know about Night Fighters?

Toward the end of the War, the Germans were pretty well beaten down so we did not do much chasing. Instead, we did ground work. On March 24, I was given four napalm bombs and two targets. One was a military area right next to an autobahn. Keep in mind, we did not have the precise navigation equipment that we have now, so it wasn't as easy to navigate and find where you were, especially at night over. Still, I managed to find this military area because it was next to this freeway. Because I didn't have a bombsite and hadn't had any training in dropping bombs, I had to guess at what I was doing. I did not know when to drop the bombs. I dropped two of them on this military area, but unfortunately, they sailed out over all of those buildings and hit right in the middle of that freeway. All I did was burn up a little concrete. My second target then was supposed to be a vehicle-filled military area next to a river. And I looked all over the place and I found the river, but I couldn't find that group of trucks and so I couldn't use that for a target. I needed to get rid of those two other bombs. Somebody opened a big door, and I saw a blast furnace. I said, "That's a good target." I told my radar observer, "I know one way I can hit it." So I just gained some altitude and dove right straight down on it and turned my bombs loose. I hit the darn thing right in the middle and that napalm just ran allover that building and down the sides. I did a good job with it. That's the only way I knew to hit my target.

During the Korean War, I thought maybe I was going to be called back to the military, but I was not, although my radar observer, Eddie Kopsel, was. He served a tour in radar in Korea in F-94s. Eddie liked to fly, so when he got back from Korea, he asked to go into pilot training and he trained at Greenville, Mississippi. He'd already passed his check rides and was about to graduate and get his fighter pilot's wings and was getting that last hour or so in the T-33 and something happened to the airplane. He was trying to get back into the airport but went in upside down and was killed. Here, after he had flown a bunch of missions in WWII and Korea, he got killed in that way. In 1948, I went up to Chicago and then to

560

Evanston, Illinois when Eddie's son was born. We had a little service for Eddie after his boy was born.

What do you remember of that service?

Of course, I'd talked to the family a good bit at the time. Eddie told them everything about me. We had worked together for all the time we were over in Europe. We were in every mission together. He knew just as much about me as I did. He was considered an Ace, as well, because he helped me shoot down the planes.

A day before the World War II was over, when I started to come back home, I got in a Jeep and drove up into Hanover Province to the little German town called Junde, from where my daddy had come. His brother was still living there. I went into the brother's house and there on the mantelpiece was a picture of my mother and daddy right in the middle of the mantelpiece, and then on both sides on that mantelpiece were all these German soldiers— their sons and grandsons that were in the Service.

That must have been an emotional experience.

It might have been a little bit. When I first went to this little town, I went to a house in the middle of the village and saw this lady coming down the walk. I asked her if that's where the Burgomaster lived. She said yes, that it was. So I went up and knocked on the door. This old gentleman came to the door. I had on my flight jacket and name on it, so I just pointed to my name. I didn't speak German very well, but I asked if any Ernsts still lived in the village. He just stood there. He didn't say anything. I thought, "My gosh, can't this guy talk at all?" Finally, he put his hand up and pointed at me and told me exactly who I was. He didn't say, "Are you...?" He paused. "You must be the son of Heindrick Broderick Christian Ernst, who left here when he was a young man and journeyed to America." He knew exactly who I was.

Bill Crump with a P–47 during World War II.

BILL CRUMP
A Man, His Coyote and the War

Though Bill Crump wanted to be a pilot, the Military sent him to gunnery school. Word had it that the average life span of a gunner was about 10 minutes in combat, and Bill was not looking forward to that. Finally, after gunnery shcool and within hours of the time he was to ship overseas as a gunner, his orders came through to report to pilot training. He graduated from pilot training at Moore Field, Mission, Texas in Febuary 1944. After pilot training, Bill found himself flying P-40s and it looked as if he was going to the Far East to fly P-40s in combat. Again, his orders were changed. He was sent to Europe where he flew P-47 Thunderbolts for 29 missions. In total, Bill made 77 missions in Europe, mostly flying P-47s and P-51s. He says, "A lot of people ask me how many planes I got. I tell them 'I shot down 12 trains—not planes.'"

After the war, Bill flew with unscheduled airlines, including flying in Alaska and as Bob Hope's C-47 pilot. Called back into the military, he flew the Berlin Airlift. In 1954, he flew in a C-124 in an around-the-world flight. He has flown over 25,000 hours. As I begin the interview with this engaging and witty man, I expect great things and am not disappointed.

Did you always want to be a flier?

Yes. My cousin, Buel Felts of Spokane, was my idol. He was killed in a crash after WWI, where they discovered that the stick was driven up through the stomach of the passenger—a newspaper reporter. The reporter apparently was flying and had frozen at the controls. Of course, Felts Field in Spokane, Washington is named for him. I had gone up on my first flight when I was five years old. My dad was a flight enthusiast and we went up in a Ford Tri-motor with pilot Nick Mamer. It was a 15 minute flight, but I remember looking down and seeing the Spokane River and coming over Opportunity, Washington where I was born. When I started caddying in the Seattle area, and would work all day for two dollars, I'd then take the two dollars down to Boeing Field and go up for a short flight. I did that as much as I could until I graduated from high school and got in the Air Corps in 1943.

You actually had a coyote with you during the war. Can you tell that story?

Yes, fighter pilots had to pre-qualify for gunnery by shooting skeet or some sort of traps every day. We'd train and train. It was boring. In going through this phase, we'd leave the base and go out into the boondocks to the firing range. When I came back from one of those trips, my friend, Ray Burwell, and I stopped to get a cup of coffee. When we pulled into that service station, the people gathered around us and wanted to know what we were doing with those guns. This one farmer approached me and said he had a lot of problems with coyotes eating his chickens. That farmer wined and dined us to try to get us to go out and shoot his menaces, but we wouldn't do that. I told him if he ever found a litter of them to save me one. I wanted to see if I could tame it. He said, "I've got a litter right now under the barn. I could probably get one for you now." So he went right to the barn, dug down and pulled up a litter of new-borne coyotes. One of them was wriggling like mad. I said, "Let me have that one." I put it in the pocket of my flight jacket and we headed to the base. The flight surgeon told me that the animal had rickets and gave it vitamins and other medicine, which enabled it to survive, but the coyote was very bow-legged. He'd just stand there and look at you.

I went to several more flying schools, then came time to go over to Europe on the *Queen Elizabeth*. We were issued gas masks, so I took the gas mask out of its carrier and threw the mask overboard. I opened a hole for it to breathe, and put the coyote in the gas-mask carrier. The *Elizabeth* had a room designed for two persons or newlyweds. The configuration was changed to accommodate 20 service men. I was given the bottom bunk in that room, so I put the coyote under the bed, buffered with dirty pillows all around it. I'd bring food back from the mess hall.

We had been on the ship for three or four days, when one day I came back from mess and saw these guys trying to get enlisted women to come into our bedroom. Whenever they saw a woman coming down the hall, they'd hold the coyote up to try to entice the women in. When I got there, the room was filled with women, and there was a party going on. It was no big deal, except that it ruined my secret. I figured it was going to be a matter of time anyway before someone took the coyote away.

One day I was sleeping in the bottom bunk when I heard a noise and popped up to see the tallest, meanest-looking bird colonel I'd ever seen in my life. He was army, not Air Corps, and had worked on two tours of combat. When he came in, everyone popped to stiff attention. He walked down the line. He knew I had the coyote, so I stepped forward. He said, "Let me see that damn thing."

I reached down and grabbed the chain and pulled the coyote up and set him in my arms and went back to attention. I noticed he wouldn't approach me to pet it or touch it. Finally, he said, "Well, I'll be damned." Then he told me a story about how when he was a kid he'd tried to train a coyote, but whenever it got loose it would kill the chickens, so he had to get rid of it. After that, it seemed like he disappeared as fast as he had arrived.

You're not out of trouble yet?

No, I was just waiting for another knock and for someone to claim it. By the time I got to England, I think everyone knew about it. On the troop train with thousands of troops going to stations all over England, I had the coyote on a tether. The train had a leather strap that you'd pull down, then out, to bring the window down. I would wrap that strap around the coyote's rump and when the train stopped at each station, I'd lower it down and he would do his thing, and before the train started I would bring him back in. One time, I couldn't retrieve the coyote. He was curled up underneath the train, and of course, I was inside. I thought, "Oh, boy, this is it." But the conductor who was just about to give the go-ahead sign to the train,

565

saw what was happening and held us up until I finally got the coyote in. The whole train had been stopped. That was the day the coyote stopped the war.

How did the English respond?

I was told that if and when the English got it, they'd kill it, because they would put it in quarantine for a year. When I got to my base in the 356th Fighter Squadron, I went to the squadron off the base. There we lived in temporary quarters until we could move into what was called the Castle. The coyote slept with me and it was damn cold in England. With only two blankets you would shiver most of the night. Some nights were a two coyote night!

How big was the coyote by now?

He was probably about six to eight inches nose to tail. We kept each other warm.

Did he actually fly with you?

He flew with me on five missions. I would only take him on missions where I knew I wasn't going to go to altitude and require oxygen. At altitude he would die of hypoxia. In fact, I took off my oxygen mask when I flew with him and used the throat microphone. That way I wouldn't be with oxygen and the coyote without. I would put the coyote by the cockpit heater by my left foot. He would often go to sleep by the time I'd take off. He normally slept most of the way.

I consider the coyote actually saved my life. We were up about 5,000 feet on a mission to Arnhem, Germany when he lurched real fast. I didn't know what was going on, but I looked in the rear-view mirror and saw two bursts of flak trailing me. Then I saw a third burst coming up my tail, I broke hard left and luckily it missed. The burst went off right where I had been.

So this is happening instantaneously. You wouldn't have had time to react otherwise, because you wouldn't know you were even being shot at.

Correct.

What did you do? Did you want to give coyote a bottle of champagne?

I'll tell you. He had the best food.

Were you able to bring the pet back with you?

No, he only lived a little less than a year. I would tie him outside on a long run and would fly on a mission. I'd come back and the coyote would not be there. There was a pattern. The English kids would come and take him to the village and show him off to other kids. So this time I came home and found the coyote gone. It was raining and dark. I went to the village and knocked on doors until I could find it. Then I'd put it in my jacket and pedal back.

One of these trips I came back and nobody had seen the coyote. We were having a big party in the Castle that night—with a lot of visitors. When I couldn't find him, my close friends fell in behind me and helped me look. Still, we couldn't find him. It was getting dark and we returned to the squadron. The commander learned of the problem and sent everyone out to look for the coyote. As it turned out, we found it. We had a road that went by the Castle. He was found dead on a footpath between the road and the Castle. Later, I learned a jeep had done a terrible swerve, but hit the animal.

The commander, Mike Yannel, said, "Crump, you and I are going to the bar." Then he turned around and said, "I want you guys to get the casket. I want you other guys to get the flowers. I want you others to dig a grave." I went back in the bar and got drunk. Finally, we went outside and there stood a visiting chaplain, a captain. The commander asked if the chaplain would say a few words for the burial. At the burial the honor guard officers didn't have rifles— only .50 caliber pistols, so the commander designated these officers to fire their .45s in a volley. The men had put the coyote in a casket, shrouded with flowers. The chaplain spoke and said, "We're gathered here to pay homage to a fellow American who's come over to foreign soil, flown in combat and died on behalf of his country." Everything was very formal and official. Then came the time to fire the volley of shots—the salute. Unfortunately, the guys were intoxicated, and some forgot to pull back the receivers in the guns, which would put rounds in the chambers. When the officer said, "Ready, aim, fire," only about half the shots went off. The guys immediately realized they had made a mistake, so they hurriedly cocked their weapons and fired them. As a result, we then heard a series of shots: "Bang-bang, bang-bang, bang-bang."

We were close to the village of Felixstowe and the villagers heard the shots and thought a German paratrooper had penetrated the area. As a result, the villagers came tearing into the area to capture this German. The village leader said, "I'm here to help out." The commander said, "We have just buried our coyote."

Did you shed some tears when you lost your friend?

Oh, yes. That coyote kept me warm at night, and he saved me. I was closer to that animal than I was to any of my comrades in those days, so it was a very sad affair.

He's buried over in England. Do you go see him?

Yes, I've been back twice. They have a picture of the coyote on the headstone.

Where's he buried?

Right there at the Castle. It's called Playford Hall. People will come in to see the 800 year old castle and the first thing they'll ask the owners is where the coyote is buried.

You had help with the coyote?

Yes, my crew helped me out. In those days, we fliers were superstitious. For example, we used to only get in on the left-hand side of the aircraft. Once I got in on the left-hand side of the cockpit, the crew chief named Sergeant Tancredi would come up the right side by the tail and hand the coyote to me. I would then put him down on the floor with the ring on his collar over the hydraulic pump handle.

Did you have any forced landings?

Not with the coyote, but I had several forced landings because of engine failures. Engine failure seemed to follow me every place I went. I think it was because of the tremendous maintenance load of the aircraft mechanics. I think I made a total of five downwind, forced landings. The most strenuous one was with the AT-6. I had probably ten hours in it at the time. The engine started to fail so I headed for an emergency strip. I barely made the end of the runway. That was the hairiest ordeal.

Any superiors have anything to say?

He said that I did a good job and commended me for saving myself as well as the airplane. Once we were in night formation. You're not supposed to fly too close at night. We had been flying at a three-to-five foot nose-to-tail clearance. Then we went into a dogfight with everyone on each other's tail. You would go round and round and then form up again. This guy started up on my wing and slid into me. He stuck that wing tip into my fuselage. It's lucky his prop didn't get my wing, because he was just inches from chewing up my wing.

569

How'd that happen?

He said later that his engine quit momentarily.

Any other dramatic episodes you can think of?

I heard this pilot call in, "mayday." He had engine failure and was going down in the North Sea. He planned to bail out because he had his canopy off, his safety harness and seat belt undone. He was descending from altitude and went through the undercast. Then as he saw the coast of England, he thought, "Oh, I can make that." So he stayed with the aircraft but ended up ditching in the water. Because he didn't remember to tighten up on everything, he smashed into the gun sight when he crashed. I was over him when he maydayed. I stayed with him and then as I saw his body float out of the aircraft as the plane sank, I kept transmitting to the "Duck Butt," the little emergency aircraft. It received a steer on me and came out and picked him up and took him to the emergency strip. I landed, ran over and jumped up on the fuselage of the "Duck Butt." When I looked in and saw his face, I thought he was dead. His nose was flat and his teeth were knocked out. He was a mass of blood. So we horsed him out of there. He was so stiff from the cold water that we couldn't get his chute off, so we cut him out of it with survival knives. I saw a flight surgeon put his stethoscope on his heart, and as he did, the doctor shook his head as if he knew he was starting to go. His face was just pulp. I flew back to the base and figured the guy had died. Then about 1950 he showed up at a reunion.

What did you think when you saw the guy?

I couldn't believe it. He had plastic surgery and new dentures.

Did he remember you?

He was incognito. Finally, he came up to me and said, "You don't know me, do you?" Of course, I didn't.
   He told me, "You saved my life."
   I said, "What do you mean?"
   "I was the one that splashed down in the water," he said.

You must have thought you'd seen a ghost.

Yes, and how! He didn't resemble anyone I'd seen before.

How did your life change because of the war?

I think the main thing was that I stayed in aviation. I was crazy about it. After the war, I started flying in Alaska in Lockheed Lodestars and then Gooney Birds for one year with a guy named Muriel E. Sasseen, a famous bush pilot. He always carried a putty knife around with him in his rear pocket. When we started flying together, he knew so damn many people that we'd sit around in the Nordale Hotel in Fairbanks and he would talk to the old cronies until they decided they wanted to fly to Seattle, so we'd load them up and make the trip. We were returning from Seattle once. We got a load of ice, and the de-icer was not working. We couldn't see to land. By now we had lost so much lift that we were up to almost full power, and were going down. It was getting real hairy. Sasseen went over the water so the salt spray would clear off the ice, but it didn't work. He had a Monel watch, which he took off and handed to me. He said, "Look there," and pointed to the right of the cockpit. All that was a diversion to get my face away from what he was going to do. He reached down under his seat for a fire extinguisher and swung that around and broke out the glass in his side window. He reached out, and with that cut-down putty knife, cleared off that ice and landed that aircraft like it was a hot summer day!

You flew around the world. Any story about around the world in the C-124?

At Eniwetok I had just feathered a faulty engine, then maydayed and advised Eniwetok control I was on three engines and that one engine was losing power, another engine was back-firing and the fourth engine just wasn't sounding good. I asked for landing instructions and was tersely advised that Eniwetok was conducting classified tests and that I would be unable to land. I then maydayed, turned off my radio and proceeded to land. I was placed under arrest until my classified orders were looked at and it was determined that they were more secretive and more priority than the atomic tests

What was your best flying ever?

You know what an Immelman is? It's a half loop and when you are on top, you roll out and do another half loop. That's a double Immelman. The P-51 would do a double Immelman, which in those days was a hot-rock deal.

Did you used to show off with those?

Oh, yes. And of course, I liked buzz jobs. When we were down in Marston in South England, we befriended all the nurses at the place where the military sent those who were flak-happy. We would fly down there and buzz the place, and the nurses would get all those wounded guys out on the patio to wave at us. Later, on my last mission I was going to fly through the hangar. I called the tower for clearance to make my pass. The people in the tower knew what I was planning to do. The tower said, "Negative. We have a general in the tower now." So I made a low level buzz job down the middle runway, which was heavy grass. When I landed, the crew chief said I had grass stains on the prop tips. I was lucky I didn't kill myself, but that's the way they did it in those days.

You also flew the Berlin Airlift. Any stories?

Yes, I flew the airlift out of Fassberg, Germany. Near Fassberg was the Belson Concentration Camp where bodies were still stacked up some three stories high. The British wanted to keep it there as a memorial, but there was so much public opinion on the subject they gave in. For the year that I flew the Berlin Airlift the pile was still there. There was a wooded area near the airfield, so it made it hard to see the runway. If you looked down, you could see the pile of white bones. That would be your checkpoint and reference for landing at Fassberg Airdrome.

What were your thoughts when you saw that each trip?

It was basically unbelievable, especially after we were briefed on the magnitude of the cremation effort.

You later flew the P-51 Mustang, a favorite.

I wanted to fly a P-51 again and got the chance. I flew *Miss America* a few years ago. I had a friend, Ron Smythe, who was blinded in an industrial accident and got a settlement with which he purchased *Miss America*. He had race pilots fly it for races and I became the pilot of the aircraft for air shows for almost two years.

How did you feel when you first went up in that plane?

It's something when you get back in that aircraft after all those years and after all the different things have taken place in your life. You buckle your seat belt, shoulder harness and get comfortable, go through the checklist, and then when that engine starts running with all those vibrations, sounds and smells, it all comes back to you—as if you hadn't been out of that cockpit for a day. When I flew that, I felt just as natural as if I had not left it—even though 50 years had passed.

Did you shed tears?

I'm very emotional, I think, especially with aircraft. Yes, I choked up a lot. And now when I see *Miss America* at air shows, I'll go up and kiss her, pet her, and maybe cry a tear. I hope she flies forever.

Irv Broughton is the author of eleven books, including a previous book on aviators from EWU Press, *Hangar Talk*. He is widely recognized for his interviews with distinguish writers, famous producers, and everyday folks. With degrees from Florida State University and Hollins College (now University), Broughton now lives in Spokane, Washington with his wife, Connie, and their three children.